Leonid Finberg

My Ukraine
Rethinking the Past, Building the Present

Ukrainian Voices

Collected by Andreas Umland

69 Max Hartmann
    Ein Schrei der Verzweiflung
    Aquarelle zum Krieg von Danylo Movchan
    Paperback
    ISBN 978-3-8382-2011-6
    Hardcover
    ISBN 978-3-8382-2012-3

70 Vakhtang Kebuladze (Hrsg.)
    Die Zukunft, die wir uns wünschen
    Essays aus der Ukraine
    ISBN 978-3-8382-1531-0

71 Marieluise Beck, Jan Claas Behrends, Gelinada Grinchenko und Oksana Mikheieva (Hg.)
    Deutsch-ukrainische Geschichten
    Bruchstücke aus einer gemeinsamen Vergangenheit
    ISBN 978-3-8382-2053-6

72 Pavlo Kazarin
    Der Wilde Westen Ost-Europas
    Der ukrainische Weg aus dem Imperium
    Aus dem Ukrainischen übersetzt von Christian Weise
    ISBN 978-3-8382-1843-4

73 Radomyr Mokryk
    Die ukrainischen »Sechziger«
    Chronologie einer Revolte
    ISBN 978-3-8382-1873-1

The book series "Ukrainian Voices" publishes English- and German-language monographs, edited volumes, document collections, and anthologies of articles authored and composed by Ukrainian politicians, intellectuals, activists, officials, researchers, and diplomats. The series' aim is to introduce Western and other audiences to Ukrainian explorations, deliberations and interpretations of historic and current, domestic, and international affairs. The purpose of these books is to make non-Ukrainian readers familiar with how some prominent Ukrainians approach, view and assess their country's development and position in the world. The series was founded, and the volumes are collected by Andreas Umland, Dr. phil. (FU Berlin), Ph. D. (Cambridge), Associate Professor of Politics at the Kyiv-Mohyla Academy and an Analyst in the Stockholm Centre for Eastern European Studies at the Swedish Institute of International Affairs.

Leonid Finberg

MY UKRAINE
Rethinking the Past, Building the Present

Bibliografische Information der Deutschen Nationalbibliothek
Die Deutsche Nationalbibliothek verzeichnet diese Publikation in der Deutschen Nationalbibliografie; detaillierte bibliografische Daten sind im Internet über http://dnb.d-nb.de abrufbar.

Bibliographic information published by the Deutsche Nationalbibliothek
The Deutsche Nationalbibliothek lists this publication in the Deutsche Nationalbibliografie; detailed bibliographic data are available on the Internet at http://dnb.d-nb.de.

УКРАЇНСЬКИЙ ІНСТИТУТ //ІІІКНИГИ

This book has been published with the support of the Translate Ukraine Translation Program.

First published in Ukrainian by Dukh i Litera Publishing House, Kyiv 2018.
Original title: Про різне і трохи про себе.
Translated into English by Natalia Komarova.
Published with kind permission.

ISBN (Print): 978-3-8382-1974-5
ISBN (E-Book [PDF]): 978-3-8382-7974-9
© *ibidem*-Verlag, Hannover • Stuttgart 2025
Alle Rechte vorbehalten

Das Werk einschließlich aller seiner Teile ist urheberrechtlich geschützt. Jede Verwertung außerhalb der engen Grenzen des Urheberrechtsgesetzes ist ohne Zustimmung des Verlages unzulässig und strafbar. Dies gilt insbesondere für Vervielfältigungen, Übersetzungen, Mikroverfilmungen und elektronische Speicherformen sowie die Einspeicherung und Verarbeitung in elektronischen Systemen.

All rights reserved. No part of this publication may be reproduced, stored in or introduced into a retrieval system, or transmitted, in any form, or by any means (electronic, mechanical, photocopying, recording or otherwise) without the prior written permission of the publisher. Any person who commits any unauthorized act in relation to this publication may be liable to criminal prosecution and civil claims for damages.

Printed in the EU

Contents

Acknowledgments 7

To the Readers 9

I   Interviews

1. Biography Pages 15
2. Publishing Affairs 69
3. About Moral Authorities 117
4. Around Judaic Studies 123
5. Ukrainians and Jews 175
6. On Cultural Shifts 191
7. "Despite the pain, find some ways of survival": Leonid Finberg on Books Published During the War 197
8. *Philisophical and Sociological Tought* in the Late 80s and Early 90s of the Last Century 205

II   Articles, Speeches, Opinion Polls

9. "Orange Prowess" (Expert opinions) 223
10. "Maidan. Testimonies" (Foreword to the book) 241
11. Selected Characteristics of the Soviet Totalitarian Abyss 249
12. Preface to the Issue of the Almanac *Yegupets* Dedicated to Yiddish Culture 255
13. Ukrainian Intellectuals on Ukrainian-Jewish Relations 261
14. A Warning from Hannah Arendt 273
15. Leonid Finberg's Speech at the Stanislaw Vincenz Prize *For Humanitarian Service and Contribution to the Development of Regions* (26.09.2020) 279

16. Holocaust. Babyn Yar. Present Day 285
17. Russia's Use of Holocaust History to Discredit Ukrainians and Ukraine 323

III Memoirs
18. Ivan Dziuba 333
19. Myron Petrovsky 349
20. Boris Lekar 355
    A life-long story 355
    If Socrates 369

Acknowledgments

First of all, I am very grateful to Oleksii Sinchenko, who suggested the structure of the texts and then worked with me on each of them. I am also grateful to Andriy Puchkov, who suggested changes to the second edition of the book.

I am grateful to Olena Finberg, Ola Hnatiuk, and Anna Prokhorova, who read the manuscript and whose suggestions and comments were extremely important to me.

My thanks to my colleagues: Valeriia Shulha for her help in forming the texts of the proposed version and, of course, my translator Natalia Komarova.

To the Readers

In this book, when asked by a correspondent, "Do you write books?", I answer that I don't. But now you are holding in your hands a book authored by me. Is there not a contradiction in that? If there is, it is not absolute. After all, this book is composed of interviews I have given over the years, as well as texts and expert surveys that I have prepared, conducted, and commented on. And behind all of this are certain milestones in my work, and most importantly, evidence of different stages of self-awareness and reflections on history and the present.

I received a higher technical education, but I did not receive a formal humanitarian one. I had a life that I designated as »first« and in it I was engaged in "not my own business." I connected my "second" life with the humanities.

The oft-repeated saying that "people who have to live in times of change are unhappy" is not so clear-cut. I have lived and am living in such times and realize that they have both their pros and cons. I won't dwell on the cons, because people like to talk about them more often, so I'll focus on the pros.

I, along with my friends and colleagues, have had the great honor of largely shaping the body of texts-books, films, exhibitions, and performances that marked the transition from Soviet totalitarianism to the liberal democratic present.

The books we have published over several decades are the voices of great thinkers from different cultures and eras, which were first heard in Ukrainian. Each time we open up entire planets for our readers — from Plato, Aristotle, Blaise Pascal to those closer to us — Serhiy Yefremov, Janusz Korczak, Olgerd-Ipolyt Bochkovsky, Czesław Milosz, Sergey Averintsev, Vasyl Stus... And each time we realize that we must hurry, because we have no time to delay all this — this is our spiritual weapon in confronting various forms of ignorance and barbarism.

Our projects are not only focused on the past. Although we were one of the first researchers of the most terrible events on our land — the Holodomor and the Holocaust. Without comprehending these tragedies, without burying those who were innocently killed, it was difficult to start something else. But no community can live only in the past, and therefore understanding current events and vectors of social development is no less important than knowledge of history. Hence the relevance of a number of our projects, including seminars, conferences, sociological research, etc.

All of the projects that you will read about in this book are primarily about the activities of two institutions — the Center for Research on the History and Culture of East European Jewry and the *Dukh i Litera* Publishing House. Both of my roles as director of the Center and editor-in-chief of the publishing house are part of my biography and my life universities. Judaic studies, which we managed to restore almost from scratch, helps me (and I hope others) to form my identity based on the values of Jewish civilization. Publishing gives me the opportunity to collaborate with the best humanities scholars in the country and the world and to present the best texts of world culture to society. Historians tend to communicate with historians, philosophers with philosophers, and we, as publishers, have a unique opportunity to engage with the entire spectrum of humanitarian culture.

It was this double specialization of mine that determined the structure of the book. Here are sequentially presented the pages of my biography, my publishing activities, and then the history of the formation of Judaic studies and my socio-analytical and sociological works. The book concludes with a research paper on the »nationwide discussion« of the draft of the 'Brezhnev Constitution' of 1977.

The latter is a testament to my intuitive move into the field of sociology. After all, it all started with an attempt to understand the legal consciousness of Soviet people, continued with the creation of the Ivan Lysiak-Rudnytsky Interdisciplinary Seminar, a series of expert surveys, and then with the recording of the experience of the Maidan of 2004 and the Maidan of 2013-2014. These are rather complex and resonant projects, the products of the joint activity of sometimes numerous teams. In the work on the book *Maidan. Testimonies* (2016) alone were involved more than a hundred people:

someone recorded the interviews, someone transcribed them, edited them, prepared them for publication, and printed them. Perhaps for the first time in the national history of recent decades (if not of recent century), we have managed to record quite thoroughly the unique experience of people who have been the creators of their own history.

I will not underestimate my own role, too, because I initiated most of the projects and then organized their implementation one way or another.

I tried to do it systematically and responsibly. Preparing and publishing a number of book series is important to me. The series *Library of Resistance, Library of Hope* brings together seemingly completely different books: domestic and translated, historical and philosophical, memoirs and fiction. However, in my opinion, the body of published books matches the title of this series. The titles of the series *Library of Jewish Studies* and *Cultural Figures* speak for themselves. In the former series there are already about 100 books, and the latter is just beginning. In addition to more or less successful projects, there were, of course, those that, unfortunately, could not be realized. So, at the beginning of Independence, I failed to encourage editors of Ukrainian literary journals to publish textbooks for schools that were alternative to Soviet ones; we failed to convince our colleagues from the International Renaissance Foundation that instead of ordering textbooks on humanities from domestic authors, we should translate the best foreign ones... We can go on talking about 'failed', but this is no longer relevant to the content of this book, because it is about what we have done.

As I finish working on this book, I realize that it is a kind of interim result of my activities. However, I want to testify that I have many plans. I have the following desires:

- to continue all the book series I have started;
- to promote more effective work of the school of Jewish literature translation;
- to record and publish a selection of books similar to those created by Iza Khruslinska (dialogues with Joseph Zissels and Yaroslav Hrytsak), but with Taras Wozniak, Borys

Yeghiazaryan, Yevhen Zakharov, Mykola Riabchuk, Ola Hnatiuk, and many others — the list is open;
- promote greater activity of the Vasyl Stus virtual museum, which I am sure will eventually become real, not just virtual;
- to find resources to intensify research on the history and culture of Eastern European Jewry and to publish translations of books by Ze'ev Jabotinsky, Natan Zabara, Shmuel Agnon, and Isaac Kipnis... I plan to organize a solid patronage for this.
- promote the organization of Jewish film festivals;
- organize the publication of a series of books of *Stus Library*, and eventually of the *Stus Encyclopedia*.

It is not difficult for me to continue this list, but it is worth to pause on something. Today, at least.

There is one more topic that cannot be avoided: the barbaric war that Russia has unleashed against Ukraine, which threatens human civilization and, above all, the certain stability of the world that has developed after World War II. Of course, all my roles have a minimal impact on these events, but my response to them is to continue the projects, both publishing and otherwise. With faith in victory!

I
Interviews

1. Biography Pages

How do you identify yourself: as a publisher, sociologist, or Jewish studies scholar?

I have two main roles: to the best of my ability, I promote the development of Judaic studies in Ukraine and I am engaged in publishing. These roles are mostly managerial. At the same time, I try to be an active participant in social processes, so I participate in public meetings, conferences, and seminars.

In Ukrainian intellectual circles, you have a reputation not just as a manager, but as an expert on Jewish tradition and Ukrainian-Jewish relations. Do these interests of yours come from your family?

I have a rather unusual, or maybe typical biography — I don't know. I was brought up in a traditional Soviet family. My father was a laborer and my mother was an accountant. My parents taught me to read. Of the first children's books, I remember the stories about Baron Munchausen and the adventures of Gulliver. Books were in short supply at the time, and it was difficult to buy them, but my relative, who lived and worked in Moscow, used to send me these priceless gifts. Books were written off, and when they were in such a state that it was inconvenient to use them, I got them. These were the crumbs from which I received my primary education. When I began to pay attention to the existence of books on my own (I was about 14 years old), it turned out that there were only two at home: one was titled *Daisy* and the other *The Feat of a Scout*[1]. Even now, many years later, I remember these covers and stories. So there were almost no books for adults in my family. And Jewish traditions... Apparently, they were manifested in respect for education and knowledge, in the ethics of relations between parents and relatives...

---

1   Popular Soviet detective stories.

It's a bit strange. After all, there is a stereotype that Jewish families always have a great respect for books.
My parents' family was more Soviet than Jewish. And all of my humanitarian interests are a product of the socialization of the late 60s and the following years. At first, there was envy of my educated classmates at the Kyiv Mechanical College, and then years and years of self-education...

Tell us more about your family.
My father's passport name and patronymic was Kushel Pinievich. But everyone called him Nikolai Pavlovich. During the Soviet era, this happened in almost all Jewish families—the Russification of names as part of the general Russification. I had already been formed and lived in other onetimes, and therefore it was fundamental for me to call myself Leonid Kushelevich, that is, to keep my father's real name. This was my position, reaction, resistance—to not obey a system that demonstrated a rejection of traditions ('We will build an ours world, a new one'[2]) and even the names of our parents.

My father had two brothers and three sisters. All of them had different names and patronymics in Soviet documents, which was also an aberration of those times: Zalik Petrovich and Olga Pinhusovna. During the years of intensive Jewish emigration, the Institute of Linguistics of the National Academy of Sciences of Ukraine was granted the right to confirm with certificates that Polina and Feiga, or Maria and Miriam, were the same names. This was a significant success for the Soviet bureaucracy.

My father had the highest qualifications as a turner, miller, sharpener, grinder, and so on. In the postwar years, he worked at the *KinoDetal* plant in Kyiv, where equipment for Soviet cinemas were produced, and in the second shift, after his main job, he adjusted equipment for the plants brought from Germany. This was how plants and factories resumed their activities, because in the early days of the Soviet-German war, Kyiv's factories were evacu-

---

2   A Soviet slogan.

ated to the interior of Russia. People associated with those enterprises were also taken away as attachments. There was no special evacuation for civilians.

I hardly ever saw my father on weekdays (back then, the working week consisted of six days): he left for work while I was still sleeping and came home when I was already asleep. I owe my admission to the Kyiv Mechanical College, where I studied after the eighth grade, to my father. As a worker, he dreamed that his son would become a foreman (the lowest-level manager at factories).

According to my father, in 1943, when the family returned to liberated Kyiv (during the war, my father worked at an aircraft factory in Moscow because he had received shell shock), a policeman lived in their apartment and was not going to move out. My father came to the shop where he started working, told this story to the workers he knew, and they took hammers and other "weighty" tools and went to vacate the apartment. And they did. This was how housing issues were resolved in those years.

I remember a few more conversations with my father: I was looking through his work record book—gratitudes, awards... and—stop!—dismissal for absenteeism. I ask him: 'What happened?' He answers: 'It was the post-war period, when a person did not have the right to quit at will. The manager of the plant where I worked earlier agreed to let me go because the manager of another plant was inviting me to work. But the only way to transfer was through the following algorithm: dismissal for violation of discipline.' It was a time when people were imprisoned for being late for work. When I was a little older, I asked my father: 'How did you vote at the party meeting on certain concepts of linguistics (by Academician Nikolai Marr or Joseph Stalin)?' He answered: 'Of course, we didn't understand it, but we voted as the party secretary said.'

After the war, my mother, Lia Davidovna Finberg (Braginska), worked in the department that was involved in the reconstruction of Khreshchatyk. From her stories, I remember that many German prisoners of war worked there alongside our workers, and our people treated them sympathetically. Apparently, despite everything, humanity has stronger roots in our fellow citizens than hatred. Then, for many years, until her retirement, my mother worked as an accountant in a Kyiv hospital. She was very sick and spent at least a week almost every month in the same hospital, but not at her desk, but under drips. Later, my wife Olena, a homeopathic doctor, treated my mother a bit and she began to feel better. And when my mother retired, she took care of our children, Marina and Arseniy, and Olena and I were able to work productively.

I can also tell you a few childhood memories to convey the atmosphere of that time. In the early 50s, late in the evening, neighbors would come to our yard (13 Tverskaya St.) almost every day to wait for Anton, who worked at the slaughterhouse, to arrive. He would take the bones of slaughtered animals out of the slaughterhouse under his pants. The neighbors would buy up the "meat" because they had no money for other 'delicacies.' During the war, Anton worked as a policeman in Babyn Yar, and he came to the slaughterhouse after he had served his prison sentence.

Back then, everything was in short supply, and to get, say, a kilogram of flour or sugar, you had to stand outside a grocery store for several hours, or even half a day. Our mothers would take us children with them, because they only gave us one kilogram of each product per person, including children. We usually played football somewhere nearby, and when it was our turn, we joined the mothers. The women often 'lent' us to each other in cases when they could not find their child and it was their turn. There were no problems, because everyone knew everyone, and it was all repeated year after year.

Our parents also warned us not to go near the fences of the Karl Marx confectionery factory at the end of the working day. It was at this time that bags of chocolate would 'fly' over the fence of the factory — stolen by workers and then sold at a low price.

Later, we moved into a five-storey house built at the expense of the *KinoDetal* plant, where, as I said, my father worked. What a joy it was! After a room of nine square metres for three persons, with a toilet in the yard, we got a separate apartment! The commissioning of the building was delayed due to a lack of funds for the installation of a telephone cable. I don't know how, whether it was for a bottle or a box of vodka, but it was agreed to sign documents stating that the telephone cable had been installed in the house, although it had not. So for the next 20 years, even though we could buy this cable, it was impossible to lay it according to the documents, and we went to call our friends at payphones, standing in the usual queues for a long time.

In fact, there were so many absurdities of the Soviet era that it is impossible to recount them all.

What did you want to become as a child?
A footballer! I didn't read much at the time, but I played a lot of football and was quite good at it. I was even invited to join a professional team. But it was not to be. When I turned 14 and entered the Kyiv Mechanical College, my preferences changed. It was there that I first met boys from intelligent families who had books at home. I was impressed that they were so well-read and intelligent. I had to catch up—at the expense of sleep, food...

Then I entered the correspondence department of the Kyiv Polytechnic Institute (KPI), where I was accepted only on the fourth attempt—in the previous exams I was asked to solve so-called 'Jewish' problems that had no solutions.

So you have a technical education, like many post-Soviet intellectuals?
Yes. After graduating from KPI and serving in the Soviet army, I was engaged in engineering for almost 25 years. However, gradually changing specialisations, I came closer to social sciences, which fascinated me a lot. For some time, I was engaged in what is called a systematic analysis of activities. My brilliant teachers Yuriy Chernyak[3] and Alik Linkov[4] taught me how to determine the effectiveness of various activities and develop programmes to improve actions. For example, we analysed the reserves of the *Rus-Intourist* hotel complex and found that 5 to 8 per cent of hotel rooms were empty every day (and this was despite the fact that it was very difficult to rent a room for a day in hotels in the Soviet Union). We saw

---

3   Outstanding engineer, theorist of system analysis.
4   Engineer, theorist of system analysis.

that each of the workers who serviced these rooms was interested in earning extra money: the plumber told that the taps were not working, the electrician—that he could not immediately repair the switches, and so on. This hotel served foreign tourists—about forty groups daily. All the tour buses were delivered to the hotel at ten in the morning. These were *Ikaruses*[5], which, especially in winter, would fill the area in front of the hotel so much that the surrounding space resembled a gas chamber. And tourists had to wait an average of 40 minutes to be able to take the lift down. Our proposals, which were based on the analysis, were quite elementary: for example, to change the single hour for bus arrival. But almost all of them were ignored, because there were almost no mechanisms to change the algorithm in the Soviet command and control system—it was an 'economy of scarcity'. We carried out similar work at power plant construction sites and even when studying the work of a theatre association.

It was an interesting period of my formation, and yet I have a bitter feeling that I spent my most active years doing something that was not my business. However, as Alexander Kushner[6] wrote: 'One does not choose times, one lives and dies in them...'

And when did you come to the humanities?
The technical sciences were the niche in which we lived, in which we 'hid'. In Soviet times, not only I, but also most of my peers who were not members of the party or were Jews, like me, or conscious Ukrainians, like many of my friends, were not allowed to study the humanities. And we didn't really want to: we were simply not allowed to read high-quality Western literature, and Soviet humanitarian texts of those years were ideologically corrected, and it was difficult to call them scientific.

I actually came to humanities, in the broad sense of the word, only in the 1970s. At that time, semi-free centres began to appear— youth clubs, in one of which I took an active part. In those clubs I

---

5   *Ikarus*—a Hungarian bus company.
6   A Soviet poet and essayist.

met activists of the Ukrainian and Jewish movements. Such movements were just beginning to emerge. I became interested in both Jewish and Ukrainian history and culture. There were public meetings with Ukrainian and Jewish writers and scholars. We, the youth, sought answers to questions that were difficult to obtain in Soviet times. World culture was hidden behind a solid wall. It was then that I first heard those who consciously spoke Ukrainian. Books written in Ukrainian came into my life, and I began to learn the language.

These were important years of my formation. I was looking for myself in various club projects. My friends and I, led by Yury Smirny[7], organised our own creative club named after Petro Zaporozhets, one of Lenin's associates. Only on this condition were we allowed to open and continue to operate this club. The club held discussions, meetings, and literary readings. For example, we invited Borys Antonenko-Davydovych[8] to one of these discussions, who argued for the return of the letter 'ґ'[9] to the Ukrainian language. At the time, I did not understand what kind of problem this was, and only later did I realise its scale.

We also organised an evening of Ukrainian and Jewish poetry dedicated to the Second World War. But these were isolated events — almost everything was banned. Every time we held such events, we were kicked out of clubs and libraries. We were 'educated' by communist and Komsomol leaders and KGB officers. In short, the struggle for each of these evenings mostly ended not in our favour. But we looked for other premises. One day we were allowed to gather in the basement of an inactive church in Podil, on the condition that we would clear and clean everything there. After the work was finished, we were kicked out.

In those clubs, I started reading *samizdat*, and then distributed it among my friends and acquaintances. Thank God, I avoided imprisonment, although I still remember the hours of interrogations.

---

7   One of the leaders of a cell of the social movement that started in the 1960s-1980s.
8   Ukrainian writer, linguist, long-term prisoner of the Gulag.
9   Cyrillic letter to denote the sound [g] that exists along with the letter "г" in some alphabets: Belarusian Tarashkevitsa, Urum.

After work, almost every day and almost all weekends, I went to the reading rooms of the Library of the National Academy of Sciences of Ukraine to try to understand the main events of history and to orientate myself in philosophical worldviews. I 'swallowed' book after book. I read the entirety of Alexander Twardowsky's *Novy Mir* text by text: the titles of the articles in the journal mattered little: it was important who wrote what and how.

A real 'university' for me was meeting the family of Myron[10] and Svitlana[11] Petrovsky. Their home was one of the centres of dissident thought, at whose threshold 'Soviet' values were stuck. A real culture of worldview was formed and came to life there. There, I met linguist Andrii Biletsky, historian and cultural critic Vadym Skurativsky, artist Borys Lekar, writer Yury Shcherbak, and many other free people. The Petrovsky's apartment, where the library contained many significant books of the twentieth century, where the owners kept abreast of the events of the time and discussed them lively, became very important for my formation. After all, such centres were a kind of underground university of the time. At the same time, I began to collect my own library, a large part of which I recently transferred to the National University of Kyiv-Mohyla Academy.

What brought you to the Petrovsky family?
It was more than 40 years ago. At one of the power plants (we often went on business trips), I met an intelligent engineer, Alik Kalmeyer[12]. He introduced me to Myron Petrovsky. I remember our first meeting, when Myron and Svitlana moved into a new apartment. They had been evicted from their flat in the downtown due to the reconstruction of the house. For a long time they refused to accept uncomfortable options for relocation, and eventually got an apartment on Florency Street, in the Cabinet of Ministers' dwelling house. After my first visit, I began to come to this home often. Myron recommended books to me that I was eager to read. Among

---

10   Leading Ukrainian literary critic.
11   Pedagogue in the fifth generation, honored teacher of Ukraine.
12   Engineer, dealt with the construction of power plants.

them were the famous *Milestones* (1909), a book of intellectuals' reflections on the first Russian revolution, and Arkady Belinkov's *Yury Tynianov* (1961), a kind of anti-Soviet treatise that legally made its way through the censorship of the time... Then there were many other texts that I would not have found without Myron. I became a listener to the conversations that Myron and Vadym Skurativsky[13] had with each other. Vadym, by the way, considers himself Myron's student. Back then, I became a reader of Vadym and Myron's books, and years later I became their publisher. Over time, I began to bring as many books to this apartment as I received from its owner.

Myron was once a member of the group of 'Peredelkino boys'. In this Moscow suburb, he worked as a secretary to Korney Chukovsky[14], collaborated with the *Novy Mir* journal[15], wrote about Samuil Marshak[16], Mikhail Bulgakov[17], and the *Oberiuts*[18], among others. He was thrown out of Ukrainian literature for reviewing the manuscript of a book by Bohdan Chaly[19], then the party secretary of the Writers' Union. At that time, there was a practice of closed reviews, and those who did not have jobs sometimes wrote such reviews. They were commissioned by publishing houses to figure out what to publish and what not to publish. Myron wrote a rather caustic review, presenting Chaly as a Stalinist trying to hide his views. For that, he got his wolf's ticket for many years. Later, he said that the writer Hrytsko Boyko[20] wrote to him about this: 'Myron, I have two joys lately. The first is that I did not die after a heart attack, and the second is that I read your review.' Such were the joys back then.

---

13 An outstanding Ukrainian art scholar, culturologist, historian, publicist, teacher, film actor.
14 Russian writer of Ukrainian origin and Soviet poet, publicist, literary critic, translator, literary critic, children's writer.
15 Russian and Soviet literary magazine, one of the oldest Russian monthly literature-artistic and socio-political journals.
16 Soviet Russian children's writer, poet, translator, playwright, critic. Primarily known as author of the fairy tale play "Twelve Months."
17 Russian writer and playwright.
18 Members of the OBERIU (Association of Real Art), a group of writers and cultural workers, which existed in 1927 – early 1930's in Leningrad.
19 A party leader, Stalinist.
20 Soviet Ukrainian writer, poet and translator.

Did other personalities influence your development as an intellectual?

My acquaintance and many years of meetings and correspondence with Moscow intellectuals, such as Victoria Chalikova[21] (an associate of academician Andrey Sakharov) and philosopher and publicist Yuly Schreider[22], contributed to my formation.

Victoria Chalikova was a brilliant figure who, in the 1970s and 1980s, seemed to do the impossible. Working at the Moscow Institute for Scientific Information in the Social Sciences (INION in Russian), she was an author and editor who brought out some of the best publications of the time, which were inaccessible to most people. Books in this institute were published only for members of the Politburo of the Central Committee of the Communist Party and for academics—they had to know what they were criticising, to know their enemies. The best intellectuals in the Department of Scientific Communism worked on this, adapting and commenting on texts by anti-Soviet writers from around the world. These were hundreds of compendiums with good analytical reviews, but sometimes just adequate translations with minimal bills. It is thanks to them that we were able to form an adequate (and not distorted by the presentation of specialists in bourgeois philosophy or sociology) idea of Alvin Toffler[23], Daniel Bell[24], Jan Szczepanski[25], John Griffiths[26]... These books were not published by prestigious publishing houses, nor were they on sale. They were published under the stamp 'For official use only' in a meagre edition of 200-300 copies. Each of these books had its own mark—for example, X for Brezhnev himself, a leading academic or a Politburo member, Y for an academic, Z for an ideologue. But that was only a part of the addressees (or readers?). Other recipients were philosophers and sociologists, historians and future politicians, simply those who had the good fortune

---

21 Philosopher, a person close to Andrei Sakharov.
22 Mathematician, cybernetician and philosopher.
23 American writer, sociologist.
24 American sociologist and publicist, founder of the theory of post-industrial (information) society.
25 Polish sociologist, professor of humanities.
26 Writer, sociologist.

to read Max Weber[27], Karl Mannheim[28] or José Ortega y Gasset[29]. Let me remind you that this was at a time when the government was doing everything it could to cut us off from the world behind the Iron Curtain.

Every time I came to Moscow, I came to see Victoria Chalikova. She would say to me: 'Well, this academician is already dead, so I can give you his copy. And this one is the kind of guy who doesn't ask for books, so take this one.' And I brought stacks of books from Moscow to Ukraine, which we could not even dream of at the time. For example, the six (!) issues of *Socio-Cultural Utopias of the 20th Century* (1981-1988) or the translation of the novel *1984* by George Orwell[30] with commentary. They were passed around and read to the holes. These books opened up ideas and thoughts without which an adequate understanding of the time was impossible. These books were much more informative and deeper than any dissident books, and they are still relevant today. Our intellectuals could not have written such books because they did not have the background. Most of us have been deprived of serious knowledge of humanitarian culture for more than half a century. Perhaps that is why the collection *From Under the Boulders*, edited by Alexander Solzhenitsyn[31] in 1974, began with the words: 'Most likely, what we are writing has long been known in the West, but we are discovering everything for ourselves for the first time.' Of course, I distributed this important literature as much as possible. I was glad that I could read such a book and pass it on to someone else.

Thus, taking advantage of the flaws in the established registration of numbered books and, of course, taking risks, Victoria Chalikova distributed this kind of *samizdat* to those who really needed it.

---

27 German sociologist, philosopher, historian.
28 Philosopher, one of the founders of the sociology of knowledge.
29 Spanish philosopher.
30 English writer, journalist, essayist, literary critic.
31 Russian historian and prose writer.

And was it really associated with risks?
Yes, we were afraid, because if we were caught with such a book, we could have been sentenced to prison. One of my friends never got on public transport with these books, but walked, even though sometimes he had to walk halfway across town. He was afraid that anything could happen in the transport. I remember, another friend of mine was carrying one of Alexander Solzhenitsyn's self-published, miniature books in his pocket. A policeman stopped him and asked what was in his pocket. Luckily, the policeman was so ignorant that he took one look at the book, returned it, and kept walking.

But I want to say a few more words about Victoria Chalikova. She was one of the few people in this world who, more than anyone else (personally!), was affected by the troubles of the twentieth century — the Armenian genocide, the Holocaust of the Jews, the famines in Ukraine and Russia, the bloody crimes of the empire against Prague, Vilnius, Sumgait, Baku... She wrote about it strongly and insightfully, went to demonstrations, risking losing her freedom, collected signatures of intellectuals in defence of dissidents, organised actions of disobedience... She did much more than most of her contemporaries, probably because she did not know how to live otherwise.

One of her letters to me, written after the death of Academician Sakharov, ended with the following words: 'I can't tell you how much I mourn for Andrey Dmitrievich. It is empty without him...'. I will forward these words to the author herself — she died shortly afterwards.

You also mentioned Yuly Schreider...
Yuly Schreider was one of the best researchers of the logic of knowledge and ethical issues. He had his own style: he wrote scientific articles on the most complex problems in a convincing, simple, dialogic manner. At the same time, he was not a purely academic scholar; every year he published dozens of texts in popular journals, not only for the development of science but also for its popularisation. His talent as a philosopher flourished in the era of stagnation, totalitarianism, and then in the period of rethinking the

ideology of communism and the Soviet past. Even a list of those articles would take dozens of pages. He was one of the few Russian scholars whose articles appeared regularly in Ukraine. We read his texts and passed them on to each other, translated them and published them in Ukrainian.

Yuly was a courageous man and was quite active in cooperating with dissidents, helping the repressed, distributing samizdat, and hiding texts by opponents of the Soviet regime. This includes active cooperation with Alexander Twardowski's[32] 'scandalous' *Novy Mir*, the preservation of Varlam Shalamov's[33] manuscripts, and much more. It was from Yuly that I received a collection of Shalamov's poems for safekeeping. I still keep this collection to this day.

Throughout his life, he defended morality and humanity in relationships. We weren't the closest of friends, but when Chernobyl exploded, a few days later I heard his voice on the phone: 'We invite you and your entire family to come to Moscow, to our apartment, for as long as you need. Do not hesitate and send your children as soon as possible.' This call—an offer of help—was one of the first we received in those tragic days.

In one of his answers to my expert questionnaire in 1991, which was the first historical hours after the collapse of the Soviet Union, Yulii said: '...We are on the ruins of the Gulag and we still have the psychology of "prisoners". And yet, the only thing we can all do is try to understand this burden and free ourselves from it. A great responsibility lies with the intelligentsia, which today, more than ever, is obliged to go against the tide, to defend freedom, human dignity and the principles of non-violence. The intelligentsia must be the first to understand and convey their understanding to everyone that blood and violence will kill the freedom that has barely been born; that one cannot be led by grievances (which are absolutely real) and ambitions (which are based on the inability to

---

32 Russian poet, editor of the *Novy Mir* (*New World*) magazine (1950-1954 and 1958-1970).
33 Russian Soviet prose writer and poet, best known as the author of a series of stories and essays *Kolyma stories* about the events in the life of prisoners of Soviet forced labor camps in the 1930s—1950s.

accept others, even if they are unpleasant, hostile, but who also have their human rights). Every example of resilience, confidence, human dignity and wisdom increases the freedom of each of us.'

Yuly Shreider died at his desk before he had finished his next article. But I remember dozens of our dialogues, which were extremely important to me.

I was also privileged to be friends with Anna Zavarova[34], perhaps one of the best art historians working in Kyiv at the turn of the century. It was Anna who wrote the landmark texts about the Sixties artists Hryhorii Havrylenko and Vadym Ihnatov. She gave excellent lectures at the Kyiv Art Institute (now the National Academy of Fine Arts and Architecture). Zavarova studied in Moscow and had a great school of collaboration with the best art historians. She was friends with Nadezhda Mandelstam[35], and when Nadezhda Yakovlevna visited Kyiv, she stayed with Anna. We hadn't met yet then. Zavarova kept a huge volume of Nadezhda Mandelstam's memoirs published abroad, with her invaluable handwritten comments and notes, and other controversial books. The KGB knew about this and periodically visited her with searches. Thank God, she was not arrested. After such searches, the books in her library were mostly on the floor or upside down. That's how I remember it as a metaphor for such searches in intelligent families—books upside down. Realising its value, Anna gave the book with Nadezhda Mandelstam's commentaries to one of her relatives for hiding. When he found out about the search of her home, he burned this priceless gift. Anna could not forgive her relative for such weakness. I honestly admit that at some points, when I was waiting for a search, I also burned books that might have caught their attention. However, I didn't have such valuable ones—only

---

34 Ukrainian art critic, art critic, art historian, teacher of several generations of Ukrainian art scientists. Anna Zavarova explored the work of artists of the Sixties, who were her contemporaries and in their work went beyond the strict regulations of socialist realism. These include Grigory Gavrilenko and Vadim Ignatov.
35 Memoirist writer, wife of Osip Mandelstam.

copies of texts by Ze'ev Jabotinsky or stories by the Strugatsky brothers[36].

And in general, what did the book market look like from the 1960s to 1980s?
It was a completely different book market than it is now. Scientific libraries had huge 'special storerooms' where copies of books that were forbidden to read were kept. A very limited sector was available. State-owned shops sold up to 90 per cent of propaganda literature, no matter what it was called, pseudo-history, pseudo-philosophy, and mostly pseudo-literature, as well as hundreds of books against Ukrainian nationalism and against bourgeois Zionism... However, there was also fiction, mostly from the late nineteenth and early twentieth centuries, but also largely with cuts. There were few books by our contemporaries worth reading in the 1970s. Sometimes something interesting came across in the journals *Novy Mir*, *Inostrannaya Literatura*, or *Vsesvit*. Over time, the situation improved.

However, during these dark years, we had brilliant translations of fiction. Ukrainian culture survived thanks to brilliant translators: Mykola Lukash[37], Hryhoriy Kochur[38], Anatol Perepadia, Marko Pinchevsky[39], Maksym Rylsky[40], Yevhen Popovych[41], Olga Senyuk[42], Mykhailo Moskalenko[43], and others. If writers were not allowed to say what they wanted to say, and even more so, they

---

36 Arkady (1925 -1991) and Boris (1933 — 2012) Strugatsky were Soviet-Russian science-fiction authors who collaborated through most of their careers. They developed their own, unique style of science fiction writing that emerged from the period of Soviet rationalism in Soviet literature and evolved into novels interpreted as works of social criticism.
37 Ukrainian translator, linguist and polyglot, a civic activist, and a Sixties activist. Most famous translations: *Faust* by Goethe, *Decameron* by Bocaccio, *Madame Bovary* by Flaubert, *Don Quixote* by Cervantes, Schiller's lyrics, etc.
38 Ukrainian translator, poet, literary critic, public figure, and Sixties activist.
39 Ukrainian translator and journalist.
40 Ukrainian Soviet poet-academician, translator, publicist, public figure, linguist, one of the "neoclassicists," literary critic. Member of the Academy of Sciences of the Ukrainian SSR (1943) and the Academy of Sciences of the USSR (1958).
41 Ukrainian translator, philologist-Germanist.
42 Ukrainian translator from Germanic languages.
43 Ukrainian translator, historian and translation theorist.

were 'killed by socialist realism,' translators could say: 'I am translating Cervantes or Shakespeare—it is their language.' They, of course, were also censored, but less so.

At that time, there was also an interesting phenomenon of literary hoaxes: imitating texts in the name of non-existent authors. This is how Mykola Riabchuk[44] or Les Taniuk[45] worked, for example. They would prepare texts, write on behalf of some medieval or older author who never existed, and pass these texts off as translations. Sometimes they were printed. I have a dream of collecting such texts and publishing them as a collection.

So there were few intellectual books in Soviet times?
My formation was no longer taking place in the blackest of times. The system was no longer eating people, although different things happened. There were no Ukrainian intellectual books (philosophical, cultural, historical) at all. It was believed that we should read such literature in Russian. In the 1970s, only a few serious intellectual books were published in Ukraine, and even then in small editions with significant restrictions on distribution. They were prepared in academic institutions. There were some good books on the theory of logic, but not on social philosophy. Although sometimes one book out of a thousand titles did break through. For example, Vilen Gorsky's[46] book *Social Environment and the Historical and Philosophical Process* (1969).

A real shock was the book by the prominent Ukrainian historian Mykhailo Braichevsky[47], The Origin of Rus' (1968), in which he argued that the Soviet versions of the common origin of Russians, Ukrainians and Belarusians were ideological phantoms, and very

---

44 Ukrainian publicist, prose writer, translator, laureate of the Taras Shevchenko National Prize of Ukraine 2022. Honorary President of the Ukrainian PEN Club.
45 Theater director, organizer of the Creative Youth Club, art historian, translator, public and political figure.
46 Doctor of Philosophy, Professor at the National University of Kyiv-Mohyla Academy.
47 Ukrainian historian and archaeologist. One of the founders of the Movement for Perestroika. M. Hrushevsky Prize and Omelyan and Tatyana Antonovich Foundation Prize winner, full member of the Shevchenko Scientific Society, Honorary Professor of the National University of Kyiv-Mohyla Academy.

convincingly offered adequate, in-depth, professional versions of ancient history.

I remember well the excursions around Podil in Kyiv conducted by Braichevsky. He told us about many events and facts that were suppressed in Soviet guidebooks and history books. When we passed by a house with a plaque saying that Peter the Great had stayed there, he said: 'There is not a single document about this in the archives'. And he did not stop at this house. He talked about the Balabukha confectioners from Podil, whose sweets were known throughout Europe, and much more. Of course, in those years there were also dissident texts, but there were very few of them, and the threat of imprisonment for possessing or distributing them often worked convincingly.

Would you say that the value of the intellectual content you received back then was much higher than it is now?
I am not sure that I valued books more than Olexii Sigov or Vakhtang Kebuladze do today. It all depends on the individual. We just had a lot more obstacles in front of us, and it was exhausting. For example, in one night we had to read *The Gulag Archipelago* — hundreds and hundreds of pages, re-photographed and printed on photographic paper where not all the letters could be made out. And the next night, this book was already somewhere else. At the same time, we all remembered that if someone reported this to the KGB, the consequences could range from unpleasant to tragic for both the reader and the person who provided the opportunity.

Was there anything else besides books?
There were films. In Soviet times, films were divided into five categories. The most popular ones were state-ordered. For example, the first category was assigned to a film that was distributed in a large number of copies and shown in all cinemas, and the fourth category was assigned to a film that had only one copy and was shown only once in one cinema. It included the film *Landscape After the Battle* (1970) by the brilliant Polish film director Andrzej Wajda. To watch this film, my wife, who was nine months pregnant, and I travelled

all the way out of town to the Concrete Plant Club. We had no certainty that she would not go into labour on the way, but we were eager to see the film. The fifth category was given to films that were not allowed to be distributed and were shelved. For example, *The Commissar* (1967) by Alexander Askoldov[48].

We earned the right to an intellectual book or film in different ways. For example, we really wanted to watch Andrey Tarkovsky's[49] *Stalker* (1979), which was probably a fourth category film, because it hadn't been shown anywhere for a long time. At that time, there was a regional film distribution office in Kyiv. We suggested that the management organise a clean-up day on their premises. And dozens of people worked all day to clean up the polluted yard of the film distribution centre, so that we could watch the film after work in a closed room.

How did you end up in the Soviet army after graduating from Kyiv Polytechnic?

Back then, guys who graduated from higher education institutions by correspondence had to serve for a year. So I was summoned to the military enlistment office, where, as we were told, a 'special' train was being formed to take the recruits to the North. And so it happened. A few days later, our relatives saw us off at the Kyiv railway station. It was a long journey, several days, and the commanders who accompanied us began to find out who had graduated from which universities, so that they could send us to certain military units depending on our specialisation. But it did not happen as expected. Two bottles of vodka were stolen from our commander. This led to the fact that at each next station we were all disembarked from the train, forming groups according to the alphabet of the list: those whose surnames began with A to V, then

---

48 Film director, writer, screenwriter. His film *Commissar* until 1988 was banned by the Soviet censorship. After this Askoldov was fired from the Maxim Gorky film studio with a stamp in workbook "professionally unfit," expelled from the CPSU and deprived of the opportunity to work for specialty. He worked as a concrete worker in Tatarstan.

49 Soviet actor, film director and screenwriter. The son of the poet Arseny Tarkovsky, the grandson of the Ukrainian writer Alexander Tarkovsky. His film *Stalker* is based on the brothers Strugatsky's novel *Roadside Picnic*.

the next ones, and so on until F — my letter[50]. The previous arrangements were ignored. That's how I ended up in a military settlement with the strange name of Afrikanda.

It was told that this settlement was named so ironically, because it is one of the coldest places on the Kola Peninsula. I spent there a year guarding Soviet fighter jets that were confronting the 'aggressive NATO bloc'. It was in the army that I learnt Polish, translating the aphorisms of Stanisław Jerzy Lec[51]. Twice I saw the fantastic spectacle of the northern lights. It is something incredible!

Most men are willing to talk about their service in the army, and I am no exception.

We were seven people with higher education who came there. To a certain extent, we calmed down the hazing, especially against the boys from the Central Asian republics: they were bullied and humiliated the most. When we were demobilised a year later, they were crying — they knew that the humiliation and abuse would return. The 'old men'[52] didn't touch Caucasians, they were afraid of them. They didn't touch us either, because there was a man in our group who was very good at kung fu. When one of those 'old men' offered to measure his strength against Viktor N., he would find himself sprawled on the floor in a few seconds. The speed of his movements and his knowledge of techniques were impressive. The 'old men' were afraid to even approach Viktor, and, accordingly, they were afraid to approach us, just in case, perceiving it as something irrational — better not to touch them.

And here's another story. In those days, almost everyone who read used the book ordering system. All Soviet publishing houses published thematic plans for the following years, and books could be ordered. This mechanism was used by everyone, and later even by dissidents in prison. In Afrikanda, the bookstore was located at a considerable distance from our barracks — near the place where officers and their families lived. I had written out the books I wanted to order, but I didn't know how to submit these requests to

---

50 This refers to the Russian alphabet, where the letter V (В) ranks 3rd and F (Ф) — 22nd. (Translator's note).
51 Polish poet, philosopher, satirist and aphorist of the 20th century.
52 Servicemen who served for more than a year and a half.

the bookstore. I turned to the commander, who said that the only way was to sound the alarm, and then we could go to our assignment. So, the next day, I went to that shop with all my equipment and a carbine and, calming the shop assistant down, handed her the order. But I only received the books when I returned to Kyiv.

And finally, one more army story. One day a sergeant woke me up and said: 'Let's go remove pictures of the Politburo members from the walls! Tomorrow, the inspectors are coming, and only you know who is still alive in those portraits in Lenin's room and who of them is still in the Politburo.' I had to take them down... Captain Ostapyuk agitated me to become a member of the Communist Party ('it will be much more difficult for a civilian, especially for you, a Jew') and to take an officer's course. I remained non-partisan and a private. He was also worried about me: 'You're so smart, but you're a bad shot.'

I'm not going to tell you any other stories, because everyone who served remembers dozens of such stories, maybe even more.

Then on to the next stage. You took part in the liquidation of the Chernobyl accident.
I should not exaggerate my role here. In my 'first life', I was involved in organising the construction of power plants, first thermal and later nuclear. In a secondary role in the design office, I developed recommendations on 'how to build.' I ended up joining this organisation by accident. After graduating from the college, I was not hired by no organisation — they said there were 'no vacancies.' So I went to look for a factory or plant where I could get a job in my speciality.

I had little understanding of why I was being rejected and what was happening in the country, and I looked for job offers on billboards. I was rejected in dozens of places. 'Yes, yes, we put out an advert, but we no longer need specialists' was a traditional formula for rejecting Jews or undesirable employees on other grounds: race or political activity. I later analysed such rejections. At the Centre for Jewish Studies, we have a large archive of memoirs by older people.

I have selected about a hundred cases, ranging from quite tragic ones, when people deprived of the opportunity to find work went crazy from powerlessness or starved because they had no money for food, to funny ones. The artist Mykhailo Turovsky[53], who now lives in America, told us about one of them. Back in the early 50s, he tried to enter the Art Institute. Mykhailo was friends with the rector's daughter, who told him every year: 'Misha, this year they won't accept Jews either.' But he went to the exams as if they were sports competitions; he had no choice—Mykhailo wanted to become an artist, and even internal migration was almost impossible in those years. On his third or fourth attempt, I don't remember for sure, he passed the first stage of the entrance exam and got good marks in drawing. Then there was a history exam. The professor said: 'You have a simple exam ticket, I'm not even going to ask you questions. Let's do it this way: one additional question, and if you answer it, you are a student of the institute, okay?' Mykhailo agreed. The professor asked, 'What did Karl Marx write to Friedrich Engels in his letter of 17 October 1882?' But you have to know Mykhailo! 'In this famous letter,' he said, 'Karl Marx wrote: 'My dear friend, thank you very much for the set of *Frankfurter Allgemeine Zeitung* you sent me, it perfectly complements my studies, and for supporting my theses from the *Communist Manifesto*...' After 15 minutes, Mykhailo was stopped, and he became a student.

I think that there was no such letter, and the 'inventive' examiner was not prepared for such an answer. This was one story in a hundred. It was the same for me: I read that some design bureau needed a mechanical technician. So, I went up to the fifth floor of a building on Shota Rustaveli Street, met an elderly (as I thought) Jewish intelligent man and asked him about the job. He nodded that they needed a man and took me to the head of the department. They consulted and hired me. So I started working in the design bureau of the *Pivdenenergobud* trust, opposite the Lazar Brodsky synagogue. And I worked there, changing roles, from technician to department head, as the organisation itself changed, for almost 25 years. Now I speak of this period as my 'first life'.

---

53   Ukrainian and American artist.

Our design bureau was, to a large extent, a typical Jewish organisation of the time (in large cities, where Jews were not employed by defence enterprises, they found refuge in specific fields of activity: construction, light industry, etc.)

My pen is not enough to describe the atmosphere that prevailed in such organisations, including ours. This would require, perhaps, the talent of a good writer, who would have to write it in the style of 'Schweik the Brave Soldier'. One way or another, almost all of the employees were from families of the repressed. This was not a Jewish peculiarity. In a country where the authorities between the 20s and 60s killed or forced millions of their fellow citizens into the Gulag, there were almost no 'pure' families. For example, one of my colleagues, Boris, who grew up in an orphanage, was afraid of everything, even his own shadow. He whispered to himself and wrote endless diaries of events, although almost nothing happened in that environment. Another colleague of mine, Aleksander V., whose father was shot in the late 1930s and whose older brother served his time in the Gulag and died in his youth, came to this office after he was prevented from defending his brilliant, according to his teachers, PhD thesis. So he stood behind his panel board and periodically hummed: 'Thank y-o-u, Pa-a-r-ty...' Another colleague spent more than half of his working time talking endlessly in the smoking room, and any attempts by the department head to get him to the workplace were in vain. But I've strayed a little from our topic.

We were organising the construction of power plants, and I travelled to Zaporizhzhya, Rivne and Chernobyl. At a certain stage, I became the head of the automated control systems (ACS) department. Such departments with large *Minsk-32* and *ES-1020* computers were being set up almost everywhere. It was believed that they would be able to optimise work in various areas, to increase the efficiency of the fantastically inefficient Soviet 'deficit economy'.

I remember these stations mainly because of the long construction process (it took 6-7 years before the first unit was launched), involving 20-30 thousand people. It all started with tents and ended with huge industrial complexes. Almost every weekend, funeral processions with brass bands marched through the streets with unfinished dormitories and houses: the stations were built mostly by young people who had just graduated from vocational schools and did not care much about safety. In addition, there were fights. So, as they wrote at the time, 'life was not a necessity'. When Unit 1 of the power plant started operating, several hundred construction workers were already buried in the cemetery. These were the 'foundation pits' of the second half of the twentieth century (to quote Andrei Platonov's novel[54]).

I, a non-partisan Jew, became the head of the ACS department by accident. The first head drank a lot and had to be suspended. Then the head became a party member who had few other merits and failed at everything. I was appointed acting head, and according to the legislation of the time, a person who had been acting head for three months automatically took over the position of head without the approval of the district party committee. The system had walls, but it also had holes in them.

When the Chernobyl accident happened, the director called us together and said: 'We built the plant, so we have to think about how to eliminate this accident. We are signing up everyone to volunteer as liquidators, but anyone can refuse.' No one refused. I went there twice after the accident. Dozens, maybe hundreds of organisations were working there, each doing something. Tens of thousands of people, including us. We were looking, thinking, inventing something: how to place a crane, how to make a shelter. But, as I understand it, the decisions were made not by us, but by the military and Moscow scientists who had experience in testing bombs and eliminating accidents at military training grounds and secret facilities. There was little information. People did not know

---

54   Andrei Platonov (1899-1951) – a Soviet Russian novelist, short story writer, philosopher, playwright, and poet. his principal works remained unpublished in his lifetime because of their skeptical attitude toward collectivization of agriculture (1929-1940) and other Stalinist policies, as well as for their experimental, avant-garde form infused with existentialism which was not in line with the dominant socialist realism doctrine. His famous works include the novels *Chevengur* (1928) and *The Foundation Pit* (1930).

what to fear or how to protect themselves. I then came up with a formula: the further away from Chernobyl, the scarier it is. No one knew the consequences and dangers of what was happening there. There were no adequate theories or experience.

In short, I am not a hero of Chernobyl. The heroes and victims are those who worked in the first days and months near the reactor. Svetlana Aleksievich[55] wrote about this very well in her book *Chornobyl Prayer: A Chronicle of the Future* (1997), whose translation into Ukrainian I later initiated. It was translated by Oksana Zabuzhko[56]. At first she said: 'You know I don't do translations.' But after reading the book, she called me the next morning: 'I cried all night, I'm going to translate it.'

How did your life develop after Chornobyl?
I call the stage of my life after Chornobyl my 'second life' — humanitarian. The first stage, as I said, was engineering. In the late 80s, the country was becoming different, and active social and political life began. The *perestroika* period changed a lot in the country. There was already a sense of freedom, although the last political prisoners had not yet returned from prison and exile. I was increasingly attracted to sociology.

It should be recalled that there was almost no official sociology in the Soviet Union, instead there was scientific communism. I studied sociology as a science of society on my own, chaotically selecting pre-revolutionary and then Polish sources. I learned Polish, and it became a window to the free world for me. At that time, there were no books in English in the shops, but some Polish books were available in the *Druzhba* (Friendship) bookstore. In 1977, when it was announced that a new democratic constitution, the Brezhnev constitution, would be adopted, I, an amateur, suddenly imagined that I would be able to analyse the 'national discussion' and understand the legal consciousness of Soviet citizens.

---

55   Belorussian writer and publicist. Nobel Prize in Literature 2015.
56   A well-known Ukrainian writer, poetess, essayist, publicist, teacher.

Have you conducted a whole study?

Yes, I did. Do you remember Thornton Wilder's[57] book *The Bridge of King Louis the Holy* (1927): 'This bridge fell, people died, and now I can trace the pattern of death: why these people died, what sins they were punished for.' And it seemed to me that it was at this unique moment that I would be able to identify the peculiarities of people's legal consciousness and understand more about who they were—Soviet people. So I collected and summarised thousands of citizens' proposals for the draft text of the constitution. It took me about a year, and as a result, I wrote a text. I pointed out the roles of different groups in understanding the country's laws: what workers wanted to change, what intellectuals, lawyers, humanities specialists, etc. From newspaper and journal publications, it was clear what constitutional articles Soviet citizens most often wrote about. It was interesting that there were no opinions published on political articles at all, although I think there were some. My selection of more than 10,000 texts is quite representative—Soviet citizens submitted about 400,000 such proposals. The press published mostly primitive proposals that had nothing to do with law and the constitution. For example, 'children should respect their parents, and salaries should be "adequate"', or 'retirement should be on time'. Some of the more interesting proposals that did manage to get through to the press, of course, were not taken into account and the constitutional commission did not include them in the final text. The roles of 'social work heroes' or laureate writers are interesting here—all of them were absolute apologists for the government.

When I finished the work, I realised that if I published it, I would get a prison sentence. I weighed the pros and cons and decided to show the text only to my friends. Thank God, the KGB didn't find out about it. In the late 1980s, my work was published in a shortened version in the journal *Philosophical and Sociological Thought*.

---

57 American prose writer, playwright and essayist, Pulitzer Prize winner (1928, 1938 and 1943).

Have there been any attempts by 'official' scholars to analyse the constitutional debate?
Pseudo-academic, apologetic reviews appeared a few years later. It was me who was so naive at the time, but professionals understood how risky this topic was and avoided it. In fact, my research revealed not so little. When I showed the text to my friends, historians and sociologists, they asked me: 'Did you do this yourself?' I answered: 'Yes.' — 'It's a valuable work for a whole department, and it's interesting to read,' I received a reply.

Did your interest in sociology turn into a professional activity, and did your participation in the journal 'Philosophical and Sociological Thought' become a new stage in your life?
Yes. It was a great school for me. I learnt a lot. The journal has become one of the most interesting intellectual tribunes for Ukrainian scholars, and the Institute of Philosophy, where a group of people gathered and later united in the editorial board of the *Philosophical and Sociological Thought*, has become one of the centres for the formation of new models of intellectual and, more broadly, spiritual life. I remember interesting discussions, large-scale projects and programmes, and publications that were ahead of their time. These were indeed breakthroughs, fresh thinking, quite deep and unconventional judgements. Until then, almost all academic journals were 'too clever', it was difficult to get through to the thought in the texts published there, and our experiments were starting a different tradition. Anyway, we discussed all the materials together, trying to understand the complex and dynamic social changes.

It was a time of transition: yesterday, many things were impossible, but today they have become a reality. I remember bringing the article to the editor-in-chief of the journal, Yury Pryliuk[58], and saying:

- Yury, we have never published anything like this before.
- Go ahead and publish it,' he replied.
- Read it, there's a lot of sedition.

---

58 Philosopher, Doctor of Philosophy.

- Publish it. While we are preparing it for publication, while it comes out, it will be allowed. Go ahead and publish.

Many of those with whom we formed the journal were my friends then and are now. They are known in the humanitarian life of Ukraine. These are the leading sociologist Yevhen Holovakha, Kostyantyn Sigov, with whom we run the *Dukh i Litera* publishing house, Natalia Vyatkina, who has been heading various publishing projects for a long time, Yevhen Bystrytsky, director of the Renaissance Foundation, Danylo Yanevsky, Yury Prylyuk, Natalia Panina, Volodymyr Zhmyr... All of us were under the tutelage of Myroslav Popovych[59], who, being one of the leaders of the Institute of Philosophy, was also the 'patron' of our team. In the Soviet years, Myroslav wrote books on logic. This was his niche, far from ideological issues. We worked with him for a dozen years.

Strategically, I was then engaged in expert surveys, developing questionnaires. I had hopes (as I did when I was working on the constitution) that by turning to intellectuals and asking them to answer the questions in the questionnaire, I would explain a lot to myself and to my readers in understanding the changes that were taking place in society. Among my respondents were Grigory Pomerants[60], Nina Braginska[61], Taras Vozniak[62], Myroslav Marynovych, Myroslav Popovych, Vasyl Lisovy[63] (this was probably his first publication after his release), other dissidents who had just returned from prison, philosophers, historians... In short, I gathered a lot of smart people, and they answered my 'naïve' questions about what was happening in the world and in the country. The

---

59 Ukrainian philosopher, academician of the NAS of Ukraine, Doctor of Philosophy, specialist in the field of cultural studies, logic and methodology of science, history of Ukrainian culture, director of the G.S. Skovoroda Institute of Philosophy NAS of Ukraine (2001–2018).
60 Russian philosopher, culturologist and writer. During the WWII he was a literary employee of a division newspaper. In 1949 he was arrested and sentenced to 5 years on charges of anti-Soviet activity. He was later rehabilitated.
61 Russian historian, translator of Greek and Latin ancient authors.
62 Ukrainian culturologist, political scientist, editor-in-chief and founder of the independent culturological magazine "Ї," General Director of the Lviv National Art Gallery, Vasyl Stus Prize winner (2021).
63 Ukrainian philosopher, public figure, dissident, political prisoner. The organizer of *samizdat* in the 1960s.

answers were often brilliant, accurate, and bold, both in their criticism of the communist system and in their understanding of the social changes at the turn of the 80s and early 90s. And all this was quite unusual in a country where the principle that what was allowed in Moscow was not allowed in Kyiv still worked.

For me, these were the first experiences of sociological expert surveys and editorial work, which eventually took a prominent place in my preferences. Kostyantyn Sigov offered me the role of co-editor of the journal and co-director of the *Dukh i Litera* publishing house, which has determined a lot in my life since then and up to now. After all, when preparing books or journal articles, I had the opportunity to communicate in person or in absentia with the giants of the twentieth century spirit — Hannah Arendt[64], Metropolitan Andrey Sheptytsky[65], Janusz Korczak, Sergei Averintsev, Ivan Dziuba[66], Martin Buber[67], Yevhen Sverstiuk[68], and many others. In previous decades, I did not even dare to dream about it.

What are your favourite moments of working at the journal?
Of course, the funny ones. Let me tell you a few stories from the first stages of my work. I first wrote an article for the journal in what I thought was Ukrainian. I don't remember the title of that article anymore, but I remember my first editor, Larysa Maleshevska, who actually rewrote my text in a wonderful literary language. I asked her: 'Is it possible to compare my text with yours to understand the mistakes?' She replied: 'You'd better look at the edited text, and if you have any comments on it, I'm ready to discuss it.' I had no comments.

---

64 German-American historian. H. Arendt, whose writings on totalitarianism and epistemology produced a significant influence on political theory, is considered one of the most important thinkers of the 20th century.
65 Primate of the Ukrainian Greek Catholic Church, Metropolitan of Galicia, Archbishop of Lviv (1901–1944).
66 Literary critic, second Minister of Culture of Ukraine (1992-1994), one of inspirers of Ukrainian independence.
67 Jewish existentialist philosopher, religious Judaic thinker and writer, first president of the Israeli Academy of Sciences (1960-1962).
68 Ukrainian literary critic, essayist, poet, thinker, philosopher, participant in the Sixties movement, political prisoner of the Soviet regime.

Another time, I was preparing a collection of materials for a scientific conference on Ukrainian-Jewish relations. It was one of the first international forums of mutual understanding. I submitted the materials to the editorial board. My friend, the deputy editor-in-chief, Volodymyr Zhmyr, was in charge of those texts. He categorically stated that he would not accept several texts for publication because, according to the journal's standards, publications must contain photographs of the authors. But I didn't know where to find the portraits of Ivan-Pavlo Himka from Canada and Abraham Ascher from the United States. It was the early 90s, when there was no internet and telephone calls to foreign countries were fantastically expensive. And then I asked Sergei Naboka (a well-known dissident and journalist) for a photo of him, because I thought he looked a bit like Himka, and I also took a photo of my father, who looked like Ascher, and brought them to the editorial office. 'There now,' Zhmyr said, 'and you said you couldn't find the photos!' Twenty years later, when I met Ivan Himka again, he thanked me for the article and asked, 'What is that photo where I don't look like myself?' And I told him the story.

When did you become interested in Judaism? After all, you know a lot about both Jewishness and Judaism, but you were not taught this in your family.
Of course, my grandparents knew Yiddish, but almost all of them died when I was still a child. My knowledge was minimal. I started to become interested in Jewish history and culture in the late 60s. It was a natural interest for a young man, but I had unnatural ways of finding sources of information. I read, like other people in those days, lousy Soviet books about Judaism and Zionism, and between the lines I hoped to find the information I needed, but I found mostly ideological propaganda. I would look through thousands of pages of books, newspapers, and journals and accidentally discover unedited texts by Chaim Nachman Bialik[69] or Vladimir (Ze'ev) Jabotinsky[70]. I started learning Yiddish with Polina Yakovlevna, an

---

69 Jewish poet, one of the founders of the modern literature in the Hebrew language.
70 Jewish writer and publicist, one of the leaders of the Zionist movement; co-founder of the State of Israel and its Armed Forces (Hagan).

accountant at the design bureau. However, she was soon summoned to the HR department and advised to stop our lessons. She could not disobey.

Over time, when the years of *perestroika* and then independence came, I decided for myself that the time had come—and it was my job—to help bring the history and culture of my people back into the public consciousness of Jews and others. I understood that without memory, without the heritage of generations, the future cannot be built.

In the 1980s, as I have already mentioned, various public organisations began to emerge—national, confessional, etc. I was one of those who contributed to the formation of the Jewish community. Interest in national history and culture was growing, but there were almost no relevant information sources. Then my friends and I created a centre for Judaic studies, which turned into an independent Institute of Judaic Studies, and eventually the Centre for Research on the History and Culture of Eastern European Jewry at the Kyiv-Mohyla Academy was created, but all of this is one line, more than a quarter of a century long.

We started from scratch because there were almost no people who could be our teachers. We gathered various activists around conferences and listened to what they had to say. Later, these conferences became thematic, and we had scholars from Israel and the United States come to give speeches and lectures. Later, we not only listened, but also prepared the first scientific studies ourselves. I knew neither Hebrew nor Yiddish, which is strange for the director of the Centre for Jewish Studies. Unfortunately, I still don't. So I decided that I would play the role of an organiser and manager, and over time, as experts in Judaic studies would appear, I would help them in every way possible. And I think I succeeded. Today we are one of the leading centres for Jewish studies in the country.

Thanks to our projects and self-education, I became more knowledgeable in this area. Despite the fact that I still often rely on the knowledge of my colleagues, I initiate most projects myself. Creativity is not always related to knowledge. I consider myself more of an organiser than a researcher.

Can I ask you a question that was natural for a Soviet Jew: did you ever have a desire to leave the country?
Of course, the question of 'to leave or to stay' was discussed in every Jewish family (and, probably, in most Ukrainian families opposed to the regime). I decided to stay where I was born. It was a subconscious decision. I explained to myself and others as follows: there are mononational and multinational states in this world. The multinational model, where citizenship in a country guarantees equal rights to all, dominates European civilisation. I hope that this is the right path for Ukraine as well. All my roles today are focused on this model of development. Ukraine would not be a European country without Armenian churches and Jewish synagogues, without the culture of the Crimean Tatars or Polish spiritual heritage, without Sholom Aleichem, Mikhail Bulgakov, Bruno Schulz.

In Soviet times, almost three generations of Jews had no access to books or knowledge of the history and culture of their people. As late as the late 1980s, Jews were still in the throes of a spiritual pogrom (and conscious Ukrainians were not in a much better situation).

There was not a single person who could be a teacher: most of those who had a Jewish education and knew the language and culture were killed by the Nazis during World War II and later by the ideologues of the Soviet government. And when modern times began, with Mikhail Gorbachev's *perestroika*, many Jews left for Israel or America. Nevertheless, the first steps were taken to rebuild the community: people interested in Jewish history and culture gathered together and later established religious communities, national schools, student associations, libraries, and more.

When did you first go abroad?
At some point, the European Union decided that, in addition to discussing important community documents by MEPs, it was worth organising public readings. A Ukrainian delegation was invited to Brussels, headed by Natalia Belitser[71], a well-known scholar who later became an active public figure, researcher and defender of the

---

71 A well-known Ukrainian researcher, a leading expert on indigenous peoples and national minorities.

rights of Crimean Tatars. The delegation consisted of 20-25 people: a deputy minister, a political scientist, an artist, etc. We travelled to Brussels by bus. For four days, we took part in a strange conference, so to speak: one after another, people from different countries took the floor and talked about different things.

I remember this trip because it was my first trip (as it was for many of us) to real Europe, to a city with a wonderful art museum. In those days, the city was celebrating its festival, and the residents dressed in medieval costumes staged a wonderful parade that impressed us.

We were accommodated far outside the city, at some sports base, and were given coupons that allowed us to use the metro and bus. The only thing was that they didn't warn us that the metro stops working at half past eleven in the evening, so one day we had to walk home, reaching the hotel around four in the morning. We were fed strangely at this conference—there was very little food and it was served on aluminium dishes that looked like either army or prison dishes.

The next day after the end of the conference, the World Jewish Congress was beginning, and Joseph Zissels[72] said to me: 'Stay with us (he was a member of the delegation), we will find a place for you to spend the night, and you will return with us (also by bus).'

When this first conference of ours was over, a powerfully built gentleman from our Ukrainian group, who was always short of food, said to me as he said goodbye: 'I hope the Jews will feed you.' He also suggested that all of our participants give me the bus/metro coupons they had left over. Needless to say, we had almost no money on this trip—the richest had ten dollars. So, I got about 50-60 of those coupons. I decided to sell them to someone to 'get rich'. At a flea market, a vendor was happy to buy those coupons from me, giving me half their value. With that 'big' money, I bought shoes for my children as gifts, as well as boots for myself. Those boots were warm and made of leather, but they must have

---

72 Ukrainian public figure, activist of the Ukrainian Jewish movement, executive co-president of Vaad Ukraine, Executive Vice President of the Congress of National Communities of Ukraine.

been made before the WWII. (In the following years, my wife tried to throw them away because they were a bit out of date aesthetically. In the end, she won, but it was already at a time when we could buy something at home).

Then I started looking for the location of the World Jewish Congress and went to ask at the synagogue. I had no idea the degree of security that such a gathering would require. A few hours later, I found myself in front of the Congress security people, who, after talking to me, decided that I was neither a spy nor a terrorist. That was the first time I attended a meeting of the World Jewish Congress. I remember wearing jeans and sneakers. The president of Ukraine, Leonid Kravchuk[73], spoke at the same congress, and I wrote a short note about him for the forum delegates.

I will also tell you about my first trip to America. It was associated with a very important international experience for me and, I think, for our other colleagues involved in the *Ukraine* project, which was initiated in the early 90s by David Ross, director of the American Jewish Committee's Institute for Tolerance. He was one of those who tried to promote understanding between peoples who had a difficult and tragic experience of relations. Before coming to Ukraine, where we met, he worked with Germans and Jews, with Poles and Jews. Now we have started to work with David. The delegations that were formed in both America and Ukraine included activists and community officials from both countries. This contributed to a better understanding between us.

The Ukrainian delegation included representatives of the Ministry of Education, as well as Solomiya Pavlychko[74], Joseph Zissels, Myroslav Marynovych, Taras Voznyak and others. David offered us a rather intensive programme, and every day we had meetings with representatives of the American authorities or the Ukrainian embassy; meetings at the *Voice of America* radio station and at the

---

73 The first President of Ukraine after the restoration of independence.
74 Ukrainian writer, daughter of writer Dmytro Pavlychko, Doctor of Philosophy, founder of the publishing house of translated scientific literature *Osnovy*, author of works on the theory of literature and the history of feminism. Member of the Revolution on Granite in 1990.

studios where were produced animated films, at Columbia University and the School of the Arts... Each meeting turned into a discovery for us: we learned how television creates stories for children's programmes that promote tolerant relations between people of different faiths or races. We saw how the *Voice of America* radio works and had the opportunity to hold dialogues with leading correspondents. We had numerous dialogues with scholars to discuss current issues in Ukraine, the United States and the world.

Now we live in a democratic world and have access to the internet, but back then everything was new to us. I remember we were taken to a huge shopping mall (400 stores) — it was the first time we had seen such an abundance of goods, because in our country there were almost empty stores. We didn't know what to do in those stores. The money in our pockets was symbolic. And we didn't really know much about goods. We are walking through a store with Taras Wozniak, discussing some philosophical issues, and suddenly we see shoes at the lowest prices. Taras orders them: 'I'd like purple shoes, size 35, 36 and 37'. I ask: 'Why purple?' He proudly replies: 'That's you who has democracy at home, but that's not the case with me: they will wear whatever I buy.' He was buying for his mother-in-law, wife and daughter. Then we saw that the doors of the shops were starting to close, but we didn't know how to get out of these mazes. I tell Taras: 'We're not at home, the dogs won't set on us, they'll find us somehow.' And indeed, half an hour later, we were found and returned to the hotel, happy.

The project, in my opinion, was extremely successful, at least for us. It lasted for three years until the tragic death of David, who was still a fairly young man. He died of a heart attack when the electricity was suddenly cut off in Chicago, his hometown. In the summer, it is impossible to live there without air conditioning, and David was one of almost a hundred people who died that tragic day. May he rest in peace.

Your interest in sociology and Jewish studies can be called professional, but do you write books?
No, I don't. I remember Leo Tolstoy's statement that you should write books only when you understand that you will say something

new to humanity. I don't think I have anything new to say. However, I do write articles, participate in conferences, appear on radio and television, but most often I act as a manager. I have two managerial roles. The first is the director of the Centre for Jewish Studies. This is a big job, because we are restoring Judaic studies in the Ukrainian post-totalitarian world for the first time. The second is the editor-in-chief of a publishing house. These two roles fill my life time. And for me, this is a great happiness that I have never even dreamed of before. After all, it is extremely interesting to be a compiler and editor of books that you choose for yourself. For example, a year of working on Hannah Arendt's book *The Sources of Totalitarianism* (2005) was a year of comprehending the main problems of the twentieth century in dialogue with a brilliant historian. *The Sources...* explained to me the recent past with its most terrible totalitarian regimes—Nazism and Communism.

What books do you refer to all the time?
Most often I refer to my business diaries, which I have kept for over forty years. Half of the diary is for reference, and the other half contains projects and plans for the year, month, week, day, hour. My wife sometimes asks: 'Put me in your nonsense too.' This is the book I work with the most—it is my management toolkit. It is in the diary that I create lists of projects I plan to work on, books from which I choose those to be published. I write down the most important projects in detail. Today, I am planning to publish books for various series (*Library of Judaica, Library of Resistance, Library of Hope,* and *Cultural Figures*), the activities of PEN, the Vasyl Stus, Yury Shevelov and Les Taniuk Prizes[75], the Vasyl Stus Virtual Museum, and so on. I am also planning meetings for *UkrlifeTV*—dialogues with

---

75 The Vasyl Stus Prize was founded in 1989 by the Ukrainian Association of Independent Creative Intelligentsia. Since 2016, the prize is patronized by PEN Ukraine, Kyiv-Mohyla Business School and the *Dukh I Litera* publishing house; the Yury Shevelov (the founder of modern Ukrainian essays) Prize is a literary award for achievements in the field of essay. It was founded in October 2013; the Les Taniuk Prize "For the preservation of historical memory" was established by the human rights organization *Memorial*, Les Kurbas National Center for Theatrical Art and the *Dukh i Litera* publishing house; it is awarded annually since 2018.

book authors, editors of publishing houses, artists, and scholars. By the way, this is a very interesting project that Kostyantyn Sigov and I have been running for over three years. Almost every half-hour conversation is watched by 1,500 to 2,000 viewers. We are grateful to Lyudmila Nemyria, the director of the portal, and her colleagues.

My favourite section in my diary is 'New Ideas', where I write down various thoughts that arise either from analogies with what I have heard, seen, read, or are formed in God knows how. I remember Emile Krotky's[76] formula well: 'A good idea came to him, but didn't find anyone at home, so it left.' So, I try to avoid such a situation.

As for books, I often return to the texts of Janusz Korczak. In my opinion, his humanistic ideas largely defined the twentieth century. Read, for example, his book *The Human Child*. I am also re-reading books by Svetlana Aleksievich. I not only read her texts, but also studied them. These are brilliantly written in-depth sociological studies and testimonies (almost all of which have been translated into Ukrainian) about the greatest tragedies caused by the communists: the fate of children and women during the Second World War (*War Has No Female Face*, Vivat, 2015, and *Last Witnesses. A Solo for a Child's Voice*, Dukh i Litera, 2016), the tragedy of the Soviet military occupying Afghanistan (*Zinc Boys*, Vivat, 2016), Chornobyl (*Chornobyl Prayer: A Chronicle of the Future*, Komora, 2016), and then the Soviet man who failed the test of freedom (*Secondhand Time (The End of the Red Man)*, Dukh i Litera, 2014).

By the way, about twenty years ago I met Svetlana Aleksievich in Paris. I said to her then: 'Ms Svetlana, it would be good to submit your books for the Nobel Prize.' Then she answered me: 'Come on, Mr Leonid, between me and the Nobel Prize is a distance as far as the sky'. But time put everything in its place. And the sky came closer[77].

---

76 Poet, satirist of Ukrainian origin. Published satirical works under the pseudonym E. Krotky, but lyric poems — under the real name Emanuel German. The author of many aphorisms.

77 The Belarusian writer Svetlana Aleksievich received the Nobel Prize in Literature in 2015 "for her multivocal work, a monument to suffering and courage in our time".

I also turn to texts related to the history and politics of Ukrainian and Polish dissent. At one time I was impressed by Mykhailyna Kotsiubynska's[78] book *Letters and People. Reflections on Epistolary Creativity* (2009), in which she analyses the correspondence of both early twentieth-century writers and dissidents. These are texts that the authors treated no less responsibly than their substantial publications of prose and essays. Neither Vasyl Stefanyk[79] nor Mykhailo Kotsiubynsky[80] could imagine themselves as authors of second-rate texts. And for dissidents who were imprisoned, letters were the basis of their spiritual heritage, almost the only thing they were allowed to do, and even then, with many restrictions. The researcher comprehended these phenomena at a deep level. Another interesting book is *A Talk Between a Citizen and a Priest* (2013), a record of a conversation between Jacek Żakowski[81] and the leaders of *Solidarity*: the political leader Adam Michnik and the spiritual leader (chaplain of *Solidarity*) Józef Tiszner[82]. These are very important internal dialogues between the sociologically oriented Michnik and the spiritually oriented Tishner in assessing the situation of the struggle against communist rule. The book is so well constructed that one almost feels like a participant in that conversation. Subsequently, these texts became an invaluable source for the comprehension of the Maidan events of 2013-2014.

In fact, I hardly have time to re-read books. I don't have time to prepare new ones. I can talk about each of them with enthusiasm, but this is a topic for another conversation.

---

78   Ukrainian literary critic, translator, active participant in the movement of the Sixties, Shevchenko Prize winner (2009). Niece of a classic of Ukrainian literature, Mikhailo Kotsiubynsky.
79   Vasyl Stefanyk (1871-1936) is an outstanding Ukrainian writer, master of expressionist short story, public figure, politician.
80   Mykhailo Kotsiubynsky (1864-1913), an outstanding Ukrainian author, known as an impressionist writer, entered Ukrainian literature as a master of psychological prose. As tops of his style are considered the novels *Shadows of Forgotten Ancestors* and *Fata Morgana*.
81   Polish journalist, brilliant interviewer.
82   A famous Polish philosopher and publicist, Roman Catholic priest, professor at the Pontifical Academy.

You touched upon the topic of dissidence. What does this topic mean to you personally?

Now we have created the Archive Center for Dissident Studies, whose main tasks are to collect dissident archives, to comprehend the ethos of this movement, to prepare and publish biographies of its main participants. We managed to collect archives of Eugene Sverstyuk, Roman Korogodsky[83], Alexander Feldman[84], Geliy Snegiryov[85], Ivan Dziuba... We have established contacts with other centers that deal with this topic and plan to coordinate our actions. We work on books of memoirs about Zynovy Antoniuk[86], Nadezhda Svetlichnaya[87], memoirs of Marta Dziuba[88], correspondence of Ivan Dziuba himself. Additionally, we deal with the need to tell about dissidents to the next generation of Ukrainians.

The topic of dissidents has been very important to me in recent years. Perhaps this is also because, while admiring the feat and memory of these people, I subconsciously feel responsible for not being there for them. I can explain this to myself by saying that I started to understand something much later than those who were involved in that milieu.

I really wanted to prepare and publish a book about the phenomenon of dissidence for future generations. I understand that our children and grandchildren are more interested in the events of their own lives, and they are certainly less interested in history, even if it is not so distant. The task was not an easy one, and only numerous dialogues with Dmytro Stus[89] and Oleksii Sinchenko[90], and then Myroslav Marynovych's advice, led to the formation and

---

83 Ukrainian film critic, literary and film expert, active participant in the Sixties movement.
84 Ukrainian and Jewish dissident, human rights activist.
85 Writer, film director, dissident. A close friend of Victor Nekrasov.
86 Member of the Ukrainian national democratic and human rights movement, publicist and translator.
87 Member of the Sixties movement, human rights activist, publicist, memoirist, journalist.
88 Wife of dissident Ivan Dziuba.
89 Ukrainian writer, General Director of the National Museum of Taras Shevchenko. The son of the poet and dissident Vasyl Stus.
90 Literary critic, chief editor of the series "Figures of Culture" of the Dukh I Litera publishing house, now soldier in the war with Russia.

publication of the book *Dissidents. An Anthology of Texts* (2018). My experience of publishing the anthology about the Holocaust, *Beyond Understanding* (2001) by Michael Berenbaum[91] and John Roth[92], the first significant book about those events, also helped. The price of the texts contained in it was the suicide of almost every third author, because it was often beyond human capabilities to relive those events, even in thought.

In recent years, this list has been supplemented by books that we have prepared with one of the best Ukrainian art critics, Dmytro Gorbachov[93]: *Knights of the Hungry Renaissance, Ukrainian Art Avant-garde: Manifestos, Journalism, Conversations, Memories, Letters*. Thanks to these books, the author received recognition, Canadian Peterson Literary Prize, Gold Medal of the Academy of Arts of Ukraine, awards at book forums, *Books of Ukraine* ratings.

I read and reread one of the most important books of recent years: Amir Weiner's *Understanding the War: World War II and the Fate of the Bolshevik Revolution*. This book, in fact, is an encyclopedia of events and participants in the Second World War. There was nothing like this in Soviet times, and even after that, because the Second World War was presented to us as a confrontation between Nazi Germany and the Soviet Union, we did not know practically stories about other events of this war and its other participants. And even that part of the stories about the Nazi-Soviet confrontation consisted more of false myths than of the truth of history.

Can your interest in fine art also be called professional?
I have been interested in art history for a long time and quite consistently. My private library has a lot of art albums and is replenished also with our publications: *Culture League: Artistic Avant-Garde of the 1910s and 1920s* (2007), *Collage. Assemblage. Object* (2013)

---

91 Famous Holocaust researcher and former head of the Holocaust Memorial Museum in the United States.
92 American writer, editor, professor emeritus at Claremont McKenna College, director-founder of the Center for the Study of the Holocaust, Genocide and Human Rights.
93 Ukrainian art critic, historian of Ukrainian art, international expert of art works, professor. Honorary Academician of the National Academy of Arts of Ukraine (2023).

by Sergei Parajanov, *Kyiv Collection. The Jewish Theme in the Works of Ukrainian Artists from the 1950s to the Present* (2015) and many other albums by contemporary Ukrainian artists.

I have also communicated and communicate with many artists. Many of them are not just talented, but in my opinion, genious.

Many years ago I met an extremely interesting artist, Boris Lekar[94]. We became friends. He told me about the history of art, which he knew very well, gave me his works when he lived in Kyiv, and I organised his exhibitions in the city's galleries. I don't know anyone else with such fine watercolours as Boris. I tried several times to publish an album of his works, but I failed. The printing capabilities of the late twentieth century did not allow to convey the subtle nuance of light colours in his paintings. He found a very interesting method of multi-layered painting, when light (mostly in portraits) was shed as if from inside the work. Later, Boris Lekar moved to Israel, and we continued to communicate: both during his visits to Kyiv and when my wife and I visited Israel. After his death (2010), Selim Yalkut[95] and I prepared and published a book (*The World of Boris Lekar*, 2012). But while the artist was still alive, we managed to publish a wonderful album, *Boris Lekar* (1999).

My wife and I have been friends with Olga Rapay-Markish[96] for several decades. In my opinion, she is one of the best ceramicists not only in Ukraine but also in the world. Her work includes thousands of wonderful ceramic sculptures that will be rediscovered by our contemporaries and future generations, understanding the scale of the master. While Olga Rapai-Markish (1929-2012) was still alive, we published a wonderful album with reproductions of her works (2007), and organised a number of exhibitions of her works, the best of which was held at the National Art Museum (2007). In 2014, after Olga's death, the film director Tamara Boyko and I made a documentary about the artist. The film includes unique footage—

94　Ukrainian and Israeli painter, graphic artist, architect.
95　Writer, compiler of several artistic albums of painters, in particular the books *The World of Boris Lekar*, *The World of Zoe Lerman* and others.
96　Ukrainian sculptor, one of the most famous figures in the field of Ukrainian ceramics. Daughter of a Jewish writer Peretz Markish, killed by the Stalinist regime, and translator Zinaida Joffe.

recordings of Olga's own memories. She talked about the murder of her father as a Jewish nationalist, the murder of her stepfather as a Ukrainian nationalist, and the life in exile, both her own and her mother's. There are striking moments in those memoirs: Olga as a child along with her mother were sent into exile as members of the family of an 'enemy of the people', and upon arrival they received a document that stated: 'eternal settlement'. To the question: 'But the court sentenced us to ten years in exile?' they replied: 'We have no other forms'. We have recently published a book-album of memories about her with reproductions of her wonderful works called *Olga Rapai-Markish: Life and Work* (2018).

I would also like to mention Vadym Sydur[97], one of the best sculptors of the second half of the twentieth century. The Soviet government hated him for his outspoken anti-totalitarian sculptures, so he never had a single solo exhibition during his lifetime. At the same time, already in the liberal years, people who lived in Moscow or came to the city knew the basements where the artist worked on his works. Later, some of them became symbols of the time: 'The Unconquered', 'In Memory of the Children Who Died in Babyn Yar', etc.

I did not meet Vadym Sydur during his lifetime, I only knew his son, who took care of his father's legacy. For some time, he managed to publish brilliant albums about his father's work at public expense, which he gladly gave to me, and I gave to friends in Kyiv and Ukraine.

Vadym Sydur's work has always gone beyond the established official framework. We know how the Soviet government interpreted and glorified the canonised, socialist-realist image of the victor. Vadym Sydur offered his own version, which, in my opinion, is much more convincing and adequate: a naked, exhausted man without a leg. It is understandable how this irritated the authorities and 'art critics' in uniform. He brilliantly illustrated a wonderful book by a Lithuanian writer in Russian translation by Icchokas Meras: *On What the World Holds. A Draw Lasts a Moment* (1966). He left

---

97 Artist, sculptor, avant-gardist, poet and prose writer. One of the classics of sculpture of the 20th century.

a large series of very talented erotic drawings, an exhibition of which we once organised in Kyiv with the assistance of his son.

I highly appreciate the work of Ludmyla Bruyevych[98], who, in my opinion, is one of the most interesting graphic artists in contemporary Ukraine. I got acquainted with her work at the *Triptych* gallery some twenty years ago, when it was located on Andriyivsky Descent. I was impressed by her works — it's a fantastic combination of, on the one hand, the traditions of high graphics, on the other — national artistic traditions in some strange interweaving that only true masters can create. I was then a member of the board of the International Renaissance Foundation and suggested to my colleagues that we publish a calendar for the foundation with reproductions of her works. My colleagues agreed with this idea, and I think we did a good deed by telling our friends and colleagues about the work of a very talented artist. Ludmyla works on each of her pieces for a year, sometimes two. This responsibility for the image goes against modern trends. Her colleagues mostly complete their works in a much shorter time, and her way looks like an atavism. But she does what she does. And we know that one of the most interesting artists of our time is working next to us. By the way, Mykyta Puchkov, together with Diana Klochko[99], made a film about her work.

I was lucky enough to meet other talented artists — Ivan Ostafiichuk[100], Viktor Hukailo[101], Oksana Tsiupa[102], Oleksa Zakharchuk[103], Ada Rybachuk and Volodymyr Melnychenko[104],

---

98 Ukrainian artist, works in the field of easel graphics, uses an author's technique based on a combination of etching, watercolor and calligraphy.
99 One of the most famous experts on the history of Ukrainian art, author of the book *65 Ukrainian masterpieces. Recognized and implicit*, Yury Shevelyov Prize winner.
100 Ukrainian graphic artist and painter, Shevchenko Prize winner (2007).
101 Ukrainian painter, illustrator, graphic artist, stage designer, decorator.
102 A well-known craftswoman who works in the unique technique of textile dolls.
103 Ukrainian painter, master of landscape painting, graphic artist.
104 Ada Rybachuk and Volodymyr Melnychenko are Ukrainian artists who worked in tandem and among another worked together on a series of panels in the Kyiv Palace of Children and Youth and the Kyiv central bus station, and also created a Park of Memory at the Baikove Cemetery.

Mykhailo Epstein, Yakym Levych, Halyna Hryhorieva, David Myretsky[105], Pavlo (Pinchas) Fishel[106], Boris Yeghiazaryan[107] and many others. But this is probably a topic for a separate conversation, or perhaps a book.

Not only are you interested in art, but you also have your own diverse collections. How did your famous brick collection come about?
I like to collect a lot of things. I have dozens of different collections. When we were moving to Mohylianka, Vlada Osmak, a researcher of Kyiv history and one of the best experts and guides in the city, came to the Centre for Jewish Studies and said: 'Leonid, the reconstruction of the late nineteenth-century building is underway, and you are not looking at the bricks!' I said: 'Vlada, it's my fault, I'll fix it'. I did go through the bricks and found nothing. However, I liked the idea of looking for history in stone. Later, a hotel was going to be built here, right next to the university, for the European Football Championship. Nothing was built, but four or five old houses were destroyed. I went there, found a brick with an inscription, and brought it back. Then I came again, and this time they set dogs on me, but when I said that I was the head of the Department of Archaeology at the Kyiv-Mohyla Academy, they chased the dogs away. I found a few more bricks. My colleagues and I came again and again until we met the foreman, whom I told about the collection. And he began to carry bricks for us himself. So we got five items from there for our self-made exhibition. Collecting is fascinating—you drive around the city, see a house being dismantled, and find something. And our friends know that we collect, they bring us bricks. You just have to start, and then it somehow continues itself.

---

105 Painter, graphic artist. He was arrested by the KGB in 1973 in Moscow for conducting a personal exhibition and in 1974—in Kyiv during the laying of flowers in Babyn Yar. Lives in the USA.
106 Ukrainian and Jewish artist, designer, sculptor and graphic artist, author of numerous works of modern Judaica.
107 Ukrainian graphic artist, painter and collage artist of Armenian origin.

How many bricks with stamps do you have now?
About 60. In total, there were about a hundred brick factories in Kyiv. Gradually, we got to know those who studied this topic, and we learned a little about the history of the city. We also came across one fake brick with the inscription 'Finberg' on it, which is indistinguishable from the others—it was a gift from the artist Pavlo (Pinchas) Fishel. I treasure my collection of bricks. It is indeed a national heritage. Of course, eventually I will donate this collection to Kyiv-Mohyla Academy, but it's me who will collect it. However, I value the collection of typewriters much more. These are the tools of very worthy people, and I want to choose myself who will be represented in the collection.

I know that this collection already includes about fifty items. Who worked on them?
When the computer age came, I realised that no one (except me) needed these writing tools anymore. So I started asking scholars, writers, and dissidents if they would donate their typewriters to our collection. Authors gave them to us, or their descendants gave them to us, and that's how our collection was formed.

Later, the machines were brought to the collection without being asked, because they were given to 'good company'. Les Taniuk's daughter, Oksana, came and immediately said that she would give me her father's typewriter. Prof. Natalia Yakovenko[108] also responded to my request...

You can still feel the warmth of their owners' hands on these typewriters. Currently, the collection includes about fifty items. Some of them are from dissidents: Geliy Snegiryov, Serhii Naboka, Valery Marchenko, Zynovy Antoniuk, Ivan Dziuba, and others are from translators: Hryhoriy Kochur, Anatol Perepadia, Andriy Sodomora, Mar Pinchevsky, and also from writers and scholars: Yury

---

108 Historian (Doctor of Historical Sciences), translator, since 1992 head of the Department of History of the Kyiv-Mohyla Academy.

Shcherbak[109], Inna Lisova[110], Kost Moskalets[111], Taras Prokhasko[112], Oleksandr Irvanets[113], and Myron Petrovsky.

We also have typewriters that were given to us by the Ukrainian community in Germany. The historian Vladyslav Verstiuk once came to us and said: 'Well, where else would you keep the typewriters of Ukrainian nationalists? Of course, in the Centre for Jewish Studies! They will preserve both their heritage and ours.' We also have typewriters with Yiddish fonts from Isaac Kipnis and Matvey Talalayevsky, with Armenian fonts from Zaven Sargsyan, the builder of the Parajanov Museum in Yerevan, and even with Braille fonts for the blind, a gift from Lesya Litvinova.

Once Yaroslav Hrytsak came to us. He looked at our exposition and admitted that he had a typewriter belonging to the famous historian Ivan Lysiak-Rudnytskyi[114]. I immediately asked: 'Will you give it to me?' He agreed. We put various photographs or documents on each typewriter that are not necessarily related to the former owners—just a kind of exhibition. The next time Yaroslav visited us, he noticed a photo of Czesław Milosz[115] on one of the typewriters. 'Do you have a Milosz typewriter?' he asked. 'Not just Czesław Milosz, but all the other Nobel laureates,' I replied. But I have to confess to you that I don't have them all yet.

We record stories about each typewriter: in some cases, it is the owner's text, in other cases, the history of the machine or the text that was printed on it.

---

109 Ukrainian writer, diplomat, activist of the ecological movement, epidemiologist.
110 Writer, artist and sculptor-puppeteer.
111 Ukrainian poet, translator and literary critic.
112 Ukrainian writer, journalist, one of the representatives of the *Stanislav phenomenon*.
113 Ukrainian poet, playwright and translator.
114 Ukrainian scholar, historian of Ukrainian socio-political thought, political scientist, publicist. The author of historical works that opened Ukraine to Europe and the world.
115 Polish poet, prose writer, translator. Nobel Prize in Literature 1980.

What is your Kyiv like and what connects you to it?
My family has lived here for several generations. My grandfather, who was in the militia in 1941, died here — one of half a million citizens who were thrown unarmed against German tanks.

Here, in 1976, I married my wife, Olena, and we have been living together for 46 years. If I have managed to do anything in my life, it is largely thanks to my wife. She is the builder of our home life. I hope that I help her too. Her services to the Ukrainian intelligentsia are much more significant than mine: as a doctor, she takes care of almost all our friends — quietly, professionally, responsibly. She also takes care of all our family ties much more than I do.

Our children, Marina and Arseny, were born and raised in Kyiv, and they gave birth to their children, our grandchildren... Olena and I are rich people — we have five granddaughters and a grandson. I like the joke that you should have grandchildren before you have children, because then you have much more time to spend with them. Although this is only theoretical. Because both Olena and I are still working quite intensively and don't have much time for that.

In recent years, Olena began to write very interesting, in my opinion, blogs on various topics, not only medical. In my opinion, these are good deep texts, a reflection on problems of confronting Russia's barbaric war against Ukraine. And unexpectedly for me (I think that also for herself) she wrote wonderful books for children about the war: *Incredible stories of Buchik the Cat*, *Buchik the Cat in the City of Lion*, *London Diary of Buchik the Cat*. I share not only my own impressions of these books, they also received interesting feedback from historian Elena Styazhkina[116], philosopher Miroslav Marynovych, writer Yuri Shcherbak.

Our children are like-minded, each of them already has their own interesting professional and — what is especially important for us — moral roles in this life. Probably, my and Olena's attitude to the city, its history and culture, influenced my son's choice. He set up a travel agency called *Interesting Kyiv*, which offers more than 200 city

---

[116] Ukrainian writer, publicist, professor of history. Previously Professor at the Department of Slavic History of Donetsk National University.

tours in dozens of languages. Marina inherited Olena's profession—she is a doctor.

That's why Kyiv is mine. Maybe it's also because I left it only for a year when I was in the army, and for another four months when I went to Geneva. It was a trip at the invitation of Prof. Georges Nivat[117]. He offered me to give a series of lectures on the socio-economic problems of Ukraine at that time: one series of lectures in English and another series—on the political history of Ukraine in the twentieth century—in Russian. Georges Nivat invited me to stay for six months, but I categorically refused. I only agreed to stay for one semester. I was afraid that my country would go somewhere in the wrong direction without me. It doesn't seem very serious today, but it's true, at the time I thought you shouldn't to be away from the events of that time for so long. The fact that I was being paid $5,000 a month, compared to a Ukrainian salary of $15-20, was not an argument for me. We (at least our circle) were not taught to value money. We dreamed of reading banned books and travelling abroad, but we had no idea how to start our own business (found a publishing house or open a restaurant). A cohort of talented artists: Hryhorii Havrylenko[118], Olga Rapai-Markish, Volodymyr Melnychenko, Ada Rybachuk, and others, hardly ever sold their works. They gave them as gifts. But not to sell! Many times I witnessed meetings of the above-mentioned masters with foreigners who wanted to buy paintings, but the artists refused to sell them. Perhaps this was an echo of Soviet traditions, when any trade was condemned as speculation.

In the Geneva archive of the Red Cross, I was looking for at least some materials about the Holodomor. I found almost nothing. The Soviet regime worked effectively and blinded even the representatives of this organisation in the Soviet Union. But let's get back to Kyiv.

---

117 Slavist, member of the European Academy (London), professor at the University of Geneva, president of the International Geneva Meetings, honorary professor at many European universities.
118 Ukrainian artist; member of the Union of Soviet Artists of Ukraine since 1960. Representative of Ukrainian avant-garde art.

In all other cases, I have only left the city for short periods of time. Thanks to my current role, I know a lot of humanitarians who work in this city. Museums, concerts, exhibitions... Perhaps the most memorable events of different years are the landmarks.

Kyiv in the 1970s was a special place for me, when the *Druzhba* theatre and concert agency was active, organising tours of the best theatres of the Soviet Union in our city. Thanks to its director and team, we had the opportunity to see the best performances of the leading theatres of the Soviet Union. For several years, I collected information about upcoming events in almost all the theatres and cultural centres of Kyiv at that time, having my own correspondents there. Then I compiled it into a single newsletter and printed several dozen copies on tissue paper. Perhaps this was one of the first bulletins that summarised what was happening in the culture of Kyiv at the time. Unfortunately, not a single copy has survived. At the time, performances by the Georgy Tovstonogov Bolshoi Drama Theatre, Rezo Gabriadze's Tbilisi Puppet Theatre, Vilnius Theatre, and Yury Lyubimov's Moscow Taganka Theatre were brought to Kyiv.

In the late 1970s, the famous Russian poet Arseny Tarkovsky[119] came to Kyiv. He was already well over 60 when we found out that he was a poet, because before that we knew him only as a translator. He had his own sentiments about Kyiv and Ukraine — he was especially interested in the figure of Hryhorii Skovoroda[120]. I was one of those who accompanied him in the city. Mykhailo Braichevsky[121] told him about the history of Kyiv and took him around the streets. Together with Tarkovsky, we visited the ceramic workshops where the wonderful craftswoman Halyna Sevruk[122] and her colleagues worked. The head of the workshops

---

119 Father of film director Andrei Tarkovsky, poet and translator.
120 Famous Ukrainian philosopher-thinker, musician, belongs to the most prominent Ukrainian figures of the 18th century.
121 An outstanding Ukrainian historian and archaeologist, one of the founders of the *Movement for Perestroika*.
122 Ukrainian artist, ceramist-monumentalist. Member of the Club of Creative Youth (1960-1964). Co-author of the stained glass window "Shevchenko. Mother "at Kyiv University. 1968 expelled from the Union of Artists of Ukraine for signing the "Letter of Protest 139" in defense of the repressed.

told us a long and tedious story about how during the years of Soviet rule, ceramists dreamed of a ceramics department at a university, a ceramics museum, or an academy, but the change of leaders, the war, the post-war years, and something else got in the way. When she finally finished, in the silence that followed, Arseny Tarkovsky said: 'The main thing is that they don't take the clay away from you.' It was like an electric shock to hear that phrase. He, who belonged to a generation whose 'clay' had been taken away for many years, and often their lives, had created an absolutely precise metaphor for that generation.

From that time I remember also some barbaric actions: the destruction of the *Wall of Memory* memorial at Baikove Cemetery (by Ada Rybachuk and Volodymyr Melnychenko), the ceramic *Tree of Life* near Taras Shevchenko University by Halyna Sevruk, fires in libraries — the destruction of the Ukrainian collection and the department of old books in the State Public Library of the Academy of Sciences of Ukrainian SSR (now the Vernadsky National Library), and book rarities in the Vydubytsky Monastery.

My Kyiv became even more dear to me and many other Kyiv residents and guests when, as a result of Russian aggression against our country, there was a real danger of losing the city in the first stages. The enemies were rebuffed and they rolled back to the South and East, but now they are getting us with bomb strikes. There are killed, wounded, there are symbols of this barbarism — a missile strike on Babyn Yar, a missile strike against a building of *Okhmatdyt*[123]. The first month after the attack, I, my wife, children, cats and dogs moved in with our friends. But within a month we returned, feeling that this is our city, where our friends, colleagues live, where we worked and will work and, as much as possible, will help our military to expel this evil spirit from our country. The war exacerbated our feelings and what was once perceived more calmly is now felt sharply: the beauty of our city, and its culture, which continues in spite of all circumstances. Kilometer queues for the

---

[123] The largest children's hospital in Ukraine, a specialized multidisciplinary medical and diagnostic institution for children.

Book Arsenal[124] and dozens of wonderful performances in the theaters of the city are just some of the evidence of this.

Was it your initiative to rename the streets after famous Kyiv residents?
I think this idea was in the air. I, like you, find it much more pleasant to walk down the streets of Ivan Svitlychny[125], Oleksandr Arkhypenko[126], Sergei Parajanov[127], Yevhen Sverstiuk and others. Some have already been renamed, some are still in our dreams. This is nice and adequate in relation to national memory and the values of the civilised world. We used to walk along streets named after Bolshevik 'heroes' — often murderers or people whose biographies were invented by Soviet leaders.

In renaming, it is important to focus on verified names. You said that we are talking about renaming Kyiv streets after Kyivans. But Kyiv is the capital of Ukraine, and therefore it is necessary to immortalise not only the names of Kyiv residents, but also the names of other figures of Ukrainian and world culture. I think it would be a pleasure to live on the streets of Antoine de Saint-Exupéry, Jerzy Giedroyc or Blaise Pascal.

National memory consists of many factors and elements. Among them are certain signs, memorial plaques, names of institutions and streets that are fixed in memory. Of course, provided that it is not only about the names of people, but also about the knowledge of what these people did. Therefore, Ukrainian cultural figures are faced with the task of correctly formulating such proposals and, in one way or another, contributing to the presence of streets named after Mykhailo Braichevsky, Hryhoriy Havrylenko,

---

124 The largest annual book fair in Kyiv.
125 Ukrainian literary scholar and critic, linguist, poet, translator, was repressed in Soviet times.
126 Ukrainian and American sculptor and artist, one of the founders of cubism in sculpture.
127 Ukrainian and Armenian film director, screenwriter. One of the representatives of the wave of Ukrainian poetic cinema. Known as the director of the film *Shadows of Forgotten Ancestors* (1965).

Oleksa Zakharchuk, Lyudmyla Protsenko[128], Les Kurbas[129], Yury Ilienko[130]... After all, we live in years when the pantheon of national culture is changing. Pseudo-leaders are gradually being forgotten, but it is very important to immortalise the names of real figures of history and culture. It is important that they become known not only to intellectuals, but also to the public. When discussing this issue in PEN Ukraine, we identified, first of all, those most important personalities for Ukrainian culture whose names have not yet been immortalized: Vasyl Barka[131], Ivan Bahriany[132], Mykhailyna Kotsiubynska, Ze'ev Jabotinsky, and others. I can offer a whole list. It is quite long. It seems to me that this should be initiated. We, as PEN Ukraine, decided to make our contribution to this cause. We agreed to cooperate with the Institute of National Memory.

We already have examples of effective measures. Svitlana Petrovska brilliantly organised a campaign in support of renaming Bauman Street to Janusz Korczak Street: there were festivities and the *Shchedryk* choir sang there. I think we should do the same with other streets. For example, not only to name a street after Sergei Parajanov, but also to show his films on that street!

I will mention a few more initiative examples of memorial plaques. Kostyantyn Sigov, who initiated the publication of the works of Father Oleksandr Glagolev[133], the last rector of the Kyiv Theological Academy, proposed to create a memorial plaque to the Glagolevs — Father Oleksandr, known for his humanistic views and murdered by the Soviet authorities, and his son, also a priest, Oleksii, whose family saved Jews during the Holocaust. I was

---

128 Ukrainian historian, archivist. She created more than 80 scientific papers on the history and methodology of archival studies.
129 Ukrainian actor, director, playwright, founder of the *Young Theater* and the *Berezil Theater*.
130 Ukrainian director and cameraman, author of films of Ukrainian poetic cinema.
131 Ukrainian writer and poet, representative of the Ukrainian diaspora in the United States. One of the first to speak about the Holocaust in Ukrainian lands.
132 Ukrainian poet, prose writer, publicist, politician. Taras Shevchenko National Prize of Ukraine winner (1992, posthumously), nominee for the Nobel Prize in Literature (1962).
133 Archpriest, philosopher, theologian.

happy to respond to this idea, and we turned to the artist and sculptor Ivan Grigoriev, who came up with a wonderful image for this plaque.

In order to install it on the facade of the Academy, we had to obtain a decision from the city authorities, which is always difficult. When we came to the then president of Mohylianka, Viacheslav Bryukhovetsky, and told him about our idea, he suggested: 'Let's hang a plaque on the academy's premises, and then all these competitions with officials can be bypassed.' So we did, and since then all the students, teachers and guests of the Academy pass by this plaque and remember the good deeds of the Glagolev family.

This year, we installed a plaque in memory of Osip Mandelstam[134] and his wife Nadezhda. Many Kyiv residents dreamed of having a memorial plaque in our city to commemorate this family, so a wonderful image by Svitlana Karunska now adorns Maria Zankovetska Street. These names are iconic among the Kyivan intelligentsia. Osip Mandelstam's poems were, are, and will remain examples of the best poetry of the twentieth century, symbols of rejection of despotism and totalitarianism. For many of us, the memoirs of Nadezhda Mandelshtam (Khazina) are also one of the most convincing testimonies to the life of intellectuals over several generations in the Soviet Union. Nadezhda Khazina was born and studied in Kyiv, worked with Ukrainian avant-garde artists in the early twentieth century, and met Mandelstam there. The great poet dedicated several poems to Kyiv. We published a thorough and skilfully written by Andrii Puchkov[135] book about it, *Osip Mandelstam's Kyiv in Intonations, Explanations, and Pictures* (2015). The unveiling of this plaque is another step in changing the image of Kyiv from a Soviet city to a cultural, Ukrainian, and European city.

---

134 Poet, prose writer, essayist, translator. One of the most prominent representatives of modernism of the 20th century.
135 Cultural expert, historian. Since 2018 — professor of the Department of Theory and History of Art of the National Academy of Fine Arts and Architecture. The author of more than 700 published works, in particular several dozens of monographs.

In 2007, together with Mustafa Dzhemilev, you received the Ï journal's 'For Intellectual Courage' award. A very unexpected and apt formula—intellectual courage...

To be honest, I generally take awards calmly, often ironically, as many awards are compromised. However, the award of the journal Ï has a different reputation: the names of Vyacheslav Bryukhovetsky[136], Yevhen Zakharov[137], Natalia Yakovenko, Myroslav Marynovych, Valentyn Silvestrov[138] are iconic for today's Ukraine. It was a special honour to accept this award together with Mustafa Dzhemilev[139]. After all, he is a prominent political leader of the Crimean Tatar people. And I stand in solidarity with Myroslav Marynovych, who said that day: 'I would even trust Mr Dzhemilev with the whole of Ukraine—he is a man of fierce will and absolute integrity'.

And then there were other awards...

Yes, there were. An Antonovych Foundation Prize, from the Ukrainian diaspora in America, the Silver Cross of Merit for Poland, an award from the Polish-Ukrainian Paderewski Foundation... At the Antonovych Foundation's award ceremony, I delivered a speech that was important to me, summarising the achievements of Ukrainian intellectuals over the past decades—the establishment of a school of humanitarian translation from many languages, professional scientific schools in philosophy, history, and cultural studies, the building of a publishing network; I tried to identify the main challenges of the times and outlined the desired vectors of development. It was a great honour for me to receive this award.

---

136 Literary critic, teacher, one of the initiators of the creation of the People's Movement of Ukraine, one of the members of the initiative group *December 1st*, Honorary President of Kyiv-Mohyla Academy.
137 Chairman of the Board of the Ukrainian Helsinki Human Rights Union, Director of the Kharkiv Human Rights Protection group. Member of the dissident movement of the 1970-1980s.
138 World-famous contemporary Ukrainian composer (b. 1937).
139 One of the leaders of the Crimean Tatar national movement, human rights activist, member of dissident movement, political prisoner.

But there are funny things that happen along with recognition. Once I received a phone call to say that according to the rating of *Novoe Vremya* journal, which annually identifies leaders in various fields of activity, I was named Publisher of the Year. On the cover of that journal, the word 'Rednecks' was written in big letters. It turned out that the main topic of the issue was the publication of materials about the wealth of Ukrainian MPs, and this characteristic on the cover was related to them. However, we, entrepreneurs, actors, directors, journalists, including me, now have to tell everyone that we are not the 'rednecks'. But seriously, the highest reward for me is the support of family and friends.

In Ukraine, in recent years, there have been more and more various awards that are of great importance for the development of culture — in particular, the Vasyl Stus Prize, the Yury Shevelyov Prize, the Gongadze Prize for journalists, and awards of film and theater festivals. It is very important that many of these awards are non-state, and in recent years they have gained some authority and respect from society — unlike many state awards (Shevchenko Prize), a significant part of the commissions of which consists not of cultural figures, but of officials, and the criteria for determining the winners are often unclear. A number of scandals around the awarding of these prizes (one of the last — around the Maxim Rylsky Prize with a reward for helpless plagiarism) are proof of this. Soviet traditions still sit deep in our society, but I am sure that we will overcome them.

2. Publishing Affairs

How did the Dukh i Litera publishing house come about?
The *Dukh i Litera* project began in 1997. I was approached by Kostyantyn Sigov, who actually created the publishing house, and offered to be a co-editor of the journal of the same name. I didn't agree at first, but later I got involved not only in the publication of the journal, but also in the publication of books. I became co-editor and then co-director of the publishing house. For more than two decades, *Dukh i Litera* has become an active and quite powerful publishing house.

We were among the first in Ukrainian culture to translate philosophical, historical, and cultural literature from English, Polish, French, Italian, Japanese, Spanish, German, Hebrew, Yiddish... Today, Ukraine is living a rather vigorous intellectual life and is involved in the heritage of the free world, European civilisation, whereas in Soviet times we were cut off from all this by barbed wire. Translations of such books used to be exclusively in Russian. Sometimes you could see something in the *Vsesvit* journal, but it was a drop in the bucket compared to what existed in other countries in these areas.

Over the years, we have published in Ukrainian fundamental works that proclaim the value of the individual, the principles and mechanisms of democracy and the rule of law, the foundations of human morality, the principles of coexistence of religions, nations, and states... Today, we already have translations of texts by Blaise Pascal, Emanuel Levinas, Timothy Snyder, Michel Montaigne, Hannah Arendt, Sergei Averintsev, Paul Ricoeur, Reichart Kozelek[1], Amos Oz[2], Janusz Korczak, Michael Berenbaum and others — these are steps in our growth. Kostyantyn Sigov initiated the publication of the *European Dictionary of Philosophies: A Lexicon of Untranslatability* (four volumes have already been published — 2009,

---

1 German historian and theorist of historical science.
2 A leading Israeli novelist and essayist, wrote in Hebrew. Participant in the Arab-Israeli wars of 1967, 1973, later an activist of the anti-war movement for reconciliation between the two peoples.

2011, 2013, 2016), which is perhaps the most ambitious and large-scale project of our publishing house. Philosopher Oleg Khoma, one of the editors of this edition, said at the presentation: 'While working on this dictionary, we have travelled from the nineteenth to the twenty-first century.' For this dictionary, the French have chosen categories from different cultures that are not literally translated into other languages. The original book contains more than a thousand pages. Our edition is the first translation of this book in the world. The translators and editors are Ukrainian scholars who studied at the Sorbonne, Oxford and Harvard. They did their job very well. And when someone now says that some things cannot be translated into Ukrainian, I say: it's not true — today this is possible!

During the existence of our publishing house, we have come a long way, with many mistakes, and now, in my opinion, there are fewer and fewer of them with each of our new books. We have refused to have semi-professionals involved in the creation of our publications. We usually work with true professionals (by the way, many of the participants in our projects have become even better professionals during their time with us). Today, we employ people who are skilled not only in foreign languages but also in the art of translation. We are publishing extremely complex texts by historians and philosophers, and we are doing this for the first time in our national history. Once we had a visit from a Canadian professor who told us that our publication of the book *Soi-même comme un autre* (*Oneself as Another*) by the prominent French philosopher Paul Ricoeur (2002, edited by Kostyantyn Sigov) in Ukrainian caused a real shock in Canada, because there was no English translation of this book yet, but there was already a Ukrainian one. For us, this is evidence that our seemingly 'internal editorial' strategies sometimes have a positive impact on the image of Ukrainian culture in the world.

Of course, when we take on the translation of highly complex works of Western European humanities, there are many problems. But we have developed a certain mechanism of work. First, we have a qualified translator, followed by a scientific editor, then a literary editor, then a proofreader, and then an executive editor proofreads the entire book. This multi-level work with texts contributes to the quality of publications.

It is clear that other publishing houses that have just started working on book translations often lack these years of experience. They have to go their own way until they master professional technologies. They should listen to the weighty criticism of reviewers, understand and choose something from the experience of others, so that their path to an educated reader is shorter. When they contact us, we help them as much as we can.

But there is one factor that can affect the quality of a translated book: the rather strict publication deadlines set by the grantors' conditions. When we don't meet these deadlines, we write letters to our sponsors asking them to extend the deadline for the sake of the book's quality. Usually, they meet us halfway, realising that rushing into such a matter can negate all efforts. The fact that the book will be published late will be forgotten, and if it is of poor quality, the blame will be on us.

A translated academic book can rarely survive without sponsorship. And this situation is not unique to Ukraine. In all civilised countries, there are special funds that promote book publishing. Publishers that have 'found their feet' and publish hundreds of books a year sometimes become sponsors of intellectual books themselves, publishing them at the expense of profits from mass literature. We didn't go this route because, publishing 50-60 intellectual books a year, we don't have the energy to work on any popular 'pulp fiction'. Or maybe we are subconsciously afraid of being 'drawn in' by the perspective of massive scale, of profits... We are closer to the practice of academic publishing houses, and we are looking for both partners and funds, focusing on this tradition. We often sell our books cheaper than they cost the publisher. The rest is compensated by sponsorship. Because only at this price can Ukrainian readers buy them. We try to respond adequately to any professional challenges — we keep our finger on the pulse.

I was once asked how Kostyantyn Sigov and I work, how we choose what to publish. I answered: 'We sit down at a table, and he names one Nobel Prize winner, and I name another.' 'Really?' 'Almost,' I replied. And so it has been for over 25 years. In fact, we and our friends keep a pretty close eye on the world's humanities, choosing what we think is the best, the most relevant.

So the main areas of the publishing house are philosophy, religion, and history?
Not quite so. Kostyantyn Sigov and I work together, although we have different priorities. The group of specialists led by him prepares for publication mainly contemporary French and German humanities, while the group led by me prepares for publication Judaic studies and Ukrainian and Polish liberal democratic literature.

Why Ukrainian and Polish?
After the collapse of the USSR, it seemed that everyone would publish contemporary Ukrainian authors. However, this did not happen. We decided that we had to do it. We started with a book by Vadym Skurativsky, a well-known researcher and publicist in Ukraine. As a scholar and polymath, in the difficult Soviet years he taught dozens of courses at various universities — philosophy, psychology, literary studies, history... Usually, after a few lectures, he was fired from his job. We published a collection of his articles *History and Culture* (1996), where the most interesting are devoted to the work of Taras Shevchenko. We published a collection of essays by Ivan Dziuba, *Between Culture and Politics* (1998) — there are not many intellectuals of this level in Ukraine, and each of his texts is very valuable. We also published the book *Letters from the Freedom* (1999), which contains texts by three dissidents — Zynovy Antoniuk, Myroslav Marynovych, and Semen Gluzman. The title of the book is symbolic and at the same time eloquent — these people behind bars, in conditions of long exile, managed to preserve their sense of dignity and freedom. Their fates are a unique experience of resistance to an immoral system in defence of dignity. In those inhumane conditions, they were able to defend their beliefs and, most importantly, after returning from the camp, find the strength to continue their intellectual work, defending moral values.

One of the first books by dissidents that we published was also *The Denunciation Novel* (2000)³ by Geliy Snegiryov. I didn't know Geliy personally, but I know his son, Philip. Philip called me and told that he had managed to get his father's manuscript back from the KGB archives, a diary from the time when his father was subjected to repression and persecution. He asked me to look at it and tell him if I would be interested in such a publication. I read the manuscript very quickly, and it was impossible to put it down. There are not many testimonies of this kind. Of course, I said that we would be honoured to publish such a book. The Ukrainian Memorial, headed by Les Taniuk, helped with the publication. And quite quickly (or maybe it seems so from the distance of years) we published this book in five thousand copies.

Geliy Snegiryov wrote his diary, in fact, in the last persecuted years of his life. He wrote it accurately, because he was one of the best Ukrainian writers and screenwriters of the time. During the presentation, the then president of the Ukrainian PEN Club, Yevhen Sverstiuk, said that this diary probably best conveys the psychological atmosphere in which the dissidents lived. Today this book is already a rarity—I have the last copies for my closest friends. It needs to be reprinted. Over time, together with Philip Snegiryov, we published another book by his father, a collection of prose called *Self-Portrait 66* (2001). By the way, it was Geliy Snegiryov's typewriter that started our collection of typewriters— 'grandmothers of computers', as my grandchildren call them.

In 2015, we reissued Dmytro Stus's biographical book about his father, *Vasyl Stus: Life as Art*. I recommend reading it to anyone who wants to understand something about Ukraine in the second half of the 20th century, who wants to hear great European poetry written in Ukrainian. Vasyl Stus is a genius, and who else but him should be an iconic figure of Ukraine and Ukrainians of our time.

---

3   An Ukrainian dissident novel-report, which became the main work of the author's life. In the preface, this novel is called "report with a noose around the neck."

We discussed with Dmytro Stus the fate of his father's legacy, the publication of materials about the poet, and so on. I don't remember who was the first to suggest—it doesn't matter, because the idea was in the air—that we should create a virtual museum of Vasyl Stus. Dmytro was thinking about it, but he didn't know where to get enough money to create the software for such a museum. I suggested that we turn to my friends, who had set up an IT firm more than 25 years ago that is now one of the country's leading companies. 'I think,' I said, 'that they will join this project. And so it happened—Olexiy Sigov and Andriy Anisimov, the heads of *Infopulse*, gave Dmytro the necessary software in a short time. The museum is now open, but even though it is virtual, there are years and years of work to be done. The 2017-2018 calendar with Vasyl Stus's poems printed on the pages with the numbers of the month and artworks by the poet's contemporaries on the reverse side is an addition to this virtual museum. The idea is simple, but a little unusual—the hope that a person looking at a poem for a month will if not learn it by heart, then at least read it. This is also our joint project with *Infopulse*. This year we published the book *Dissidents. An Anthology of Texts* (2018), the first attempt to present the movement more or less systematically in the most important texts by the authors. We open the book with poetic works that often served as 'evidence' in the courts, followed by speeches before the announcement of the verdict, texts written in prisons and camps, and finally, the reflection on the experience by those who were lucky enough to survive. In my opinion, the book is a success. In a few years German publishing house *ibidem-Verlag*, which publishes books in German and English languages, published this book in English.

As for Polish literature, almost every year the books we publish include new translations from this language. We owe these projects to a number of factors: the special interest of Ukrainian society in Polish affairs, the activities of the Krakow Book Institute and the Polish Institute in Kyiv, personal contacts with Henryk Litwin, Polish Ambassador to Ukraine until 2017, and his wife Anna Litwin, as well as with the Consul General of Poland in Kyiv, Rafał Wolski. We have cooperated succesfully with our Polish colleagues before, especially when Ola Hnatiuk[4] worked at the Polish embassy, but the last few years have been extremely fruitful. Firstly, we have published a dozen or so very important Polish books, and secondly, Anna Litwin has written and we have published an interesting modern guide to Kyiv in Polish. When we were looking for a place to organise an exhibition of Anatoliy Kaplan's[5] book graphics, illustrations for Sholem Aleichem, Henryk Litwin suggested that we hold it in the halls of the Polish embassy. Someone said that he would be called the Ambassador of Israel (although Kaplan had nothing to do with Israel). Henryk replied: 'I will only be proud'. Rafał Wolski initiated the publication of Mariusz Kożeniewski's book *Beyond the Golden Gate. Social and Cultural Activities of Poles in Kyiv in 1905-1920* (2015) about the history of Polish culture in Kyiv in the early twentieth century. Afterwards, he organised a number of art exhibitions of Ukrainian artists in Poland. In cooperation with colleagues, the personality of the partners, their education and interest in the work we do together is of great importance.

So, in this area, we already have something to boast about, too. I once joked with Poles that Polish literature in Ukrainian is more interesting and deeper than in Polish. Only because we choose the best and translate them—Czesław Milosz, Zbigniew Herbert, Julian Tuwim, Bruno Schulz, Janusz Korczak.

Almost all of Bruno Schulz's works are represented in Ukrainian. We have published his journalism (*Literary and Critical Essays*, 2012), correspondence (*The Book of Letters*, 2012), and artistic works (*The Book of Images*, 2014). And also a book by Jerzy Ficowski (*Regions of the Great Heresy and the Suburbs*, 2010). It was Jerzy Ficowski who collected and published Bruno Schulz's manuscripts, both prose and drawings. The previously almost unknown author, who

---

4   Polish researcher in the field of Ukrainian studies, translator and popularizer of Ukrainian literature, employee of the Institute of Slavic Studies of the Polish Academy of Sciences, professor of NaUKMA, chairman of the Promotion Society of Ukrainian culture in Poland and Polish in Ukraine.
5   An artist whose work throughout his life was closely connected with Jewish folklore and Yiddish literature, author of illustrations for the works of a number of Jewish writers, in particular classics of Jewish literature, as well as for Jewish folk songs.

was killed during the Holocaust, has become a classic of European and world culture. I am glad that in Ukrainian culture he has taken a prominent place in good translated editions. *The Schulz Dictionary* — in fact, an encyclopedia about the writer and artist — is one of our last books, which is a very interesting representation of the great master. We are sincerely grateful to our Polish partners who gave us the opportunity to translate and publish this book in Ukrainian.

Another author read by Ukraine is Janusz Korczak. He stayed in Ukraine during the First World War and completed his programme book *How to Love a Child* here. In 2012, we published two volumes of his selected works, *The Human Child* and *The Right to Respect*, translated by Sashko Irvanets, Kostya Moskalets and Volodymyr Kadenko. Sashko delayed his translations — *Alone with God. Prayers of those who do not pray* and *Children of the Bible. Moses* for several months. But he explained: 'I wasn't lazy, my responsibility to these texts was absolute.' I agreed — these are brilliant translations of brilliant texts. Some time ago we were given brilliant illustrations for *Prayers of those who do not pray*, made by one of the best Ukrainian graphics Serhiy Yakutovych. We will prepare this edition, because when the texts of one genius are complemented by works of another genius, it is usually extraordinary.

In 2021, we published a book by one of the most interesting contemporary Polish historians, Andrzej Nowak, about the Russian empire: *How did the 'empire of evil' arise? Experience of Central and Eastern Europe*. In my opinion, this is one of the most interesting studies of this topic. Poles, like Ukrainians, are well aware of the worst imperial and chauvinist theories and actions of Russia in recent centuries.

We belong to a generation that does many things for the first time. And being first also means being responsible.

You publish a lot of books, is there a growing need for professional editors?
We started with translations of French philosophers, with small brochures, which I don't dare to show now, because neither the level of those translations nor the level of publication satisfies us

today. But it doesn't happen otherwise, we all started from scratch. Today, no summary in the books of our authors is published without editing by a native speaker, and if we don't have a good editor, we won't publish the book. But I hardly remember any such cases. We have a certain circle of editors of philosophical, historical and sociological literature around us who cooperate with us quite well. We have recently published two books, *Maidan. Testimonies. Kyiv, 2013-2014* (2016) and *Maidan. Testimonies. Help for the victims. International Solidarity* (2018), where three editors worked on each text, and together with the compilers we read all the texts and knew them almost by heart. I have always remembered the words of Prof. Roman Shporlyuk: 'Nothing discredits Ukrainian books abroad like a summary in supposedly English.'

Working on our books, our editors from good professionals became brilliant. These are Yury Vestel[6], Andrii Puchkov, Olexii Sinchenko, Olexii Panych[7], Igor Vinokurov[8].

In recent years, we have published hundreds of books, and many humanitarians in the country cooperate with us. We are rich in partners, colleagues, friends, and interested readers... But at the same time, we continue to learn.

Dukh i Litera is not just a publishing house, but also a centre that strives to create an intellectual infrastructure that would connect intellectuals, publishers and readers. How does this creation process manifest itself?
First of all, in the organisation and conduct of the Ivan Lysiak-Rudnytsky Interdisciplinary Seminar, which was launched in 1996 and continued for several years. We named the seminar after Ivan Lysiak-Rudnytsky, because it was then that the *Osnovy* publishing house and the creative team led by Yaroslav Hrytsak published a brilliant two-volume work by this historian and sociologist, one of the best Ukrainian scholars of the twentieth century. Back then, his name was almost unknown in Ukraine. It is a great injustice that it did not become a symbol of intellectual freedom, intelligence, and

---

6 Science redactor of the *Dukh I Litera* publishing house.
7 Historian, translator, leading researcher at the *Dukh I Litera* publishing house.
8 Translator, researcher at the *Dukh i Litera* publishing house.

a certain professional level for all those working in the social sciences.

The seminar arose out of the need of Ukrainian intellectuals to comprehend the problems of our time. Most of these problems are difficult to correlate with the scope of any one social or humanitarian discipline. Brainstorming among representatives of different fields of knowledge is the best way to understand what is happening. Not only do the methodologies of different sciences complement each other, but also different methods within each field of knowledge work.

At the first meeting of the seminar, I spoke on behalf of the initiative group — Solomiya Pavlychko, Volodymyr Kulyk[9], Semen Gluzman[10], Oleksandr Kryvenko[11] and Volodymyr Ruban[12] — and welcomed the participants.

We have been thinking for a long time about the need for an interdisciplinary seminar that would bring together historians and sociologists, cultural studies and economists, lawyers and literary critics to think together about the most complex social problems, which are definitely interdisciplinary. We wanted this seminar to be named after Ivan Lysiak-Rudnytsky and to become a live discussion. Therefore, we proposed a certain form of meetings. First, the topic was defined, and then the author's (mostly my) development of a number of questions that would allow us to systematically analyse the phenomenon. We had two speakers who were given 10-12 minutes each to present their vision of the problem under discussion. All those present (including the meeting participants and specially invited experts who had five minutes to speak) could ask questions or participate in the discussion, with a maximum of five minutes. Afterwards, those who started the discussion summarised

---

9 Ukrainian political scientist, historian, journalist, doctor of political sciences.
10 Human rights activist, former dissident and political prisoner, well-known psychiatrist.
11 Ukrainian journalist, publicist, political and public figure. Editor of Lviv newspapers *Progress* and *Post-Progress*.
12 Ukrainian journalist, one of the founders of UNIAN news agency (1993) and several well-known Ukrainian media.

the opinions expressed and formulated the conclusions of the discussion.

I borrowed the method of discussion from a seminar in Ebenhausen, Germany, where I was invited along with other researchers and politicians from Ukraine and Russia in 1990. At that time, we were the experts for German researchers in terms of knowledge about these countries and issues. The organiser of the meeting was one of the best experts on Eastern Europe, Prof. Klaus Segbers.

The seminar was attended by the most famous Ukrainian intellectuals: historians Orest Subtelny[13], Natalia Yakovenko, Zynovy Antoniuk; philosophers Myroslav Popovych, Kostiantyn Sigov, Viktor Yelensky[14], Oksana Zabuzhko, Viktor Malakhov, Myroslav Marynovych, Yevhen Bystrytsky[15]; sociologists Yevhen Holovakha, Valery Khmelko, Iryna Bekeshkina; political scientists Volodymyr Kulyk, Mykola Riabchuk, Maksym Strikha, and Oleksandr Kryvenko; cultural historians — Vadym Skurativsky and Oleksandr Hrytsenko; literary critics — Ivan Dziuba and Solomiya Pavlychko. In addition to the Ukrainian participants, the seminar was attended by Prof. Georges Nivat (University of Geneva), Prof. Roman Shporlyuk (Harvard University), writer Svetlana Aleksievich (Belarus), Prof. Pierre Asner[16] (Sorbonne), Prof. Evgeny Rashkovsky[17] and Yury Tabak[18] (Russia), and others.

The aim of the seminar was to analyse the most complex social processes, of which we were all witnesses and often participants. Discussions were held, for example, on the following topics: faith and religion in the modern world and in Ukraine, law and lawlessness in Ukraine, etc. One of the seminars attempted to analyse the decade of independence — victories and defeats. A discussion ensued, which, due to the lack of terminology and approaches for an

---

13 Ukrainian-Canadian historian, Ph.D. Author of the first history textbook after recovery of independence of Ukraine in 1991.
14 Religious scholar, publicist, teacher, Ph.D.
15 Ukrainian scientist, Ph.D. Since 1998, Executive Director of the George Soros' International Renaissance Foundation.
16 French political philosopher, expert on international relations.
17 Soviet and Russian orientalist, religious scholar, translator, historian of science, education and Russian philosophical thought.
18 Religious scholar, translator, journalist.

objective description of this field, pointed to the fragmentation of the research that has been done, for example, in the field of sociology. Sometimes, the Lysiak-Rudnytsky seminar was a more effective mechanism for understanding problems than traditional conferences. Thus, the analysis of the topic of social tension in society began with speeches by sociologists Yevhen Holovakha and Valeriy Khmelko. They analysed the way in which modern social conflicts are growing in Ukraine. The topic was continued by historians Natalia Yakovenko and Vadym Skurativsky, who described how major social conflicts took place in Ukraine in different historical periods and under what conditions. Next, economists Oleksandr Paskhaver and Viktor Lysytsky tried to analyse the dynamics of social tension in relation to the state of the country's economy. The discussion was complemented by reports from psychiatrists, including Semen Gluzman, whose research proved that the growth of social conflicts and a sense of destabilisation had an impact on the increase in morbidity among certain groups of patients, such as drug addicts and mental patients. This was perhaps one of the most successful meetings.

At that time, each issue of *Dukh i Litera* journal began with a presentation of the recordings of discussions from our seminars. We published a separate book, *Dialogues on the Turn of the Century* (2003), which contains transcripts of more than twenty Ivan Lysiak-Rudnytsky seminars held between 1996 and 2000.

I will name only the topics of some of them: 'Intellectual Freedom in Today's Ukraine', 'Public Roles of Intellectuals', 'Law and Lawlessness of the Present', 'National Security of Ukraine', 'Faith and Religion in Modern Ukraine', 'Historical Roots of Modernity', 'Global Contradictions of the Modern World and Ukraine', 'Mass Culture in Modern Ukraine', 'Europe on the Threshold of the Third Millennium', 'Events in Yugoslavia and Possible Geopolitical Consequences of the Conflict'.

We began these seminars with the problems of intellectual freedom in Ukraine and ended with a discussion of Sergei Averintsev's *Sophia-Logos* dictionary. This dictionary-encyclopedia is one of our most successful publishing projects. The high demand for this book proved the need for such literature in the Ukrainian publishing market. A modern person subconsciously looks for those texts that bring him or her back to the world of values of European civilisation, which the Soviet system destroyed for three generations. Liberation from the constraints of totalitarian thinking is impossible without a reassessment of the foundations. Sergey Averintsev's book was recognised as the *Book of the Year* at the Lviv Forum. 'Ten słownik jest niezbędny zwłaszcza dla wszystkich postsowieckich krajów' — wrote the reviewers[19].

In the following years, our contacts with colleagues and readers grew into numerous academic conferences and public presentations of the publications at book forums, in TV and radio projects, and in various interviews for newspapers and journals. Perhaps the most successful were the discussions of the *European Dictionary of Philosophies*, volume after volume, as well as the brilliant speeches by well-known authors such as Prof. Roman Shporlyuk, the Nobel Prize winner Svetlana Aleksievich, and the author of the famous *Ukrainian Silhouettes*, Mykhailo Heifetz... The mini-performances were also great — the actors of the university theatre on stilts read texts by Blaise Pascal or Stanisław Jerzy Lec.

In your opinion, are universities in Ukraine intellectual centres?
All I can say is that we have real centres of spiritual life, such as the Kyiv-Mohyla Academy. Here you will see dozens and dozens of announcements every day about speeches by politicians, national and foreign scholars, book presentations, interest clubs, informal meetings over coffee, art exhibitions and performances, scientific seminars, discussions, theatre performances, and music concerts...

However, in my opinion, the potential here is much greater than we are using it. Knowing a little bit about international experience, I miss large-scale projects. I would like to see a seminar of world intellectuals in Mohylianka, similar to the one that has been operating in Geneva for many years. I also dream of public lectures by the world's leading scholars and large-scale dialogues around the best Ukrainian films and books... Hopefully, all this will still be

---

19 This dictionary is important for all citizens of post-Soviet countries (from Polish).

the case—young people are more educated than we are, more energetic... A similar spiritually rich life takes place at the Lviv Catholic University, with whose professors we have good academic and social contacts.

In addition to real universities, there are many others that are also called universities, but they remain Soviet in spirit. Students there only dream of lectures by real professors. I also know of educational institutions where the pseudo-business of 'me to you, you to me' has become the priority 'discipline' for all participants in the process, and where the acquired knowledge and freedom of thought and will are abstract concepts. Well, we live in a time of transition, with all its contradictions. Real universities are great developments.

However, spiritual and intellectual life is not only concentrated in universities. One of the manifestations of active intellectual life is associated with academic seminars and summer (or winter) schools. In 1995, Natalia Yakovenko, the head of the Department of History at the Kyiv-Mohyla Academy, introduced historical seminars for young scholars. This is a very effective way of historical understanding—scholars need to be in dialogue. At each seminar, reports are presented. From these reports, articles gradually grow. And so on, year after year. This is a real scientific environment. Today we are talking about them as one of the best schools of historians in the country. The annual *Assumption Readings* by Kostiantyn Sigov and his summer school in Lyshnya, near Kyiv, are in the same line. The most authoritative world philosophers and theologians spoke at those readings: Don Francesco Braschi, professor at the Ambrosian Academy in Milan; Dagmar Heller, professor at the Bosse Institute; Georges Nivat, Swiss thinker and Slavic scholar; Adriano dell'Asta, Italian philosopher; Adalberto Mainardi, theologian of the Transfiguration Monastery of Bose; Russian philosophers Anna Yampolskaya and Alexander Markov; and Ukrainian priests, philosophers, and theologians: Mykhailo Dymyd, Bohdan Ogulchansky, Andriy Dudchenko, Andriy Baumeister, Oleksandr Filonenko...

It is worth noting that a certain environment of intellectuals is formed by publishing houses and journals. For example, the

Smoloskyp publishing house, in my opinion, is one of the most important projects in Ukrainian humanities. It was created and developed by Osyp Zinkevych. Together with his colleagues, he published dozens of volumes of memoirs of dissidents, texts about the Ukrainian literary process of the 20s and 30s, and founded schools of writers that are still active today. The same can be said about the *Rodovid* publishing house, which has presented Ukraine and the world with the fantastic artistic heritage of the people. Their contribution includes stories about glass paintings, Carpathian candlesticks, Ukrainian artists in Paris... Almost every one of their books is a discovery, and in terms of quality and professionalism, none of them is inferior to outstanding publications in any other country in the world. Are worthy of mention, in particular, such publications as *Narbut. Studies. Memories. Letters* [Reconstruction of the *Narbut Collection* destroyed in 1933], *Bogomazov in Finland. One hundred years later*, *Olexandra Exter* and others.

Among the intellectual publishing centres, it is worth mentioning the *Krytyka* publishing house with its eponymous journal. Their texts, especially from the 2000s, are a brilliant collection of humanitarian thought, both national and international, presented in numerous translations.

The Lviv-based journal *Ï* is also worthy of special attention. Its extensive thematic and topical selections are, indeed, good quality food[20]. *Ï* is not only a journal, but also a discussion club, a place for seminars and conferences, and an active website. I have been friends with its founder and editor-in-chief Taras Voznyak for a long time. We were once introduced by Leonid Cherevatenko[21], who later gave me Taras's philosophical texts. We published them in the journal *Philosophical and Sociological Thought*. I told my colleagues at the time that these were some of the best philosophical texts that the editorial office had ever received.

Taras Voznyak started the now famous journal *Ï* in the late 1980s, and its first issues were printed in Lithuania. Back then,

---

20   *Ï* is a specifically Ukrainian letter. With it begins, in particular, the word *їжа* (food).
21   Ukrainian poet, art critic, film critic, screenwriter.

Taras used an interesting design technique: each issue contained coloured pastes. Once, in my presence, Taras Wozniak was asked: 'Who is sticking these cards in?'. He replied: 'My wife'. The next question was: 'How many of them do you have?'

Today, libraries already have about a hundred issues of this journal, and this is a whole era of the country's life: philosophy, political science, literature, local history. It's hard to imagine that all this was done by one person, even with a good team of like-minded people.

One of the leaders in today's book market is the *A-BA-BA-HA-LA-MA-HA* publishing house. Their anthology of Ukrainian poetry, which has dozens of volumes, is a reliable reference point for intellectuals, it consists of collections of poems made with great taste and accompanied by good comments. In my opinion, the format and design of these publications are brilliantly chosen. And this is only one facet of their activities, led by Ivan Malkovich. There is also a whole library of wonderful prose published by them. In addition, *A-BA-BA-HA-LA-MA-HA* is one of the leaders in the production of excellent children's literature in Ukraine.

In this list, you have not yet mentioned the Dukh i Litera journal...
Thank you for reminding me. I didn't forget, I just put it off for later. However, without undue modesty, I will say that *Dukh i Litera* is an unusual phenomenon in the Ukrainian media. This is a journal of public opinion, where the isolation and split between the 'sciences of the spirit and the sciences of the letter' (Kostyantyn Sigov) are reduced to nothing. Along with semiotics, linguistics and law, it includes history, philosophy and sociology. Twice a year, since 1997, readers have received 500 pages of texts — a thick intellectual broth. The main sections of the journal were: 'Ukraine Today', 'In the Shadow of Empires', 'The Law of Power and the Power of Law', 'Kyiv Circle', 'Personality', 'What is Truth', 'Bibliography'... In my opinion, the most interesting were the thematic issues — 'Celan's' (No. 5-6), 'Averintsev's' (No. 11-12), 'Grosman's' (No. 13-14) and one dedicated to the memory of the philosopher Serhiy Krymsky (No. 15-16).

Paul Celan[22] felt the immense weight of history in his native and ancient city of Chernivtsi. And these feelings and experiences were reflected in his poetry. In one of our issues, we devoted a whole section to this aspect, entitled 'Paul Celan and Chernivtsi'. Prominent scholars and artists not only from Ukraine but also from around the world — Petro Rykhlo[23], Leonid Cherevatenko, Jean Bollack[24], Alex Nuss[25], Thomas Spahr[26], and others — told about the poet and his work. Vadym Skurativsky very aptly noted that Marina Tsvetaeva's expression 'in the middle of the world' is the best way to describe Paul Celan's location.

The legacy of Sergei Averintsev is a treasure for us. His ability to analytically evaluate any material is simply amazing. This was the main key for us in selecting the articles published in the journal. The first of these is an inaugural lecture on the occasion of Averintsev's being awarded the academic title of Honorary Professor at the National University of Kyiv-Mohyla Academy. The second is a reflection by the scholar, which presents his vision of the future of Christianity. At the same time, Kostyantyn Sigov came up with a great idea to publish all his encyclopaedic texts. Kostyantyn has an amazing eye for talented authors. I immediately agreed to this idea, although I realised that we would not be able to keep up with our obligations to our sponsors with this book. And then, for the first time in our practice, we made a 'doll' (one copy of the book) for the presentation, and soon we released one of the most successful and profound books of our publishing house. Later, we published a

---

22 Poet and translator. Literary critics consider Paul Celan one of the best European lyrical poets of the post-war period.
23 Ukrainian literary critic, teacher, translator. Published in Ukrainian, German and Russian languages in periodicals and special editions of Ukraine, Austria, Germany and other countries dozens of books and more than 800 scientific articles, literary texts, translations, explorations, prefaces and postscripts, comments, glossaries.
24 French philologist, philosopher, historian of Greek philosophy, translator.
25 Professor of general and comparative literature at the University of Aix-Marseille (France).
26 One of the first theorists of utopian socialism, philosopher, writer and political thinker.

Ukrainian version of this book, many of whose articles were translated by Mykhailyna Kotsiubynska. She wanted to translate these texts herself and, of course, she did it brilliantly.

Eventually, we published four volumes of works by Sergei Averintsev, one of the most profound Christian thinkers of the second half of the twentieth century (*Translations: A Precious Pearl*, 2004; *Translations: The Gospels. The Book of Job. Psalms*, 2004; *Connection of Times*, 2005; *Sophia-Logos. Dictionary*, 2005).

Important for us were the texts of the French philosopher Paul Ricoeur, whose practical philosophy is the pinnacle of rethinking the problems of human identity in the context of the tragic experience of the twentieth century. In the journal, we published several of his articles, as well as an interview in which the philosopher talks about his book *Oneself as Another* (the book was just being prepared for publication in our publishing house). 'I was present when it happened,' wrote Paul Ricoeur, referring to the witnesses of various phenomena of our existence, including the twentieth century. Paul Ricoeur's texts are the guiding principles for our oral history projects.

The list of authors and texts can go on for a long time. I hope that I have managed to reveal at least a little bit of the main content line of the *Dukh i Litera* journal, which is based on scientific and journalistic texts in philosophy, sociology, political science, philology, and history; these texts are well-known and not so well-known, but—without exaggeration—written by genius authors.

Was there really no such journal in Ukraine?
Indeed, there were not. Traditionally, social and humanitarian texts were published in the journalism sections of literary journals or in special professional philosophical, historical, and sociological journals. It was only on the pages of *Dukh i Litera* that they came together for the first time, complementing each other in understanding history and the present. Of course, we are following European traditions here. We, like the above-mentioned centres, have been gradually changing the established paradigms as we have moved away from the Soviet era.

Isn't there a suspicion that these intellectual centres are islands of almost imperceptible influence on society?

Yes and no. The contemporary world does not listen to intellectuals very closely, and the post-Soviet, post-totalitarian, post-atheistic world even less so. To what extent did contemporaries listen to Moses or the prophets, Dante or Thomas Mann, George Orwell or Les Kurbas? This is a rhetorical question. And yet... Dissident self-published books[27] had several copies — depending on the thickness of the paper, from 6 to 10 copies, but were read by hundreds and thousands. We print thousands of copies, and tens of thousands read them. We can see how the ideas of our authors are assimilated in the references to our publications. There are hundreds and thousands of them in the texts of our contemporaries. We do what we can, and then, as Soviet doctors used to say, 'the autopsy will show'.

I would very much like to see many more islands of thought in Ukraine, so that the names of Mykhailyna Kotsiubynska, Ivan Dziuba, Yevhen Sverstiuk, Roman Shporliuk, Joseph Zissels, or Vasyl Stus become symbols of modern life, so that these moral authorities are increasingly listened to...

To a certain extent, the work of Jerzy Giedroyc's Parisian *Kultura* was a guiding light for me personally. I'm not talking about the scale, but about the experience, about worldview guidelines. The influence of the intellectuals of this centre on the culture and politics of post-war Europe was significant. No other collective from Eastern and Central Europe has created such a powerful corpus of top-quality texts (both the journal and the journal's libraries) and has had such a significant impact on the development of both political events and cultural processes in the region.

Kultura consistently upheld the fundamental principles of humanism, democracy, tolerance, and understanding between people and nations in the dramatic post-war years and during the decades of communist terror. It was not only a tribune of the Polish intelli-

---

27   Published out of censorship (including in the USSR) underground leaflets, brochures, books and periodicals were one of the manifestations of the resistance movement.

gentsia (which is a great value in itself), but also a space for dialogue between scholars, writers and publicists of free Europe and the enslaved peoples of the continent. The intellectuals who united around the journal were breaking down the fortresses of communist captivity step by step. Their contribution to the overthrow of numerous Gulags and the Berlin Wall will be appreciated. *Kultura* had another special role: to develop models of cooperation between the states and peoples of our part of Europe, and the present confirms the importance of these developments.

In 2015, we published Jerzy Giedroyc's book *Autobiography in Four Hands*, which demonstrates the daily activities of this leader and of the *Kultura* team. Step by step, they shaped and implemented humanistic principles, looking for ways of understanding in a world often dominated by other trends — aggressiveness, categoricality, populism. To a certain extent, the creation of a united Europe and the more or less peaceful decades of the post-war period are a victory for Giedroyc and his like-minded people around the world. What we have inherited in modern times are new challenges, and these are our problems. As you know, freedom does not last forever. It has to be defended every day.

And in this context, I would like to say a few words about Bohdan Osadchuk, a Ukrainian intellectual of European standing, and his texts for *Kultura*. His voice, which informed the world about Ukrainian captivity and Ukrainian hopes, despite the arbitrariness of the communist regime, was the voice of contemporaries who did not submit to the authorities and served their sentences in prisons and camps — such a role is difficult to overestimate. Osadchuk's articles are analytical journalism. Sometimes it is difficult to tell where in-depth research work ends and where journalistic skill complements it. He is sounding the alarm at a time of another pogrom against the Ukrainian spiritual elite and culture. As a chronicler, he records terror and Russification with pain, addressing the civilised world and hoping for at least some understanding and solidarity with the repressed.

In other, somewhat calmer historical moments, Bohdan Osadchuk rejoices in the sprouts of a new generation of Ukrainian intellectuals. His hopes are unwittingly reminiscent of Hannah Arendt's optimism during the Nazi years: children are born, and they will have a chance for a different life.

Osadchuk's special role, in his own words, as a Ukrainian Polonophile, is to consistently, honestly, and without hiding uncomfortable facts and events of history, defend the value of Ukrainian-Polish understanding for the sake of the future. Despite the fact that everyone on both sides of the border has their own truth and is ready to stand for it to the end, there are 'things more important than truth,' as another famous Ukrainian poet, Leonid Kiselyov, wrote. The past cannot stand in the way of the living forever — it is a dead end, a stupor. The living need life-affirming energy.

And yet the situation in which our intellectuals find themselves is not something exceptionally comfortable in the European or global context...
In fact, we are following the general trends of our time: the world acquires a mass character, and intellectuals often live somewhere on the outskirts of this world; the world is becoming a mass media world, turning, in the apt phrase of Hermann Hesse, into a 'feuilleton civilisation'; the world is becoming telephone and computer-based, often virtual — there are no reserved comfortable places for contemporaries. 'Fit in with influential circles,' Stanisław Jerzy Lec recommended. So, the direction of action has been determined.

However, there is more to the world: for example, there are more than a hundred monographs devoted to the ideas of our contemporary, the prominent French philosopher Paul Ricoeur; there are influential international intellectual journals, thematic seminars (Geneva, in particular), and other forums of European and American intellectuals. Unfortunately, our presence there is still minimal. However, it is growing every year.

Again, to return to your question about intellectual islands... I think that the key here is the measure — how many and what level of universities, publishing houses, journals, scientific seminars we have; how much they influence the life of society; what place people of conscience occupy in the life of the country.

Once I was lucky enough to attend the event where Bohdan Osadchuk was awarded the *Man of the Borderland* award. It was a wonderful ritual: a scientific conference, exhibitions, and artistic events. An announced keynote speech by Bohdan Osadchuk himself entitled 'What Awaits Ukraine in the 21st Century'. He came to the podium and said: 'What, do you think I am so stupid that I know this? I'd rather share my memories of Berlin in the 1950s'.

Here, we need sociological research to help us calculate the measure of what is expected and what is real. I understand that the intellectual life of Paris, New York, or London is more intense than ours, but for me it is much more important to compare it with what we had yesterday. After decades of totalitarian and imperial genocide, it is not easy to restore and rebuild the infrastructure of spiritual and moral life. It will take decades, the next generations will bear this burden, and no one can guarantee only positive results. But in these processes, it is important to have development vectors. Today, I think we have positive ones.

Back in the early 1990s, some people believed that the kingdom of freedom was close, that the path to Europe was easy and short. More sensible people understood that we had only been given a certain historical chance. Whether we take advantage of it will depend on many factors, including our consistency, strength, and courage in defending human rights, democracy, and independence. When perestroika processes began in Ukraine, and then it became independent, it turned out that the intellectual potential of opposition centres was not as significant as it seemed. Alexander Solzhenitsyn once wrote about this, realising that all of us, including dissidents, were outside the processes that were taking place in the European intellectual world. The dissidents' texts covered only fragments of the knowledge necessary to understand the times. Dissident opposition groups were not able to automatically turn into 'animators' of intellectual life because they did not have the power to create publishing houses, European-level universities, or initiate national discussions. It takes time to form new communities capable of comprehending the latest trends and proposing development strategies.

The texts of Sergei Averintsev remain relevant in this sense. He understood much better than anyone else how difficult it would be to move away from the Soviet fever, which was aggressively atheistic and violent, and to move towards a more humane and tolerant world. He repeatedly asserted the need to rely on the achievements of the Judeo-Christian civilisation, the cultural and spiritual heritage of generations. Let us also listen to Myroslav Marynovych, Timothy Snyder, David Sutter, Svetlana Aleksievich, Serhiy Zhadan, and others.

In many post-communist countries, intellectuals are trying to initiate a discussion about the experience of totalitarianism. Is there a similar demand in Ukraine?
This is an important and complex problem at the same time. Usually, we are asked this question by people who were not affected by communism or were affected to a lesser extent. In Ukraine, 'communism' was an almost total phenomenon, especially between the 1920s and 1970s. The system, as unfortunate as it may sound, changed people. There are almost no people left who are free from the influence of this system. Therefore, when the time came for liberation from totalitarianism and it was possible to analyse or get even with the past, it turned out that few people had the moral right and strength to do so. Each of us is infected, there is no one who does not have this sin. Quite often, those who stood in opposition to the system had the burden of collaborating with it behind them. Most people were imbued with communist ideas and the absurdities of the system. Even now there is little chance for an objective trial of communism, because it is very difficult to find those who could become judges. At one time, Myroslav Marynovych wrote an article entitled 'The Atonement of Communism,' which we published in the collection *Letters from the Freedom* (1999). Before accusing someone, one should honestly ask oneself, and comprehend one's own guilt for the tragedies of the past and the problems of the present. There are no simple solutions. Social processes are extremely complex—it is dangerous to act with a scalpel. 'It is better to live in a disingenuous "friendship of nations" than in sincere inter-ethnic hatred,' writes Myroslav Marynovych. And this is true.

The point is not that we have renamed the communist system rather than changed it, but that we have no system. And this global problem haunts us. For many people, it is easier to call a country ruined and fight against this 'ruin' than to set a new goal and identify areas of change. However, without adequate, creative thinking, there is little hope for change.

The absence of condemnation of communism at the beginning of Independence, the silence of this problem, was not only a political problem, but also a defensive activity of people associated with this system. And more broadly, it was a self-defence mechanism of society as a whole, because if it had come to exposure then, it would have ended in a civil war. Only partial convictions of those directly responsible for the repression were possible, but this did not happen, too. At the same time, there was complete confusion. For example, in one presidential election, some former political prisoners who had spent many years in camps and prisons campaigned for a candidate who was a former KGB general. So we understood that in our circumstances, we had to speak primarily about the intellectual and moral condemnation of communism.

Could it be that some changes in society, in people's minds, have become irreversible under the pressure of totalitarianism?
The influence of the totalitarian world on society was virtually total. Several generations of people lived cut off from the outside world in an atmosphere of communist poison (almost in pressure chambers) and became carriers of totalitarian ideas. This was evidenced by many events and processes of the 20s, 30s, 40s, and later. For example, people who had themselves carried out repressions in the 20s fell under the machine of repression in the 1930s. They died, for the most part, without ever getting rid of their pseudo-belief. And there are many similar examples. The totalitarian ideology became part of the worldview and language of those times, the so-called 'new language', and it is quite difficult to change all this. After all, what was then called an election was not an election, and the Bolshevik coup was not a revolution...

And yet, we can hardly talk about a dead end. I think that under favourable conditions, we will be able to return to the normal traditions of public life. Many of the younger authors are much more educated (and, hopefully, more moral) than previous generations. I remember when Viktor Yanukovych became President, I had a thought: 'Well, let's get over it, we've been through worse. We'll look for new niches (stokers, working roles, etc., as it was in the 60s and 70s[28]) and hope for something better.' And I am very glad that our children did not accept this and decided otherwise — they organised resistance. The Maidan was our common victory. And these were the very favourable conditions that led to encouraging changes. Civil society emerged and grew. For some time, the influence of this society was, and sometimes still is, as great as that of the official authorities. Despite all the contradictions, the current judicial system is fairer and more professional than in previous years. The education system has changed significantly. Today, there are many public and especially private schools where children receive a good education. Sometimes there are shifts in the higher education system, at least in some higher education institutions. It is very important that the Ukrainian army has been formed, which is now resisting aggression from Russia. Another achievement is the emergence of modern security structures. But I will stop here because there are trends that speak not only of our successes.

Were dissident centres important in the first years of independence?
In Ukraine, most of the first political parties were created by dissidents, and in the cultural sphere they and their like-minded people played an important role in the life of the country. The list of people who in various ways defied the system is not so short. However, it is difficult to hide the fact that resistance to the communist machine united quite different people. Among the dissidents were not only democrats, but also people of extreme right or left views. We should also not forget that some of the dissidents who were unable to adapt to the new realities joined the fight against everyone and

---

28 People who were in opposition to the government often could not work in their specialty and their refuge became the jobs of stokers or movers (if there were forces) and this gave at least minimal money for survival, so as not to die of hunger.

with everyone. A bright portrait of Ukrainian dissidents is made up of the names of Zynovy Antoniuk, Mykola Horbal, Mykhaylyna Kotsiubynska, Joseph Zissels, Myroslav Marynovych, Vasyl Ovsienko, and Yevhen Sverstiuk. It was they who laid down the ethos that modern Ukraine needs. For example, for many years, until his death, Yevhen Sverstiuk uncompromisingly opposed any clumsy and inhumane actions and statements by the authorities. He opposed all forms of discrimination against national and religious communities. Through his activities, Yevhen Sverstiuk promoted trust in the church, as he was an extremely spiritual, honest and decent person. He headed the Ukrainian PEN Club, was the head of the Vasyl Stus Prize jury, and wrote extremely thorough texts about Ukrainian cultural figures.

I was lucky enough to know Sverstiuk. We often met and talked. I supported Yevhen in organising evenings dedicated to Ukrainian dissidents, and later, together with Ola Hnatiuk and Yevhen Zakharov, I helped him hand over the leadership of PEN to Myroslav. I remember one of his stories, told after farewell to Anatol Perepadia. Yevhen Sverstiuk was friends with Arie Vudka, one of the Jewish dissidents with whom he was imprisoned in the camp. There were many people among the political prisoners who wrote poetry. Arie Vudka learnt these poems by heart and, when he was released, wrote them down. The collection *Poetry from Behind the Barbed Wire* was published in Munich in 1978 with these poems. I suggested that this story be published in our almanac *Yegupets*. 'But everyone knows about this,' Yevhen Sverstiuk told me. I rebutted him. Now that it has been recorded and published, many more people know about this page of Ukrainian-Jewish solidarity...

Myroslav Marynovych became one of the leaders of the Ukrainian Catholic University, and his texts serve as beacons for solving many social problems.

For many years, Joseph Zissels has been the head of the most active Jewish structures in Ukraine, organising youth projects that promote European values and tolerant behaviour, and promoting interfaith and interethnic dialogue in modern Ukraine.

Vasyl Ovsienko has been recording the history and experience of the dissident movement and promoting it over the past decades[29].

One could go on and on about everyone, growing the list of names and what they did.

Has the role of the intelligentsia changed in modern Ukraine?
It is difficult to answer this question unequivocally, because not enough time has passed to make a comprehensive assessment. Slowly, processes similar to those in Western countries are beginning to dominate in Ukraine. At the end of the twentieth and in the twenty-first century, there are almost no universal roles for intellectuals. Knowledge has become highly specialised, and roles in society have become national. In addition, most professions have become mass professions, which also affects the specific roles of a particular person. But this is not specific to the Ukrainian situation. Almost all European communities are developing in this way. Nevertheless, there is a need for moral leaders (after all, this is what characterises the intelligentsia in society to a greater extent than before). The dynamics of social processes are frantic, decisions need to be made quickly, and changes in the world do not allow for relaxation. The activities of new structures show how traditional roles are changing. And we are no exception to the rule. The roles of the intelligentsia are different, but the mission is the same: responsibility for the moral life on earth.

How dynamic are the changes in Ukrainian book publishing?
Book publishing is gradually developing. Today, if you go to a good bookstore—in particular, to the Є bookstore—you will see that almost all areas of humanities are already filled with Ukrainian books. The quality of these books varies, but twenty or even ten years ago this was not the case—they were 90 per cent Russian books and 10 per cent Ukrainian. Today, perhaps 80 per cent of books are already in Ukrainian (I mean academic literature). It's not

---

29 Unfortunately, a year ago he passed away and today we are already looking for materials for memories of him and his unpublished texts.

just about the language of the publications, but also about the quality of the books: great children's literature from *Staryi Lev Publishing House*, *A-BA-BA-GA-LA-MA-GA*, *Mamino*, etc.; quality fiction from the *Family Leisure Club*, *Folio*, *Staryi Lev Publishing House*, and *Book-XXI*; creative and innovative art books from *Rodovid*, *Staryi Lev Publishing House*, etc.); books about Ukrainian literary and artistic life in the 1920s and 1930s and memoirs of dissidents from *Smoloskyp*; high-quality humanitarian books from *Krytyka*, *Naukova Dumka*; a library of books by Nobel Prize winners from *Zhupansky Publishing House*; and a library of Ukrainian poetry from *A-BA-BA-GA-LA-MA-GA*.

I've mentioned only a few of the books worth reading. In the Є bookstore, you can find literature from the US and Europe. And then there's the Internet, and the idea that the Internet will save humanity — in this case — seems to me to be reassuring.

What kind of books does Ukrainian society need in terms of content?
I think that what is most needed is adequate research on what is happening in society. The research that is being conducted is mostly inertially focused on the structures formed in Soviet times. For example, the Institute of Party History under the Central Committee of the Communist Party of Ukraine was renamed first the Institute of National Relations and Political Science, and then the Kuras Institute of Political and Ethnic Studies of the National Academy of Sciences of Ukraine. But all the personnel who wrote there against Ukrainian nationalism and Zionism continued to work there in the following years, and perhaps still do. Funds in the Academy of Sciences system have been distributed over the years among these institutes almost without competition, although there may have been some formal competition. There are few serious studies that do not relate to purely political science and election-related areas. The ability of university departments and independent research centres to participate in various competitions, receive grants and funding, and study what is happening in society is several orders of magnitude less than in developed societies. Our society knows much less about itself than we would like. And this is

also in circumstances of extreme complexity and drama of all our transformations. We also lack world classics in the humanities. Although a certain amount of literature is published through the efforts of international foundations and embassies. With their support, several hundred books are published a year, but what is several hundred? I once visited the Harvard Library, where the sociological shelves contain hundreds of thousands of volumes. Our sociological library has only a few thousand books. Today there are already many independent publishers. However, there are very few publishing houses that would work professionally with the world's current humanitarian literature. There is an urgent need for translations of contemporary books on the latest trends in the world's development, such as informatisation, international relations, modern technologies, the experience of successfully developing countries, etc. However, I would like to point out that the breakthrough made by Ukrainian scholars and publishers in recent decades is worthy of all respect. If in the 80s and 90s we were talking about creating a publishing system, today we are talking about expanding it.

What impact do academic publications have on society?
It is difficult to track. There are almost no such studies. Dissident texts that were published in six or twelve copies influenced many intellectuals in the country. Today, when a book is published in even a thousand copies (such editions are traditional for Ukrainian publishing), I think that they also do not bypass society. It's hard to say how they influence. In general, books on the level of Paul Ricoeur or Hannah Arendt are not widely read in any society. But in many Western universities, they are required reading for humanities programmes. And in a few high-quality universities in Ukraine, such as Kyiv-Mohyla Academy and Lviv Catholic University, these books are prominent in professors' lectures and on the list of recommended reading.

Many philosophers, historians, art and literature researchers, and journalists revolve around us in one way or another. From Kyiv, Lviv, Kharkiv, Odesa, Vinnytsia, Chernivtsi, Drohobych, Chernihiv... They also propose many books for publication, take part in their preparation, and then in their distribution and popularisation. I can say that some of our recent books have been widely distributed in society. For example, Olya Hnatiuk's book *Courage and Fear* (2015) sold over three thousand copies and received about a dozen reviews. The book was presented on Internet television and several radio channels and the *Espresso* TV channel. Similarly, the book *Catching an Elusive Bird: The Life of Hryhorii Skovoroda* (2017) by Leonid Ushkalov: a series of presentations in the Є bookstore chain (the first presentation alone was attended by over a hundred people), reviews, speeches, and the sale of three thousand copies. And I'm sure it will continue. There is a peculiarity in publishing practice: if a good book is published about significant events or significant figures in national history, the attention to it is very high. There is a certain regularity that we have already observed: the more intellectual a book is (of course, when it is of high quality), the better it is sold. In our case, in addition to the books mentioned above, this also applies to the *European Dictionary of Philosophies* and Henryk Litwin's study *From the Rus' People. The Nobility of Kyiv, Volyn, and Bratslav (1569-1648)* (2016), the two-volume *Jewish Civilisation. An Oxford Textbook of Judaic Studies* (2012), and Mircea Eliade's research *A Treatise on the History of Religions* (2016), etc.

Do you think that Ukraine has already formed an audience for the perception of intellectual literature?
I'm sure it is. There is such an audience and it is quite numerous. Our thirst for serious humanitarian literature is special: we need it no less than citizens of other civilised countries. But while in most of these countries these texts were formed over decades and centuries, in our country we have had either false texts or a gaping void for a long time. Ukrainian civil society, which has confidently asserted its rights, especially after the Maidan of 2013-2014, needs knowledge on the level of the best contemporary texts known in the world. This is a certain challenge for us, the publishers, and we are trying to find adequate answers as best we can.

What is the definition of an intellectual book?

I think it's a book that helps you live in the modern world, based on the experience of previous generations. And this depends not so much on the genre of the book as on its author. We know this from our own practice, because *Dukh i Litera* has been publishing intellectual books for over 20 years, and more than five hundred of them have been published. In my opinion, an intellectual book can happen in any field. At the same time, there are more and more books on the Ukrainian book market today that can be called intellectual and are no worse than books in other developed countries. What kind of books they are can be found out from honest and prestigious awards, both state and independent, both Ukrainian and international. Among the Ukrainian ones, for me, these are the Shevchenko Prize, Vasyl Stus and Yury Shevelyov Prizes. I can name a few books that I include in this series: *Descartes' 'Meditations' in the Mirror of Modern Interpretations: Jean-Marie Beysad, Jean-Luc Marion, Kim Sang-On-Wan-Kun* edited by Oleg Khoma (2014), Natalia Yakovenko's books *Outline of the History of Ukraine from the Ancient Times to the End of the Eighteenth Century* (Genesis, 1997) and *Introduction to History* (Krytyka, 2007), Yaroslav Hrytsak's *A Prophet in His Fatherland. Franko and His Community (1856-1886)* (Krytyka, 2006), philosophical essays by Taras Vozniak *Philosophy of Language* (2009) and *JUDAICA GALICIENSIA* (2017), *Jewish civilization. Oxford Textbook on Jewish Studies,* books by Petro Rykhlo about Paul Celan, books by Andrii Puchkov *Between Navigation Masts: Profiles of Ukrainian Art Critics (Architecture and Visual Art)* and by Leonid Ushkalov[30] *The Charm of Energy.*

Thus, a philosophical book can be intellectual or anti-intellectual. For example, I have seen such scholastic philosophical texts from the Soviet era that you cannot understand anything in them. They seem to fit the standard definition of an 'intellectual book,' but they are not.

---

30 An outstanding Ukrainian researcher of the life and work of Hryhorii Skovoroda, Mikhailo Drahomanov and others.

The traditional history of philosophy is a science that contributed to the understanding of man in this world, and in Soviet times, a number of philosophical works were aimed at preventing this understanding. The techniques were different: tautologies, absurd things, correct attitudes from which wrong conclusions were then logically derived, and so on. This is a separate area that should be studied, because the anti-intellectualism of traditional Soviet books, especially of the most terrible times, is a separate topic.

At that time, there were no books by Andrey Platonov, Jorge Luis Borges, Mikhail Bulgakov, George Orwell, Osip Mandelstam, Viktor Petrov (V. Domontovich), or Nadezhda Surovtseva. When they started printing them, they did so with huge cuts. For example, the Bulgakov's novel *The Master and Margarita* was published, but then in the *samizdat* one could find 50-60 pages of inserts — each page from which a certain fragment of the text was removed.

In Sholem Aleichem's *Tevye the Milkman*, much of the original text is not available in either the Russian or Ukrainian translations of the Soviet years. Publishers and censors removed everything that did not conform to the ideological tenets of the authorities. Such 'corrections' were made in almost every publication of the Soviet period, and, of course, they concerned not only Jewish literature.

It was at that time that books that were not supposed to be published were accidentally published. Thus, the USSR Academy of Sciences published the book *Textology of Works of Soviet Literature* (1967). It contained a literary analysis of how the texts of classic Soviet books, such as Alexander Fadeev's *The Crush*, Fyodor Gladkov's *Cement*, and others, were changing. Readers of subsequent generations have mostly never even heard of these books (perhaps for the best). But they were reprinted 20-40 times and rewritten each time, but people who read these books in the 50s and 60s could not understand why they were read in the 20s and 30s. In the original version, despite their ideology, the texts had some life in them, but after hundreds of cuts, there was nothing left.

Nowadays, these subjects are studied little, leaving out the topics of Soviet ideology and life, book publishing, literature... How do you feel about this?
I think we need to study both the positive and negative pages of our country's life. Memory is one of the most important mechanisms of human existence, which is why it was very important for me to capture the memory of the Maidan. In Soviet times, people were not allowed to preserve their memories: during the war, diaries were banned, letters were completely censored, and correspondents were not allowed to film or write about the retreat of Soviet troops. What can we say about the 1930s, when everyone and everything was simply destroyed! People were afraid to tell their families about the famine because they knew they could be punished for it. That is why we in Ukraine lived almost the entire twentieth century without texts of memory, with suppressed memory. The rare texts of honest diaries or memoirs that have survived are worth their weight in gold. It is very good that such publications have recently appeared.

However, in German, French, and other European cultures, almost every family has diaries of their relatives. In our country, people were afraid to trust the texts on paper, afraid to keep letters. As for the dissident correspondence, we need to know the keys to understand what the authors of the letters really meant. And remember that Vasyl Stus was forbidden to send poems to his family during the last years of his imprisonment...

Where can we find these keys?
Read the memoirs of Myroslav Marynovych, Yevhen Sverstiuk, Vasyl Ovsiienko, Svitlana Kyrychenko, Semen Gluzman, Iryna Zhylenko — they have these keys. These are books of 500-800 pages, which are extremely interesting to contemporaries of the events. But it is difficult to imagine that they will be read carefully by the next generations — they have a different life experience. There should be some kind of digests, abridged versions, because it is clear that young people are primarily interested in their lives, their time. Therefore, in the strategy of book publishing, in the culture of

the new time, it is very important to find adequate methods of transmitting memory to the next generations.

I also feel guilty for not writing my own memoirs. But I didn't, because in my 'first life' I built power plants and did drawings, and in my 'second life' I became a humanitarian. And in order to catch up with what modern young people get at universities, having the opportunity to go abroad to study, I have to work three times as hard. The gaps in my knowledge are huge. That's why I don't have much time to do what I'm doing and write down my memories. But it's not yet too late.

In developed cultures, these chains are more tightly connected and more organically preserved. When we have to recreate a culture that almost three generations of people could not even touch, it takes extraordinary efforts.

Has the position of the intellectual book changed since independence?
A serious Ukrainian intellectual book has appeared only in recent decades. Earlier, such books also appeared as an exception, in particular historical works, but this only confirms the rule. I think that hundreds of Ukrainian books have been published over the decades, and among them, dozens still fit into the context of world culture. I am sure that each of us has our own recommended bibliography on this topic. I'll try to name the books that are important to me. Among those published by our publishing house: Myron Petrovsky's *Master and City. Kyiv Contexts of Mikhail Bulgakov* (2001), Mykhailyna Kotsiubynska's *My Horizons* (2004), Andriy Puchkov's *Under the Open Sky: Kyiv Essays* (2017) and *Osip Mandelstam's 'Kyiv' in Intonations, Explanations, Pictures* (reprinted in 2018), Olgerd Ippolit Bochkovsky's *Selected Works* (2018); among those published by other publishers: Myroslav Popovych *Essays on the History of Culture of Ukraine* (ArtEk, 1998), Ihor Shevchenko's *Ukraine between East and West* (Institute of Church History of Lviv Theological Academy, 2001), Larysa Masenko's *Ukrainian Language in the Twentieth Century: The History of Linguicide* (Kyiv-Mohyla Academy Publishing House, 2005), and almost all books by Natalia Yakovenko, Yaroslav

Hrytsak, Natalia Starchenko, Tetiana Vronska, Viacheslav Bryukhovetsky, Eleonora Solovey, Volodymyr Panchenko, and Vladyslav Hrynevych...

In the same vein is Olena Stiazhkina's small but, in my opinion, very powerful novel *In the Language of God* (Dukh i Litera, 2016) about the moral choices of people during the Russian occupation of Donbass. Olena Stiazhkina is a brilliant historian, a researcher of women's behavioural patterns in the occupied territories during the Second World War, who creates an alternative to the vulgar and misleading Soviet interpretations of those events.

The list goes on and on... But, of course, the mainstream is still translations. A number of publishers, including ours, work in this area.

Can an intellectual book be commercially successful in Ukraine?
We always want both a cinema ticket and ice cream. But we have resources for one thing only. We want to publish both intellectual and popular literature. But popular literature can only appear when there is intellectual literature.

Once upon a time, my colleague, Prof. Martin Feller, who has done much to promote Jewish studies in our time, suggested that we create a popular encyclopedia of Ukrainian Jewry. I was against this idea. It seemed to me that a popular encyclopaedia could appear only when there is a high-profile, academic one, when there are solid materials and research. That project did not result in an encyclopaedia, although many good texts were collected. At the same time, there are certain areas where the existence of popular literature is essential.

In this regard, we have the following experience: we wanted to publish an anthology of texts about the Holocaust, *Beyond Understanding*. I asked Michael Berenbaum, the man who created the Holocaust Museum in Washington and was the author of this idea, to give us the right to publish the book. He asked, 'Why would you want to do that? Take any popular book on the subject.' I replied: 'It's your society that needs more popular texts on this topic, but ours needs basic books first and foremost.'

And yet we have more or less popular books. After all, the line between popular and intellectual literature is a shaky one. We shouldn't show false modesty — there are many educated people in Ukraine who work at the level of the world's leading intellectuals.

When a person comes to me and brings me a book that interests me, we will definitely publish it, because I am sure that today any book can be self-sustaining. You just need to adequately assess the manuscript and its prospects.

The days when it was impossible to print a good book are over. A person who has no sponsors can learn how to make a book on a computer and publish it in 1-10 copies. It is also possible to make an electronic version of the book (usually for young people).

Currently, the publishing house receives back about 50 per cent of the money we invest in the publication. The other 50 per cent we find thanks to grants or philanthropists. However, if we publish, say, 40 books one year and 60 books the next, we have some potential to publish five more books that we wanted but did not have the funds for. However, there is a serious competition between what we want and what we can publish without targeted funding. We are, of course, talking about editions with large numbers of copies.

In the context of our conversation, I would like to talk about certain books that have received publicity. One of them is a translated book, 'Rebellion of a Generation: Conversations with Ukrainian Intellectuals.'

The Rebellion of a Generation... (2004) is a book based on the method of *oral history*, memoirs. Consistent stories of contemporaries become significant sources of history. The events of the past appear not only as the actions of generals and national leaders, but also as individual human destinies.

The heroes of this book are iconic figures of modern Ukrainian history: Ivan Dziuba, Mykhailyna Kotsiubynska, Mykhailo Horyn, Yevhen Sverstiuk, and Mykola Riabchuk. The publication is based on their stories and dialogues with brilliant experts in ancient and modern Ukrainian history, Ola Hnatiuk and Bogumiła Berdychowska. The conversations recreate the dissident times, the moral choices of the protagonists, and portray the figures of people who challenged the totalitarian government. Today we know that they won, but behind bars they even defended the right to dispose of their bodies after death (Semen Gluzman, Mykola Horbal), because many were killed and buried in mass graves without even being identified.

Why is this the title of this book?
The title was suggested by the authors, and we, the publishers, agreed with it. Because it was really a rebellion of people who did not want to become the humus of the totalitarian system.

Not everyone took part in the rebellion, but many people were involved in it: they helped relatives of dissidents, distributed or hid books, read and retold dissident texts to their friends.

We were talking about contemporary centres of intellectual thought. I am sure that they all come from the same dissident 'overcoat'. Natalia Yakovenko, Taras Voznyak, Vyacheslav Bryukhovetsky, Mykola Riabchuk...

I would like to see the dissident heritage take an adequate place in contemporary Ukrainian culture. I think this would clarify many problems of history and the present. I hope that in time these texts will be included in educational programmes.

How did you come up with the idea to publish Kobzar with illustrations by Vasyl Sedliar[31]?
A lot of people knew about this book, but very few people have seen it. Its history is as follows: in 1931, the first edition of the book was published, and in 1933, the second edition. When the persecution of the Ukrainian intelligentsia began, the book was destroyed, removed from all libraries, from all collections... Then the artist was killed and the publishers were repressed. Since then, references to the book have disappeared and resumed only in studies after the 1960s. Most intellectuals from my circle of acquaintances at the

---

31 Ukrainian monumental and graphic artist, art critic, teacher from the times of the "executed Renaissance", belonged to the creative group of "Boichukists." Victim of Stalin's terror.

Kyiv-Mohyla Academy, including Natalia Yakovenko and Volodymyr Panchenko, had heard of this legendary book but had never seen it. One day Sashko Irvanets, who, by the way, knows the *Kobzar* by heart, came to us and saw this book for the first time. Sashko sat over it for half an hour, and then looked up in amazement and asked: 'Did you know about this book?' I said: 'No.' 'Who did?'

I am pleased that we have returned to Ukrainian culture the work of this great master, a favourite student of Mykhailo Boichuk, whose legacy includes only a few works.

It all started when Artur Rudzycky showed me his family's copy of the book and said that he would like to republish it. I looked at it and said: 'Me too'. In my opinion, these are drawings of the level of Matisse, Picasso, the great masters of that time. The Boychukists knew the art of their time, travelled around Europe, and were real masters themselves. We started working on preparing *Kobzar* (2011) for publication. But the task was not so simple. At first, we wanted to make a facsimile of the first edition, and then we saw that the original had falsified Taras Shevchenko's texts. This is how books were published in the 1930s. It was easy to write 'Tatar invaders' instead of 'Moscow invaders' — and this is not the only example. So, we decided to recreate the aesthetics of the book, but also make it modern. Of course, we had to write about the fate of the artist and the fate of the book, and that's what we did. This work was done by Artur Rudzycky and Stepan Zakharkin, the editor of this book.

We worked on the book for a year and a half. I generally like books that take a long time to edit and publish. They usually turn out to be of high quality. If you do something quickly, there are always mistakes and shortcomings. I think there are fewer of them here. We discussed the concept of the book many times. The first edition was in black and white, the second edition had colour pictures, but very interesting division markers between different texts of *Kobzar* were removed. There was another problem: the original drawings had not been preserved, neither in black and white nor in colour. So we decided to make our own — the third — edition, essentially combining the advantages of the two previous ones. Then experienced designers worked on the book and cleaned the drawings, because when a book is prepared without the original drawings, it is difficult to ensure good quality. In short, a lot of work was done, and so the book came out at a high level. The layout was ready, and we were looking for money for printing. I turned to our partners, the managers of the *Oranta* printing house (now *Master of Books*), with whom *Dukh i Litera* has been working fruitfully for several decades. They are reliable and responsible partners who produce high-quality books. The head of the printing house is an educated and proactive intellectual, Pavlo Sachek, to whom I brought this book and said: 'Pavlo, let's divide the costs: we'll take care of the preparation, and you'll take care of the printing. Then we will divide the circulation in proportion to your and our expenses.' He looked at it, looked at it, and answered: 'Let's do it!' And so it happened. The book won two of the most prestigious awards at the Lviv Forum. Then we received another award from the Arseniy Yatsenyuk Foundation. The head of the printing house is an educated and proactive intellectual, Pavlo Sachek, to whom I brought this book and said: 'Pavlo, let's divide the costs: we'll take care of the preparation, and you'll take care of the printing. Then we will divide the circulation in proportion to your and our expenses.' He thought for a while and answered: 'Let's do it!' And so it happened. The book won two of the most prestigious awards at the Lviv Forum. Then we received another award from the Arseny Yatseniuk Foundation.

When the National Art Museum found out that we were preparing to publish *Kobzar* with illustrations by Vasyl Sedliar, they extended the exhibition schedule and gave us space in one of their best rooms. Together with the museum, we made a good exhibition dedicated to the work of Vasyl Sedliar. There were photographs of the time, documents, enlarged colour illustrations and the master's works that are kept in the museum. In addition, a small catalogue was published. In short, the great book of Ukrainian culture was given a new life.

One day I read that David Hofstein once translated *Kobzar* into Yiddish. An idea came up: to publish a bilingual version of *Kobzar* and illustrate the book with Vasyl Sedliar's brilliant drawings. Today we already have this edition, which was published in 2018. When preparing the texts, we checked them with the originals, and here the editors report to me: "Here Hofstein has such lines that Shevchenko did not have." We smiled and left it as it was with Hofstein, but in the practice of those years both adding and changing of texts were usual (this phenomenon of socialist realism still needs its researchers).

What is special about Blaise Pascal's book Pensées?
This book is well done. It was translated by Anatol Perepadia, one of the cohort of brilliant Ukrainian translators who essentially preserved Ukrainian culture in the dark times of the mid-twentieth century. He has translated from French, perhaps, more than any other translator of any other culture in the world. He presented Ukrainians with six volumes of Marcel Proust, three volumes of Michel Montaigne, texts by Blaise Pascal, Albert Camus, Antoine de Saint-Exupéry, François Rabelais... For his French translations, Anatole Perepadia was awarded several French orders — the Order of Arts and Letters and the Order of the Palmes d'Or. He translated fantastically. In order to recreate the language of the seventeenth or eighteenth century, he immersed himself not only in French texts but also in the corresponding Ukrainian texts of the same period.

When Mykola Lukash died (in 1988) and did not have time to finish the translation of *Don Quixote,* Anatoliy Perepadia completed it. We worked together with pleasure for many years. Together with him, we published Michel Montaigne's *Essais* in 3 volumes (2005-2007). Blaise Pascal's text was the last manuscript that he managed to pass on to us. One of the philosophers of the new generation, Oleg Khoma, worked on the book. Today, you probably cannot name another book that contains four hundred pages of text and two hundred pages of commentary, indexes... And the design of the book is of a high standard, made by Iryna Pasternak. So this book is a success. I'm glad that it was once recognised at the Lviv Forum as one of the most interesting books of the year.

Your publishing house has launched a series of books. Is the 'Library of Resistance, Library of Hope' series a spontaneous idea, or has it been maturing for years?
This is one of our most important projects. It consists of books that help us to grasp the twentieth century and understand the challenges of today. It has already included more than 15 books, two of which have won top awards: *Second-Hand Time (The End of the Red Man)* (2014) by Svetlana Aleksievich won the Nobel Prize in literature (including for its Ukrainian translation), and *Courage and Fear* by Ola Hnatiuk won the Grand Prix at the Lviv Book Forum (2015) and the Warsaw City Prize (2015).

Back in the 60s and 70s, I tried to understand the pages of Ukrainian history by reading 'between the lines' of anti-Ukrainian books that were published then in hundreds of thousands of copies, hundreds and hundreds of titles. Gradually, I began to make lists of books that I wanted to make known not only to my friends but also to the wider public. Later, while working as an editor at the *Dukh i Litera* publishing house, I learned more about contemporary trends in humanitarian thought and about European and American authors who could form the basis of such a library.

And now we are looking for answers to the challenges of our time. There are a lot of good political science texts, excellent Maidan journalism. However, to understand the reasons for the current situation, it is necessary to delve into historical events, into works on sociology and philosophy. At first, I called it the *Library of Anti-Soviet Literature*. I thought about the concept for a long time, consulted with my teachers and partners: Ivan Dziuba, Yaroslav Hrytsak, Ola Hnatiuk, Yevhen Zakharov, Kostiantyn Sigov, and many others.

Are these texts both contemporary and of the last century?
I wanted to see memoirs, philosophical works, historical books, and essays in this library... At the same time, there are certain limitations. In particular, it is necessary to find considerable funds to publish dozens of books. We should look for realistic prerogatives. For example, there is a programme called Skovoroda to support translations from French. It is known that French culture has brilliant texts that are adequate to this idea. We have good cooperation with

Polish structures (as I have already mentioned), and I ask my Polish friends to recommend some of the best Polish works. The books of Hannah Arendt or Timothy Snyder are very high standards of intellectual reflection. It is very difficult to choose just a few texts from the rich Ukrainian spiritual heritage. I would like the library to contain books of the same level about the important Ukrainian experience — the struggle for independence in the early twentieth century, resistance to totalitarianism, dissidence in the 60s to 80s...

Is it difficult because the most creative intellectuals were killed or isolated in camps for decades?
I think that's not the only reason. It's just that the generation of contemporary Ukrainian historians is perhaps the first to have access to world literature. I once came across a book in a second-hand bookshop called *The Struggle Against the Anti-Soviet Underground in 1921-23*. I was excited: I would finally find out who was fighting against the Soviet regime! But all the references in that 500-page book were to Karl Marx, Friedrich Engels, Vladimir Lenin, and to the decisions of the Communist Party congresses. The primary sources were not available. There is a joke: a pillar is a well-edited tree. Similarly, the 'history book' was turning into something quite the opposite, which had nothing to do with this science. Therefore, it was difficult to expect serious works from historians who were cut off from world culture and sources.

What kind of 'resistance' and what kind of 'hope' are referred to in the title of the series?
I think that the publications of this library are a resistance to the totalitarian concepts of history, philosophy, and humanities in general, which are still present in our school and university textbooks, in the speeches of public figures, and in the public consciousness. Instead, we provide our compatriots with up-to-date knowledge about the patterns of history and contemporary life in the world and in Ukraine. And 'hope' is the joy of understanding, a way of comprehending time for the sake of adequate answers.

Is showing other relationships — interaction in society and solidarity — also resistance?

Absolutely. When you talk not about the abnormal mechanisms of people's lives, but about the values and ways of building a normal society that were born and exist in modern Europe and democratic America. But first, we need to reckon with history. With what is still our previous 'knowledge', our psychological attitudes. We have to squeeze the slave out of ourselves, so to speak.

People such as Sergey Averintsev, Yevhen Sverstiuk, Yury Lotman[32], Mikhail Gasparov[33], Vasyl Stus, and Emanuel Levinas told their contemporaries that there were 'other spiritual worlds' with other values — morality, the rule of law, and the ethics of Judeo-Christian civilisation. The dissidents were 'anti-Soviet,' but this 'anti-' was still part of the 'Soviet', albeit the opposite. Therefore, the main focus of the *Library of Resistance...* is not only a reckoning with the past, but also value guidelines for the present.

It is important for Ukraine to know the book *Utopia in Power* by the classics of anti-Soviet history Mikhail Geller and Alexander Nekrich. The book presents an alternative version of national history to the Soviet one, as seen by the modern European world. The Bolshevik coup in Petrograd is not called the 'Great October Revolution' here, Russia's occupation of Ukraine is not covered by the euphemism 'civil war,' and the Second World War is not hidden behind the well-established Soviet term 'Great Patriotic War.' It is equally important not to overlook the only publication to be published in Russian in this series, *The Gulag Handbook* (1987). It was compiled by the French researcher Jacques Rossi, who, having served his sentence, collected many memoirs of fellow camp inmates and compiled an encyclopaedia explaining the concepts associated with this shameful and horrific page of Soviet history. For example, it contains information about the punishment cell, its types, equipment, who was punished and for what. Or information

---

32 Soviet and Estonian literary critic, culturologist and semiotician of Jewish origin.
33 Soviet and Russian literary critic and classical philologist, historian of ancient literature and of Russian poetry, translator from ancient and new languages, literary theorist.

about the concept of the Belomorkanal—when it was started, who built it and how, how many people died, what technologies and what punitive measures were used. There is no point in translating this book because the entire Gulag is written in Russian.

You also have another book series called 'Cultural Figures'...
Yes. The national memory of every nation should include not only knowledge of history, but also biographies of prominent people. Initially, I conceived it as a series of biographies of prominent Ukrainian figures. But I decided that knowledge about Ukrainian intellectuals was the most deficient. For several years in a row, I spoke publicly about the need for such a series of books for contemporary Ukrainian culture. One of my friends asked me how much money I needed to start such a series. I told him a rather modest amount, but it wasn't that small. And our friends, Olga and Andriy Anisimov, decided to sponsor the publication of a number of books in the *Cultural Figures* series. Many thanks to them: from us, the publishers, and, of course, from the readers.

Thus, we launched the *Cultural Figures* series and have already published the first books. We opened the series with Roman Korogodsky's book *To the Gates of Light* (2016), which contains portraits of Ukrainian cultural figures. They are written as well as, unfortunately, few people have written about himself.

The second book in the series is Leonid Ushkalov's *Catching an Elusive Bird. The Life of Hryhorii Skovoroda* (2017). Ushkalov devoted the lion's share of his life to studying the legacy of Hryhorii Skovoroda. His book is written in a light (journalistic) style and presents one of the most interesting thinkers of the eighteenth century very well. It is filled with the voices of the era—students, teachers of the Kyiv-Mohyla Academy, residents of the city... and, of course, with texts by Hryhorii Skovoroda himself.

There is also a biography of Mykola Lukash, the translator of *Faust* and *Decameron*, entitled *Under the Star of Lukash* (2018), which was prepared for publication by Bohdan Zholdak. At the presentation of this book, I recalled that during the farewell to Mykola Lukash I was struck by the fact that there were very few people and the tombstone was in Russian with mistakes. But this was Mykola Lukash—one of the greatest national geniuses...

Then there was Yury Vilensky's book *Viktor Nekrasov. Portrait of a Life* (2018), which is largely based on Nekrasov's own texts. This is our attempt to remind our compatriots of a talented, honest writer and a courageous man of Ukrainian culture.

And this is only the beginning, as the editorial office is preparing new manuscripts about Ukrainian literary critics, art historians, modernist artists, and others for publication.

To date, more than 30 books have been published in this series. Outwardly, it seems that this is easy to do, but in fact, behind each of the books there is a separate story, a separate choice, the talent of a particular writer or compiler. I will dwell only on a few books in this series and this does not mean that others that I do not remember are worse. One of the largest books in this series is the biography of Mykola Zerov, authored by Volodymyr Panchenko. Zerov is an iconic figure of Ukrainian literature and culture of the early 20th century and it is no accident that Panchenko wrote his biography. As for me, this is one of the best books of Ukrainian culture of recent decades. Three books by Petro Rykhlo were also published in this series—about Paul Celan and other Jewish writers of Bukovina. It is very important that Rychlo's texts introduce Paul Celan into Ukrainian culture, tell about very interesting writers who lived in Chernivtsi and wrote in German. This is an important part of Ukrainian cultural heritage. For these efforts, Petro Rychlo was awarded the Stanislaw Vincenz Prize 2021.

In the same series there is a book prepared by Andrii Pavlyshyn, one of the best Polish translators, who was awarded the prize "Translators of Jewish Literature." It is very important that these people who lived in Lviv, where Polish, Jewish, Ukrainian cultures met, today become part of high Ukrainian culture.

Some of the books in this series are stories by Ivan Dziuba. Recently, a book by Martha and Ivan Dziuba about Parajanov was published. This is, on the one hand, Ivan's remarkable research and on the other, Martha's memories. This book belongs to the best portraits of Sergei Parajanov—one of the best filmmakers in the world of the turn of the century.

Kateryna Rapay[34] prepared several books for this series, namely: *The Circle of Yakutovych*, *The Age of a Leader*, *Double Exposition*. Ukrainian art of this period is one of the most interesting in modern culture. Intellectuals know about this, but it is very important that wider layers of readers learn, including abroad.

The publication of books in this series is very important for us, because in previous years Ukrainian society managed to get acquainted with the main stages of its history, but we know much less about the people who created it. The purpose of the publication is to get readers acquainted with as many biographies of philologists, artists, dissidents, theater and cinema figures (whom only the national community knows) as possible. To the best of our ability, we try to achieve this by printing the books of this series.

In order for a selection of your serial books to end up in university libraries, do you need a patron to buy them?
First of all, you need the willingness of the institution's teachers — this is perhaps the most difficult, although leading universities and centres already have such collections — books from the *Library of Resistance...* are often cited.

We send 10-12 copies of each of our books to the main libraries of Ukraine. There is also a programme of state support for book publishing, but I was careless enough to see those thick volumes published for fabulous money with lots of photos and gold embossing. True books are the exception, not the rule. At one time, Shevchenko Prize winners had the right to have their books published at public expense for libraries across the country. Mykhailyna Kotsiubynska was awarded the National Taras Shevchenko Prize in 2005 for her two-volume book *My Horizons* (2004), which we published together with the Kharkiv Human Rights Group. Therefore, as part of this programme, she decided to republish her book *Fixed and Imperishable* (published in 2001), in which she presented and analysed the correspondence of early twentieth-century writers and dissidents as a great national cultural heritage. For two

---

34 Ukrainian artist, the daughter of the famous ceramic artist Olha Rapay-Markish and the prominent Ukrainian sculptor Mykola Rapay.

years, the State Committee fooled us, but eventually everything was somehow resolved. In 2009, the book was published under the title *Letters and People. Reflections on Epistolary Writing*. But after that, Mykhailyna Kotsiubynska, an elderly woman, spent six months trying to get at least one copy of her own book for herself, or to find out which libraries had it. It was a difficult search. There is a chance that now, in the new environment, things will change for the better.

Taking into account Ukrainian book publishing, what 'diagnosis' would you give to Dukh i Litera: is it surviving, living or thriving?
Well, we are still a long way from prosperity: both the country and the publishing house. But we are living. We live interestingly, intensely. After the Soviet 'famine', we have been doing proportionately more than our foreign colleagues who work in more favourable conditions. And so it has been for almost thirty years, for which we can report to Ukrainian society with a clear conscience.

3. About Moral Authorities

"We must think today about who will be moral authorities tomorrow": Interview of Leonid Finberg to the *Kraina* (*Country*) magazine
Interviewers: Sergey Demchuk, Angelina Kovanda

January 21, 2019, for the first time since independence, a bas-relief dedicated to the head of the UPR[1] Directorate Simon Petliura[2] was unveiled in Kyiv. How would you describe this event?
This is the stage when we recognize not the Russian, but our own version of history. For me Petliura is an intellectual who took responsibility in difficult times. He did a lot to make the Ukrainian state happen. But the circumstances were more powerful than his will. He could not stop the madness of *khokchlocracy* (from the words "ochlocracy" — the power of the crowd and "khokhol" — an unconscious Ukrainian. — *Kraina*). During the post-war impoverishment, the Bolsheviks promised to share all the wealth. It was impossible to stop those who believed in these unrealistic socialist utopias. No sober voices were heard. Today we are also under this threat.

In the film The Secret Diary of Simon Petlyura released in 2018 the issue of Jewish pogroms committed by the UPR army is raised.
Petliura tried to stop them with harsh methods. But he lost control over the situation. The *Otamanshchyna*[3] began. Pogroms of those years are called Petliurian, but they were also carried out by the

---

1 The Ukrainian People's Republic (UPR) was a short-lived state in Eastern Europe. Prior to its proclamation, the Central Council of Ukraine was elected in March 1917 as a result of the February Revolution, and in June, it declared Ukrainian autonomy within Russia.
2 Ukrainian state, military and political figure. Member of the General Secretariat of the Ukrainian Central Council as Secretary General for Military Affairs (June 28 – December 31, 1917).
3 Otamanshchyna or Otamania — the presence on a certain territory of a large number of partisan detachments led by their atamans, the actual military and political power in the absence or insufficient power of the centralized apparatus of state power.

Bolsheviks and Denikinians[4]. And not only against Jews — these gangs robbed everyone.

How has the attitude of Ukrainians to their history changed in recent years?
We've made huge strides, but there's an even bigger path ahead. In countries, where there was no strong imperial pressure, humanitarian disciplines developed gradually. Libraries in France or America count millions of books and tens of thousands of them are about history. They evolve, depending on how the search methodology changes or new archives are opened. This is the normal way. But we have a different situation.

We need to turn the pages with lies. There was no Great October revolution, but a coup in St. Petersburg. There was no Bolshevik revolution in Ukraine, but an occupation. There were no elections in the USSR, but appointments. Pseudohistory entered the language. We have none Ukrainian book about the Second World War. As a publisher, I really want to do this.

My personal answer to the challenges of historical memory were several series of books. For example — *Library of resistance, library of hope*. It includes about 15 books. These texts should be known to understand the 20th century, to navigate in the present. For example, the works of Svetlana Aleksievich (Belarusian writer, Nobel Prize in Literature 2015. — *Kraina*) about Soviet history or journalism by Sergii Yefremov (Ukrainian politician, literary historian; repressed in 1930. — *Kraina*).

In the USSR there were no philosophical or historical books in Ukrainian. They believed that there were enough Russian-language ones. We managed to change the situation — Ukrainian-language non-fiction literature took place.

---

4   Anton Denikin was a general who led the anti-Bolshevik ("White") forces on the southern front during the Russian Civil War (1918–20).

How do you assess decommunization?
It is not enough just to remove monuments and blame communism for millions of victims. It is necessary to prepare literature, films, new textbooks. It will take decades.

In honor of whom it is necessary to establish monuments and to name streets?
We must move from the Soviet pantheon to one that would meet our current values. Streets are called by the names of Ukrainian prominent politicians, but people of culture are not honored enough. This year marks the 100th anniversary of the birth of the brilliant Mykola Lukash[5] (he translated into Ukrainian, in particular, Flaubert's *Madame Bovary*, Goethe's *Faust*, Boccaccio's *Decameron.—Kraina*). It would be nice if a street was named after him. The list can be long: writers Vasyl Barka, Victor Domontovych, Yury Shevelyov, artists Olexandr Arkhypenko, Olexandr Murashko. We have a great culture that has been abandoned. We do not know it well, and there is a lot of evidence about this.

What do you value most in today's Ukraine?
Solidarity of intellectuals. It manifests itself not in the Writers' Union, where they constantly cannot divide something between them, but in joint projects, films, actions, publications. That is our hope. The dignity of a considerable part of society was manifested on the Maidan. I don't really hope for politicians. Their behavior impressed me when martial law was introduced. They talked not about the danger and captured sailors, but about the struggle for power. I don't want such people to get it.

What should be fixed in the country immediately?
It is important to establish democratic mechanisms for solving problems. We can survive as a country only on the condition that the rule of law will be the main thing in our society. The authorities should feel and know what is happening in its various layers. Everyone should be heard. Discontent and the arrival of populists in

---

5   Ukrainian translator and linguist.

many countries, including the United States, suggest that liberal democratic leaders do not listen to the poorest.

Does Ukraine adequately withstand these tests?
We must compare the present not with what is in other countries, but with what we had yesterday. We didn't notice how we had changed. Our industry today is much freer, businessmen say. Exports to Europe increased. We entered the markets of Brazil and Africa. Dependence on Russia has decreased as much as possible.

We have an interesting Ukrainian cinema and theater. Only in Kyiv there are 50 theaters and performances that are not a shame to show in any capital of the world. I especially like *Morituri te salutant* based on the works of Vasyl Stefanyk (performance of Ivan Franko National Academic Drama Theatre. — *Kraina*) and the brilliant performances of Vlad Troitsky at the *Dakh* Theater.

Museums have changed a lot. They are led by competent people. Lviv Art Gallery is run by Taras Vozniak, one of the country's best intellectuals. Dmytro Stus makes interesting programs at the Taras Shevchenko National Museum. To record my granddaughter at a lecture at the Khanenko Museum, I had to wait six months. They fantastically talk about art — you can even envy the children.

Will we get along with Ukrainians from the occupied territories after their return?
These territories can be returned when Ukraine becomes more powerful than Russia. There live people who consumed Soviet information food. Anti-Ukrainian stereotypes were imposed on them. It's hard to overcome. If it becomes obvious for the occupied Donbas and Crimea that we are developing democratically, that our standard of living is increasing, they will begin to look in our direction. There is not enough Ukrainian propaganda directed at those regions. I was told that the most demanded profession there is a Ukrainian language teacher. Because children from there go to us to study, and for this they need to know the state language.

Are you disappointed or impressed with the changes over the past five years?
Maidan and the war mobilized the best part of society. Ukrainians as a society have become much healthier. It is necessary to consolidate the moral spirit and the enthusiasm that the Revolution of Dignity gave.

Does the quality of the elite prevent the state from making a rapid breakthrough?
The days when intellectuals were people of universal knowledge are over. This is a global trend. In addition, in Soviet times, we read a lot, because there was no opportunity to act. Now I do what I love more.

We want a rapid jump. But it cannot be. They say we need an army like in Israel. But a few years ago we didn't have any. We do what we can. It is dangerous to jump over the necessary stages of development. This year's elections are an exam for Ukrainian society: will we be able to soberly assess our capabilities or will we follow the populists? In the 20th century, we did not pass this exam and got a collapse.

Those who are not going to go to the polls are also disturbing. The worst periods of history were due to the indifference and inaction of people who believe that they do not affect anything.

According to sociological studies, a third of Ukrainians have not read a single book in a year.
Now people are more focused on visual information — cinema or the Internet. Poles have a non-reading rate of 50 percent. When cinema appeared, everyone said that the theater would disappear. But this did not happen. With books it is the same.

Should the state promote the Ukrainian language?
Officials must speak the state language. In private areas, nothing should be enforced. When Ukraine gained independence, a sociological study showed that the Russian-speaking population prevailed. Most said they were not ready to switch to the state language. But 80 percent of parents agreed that their children should

study in Ukrainian. The best option for us is a soft Ukrainization with an emphasis on education. In Israel, it took seventy years for Hebrew to become the national language. We are moving in the right direction.

What question do you often think about?
I worry about less moral guidelines in society. In recent years, Cardinal Lubomyr Husar, writer Yevgeny Sverstyuk, philosopher Miroslav Popovich have passed into eternity. The super-challenge for Ukraine is the formation of elites whose morality will be important for society. This should be recognized as a national problem and we should think today about who will be the moral authorities tomorrow.

Which contemporary writer has the greatest influence on society?
Now it is Sergii Zhadan[6]. In 2017, he received the Vasyl Stus Prize[7]. I am involved in the process of awarding this prize. We focus on the morality and influence of potential laureates. It is necessary that the names of our cultural figures become better known to the general public.

---

6   An outstanding Ukrainian writer, public figure, frontman of the rock bands *Zhadan and Dogs* and *Mannerheim Line*.
7   For a special contribution to Ukrainian culture and stability of civic stance.

4. Around Judaic Studies

How do you, the director of the research centre, define 'Judaic studies'?
It is a set of sciences that studies the history, culture and modernity of the Jewish people. You can draw a comparison with Slavic studies, the field that studies Slavic peoples.

Please tell us about the activities of your Centre, when it was established, and what issues are most important to you today?
We emerged in the early 1990s as the Vaad Judaica Centre of Ukraine, and then became an Institute. Today we are called the Centre for Research on the History and Culture of East European Jewry at the National University of Kyiv-Mohyla Academy.

When we started, there were no clues, and we had nowhere to get them from—everyone who was involved in Judaic studies in the 1920s and 30s was gone: some were shot, some died, some emigrated. We began to gather enthusiasts—all those who were interested in Jewish history and culture, and especially those who had reached Judaic studies on the periphery of their humanities research. Gradually, the topics of the first studies and the first conferences were identified. Friends and partners, Israelis, Americans, and colleagues from Russia, who were solving similar problems, helped us. Over time, our steps became more and more professional, and now we can talk not about the beginnings, but about the history of our activities and certain results. Over the years, we have published many books. Of course, I would like to rewrite the first of them today, but I am not ashamed of the next ones. Every time I face a dilemma—I want to talk about almost every one of our books, because each one has its own story, but due to lack of time, I have to talk about only a few.

Probably, like all our colleagues from post-Soviet countries, we started by understanding the Holocaust. The wounds were still fresh, and we were still tormented by the conscience that we had not buried our relatives, the innocent victims, with dignity. Therefore, an important publication for all of us was the anthology of texts by philosophers and theologians *Beyond Understanding. Theologians and Philosophers on the Holocaust* (2001), edited by John C. Roth and Michael Berenbaum. I think that even today, this is the best book for anyone who finds the strength to understand the Shoah tragedy. The price paid by the authors of the texts — one in four, unable to bear the attempt to go through those horrors again, even if only in their minds, committed suicide — is evidenced by the Hamburg account. We continue to research and publish texts about the Holocaust. But today, more and more, we are collecting and opening up the world of Jewish values for ourselves and our readers.

We have published an impressive memoir, *Diary of the Lviv Ghetto* (2003), by David Kahane[1], a witness to the terrible life and death of the Lviv ghetto and the Janowska concentration camp. Few books on this topic have the power and accuracy of this one. Kahane's text is a book by an educated and courageous man who gave voice to the tragedies of tens of thousands of people. Without his memoirs, this experience would have remained unknown to the world. The author was rescued by the Studites in their monasteries, and Metropolitan Andrey Sheptytsky, after David escaped from the ghetto, hid him in his own library.

At the same time, we published *Humanity in the Abyss of Hell* (2009) by Zhanna Kovba[2], a study of people who helped Jews in western Ukraine during the war. It is a wise and delicate book. One reader, who was 85 years old at the time, said: 'I have been waiting for a book like this all my life after the war. I thank the author and the publishers.'

Two anthologies of Yiddish and Hebrew poetry translated into Ukrainian have become a certain achievement. The first of these, the 600-page *Anthology of Jewish Poetry*, was compiled by Velv Chernin[3] (Israel) and Valeria Boguslavska[4] (Ukraine). For the first time, Ukrainian readers had the opportunity to get acquainted with

---

1   Polish-Jewish religious teacher, doctor of philosophy
2   A historian, Senior Research Fellow at the The Center for the Studies of History and Culture of East European Jewry (Judaica Center).
3   Israeli poet, and historian.
4   Ukrainian translator and poet.

the works of nearly 90 poets who wrote in Yiddish in Ukraine and Australia, in Palestine and America, in Austria and Belarus... What giants gathered under one cover: Perets Markisz[5] and Ivan Franko[6], Itzik Manger[7] and Maksym Rylsky[8], David Hofstein[9] and Lina Kostenko[10], Uri Zvi Greenberg[11] and Stanislav Telniuk[12], Chaim-Nachman Bialik[13] and Pavlo Tychyna[14]! The experience of working on this book has taught me that the best poems are not those for which knowledge of the language is mandatory, but those where the translator is a talented poet. Hence the idea of inviting the best Ukrainian and Israeli poets of our time to translate each other and publish anthologies of Hebrew and Ukrainian poetry in Ukraine and Israel, respectively. We have done our part in this work. We offered our poets word-for-word translationi from Hebrew with detailed commentaries and audio recordings of the readings of those poems in Hebrew. Each of the Ukrainian authors chose a counterpart who was the closest to their spirit. After the translations, our experts checked the adequacy of the Israeli texts and suggested certain corrections, if necessary. The book contains quite detailed and interesting texts about each of the authors and translators. My colleagues have done a brilliant and great job. Thanks to

---

5 A poet and writer, he was arrested as a member of the presidium of the Jewish Anti-Fascist Committee. He was convicted by a military tribunal in a closed trial. On August 12, 1952, he was shot in Butyr prison.
6 Ukrainian poet, writer, social and literary critic, journalist, translator, economist, political activist, doctor of philosophy, ethnographer, and the author of the first detective novels and modern poetry in the Ukrainian language.
7 A prominent Yiddish poet and playwright, a self-proclaimed folk bard, visionary, and 'master tailor' of the written word.
8 Ukrainian poet, translator, academician, and doctor of philological sciences.
9 Yiddish poet. He was one of the 13 Jewish intellectuals executed on the Night of the Murdered Poets.
10 Ukrainian poet, journalist, writer, publisher, and former Soviet dissident.
11 Israeli poet, journalist and politician.
12 Ukrainian poet, novelist and literary critic. Father of Ukrainian singers Lesya and Halya Telnyuk, members of the Telnyuk Sisters duo.
13 Jewish poet who wrote primarily in Hebrew and Yiddish. Bialik is considered a pioneer of modern Hebrew poetry.
14 Ukrainian poet, translator, publicist, public activist, academician, and statesman.

Yulia Morozyuk and Anna Dubinska, the editors, and to the brilliant translators — Bohdana Matiyash[15], Mariana Savka[16], Marianna Kiyanovska[17], Yury Andrukhovych[18], Halyna Kruk[19], Ivan Malkovych[20], Petro Rykhlo, Volodymyr Tsybulko[21], Vasyl Herasymiuk[22], and others.

I want to mention a few more books that are significant for me. One of the first was *Field of Despair. Field of Hope* (1994), with which we actually launched a publishing series on Judaic studies. It was compiled and prepared for publication by Roman Korohodsky. The book is based on Mykhailo Heifetz's[23] memoirs *Ukrainian Silhouettes*, translated from the Russian. Among them are brilliant essays on Vasyl Stus and Vyacheslav Chornovil[24] (the latter Heifetz called a general long before his political role in independent Ukraine) and other impressive texts. One of the first was a book by Shimon Markish, whom I met when I taught at the University of Geneva at the invitation of Georges Nivat. In France and Switzerland, Shimon Markish published a number of texts about the work of Russian-speaking Jewish writers. I read these texts and suggested that Markish publish them. He said: 'I've been in exile for a long time, I don't know what's going on there. Select the articles, and I will prepare them for publication.' And that's what we did. A year later, the book *Babel and Others* (1996) was published, which, in my opinion, is one of the most interesting books on this topic.

One of the best researchers of bookplates (and not only), Yakiv Berdychevsky, prepared for us, and we published the manuscript

---

15 A translator from Belarusian and Polish into Ukrainian.
16 Ukrainian poet, children's writer, translator and a publisher.
17 Ukrainian poet, translator and a literary scholar and is a recipient of the Shevchenko National Prize (2020) and the Zbigniew Herbert International Literary Award (2022) for the poetry book The Voices of Babyn Yar.
18 Ukrainian prose writer, poet, essayist, and translator.
19 Ukrainian writer, translator, educator and literary critic.
20 Ukrainian poet and publisher.
21 Ukrainian poet and politician.
22 A prominent Ukrainian poet.
23 Ukrainian and Jewish political prisoner.
24 Ukrainian politician and Soviet dissident. As a prominent Ukrainian dissident in the Soviet Union, he was arrested multiple times in the 1960s, 1970s, and 1980s for his political views.

The People of the Book (2006) in very good printing quality. These are stories about book collectors and their bookplates that Berdychevsky collected. These are short and very accurate biographies of intellectuals from the nineteenth century to the present day. At the same time, this book is a wonderful catalogue of book graphics.

We published two volumes of texts by David Harris, the executive director of the American Jewish Committee, one of the most profound intellectuals I know. These books consist of brilliant essays that, in my opinion, reach the level of Ze'ev Jabotinsky's journalism. They deal with the most painful and urgent problems of the modern world. David Harris was one of the first to warn about the threat to the world from post-Soviet Russia many years ago—but he was not heard.

I should also mention:

- the multi-volume edition of *Jews and Slavs* edited by Prof. Wolf Moskovich, some of which we compiled together;
- a map, and subsequently the book *Jewish Addresses of Kyiv* (2012) by Mykhailo Kalnytsky;
- the translation of *Jews and Words* (2017) by Amos Oz and Fania Oz-Saltzberger, which was done very well by Yaroslava Strikha, and so on.

Among other landmark publications is a book by one of the brightest Ukrainian intellectuals, Vadym Skurativsky, about the authorship of the famous forgery, *The Protocols of the Elders of Zion*. Many have previously named Matvey Golovynsky as one of the possible authors, but no one has ever proved his authorship in as much detail as Vadym Skurativsky has. Other names were also mentioned. Skurativsky found other texts by Golovinsky and conducted a comparative textual analysis. After this work, the question of the authorship of the forgery is, in my opinion, closed. Vadym Skurativsky's arguments are irrefutable.

The areas of our work are very closely intertwined. For example, we conduct quite serious archival searches, which usually result in the publication of books. We work with the archives of the Cheka, GPU, and NKVD (20s, 30s, and 40s). There are a lot of documents about the persecution of Zionist and other Jewish parties and the dispersal of Jewish organisations. Interestingly, when Soviet officials were evacuating or trying to evacuate various archives during the Second World War, they first took out the archives of the NKVD and the Communist Party, and destroyed what they could not, because they were most afraid of the truth. Today, the vast majority of archival materials and documents that were inaccessible in Soviet times have been opened in Ukraine. If only there was someone to work with!

Thus, the work with the archives resulted in the work of Mykhailo Mitsel[25] (now living and working in the United States), *Communities of the Jewish Faith in Ukraine* (Kyiv: Library of the Institute of Judaica. 1998). The book tells the story of the Jewish communities of Kyiv and Lviv under Soviet totalitarianism. This is a bloody story that we look at through the crooked mirror of denunciations to the authorities by synagogue elders and commissioners for religious affairs. Despite the specificity of the source, even through these texts we can see an infinitely heroic and equally tragic story, because the research was completed only up to 1942, because after that there were practically no Jews left in western Ukraine... By the way, it is little known that the number of ethnic Ukrainians in this region also decreased by three times.

The American-Russian-Ukrainian project to describe Jewish heritage archives was very important. Three or four volumes of inventories were prepared and published, and hundreds of researchers, led by Yukhym Melamed, worked on them for many years. These are very good guides for scholars. However, we are increasingly facing the following problem: almost everything has already become available (the Ivano-Frankivsk Oblast archive alone contains materials on the activities of more than a hundred Jewish organisations of the interwar period), while researchers can be counted on one hand.

In addition to scientific research, which most often resulted in the publication of books, we organised and held several dozen con-

---

[25] Senior Archivist at the American Joint Jewish Distribution Committee (Joint) in New York.

ferences, the materials of which were published in separate collections. We also organised dozens of art, historical and cultural exhibitions. Regular exhibitions by artists who are interested in Jewish themes have become a tradition in the cultural life of Kyiv and beyond. For many years, our mobile historical and cultural exhibitions have been travelling around Ukraine. One of the most interesting is about the solidarity of people of different nationalities and faiths in the darkest times of history, such as the years of Nazism or Stalin's terror. It was dedicated to people who build bridges between nations and cultures. The highlight of these exhibitions is that they are exhibited in schools in different cities of the country and local children, whom we specially train, act as guides. This is a unique project of Yulia Smelyanska.

Since 1995, we have been publishing an annual artistic and journalistic almanac called *Yegupets* (as Sholem Aleichem called Kyiv). It is one of our 'tribunes,' each issue containing 400-500 pages of good, in my opinion, prose, poetry, and journalism... For example, in the almanac we published the drama *Dibbuk* by Semen Ansky (the author of the material is Yohanan Petrovsky-Shtern), written at the beginning of the last century, but previously absent from our literary discourse. We are constantly publishing translations from Yiddish, Hebrew, and Polish (Deborah Vogel, Edgar Keret, Hanna Kral...)

The first editor and regular contributor to the almanac was Gelii Aronov, an extraordinary person, Doctor of Medicine, writer, author of a dozen books, and a famous athlete in his time. Other authors include writers, poets, historians, and researchers from Ukraine, Israel, Russia, and the United States. I will name just a few of them: Yakov Lotovsky, Myron Petrovsky (incidentally, he was also one of the first editors of the almanac), Alexander Kantor, Selim Yalkut, Amos Oz, Shimon Markish, David Harris, Michael Berenbaum, and others. I consider the prose of Inna Lisova, a Russian-language writer on Jewish topics, to be a kind of our discovery. Later we published her novels *Bessarabian Romance* (2003); novels and stories *A Lady Checked In Her Luggage* (2003); stories *The Four Ladies Solitaire* (2006); and a collection of poetry *On the Asphalt Bank* (2010).

It soon became apparent that one of our main tasks was to collect Jewish heritage. This is the basis on which other projects can be built. And now, many years later, we are intensively collecting what can still be collected: we are describing the archives of organisations, social movements, libraries, private collections, collect the archives of artists and writers, family archives...

Would you say that the purpose of your Centre is primarily educational?
Not only, but it is also educational. To promote knowledge, one must first study, then research, and only then tell others about it. We are doing all of this as best we can, having defined three main areas of activity: research work (historical and archival research and research of the present); organisation and holding of conferences, seminars, exhibitions; publishing; and collecting archives of history and culture.

Your Centre is officially called the Centre for the Study of the History and Culture of East European Jewry. Can we talk about the phenomenon of Eastern European Jewry?
Undoubtedly, and there are several reasons for this. First of all, it is about changing borders. They are not the same now as they were, say, a hundred years ago, and the countries they outline also have different names. We are talking about a territory that is difficult to define within the borders of the current nation-states. In addition, there were developed 'horizontal' connections between Jews living in different parts of Europe. It happened, for example, that a book was prepared in Warsaw and published in Zhytomyr. This gives grounds to speak of Eastern European Jewry as a phenomenon.

You have listed many interesting books about Jews, and yet there are very few Jews left in Ukraine...
Both few and many... It depends on how you count. There are about 50,000 Jews in Kyiv and several hundred thousand in Ukraine. In the Soviet years, more than 90 per cent of children in mixed Jewish-Ukrainian and Jewish-Russian marriages renounced their Jewishness. It is difficult to estimate how many of them are returning to

their Jewish roots today, but there are many. But I am sure that our books, including Judaica, are read by citizens of Ukraine of various faiths. It is impossible to master the Christian spiritual heritage without going through the Old Testament, the Jewish component of the major world religions. Similarly, I have no doubt that people do not choose to read Taras Shevchenko and Sholem Aleichem, Ivan Franko and Chaim Nachman Bialik, Yuri Andrukhovych and Inna Lisova on the basis of their nationality. Ukrainian readers need Elie Wiesel[26] as much as Jewish readers need Vasyl Stefanyk. I remember reading Stefanyk's stories about Ukrainians leaving for America during the years of Jewish emigration to Israel. One of Sergey Averintsev's articles, which we published in our almanac *Yegupets*, was entitled 'Solidarity in the Persecuted Faith.' Our great contemporary was well aware of the priority of humanity over all differences based on faith, ethnicity, age, etc.

During the years of Soviet rule, much was turned upside down, shrouded in myths and supported by fictitious evidence. Therefore, as it turned out, the whole of Ukrainian culture is poorly understood, not just its Jewish component. Some of our projects and publications have contributed not only to contemporary Jewish studies but have also expanded traditional versions of Ukrainian history and presented it as multicultural. For example, the *Kultur-Liga* phenomenon of the 1920s goes beyond the scope of purely Jewish studies. It is an asset of both Ukrainian and world culture. A lot has been done in recent years, and today the intelligentsia perceives Jewish or, say, Crimean Tatar art as part of the national Ukrainian culture. We should hardly expect a miracle, but the process is underway. Through the joint efforts of liberal circles, including scholars, writers, filmmakers, journalists, and theatre artists, we are gradually moving towards Europe, step by step, restoring or assimilating the values of Judeo-Christian culture. We have many partners on this path: Ivan Dziuba, Myroslav Marynovych, Taras Voznyak, Kostyantyn Sigov, Andriy Pavlyshyn, Akhtem Seitablaev,

---

26 Romanian-born American writer, professor, political activist, Nobel laureate, and Holocaust survivor.

James Timerty, Paul-Robert Magocsi, and Yaroslav Hrytsak. This list can be easily extended, and it is very important.

Of course, given the current state of our Jewish communities, we cannot help but feel seriously concerned. Their average age is well over 60, and for several generations they have had no access to the sources of Jewish history and culture. However, our situation is not unique. Minorities in other countries of the world live in a similar way. In this situation, we, 'people on the border of cultures' (as sociologist Igor Kon put it), associate ourselves with two, sometimes more, communities: the dominant nation and our own. The communications of the modern world in democratic countries allow us to combine this quite effectively.

I once gave a lecture at Harvard on the state of Jewish communities in Ukraine. I cited sad figures: for every child born to a Jewish mother, there are ten deaths of older people... We are an ageing community. We are shrinking like a shagreen skin. Our average age is retirement age...

However, when I was asked after the lecture what my forecast was, I replied: 'Under normal circumstances, the Jewish community in Ukraine will probably exist more or less fully for at least more than one generation.' Then Prof. Roman Shporlyuk, director of the Ukrainian Institute at Harvard, exclaimed, 'Leonid, but for you and me, two generations is an eternity!' I could not disagree with him... But we have to hurry...

Are non-Jewish scholars interested in the history of Eastern European Jewry?
I am among those who believe that the main stage in the history of the Jews of Eastern Europe, when the vast majority of the world's Jews lived there, is largely behind us. However, this does not affect my attitude to the study of this period of history. There is a regularity that people learn more and more about a certain ancient period in history over time. And the greatest experts are not those who lived then, but those who live today.

Interestingly, until the eighteenth century, Jews practically did not study Jewish modern (post-biblical) history, believing that everything was written in the Bible. The Germans and the French started such studies.

Among Ukrainian scholars who address this topic, the vast majority are professional researchers. There was a time when we were all in a kind of abnormal situation: we were unable to get the appropriate education, unable to engage professionally in either Jewish or Ukrainian history and culture. It is important that, as these scholars accumulate knowledge of Jewish history, they consider it necessary to share it.

Together, we participated in the preparation of the Second Ukrainian-Jewish Conference in Jerusalem (the first was held in Kyiv in 1991), which took place in May 1993. The main topic of this meeting was relations between our peoples in the twentieth century. Ivan Dziuba and Mordechai Altshuler[27], Yaroslav Dashkevich[28] and Naftali Prat, Leonid Plyushch[29] and Mila Zigelman, Myroslav Marynovych and Mikhail Heifetz took part in this dialogue. In addition to Ukrainian and Israeli scholars, well-known researchers on this topic from Canada, the United States, and Russia came to Jerusalem.

In those years, it was only the beginning, and in the following years, there were already dozens of such forums.

What is the general picture of the development of Jewish studies in Ukraine, and what are the main problems that have to be solved?

The peculiarity of our situation is that there was a rather long period when Jewish studies did not exist in Ukraine. While in the West there was a continuous process of studying Jewish history, literature, language, art, traditions, etc. We were deprived of this opportunity. Therefore, even our current extraordinary efforts are just a drop in the bucket of what we would like to do. At the same time, we are well aware that no one else can do this work. After all,

---

27 A leading historian of Soviet Jewry.
28 Ukrainian historian, archaeographer, armenologist.
29 Ukrainian mathematician and Soviet dissident.

it is obvious that Jewish culture in Eastern Europe is largely of little interest to either Israel or America. Israelis mostly rely on their ancient Jewish roots and the heroic pages of the last decades of their history. Jews in America are happy to talk about their European roots, but they are much more interested in American history. We who live here should be aware of this and, if possible, make up for lost time.

There are two main things that need to be done: to promote the formation of young scholars, specialists in Jewish studies, and, at the same time, to conduct research. The first is extremely difficult to do because during the Stalin-Brezhnev repressions, specialists in Jewish studies were virtually destroyed. But research is necessary because society needs both historical and sociological knowledge to adequately understand the social processes that are taking place.

Of course, it is not easy for us to do science from scratch. The Harvard Library alone has millions of items on Jewish studies, while our libraries can only keep track of hundreds, sometimes thousands of books. Tens of thousands of Jewish books are published annually in the world. We, in Ukraine, were able to publish only a few hundred books. At the same time, only 20 per cent of them are serious scientific literature. The same amount is semi-scientific, and the rest does not belong to this category either. Meanwhile, our intellectual needs are no less than those of our Western colleagues. So in such a situation, we have 'no choice but to plough on'. This is what we are doing, hoping to publish more books every year, conduct more research, conferences, exhibitions, etc.

Formally, as a Centre, you are part of the structure of the National University of Kyiv-Mohyla Academy. How important is this for you?
Indeed, we used to be an independent structure, but now we are part of a university. It is obvious to me that Kyiv-Mohyla Academy is a leading humanitarian institution in Ukraine. Famous humanities scholars have worked and are working here: Mykhailyna Kotsiubynska, Serhiy Krymsky, Natalia Yakovenko, Viktor Malakhov, Volodymyr Morenets, Volodymyr Panchenko, Maryna Tkachuk, Mykhailo Kirsenko, Valery Khmelko, and others. And, of course, I

wanted to work with the best. In addition, I have known the first President of the Academy (today's Honorary President), Viacheslav Bryukhovetsky, for a long time, since the days of the *Rukh* [Movement]. And when Leonid Nevzlin, who worked with Mikhail Khodorkovsky before he emigrated to Israel, gave us a grant for academic Judaic studies, I asked Bryukhovetsky if he wanted us to be in the Academy. He replied: 'You are most welcome.' Thus began a new stage of our activity, now as a university department.

The university is a space of science, a dialogue between generations, a field of freedom of thought. It is important and honourable to be part of such a structure. We found the premises for the Centre, where we have been working for more than ten years, in the semi-basement of the 5th building of the NaUKMA. For many decades, these areas had not been used, but according to experts, they were suitable for office arrangement. Kyiv businessman Igor Kerez said: 'I want Judaic studies to appear in Mohylianka and I will cover all the costs of setting up an office.' Those who are versed in this matter will understand: it's a lot of money. We are grateful to Igor for his invaluable help.

What is the direction of cooperation with NaUKMA?
We work with various departments. First of all, with the Centre for European Humanities Studies, with the Master's and Certificate Programmes in Jewish Studies, with the Scientific Library, with the Cultural and Artistic Centre, and with the *Dukh i Litera* Publishing House.

We have a number of joint projects with the Master's and Certificate Programmes in Jewish Studies: lecture courses delivered by Natalia Ryndiuk, the preparation of the first textbooks and manuals for teaching Jewish studies in Ukrainian history: *Jewish Civilisation. The Oxford Handbook of Jewish Studies*, edited by Martin Goodman (2015) and Dmytro Tsolin's *Aramaic of Biblical Texts and the Targum Onkelos* (2017), books on Jewish history and culture (*Polin. Studies in the History and Culture of the Jews of Eastern Europe,* edited by Anthony Polonsky (2011); *The Shoah in Ukraine: History, Testimony, Memorialization,* edited by Ray Brandon and Wendy Lauer (2015);

Henry Abramson, *Prayer for Power. Ukrainians and Jews in the Revolutionary Era (1917-1920)* (2017)), and others. We jointly hold presentations of projects and programmes, and facilitate students' work with our archives. Some of the Centre's staff today are graduates of the Master's degree in Jewish Studies.

At one time, from 1997 to 2000, on the initiative of Prof. Tetiana Balabushevych, I taught a course of lectures on Jewish civilisation for masters of history at the Faculty of Humanities. It was an interesting experience, but at some point I gave up this practice. I decided that as a manager, not a teacher, I could do more. But we do cooperate with the departments of the National University of Kyiv-Mohyla Academy. Together with the Department of Political Science, we are describing a collection of thousands of leaflets of all types of Ukrainian elections — from 1989 (elections to the Supreme Soviet of the USSR) to the present day; with the Department of Sociology, we published Olena Bohdan's book *What Should You Know About Sociology and Social Research? A Handbook for Civil Activists and All Those Interested* (2015), and our researcher Anna Prokhorova is teaching a course on oral history for sociologists based on our books on the Holocaust and the Maidan.

We have joint projects with the university library, to which I donated my *samizdat* collection and then helped to attract several significant private book collections to its funds, including the library of the International Solomon University, which has ceased to exist.

I collected several thousand posters announcing events at Kyiv-Mohyla Academy since 2012. I think that this unique material will be useful for researchers of the university's history in the future.

Do you cooperate with Vaad?
Yes, we do. Vaad is a planet where many extremely important projects and programmes are operating and developing. Its leader, Joseph Zissels, is one of the people in Ukraine who understands our problems the best and helps us the most. That is why our cooperation with the Vaad includes dozens and dozens of published books on Judaic studies, the *Yegupets* almanac, and historical, cultural,

and artistic exhibitions. The most significant of them are the Chernivtsi International Conference on the Yiddish Language (2008), Metropolitan Andrey Sheptytsky and Jewish Communities during the Second World War (2015), the International Academic Conference on the 100th anniversary of the death of Sholem Aleichem (2016), the International Conference on the Preservation and Promotion of the Jewish Cultural Heritage of Ukraine (2016), and others. The participants of these conferences are the world's leading scholars of Jewish studies. And they already know that Kyiv is one of the centres on the cultural map of the world where Jewish studies are conducted, relevant conferences are held, books are published... While the materials of our first conferences were mostly conventionally scientific, in subsequent years they became serious scientific works. The most recent of these are *The Second World War and the Fate of Civilians in Eastern Europe. Proceedings of the International Scientific Conference in Memory of Metropolitan Andrey Sheptytsky* (2016) and *Jewish Cultural Heritage of Ukraine* (2018).

Do you have contacts with foreign centres of Jewish studies?
Yes, of course. We cooperate with a number of academic centres and institutions for Jewish studies around the world. At the stage of our formation, our Israeli partners helped us a lot. At the initiative of Prof. Warshawsky (Sorbonne), leading Israeli and European scholars have been visiting us for many years to give lectures. They talked about Jewish history, philosophy, literature, and cultural studies. It is difficult to overestimate this stage of our development, especially since the lecturers were well-known international researchers.

In the following years, cooperation with the Sefer Research Centre, which for many years has organised and continues to organise annual conferences on Jewish studies in Moscow with the participation of hundreds of scholars from around the world, became very important for all those involved in Jewish studies. However, after the Russian occupation of Crimea and eastern Ukraine, I and some of my colleagues no longer go there.

In 2014, we had a joint project with the Centre for Jewish Studies at the University of Regensburg, with mutual lectures. We also intensively cooperate with the Jewish community of Düsseldorf in the project 'Learning to Remember'. We organise joint seminars, prepare publications, such as the *Black Book* edited by Ilya Ehrenburg and Vasily Grossman, didactic materials on the history of the Holocaust, and Anne Frank's diary with drawings for children.

For many years, we have been cooperating intensively with the United States Holocaust Memorial Museum in Washington, D.C., exchanging archival materials and preparing joint publications. One of them is the book *The Shoah in Ukraine: History, Testimony, Memorialization* (2015, ed. by Ray Brandon and Wendy Lauer).

Over the years, we have had many interesting projects with the Vilnius Centre for Jewish Studies: the preparation and publication of the Lithuanian edition of the *Yegupets* almanac, the organisation of the exhibition 'YIVO in Vilnius. The Beginning of a Legend' (2016), dedicated to the Jewish Research Institute.

We have a number of projects with the Canadian charity foundation 'Ukrainian Jewish Encounter', including numerous conferences in Toronto and Jerusalem, New York and Kyiv, and the preparation and publication of the book *Babyn Yar: History and Memory* (2016).

One of our most ambitious projects, implemented jointly with the Shoah Foundation at the University of Southern California, is the recording of Holocaust survivors' memoirs. Over the course of several years, under the leadership of Hanna Yudkovska, we managed to record 3,500 unique interviews. On this basis, the film director Serhiy Bukovsky created his film *Spell Your Name* (2006). An interesting continuation of this project was another project initiated by the Austrian researcher and photographer Edward Serota. With him, we prepared and then recorded memoirs of Jewish life before the Holocaust in Ukrainian, Russian, and English. These materials are available on a separate website: http://www.centropa.org.

We cooperate with scholars in Israel. First of all, with the Centre for Research and Documentation of East European Jewry at the Hebrew University of Jerusalem, as well as with researchers Hillel Kazovsky, Boris Khaimovich, Zeev Khanin, Prof. Wolf Moskovich, and Lyudmila Zigelman....

And with whom do you cooperate in Ukraine, besides NaUKMA?
First of all, we cooperate with the Ukrainian Catholic University in many projects. For example, in the publication of the books *Metropolitan Andrey Sheptytsky. Documents and Materials 1941-1944* (2003), Kurt Lewin's *Journey Through Illusions* (L.: Svichado, 2007), *Dissidents. An Anthology of Texts* (2018).

I remember our work on our first book together. One day Zhanna Kovba, one of the best researchers of the history of the Holocaust in Galicia, came to me and said: 'Leonid, I think I have found the wartime diaries of Metropolitan Andrey Sheptytsky.' I asked: 'How long ago did you find them?' He said: 'About six months ago.' — 'Why didn't you say anything?' (Zhanna was an employee of our Centre.) — 'Because,' she says, 'I had my doubts. In the archive it was titled *Diary of a Ukrainian Nationalist*." I looked at these texts and quickly realised that there was no doubt that I was holding unique diary entries by one of the greatest intellectuals and moral authorities in Ukraine at the time. I called Myroslav Marynovych and told him this story, and I could tell that Myroslav did not really believe me. I said: 'Zhanna is coming to see you, tomorrow you will look at the materials together...' Soon the book was published.

We also cooperate with Myroslav Marynovych in other projects, including organising discussions about the present with intellectual leaders of the younger generation. For several years now, we have been listening to their deep, creative, sociologist-level thoughts on the problems of Ukraine's modern development and ways to solve them.

Thanks to the experts from the Ukrainian Catholic University, especially sociologist Viktor Susak, we learned how to organise oral history records. Together with Viktor, we made our first records. We now have unique archival collections. Together with Prof. Yaroslav Hrytsak, we prepared and published the book *Conversations about Ukraine. Yaroslav Hrytsak — Iza Khruslinska* (2018), and we are starting to work on a collection of Ivan Lysiak-Rudnytskyi's works.

We have experience of joint projects with the National Art Museum of Ukraine. It was with them that we organised an exhibition about the work of the *Kultur-Liga* artists. For the first time, Kyiv residents, and we ourselves, saw unique works: paintings by David Sterenberg, which had been shown only in 1912, and Solomon Nikritin from the collection of Igor Dychenko, brilliant landscapes by Robert Falk from the Donetsk Art Museum, graphic works by Mark Epstein, book graphics by Marc Chagall, etc. We presented their works of that time—paintings, book graphics and sculpture. Unfortunately, the sculpture is only in photographs, because almost nothing has survived of those unique works that could have adorned the best museums in the world. The exhibition was opened with large photographs of these strong artists, who had practically disappeared during the Soviet era: some emigrated, some were killed, some stopped being artists. The same museum also organised exhibitions of works by Zinovy Tolkachev, Mark Epstein and Olga Rapay-Markish.

In recent years, we have been cooperating extensively with the Taras Shevchenko National Museum. In its hospitable walls, we held a historical and cultural exhibition about Agro-Joint's activities in Ukraine (2013). For the first time, we learnt about the scale of assistance provided by this American Jewish organisation, which saved thousands of lives in the 1920s (2 million people received a bowl of soup at a certain time every day). Later they helped to establish agricultural farms and Jewish collective farms. It all ended tragically, with accusations, executions of their own people, and the expulsion of American consultants. We have been organising art exhibitions at the Shevchenko Museum for several years now. We called them 'Masters' (I call them 'genious masters'), and we have already held wonderful exhibitions by Boris Yeghiazaryan (2016), Oleksa Zakharchuk (2016), Olga Rapay-Markish (2017), Lyudmyla Bruievych (2017), and Halyna Hryhorieva (2018). And these are not just exhibitions, but large projects with music, choral singing, evenings of memories, and quests for children. Together with the National Museum of Literature of Ukraine, we once organised an exhibition dedicated to the life of Swedish diplomat Raoul Wallenberg. It was a unique exposition that was brought from Sweden thanks to an employee of the Embassy, Tatiana Nekrasova. The exhibition featured Wallenberg's interesting texts, his typewriter with a clicking sound effect that gave the impression as if he was typing, as well as family and research materials about the last days of his life, which ended in an NKVD torture chamber. Together with the staff of this museum, we organised an exhibition about the fate of Jewish intellectuals who left Austria during the Nazi era. This exhibition told the story of how brilliant writers and scientists became figures of other cultures because Nazi Austria rejected them as superfluous, inferior, and alien.

We also cooperate with the Holodomor Museum, the National History Museum, the National Museum of the History of Ukraine in the Second World War, the Kyiv History Museum, the Sholem Aleichem Museum... As a rule, we participate in the organisation of various exhibitions in museums by providing our archival materials.

I would also like to tell you about our cooperation with the Lviv Ethnographic Museum in creating an exhibition dedicated to Chornobyl before the accident. I was approached by MEPs Walter Mosman and Rebecca Harms with the idea of creating such an exhibition. I liked the idea, named them possible partners, and then told them something they didn't know: that Chornobyl was a Jewish town where a dynasty of Chornobyl *tzaddikim* was founded, whose descendants still live in the world. This was followed by several years of hard work and the opening of a major historical and cultural exhibition in Freiburg in 2011. The exhibition consisted of two parts: the culture of Ukrainian Polissya and the Jewish town of Chornobyl. Materials for the Jewish part of the exhibition were provided by the Lviv Ethnographic Museum and our Centre. The exhibition lasted over three months. Nina Matvienko [30] sang brilliantly at the opening. A wonderful catalogue was published, including our texts. We have and have had many projects with the

---

30 Ukrainian singer, People's Artist of Ukraine.

Lviv Centre for Urban History, the journal *Ї* and numerous art galleries.

How do you find the money to implement your projects?
At the first stages of our activity (relatively small compared to what we have now), we were most actively supported by Vaad and Joint. Over time, we learned how to do fundraising professionally — otherwise we would not have survived and would not have been able to develop. Our experience shows that effective work is only possible with large-scale fundraising.

As a rule, I initiate certain projects, while the Centre's staff do a lot of work on substantiating applications, making calculations and submitting reports. It is important for us to maintain our independence and freedom to choose projects and programmes, so we prefer to diversify our funding. We cooperate with dozens of international foundations and organisations, but we do not want to be patronised by anyone. The Claims Conference Foundation, the Rothschild Foundation, the Dutch Jewish Humanitarian Fund, the Ukrainian Jewish Encounter (UJE), the International Renaissance Foundation, the Holocaust Memorial Museum in New York, and others have helped us and continue to help us.

At a certain stage, we realised that it was harder to find money for research projects and a little easier for publishing projects. Almost every developed country has institutes and centres aimed at promoting national authors abroad — we cooperate with the American, Polish, and French embassies (the *Skovoroda* programme), the Polish Book Institute, the Goethe Institute, the Lithuanian Institute of Culture, the Polish Institute in Kyiv, and the Central and Eastern European Book Projects Foundation (CEEBP). Recently, there has been hope that Ukrainian institutions, such as the Ukrainian Cultural Foundation, the Book Institute, and the Ministry of Information Policy, will also support research and publishing projects. So we have 'first swallows'.

Who are your employees?
Today, depending on our financial support, we have between 25 and 40 employees. Most of them are people with relevant education, including Jewish studies.

This was not the case at the beginning of our activities, when we were all just enthusiasts with fragments of knowledge of Judaic studies. In recent years, we have seen a specialisation of our staff: some are more involved in Jewish literature, others in art, history, Holocaust history, etc. There are also other specialisations, such as editorial roles, design, management, archival and library staff. The most important thing is that over the past few decades we have all gained professionalism and are able to speak at international conferences without any complexes, and to prepare books that are not inferior to their analogues in other countries... Another sign of our current activity is the wide range of partners—leading experts in their fields—historians, philologists, culturologists...

One of my colleagues once asked me what language she should use to speak at the International Commemorative Conference on Yiddish Language and Culture. I naively said that it would be better to speak in Ukrainian with Yiddish quotes, but she suggested English with Yiddish. I applauded her internally.

Another small story from our HR policy. I was once asked if I hired non-Jews. I didn't immediately understand what they were talking about, but then, remembering well how Jews were not hired in our country, I guessed. It is clear that our team includes people of different faiths, nationalities, and ages.

Yiddish-speaking specialists are rare. Does anyone help you with your work with the archives? Are there any translations from Yiddish now?
There are really few Yiddish translators. At a certain stage of our work at the Centre, I realised that one of the most important priorities of our activities should be the creation of a school for translating Yiddish and Hebrew fiction and non-fiction into Ukrainian. The country is intensively Ukrainising, especially in the humanitarian sphere. The most interesting books on history and cultural studies

are published mainly in Ukrainian. Contemporary Ukrainian literature, which is also mostly in Ukrainian, is developing intensively and has already had some success. It is very important that Judaic studies and translations of the best examples of Jewish literature into Ukrainian be a part of this culture. A few years ago, we started a Hebrew and Yiddish translation school with the support of the NADAV Foundation. The first year, it was a beginner's class, with mostly those who wanted to do it. In the second year, there were those who were already able to translate to some extent and wanted to. Meetings with professional translators are an important part of the school. Lesia Lysenko, who translated Svetlana Aleksievych's *Second-Hand Time* (2014), and Yurko Prokhasko, who worked on Katia Petrovska's book *Must Be Esther* (2015), spoke about their experiences.

This is not an easy process, we need to be patient and help everyone who is involved in this very important work step by step.

In addition to a number of translations by Valeria Boguslavska (*Dark Gold*, 2008; Leiser Wolf, *Sad and Happy Songs*, 2009; Shike Dries, *The Violin Master*, 2010; Moishe Teif, *Selected*, 2011, and others), new Yiddish translations by representatives of the new generation have appeared in Ukraine in recent years. Ukrainian girls who studied Yiddish in New York and Paris, Vilnius and Jerusalem, Lviv and Kyiv have already made a name for themselves. Their translations are published in our almanac *Yegupets*. A significant success was the publication of the first Ukrainian translation of Sholem Aleichem's *Tevye the Milkman* (K.: Znannya, 2017). It was made by Oleksandra Uralova, a researcher at the Centre. I say 'first' because the texts of the 1920s to 1940s were more like talented retellings than translations. Everything that censors and editors did not like was removed or distorted. Thus, Tevye had fewer daughters in the Ukrainian and Russian versions than in the original (one of them dreamed of moving to Palestine), and there were fewer biblical texts than in the author's version, because you should fight against religion. These distortions of the author's texts were not limited to Yiddish translations, but were a common practice in those years. Even the loyal subjects of Soviet rule, the 'ideologically pure'

Fadeev, Gladkov, and Seifullina, were censored, shortened, and corrected from edition to edition.

And yet, what does the concept of 'preserving Jewish cultural heritage' mean, and how extensive and researched is the material that has come down to us?
If we are talking about monuments of Jewish material culture, about what remained on the territory of Ukraine at the beginning of the twenty-first century, these are primarily synagogues, headstones, museum collections, and books.

The paintings that adorned the synagogues are real masterpieces that impress with their colours and original symbolic images. Unfortunately, most of the murals have been lost, and they can only be appreciated through descriptions, photographs, and reconstructions. For example, the famous murals of the Khodoriv Synagogue have been reconstructed at the Diaspora Museum in Tel Aviv. We presented them in the wall calendar for 5772 (2010-2011). And yet several monuments have survived. Now it is important to explore them and open them to the world, because they are truly worth it.

In 2008, we published a book by Boris Haimovych about the Beit Tfilah Benjamin synagogue in Chernivtsi, whose murals are among the most interesting preserved in Central and Eastern Europe. Later he published a study of the Novoselytsia synagogue, whose murals were discovered by chance. We also published this book under the title *Synagogue Paintings in Novoselytsia* (2016). In addition, we contributed to the publication of a catalogue of synagogue murals prepared by our colleagues from Chernivtsi and Kharkiv, *How Beautiful Are Your Tents, Jacob. Wall Paintings of Synagogues in Bukovyna* (2016). Paintings in wooden churches can still be found, for example, in Drohobych, but there are no such synagogues left in our lands.

In general, the preservation of culture, including Jewish culture, is primarily about protecting what is valuable in material culture (buildings, artworks, household items, books, etc.) from destruction and annihilation, and in the spiritual sphere it is about describing these monuments and deciphering their signs and symbols, both in everyday life and in beliefs.

I would like to say a few words about Jewish tombstones — *matzevot*. Due to the religious prohibition on depicting people in Orthodox Judaism, we see numerous symbols that can stand for the name, field of activity of the deceased, speak of his piety, virtue, etc. There are dozens of cemeteries in Ukraine with *matzevot*, and they are amazing works of art. Experts know about them, they are described in articles and books, but they are little known to the world as masterpieces of carving art.

Another important segment of Judaica is the objects that were and are used in Jewish religious ritual: *parokhetas* (coverings) and crowns of Torah scrolls, *yadas* (pointers) for reading it, *mezuzahs*, *menorahs*, *kiddush* glasses, etc.

Such monuments are examples of traditional decorative and applied art, and their design style always contains features peculiar to a particular era, region, and author's style.

Jewish archives are another important part of the cultural and historical heritage. For obvious reasons, they were closed during the Soviet era, so all works about the life of Eastern European Jewry were written without knowledge of these archives.

Once, at the Centre for Folk Art, a gentleman shared with me a theory that there are two models of memory preservation among different peoples. The first model is when nations try to preserve signs and symbols for hundreds of thousands of years, such as the Egyptians who built the pyramids. The second model is when communities pass on their national symbols by teaching their children the technologies that allow them to recreate the art of previous generations — for example, Ukrainians teach their children to make embroidered shirts and *pysankas*.

You mentioned books as an element of cultural heritage preservation. This is probably a separate topic, because Jews are called

the People of the Book. It is known that you have managed to collect a large library.

If we are talking about the oldest publications printed on the territory of Ukraine, we are talking about the Torah (Tanakh), the Talmud, and mystical works. At one time, some Jewish printing houses were well known, such as the Slavuta and Zhytomyr printing houses owned by the Shapiro family.

It is difficult to identify any peculiarities of local book printing, although in some cases books were published with artistically designed covers. At the turn of the nineteenth and twentieth centuries, the printing level of publications increased significantly, and illustrated editions were printed more and more often. In general, Yiddish literature was printed in almost all cities and many towns on our lands.

Some examples of such products can be seen in our library, but the largest collection of Jewish books in Ukraine, including manuscripts, is at the Vernadsky National Library of Ukraine, where they are stored, described, and researched.

The book collection of our Centre's library includes over ten thousand volumes, many of which are bibliographically rarities. Dozens of Jewish book printing centres operated on the territory of Ukraine, as well as throughout Europe. It often happened that the typesetting was done in Amsterdam and then brought here and printed in Slavuta or Zhytomyr. Our collection includes books in Hebrew, Yiddish, English, Polish, Russian, and Ukrainian. Today the collection includes many books that could become an adornment of any museum. The oldest are from the early eighteenth century, printed in various European cities, but we have books from later periods from almost all centres of Jewish culture and book printing in Ukraine—Brody, Bar, Lemberg (today's Lviv), Drohobych, Odesa, Slavuta, Berdychiv, Kyiv, and many others. First of all, the corpus of religious books includes various editions of Tanakh, the Talmud, and *siddurim* (prayer books).

The total number of religious publications is about two thousand. Most of them are books donated to us by the Chief Rabbi of Ukraine, Yaakov Dov Bleich, who did a lot to restore Jewish life in Ukraine.

When restoration work was about to begin at Rosenfeld's synagogue on Shchekavytska Street in Podil, I came to him and said: 'Rebbe, you've been reading one book all your life (referring to the Talmud), give us the others.' The Rebbe, a man with a good sense of humour, agreed with me. He understood that we would keep the books and extend their life. When the synagogue was closed for repairs, he called me and said I could pick up the books and asked me what I would be driving. 'In my *Zhiguli*,' He replied. 'I'm afraid it won't fit.' We took out five cars of books. They laid the foundations of our collection — books in Hebrew and Yiddish. These books are unique to us. Of course, collectors have copies of the Talmud from the fifteenth and sixteenth centuries, but the editions of 1702 and 1720 that we have in our library are also rarities. It is interesting that the books that made up the library from the time the synagogue was built, i.e. from 1895, have been preserved.

This is incredible, given that the synagogue was closed several times under Soviet rule, and during the German occupation it was used as a stable.
And this increases the value of the preserved copies even more! The book collection on Shchekavytska Street was also replenished by the state customs: people travelled abroad, but they did not allow old books to cross the border, and the books ended up in the synagogue. For us, all these books are a wealth that is now available to all who are interested.

Surely there were other sources of replenishment?
There is an interesting and somewhat detective story connected with the removal of these books from the synagogue. There was a container on the territory of the synagogue. Since reconstruction was planned, it had to be removed. When I asked what was in it, no one could answer me. When we opened the container, we found about 1,500 books sent to Kyiv from London. A Yiddish institute had finished its work there, and everything that was left was sent to the Kyiv synagogue, where these books with stamps and numbers stood for several years. t can be assumed that the first Kyiv readers were mice, and then part of this London collection came to

us. In this library, we found first edition books by the classics of Jewish literature, such as Solomon Dubnov, Shaul Chernyakhovsky, Chaim Nachman Bialik, and many others. In addition, the container contained more than two hundred Yiddish textbooks by Gennady Estreich. These textbooks were used by everyone who has been studying Yiddish in Ukraine for the past fifteen years.

Books in similar containers were gathering dust in Joynt's warehouses, where they also found no readers. We agreed with the Mohylianka library that we would take them, describe them and make them available to students. We found there several thousand more books and journals in English and German, as well as Yiddish and Hebrew, published at the turn of the nineteenth and twentieth centuries. Often these were unique copies: for example, books about ghettos in medieval Europe, books on Jewish history by Solomon Dubnov and other authors.

The Centre's library contains about 2,000 books in Yiddish. Among them are many rarities: the first publications and collections of works by the Ahat HaAm, Peretz, Sholom Aleichem, Sholom Asha, and others—almost all the classics of the turn of the 19th and 20th centuries. The books have many inscriptions of donation, stamps of libraries and organisations, and random, but sometimes striking, inscriptions on the books of their former owners. We mostly received these books when we were collecting the heritage of Jewish writers (we are talking about Holocaust and Gulag survivors) who lived in Ukraine and wrote in Yiddish. We found their descendants and asked them to give us the archives.

In most cases, writers were frightened by endless repression. They were often afraid to teach their children Jewish languages. Defending the language was considered nationalism, just as it was for Ukrainians. They were accused of it and given prison terms. That is why none of those with whom we spoke refused to give us books, manuscripts, and photographs of their relatives. Few of them could read those manuscripts and books.

Other books in the library include publications on Judaic studies in English, Russian, Polish, Ukrainian, Lithuanian, and other languages.

Our collection contains a large array of periodicals: individual issues of pre-revolutionary and post-revolutionary newspapers and journals, many Yiddish magazines of the 60s-90s of the twentieth century; scientific and socio-political almanacs and journals from Israel, the USA, Russia, Poland, France, and Germany of the last decades. The collection of periodicals includes sets of almost all Jewish newspapers and magazines, more than 120 titles, of independent Ukraine, as well as collections of *samizdat* — original underground publications, archival documents, recordings of radio broadcasts by Radio Liberty, handwritten calendars, etc.

I'll tell you a little about a few libraries that I managed to preserve and give to my friends and community.

In the 1990s, the Israeli Cultural Centre began operating in Kyiv, and it had many wonderful books on Jewish history and culture. I was one of the active readers in this centre. From time to time, when they received new books and magazines, they would give me something.

This did not go unnoticed by the centre's management, and once, when several thousand books were brought there, the director called me and said: 'Did you ask about books? Come and take as many as you want.' Having received such carte blanche from the director, I began to form appropriate libraries for Jewish communities in Ukraine (50 to 100 books each), as well as small libraries of the most important books for Ukrainian intellectuals. Thus, not only for me or Joseph Zissels, but also for Ivan Dziuba, Myroslav Marynovych, Taras Vozniak, and many other connoisseurs, we managed to create great libraries.

I dream that someday a similar situation will happen for Ukraine's friends abroad — we will be able to give them libraries of books on Ukrainian history and culture. However, now, with the advent of the Internet, this task is not as urgent as it was then.

The second library that we managed to save from being scrapped was the library of Solomon International University. When it ceased to exist, I thought that there must be a rather large library there that would be worth preserving. It turned out that there were about 30,000 volumes. I called the head of the library, and he said that they had been looking for someone to give the books to for several months and no one had come forward yet. We responded, and about 10,000 books were added to Mohylianka's library, which now has more than a million copies.

We, the Centre for Jewish Studies, inherited our own specialised literature. The most valuable in it are books from the collection of Leonid Matsykh, a great expert and teacher of Jewish studies who taught at this university for some time.

To be honest, when even smaller libraries are left without an owner, I try to take them and distribute them to friends and colleagues. I will probably continue to do so as long as I can.

Let's continue talking about books...
The peculiarity of our collection is that the books from it have preserved their history in their margins. There are a lot of notes and inscriptions left by the owners: tragic and funny, solemn and everyday. With the passage of a century, they take on a completely different sound. On one children's book, a girl writes: 'Dad, buy me more books, I like reading very much, but don't buy my sister any, she doesn't like reading and spoils books.' When you read an inscription like this, a touching testament to the love of reading and at the same time a small denunciation, made in the early twentieth century, you realise that neither the girl nor the sister has been alive for a long time, and this book is lying in front of you, reflecting time more convincingly than official documents.

A number of publications contain inscriptions from the Holocaust. People wrote in the margins the names of their relatives who died at the front, in ghettos and camps. The President of Ukraine, Viktor Yushchenko, presented one of these books from our collection to the Yad Vashem Museum during his official visit to Israel. We translated the inscription in Hebrew, this was a curse on Hitler: 'May human memory forget his name!' Below are the names of the eleven authors of the texts who died in the ghetto and at the fronts, with the dates of birth and death, but next to his own name did the book's owner put only his date of birth... This gift was gratefully received at Yad Vashem. This man from Berdychiv was foresighted and made several identical inscriptions, so we have a similar book in our collection. We hope that someday it will take a place in the exposition of our Jewish museum. I think that even in a world-famous museum, there are not many such testimonies to the Holocaust written in both ink and blood.

The bookplates on books are very interesting, telling us about their owners, libraries, and communities. But this is a separate story.

There are also entries in the margins of *siddur* prayer books. We have hundreds of them of all kinds: specialised ones for holidays and disasters, with and without translation, published in different countries... In fact, this is an independent collection within the collection.

Of particular interest are books that, to one degree or another, reflect the history of their owners and their people as a whole. Some of the prayer books, for example, were found in the covers of Soviet books: a textbook on mechanical engineering or the collection 'Native Speech'. They were hidden in this way because in the late Stalinist and even Khrushchevian times, people were afraid to keep books printed in Yiddish or Hebrew at home.

This collection was supplemented by Yiddish books collected by Jewish writers Nathan Zabara and Itzik Kipnis. Both were book lovers, and their libraries added many volumes to ours. There are very interesting avant-garde books from the early twentieth century with illustrations by famous artists. They were published in limited editions, and only a few survived the cataclysms of the twentieth century.

In the twentieth century, the number of people who read Yiddish was shrinking for various reasons; few books were published, and book owners often gave old and new editions to each other... It seems to me that the study of gift inscriptions would be extremely interesting, and this work will definitely be carried out.

Another of our collections is Jewish *samizdat*. We have up to a hundred different texts, including Hebrew textbooks, Zeev Jabotinsky's feuilletons, re-photographed books on the history of the State of Israel, etc. Our library also has a multi-volume collection of Jewish *samizdat*, edited by Prof. Mordechai Altshuler in Israel.

And what does the general public know about these meetings?
Unfortunately, not much. But we try to hold various public events and tell people about our archives. Together with the Museum of Books, we organised an exhibition of publications of the 18th and 19th centuries based on our collections: rare books printed in the famous Slavuta printing house, copies of the Babylonian Talmud of the 18th and 19th centuries, Torah scrolls, and rather rare editions of the Talmud translated into Yiddish — the so-called women's Talmud.

The library of our publications is available at ua.judaicacenter.kiev.ua. Libraries such as ours (a scientific library) and books on Judaic studies are not aimed at the general public. They are for experts. Our library's books are used by Mohylianka's teachers and students, as well as other scholars from academic institutions in Kyiv and Ukraine. Researchers from different countries of the world — the USA, Israel, Poland — also come to visit us.

You said: a women's Talmud?
There was a short period in the late nineteenth century when it was believed that it was difficult for women to learn Hebrew, and an adapted version of the Talmud was published in Yiddish. The entire Talmud is Jewish law, and women also had to understand it.

Not all scientific libraries in the world have such editions, but we have almost all the volumes!

It is logical to move from the book collection to the manuscript collection...
We have about 50 family archives. Among them is the archive of the family of Prof. Filatov, the director of many feature films and documentaries in the mid-20th century. These archives contain hundreds of documents: birth, marriage, and death certificates, diplomas from Jewish schools and colleges, unique diplomas of education, residence permits in cities outside the Pale of Settlement, train tickets for people returning from the Gulag, interesting documents related to repatriation to Israel (*aliyah*), unique photographs, and more.

Back in the 1990s, we managed to collect the creative archives of Jewish writers in Ukraine, mostly those who wrote in Yiddish. There was a considerable chance that some of the archives might have disappeared irretrievably. Thus, we have the archives of Mykhailo Pinchevsky, Natan Zabara, Itzik Kipnis, Matvey Talalaevsky, Ikhil Falikman, Oleksandr Lizen, and others (16 archives in total, tens of thousands of storage units).

First of all, these are manuscripts of writers, their letters, books with inscriptions, personal documents, photographs, etc.

None of the Ukrainian state archives have these manuscripts, and our archive has become the largest collection of Jewish literary heritage in the country. I know that there are isolated and scattered documents in the Odesa Literary Museum, but they still need to be described, while our manuscripts, like most of the correspondence, are described and available to researchers.

Searching for and obtaining these archives for the Centre is a fascinating, sometimes detective story.

Among the largest collections is the archive of Matvey Talalaevsky, which was given to us by his daughter Iryna. It consists of about 100 folders with texts in Yiddish, Russian, and Ukrainian, slogans for military newspapers, photographs, correspondence, etc. This is a unique collection, primarily because it is complete, not fragmentary. Talalayevsky was one of those people who collected everything or almost everything (I am guilty of this sin myself). He went from Stalingrad to Berlin as a war correspondent and wrote letters home and articles to military newspapers every day. All these texts have been preserved. Like most of our heroes, he had been in the Gulag. From there he brought back scenarios for Soviet holidays, which he (and his fellow prisoners) prepared either for the anniversary of October revolution or for May Day (what else could you celebrate in a camp?). About a third of the texts are Ukrainian poems and songs. All the scenarios were, of course, approved by the camp leaders. How they managed to preserve them and bring them to Kyiv is a mystery. These are extremely interesting materials for researchers. We have eight such notebooks in our archive, and I don't think any museum in the world has such materials. There are also hundreds of his letters in Yiddish, Russian, Ukrainian...

My friends from Tallinn told me about the archive of Natan Zabara[31], sending me the address of a distant relative of the writer. I immediately contacted her and came to visit. There were priceless manuscripts and many more books on the mezzanine covered in dust and cobwebs. Natan Zabara had been collecting Yiddish books for years. When the owner asked me, 'Do you need all this?' I answered: 'Yes, very much!' She asked when I would come to pick it up. I told her that if she didn't mind, I'd pick it up now. I was afraid that tomorrow something might change: my condition, the mood of the owner, something like that...

Itzik Kipnis's[32] archive was carefully collected and described by his daughter Bella. She took a large part of the archive with her when she emigrated to Israel. However, a lot of materials remained. They were kindly given to us by the writer's son Leonid. He gave us his father's rather large library, which has taken a prominent place in our collection.

We keep the archive of Joseph Shaikin, who carefully collected materials about Jewish agricultural colonies on the territory of Ukraine. We have memoirs of participants in the events, maps of the location of these colonies, correspondence with descendants, and more.

And we also have the largest archive of Jewish musical folklore in our lands: the manuscripts of Moisei Beregovsky[33], who collected five volumes of unique ethnographic recordings: *purimshpils*, *nigunim* (melodies without words), Jewish songs, Jewish dances, and so on. Before the war, he published one of these volumes, *Workers' and Revolutionary Songs. Songs about Recruitment and War* (1932), and then there was the war, then the Gulag (how could you do without it?).

---

31   Jewish writer born in Rogachev, a shtetl located in the Zhytomyr area of Ukraine.
32   Yiddish fiction writer.
33   Jewish folklorist, musicologist and ethnomusicologist from the Ukrainian SSR who was a key figure in the study of Jewish music.

Shortly after his release, Moisei Beregovsky died. His daughter, Eda Moiseevna, requested her father's manuscripts from the KGB archives. She told me how she woke up every day thinking: 'Will I die and not give away his legacy?' That's why she came to us, and we were able to publish a huge volume of *Purimshpils*. At that time, we did not find money for the other volumes, and only after Eda Moiseevna's death did we publish all five volumes as e-books on discs. Unfortunately, I had not thought of this type of publication before. Eda Moiseevna's generous gift to our Centre was her father's priceless manuscripts. I witnessed how one of our *kleizmers* touched those manuscripts as if they were sacred.

Another unique archive is that of Zinovy Tolkachev, who participated as a Soviet army officer in the liberation of Auschwitz and Majdanek. He is perhaps the only artist to have captured the surviving prisoners of those camps from life. Hundreds of terrible, non-fictional drawings are now on display in the museums of these camps, in Yad Vashem, and in our collection. Zinovy Tolkachev often drew on forms from those camps, as there was no other paper available. Our archive contains many of his wartime letters, including several 'triangle' letters (there were no envelopes) written in Yiddish, without the obligatory mark 'censored'. That's happened, too.

By and large, these archives have only just begun to be worked on. I am sure that many discoveries await us. Unfortunately, the writers' archives contain not only works of fiction and journalism but also denunciations of Jewish writers against each other. The situation was similar in the Ukrainian literary and artistic community. People thought that they were staying within the framework of an artistic polemic, albeit a sharp one, when in fact their texts were already becoming prosecutorial indictments.

Families also give us artefacts related to the writers' creative work. Thus, we have the typewriters of Isaac Kipnis, Moisei Beregovsky, and Matvey Talalayevsky. Interestingly, when Beregovsky was recording Jewish folklore, he used Latin transliteration, while having a typewriter with a Yiddish font. Otherwise, it would have been impossible to combine the notes written from left to right with the text, which is written in Yiddish from right to left.

What other collections do you have?
We have a collection of posters and leaflets of almost all Jewish parties and movements that were active before the revolution in Ukraine. Among them are Zionist, labour, and socialist parties. Extraordinary texts and appeals are printed on them. For example, one of the posters reads: 'Jewish women! Are we going to give our votes to men? It is not enough that they solve our problems for us. We must create our own Jewish women's organisations and go to the polls with our own lists.' The language of these leaflets is interesting: in some cases, Hebrew and Ukrainian, in others, Yiddish and Russian. The Zionist parties stood in solidarity with the Ukrainian national parties, while the socialist parties were more inclined to Yiddish and Russian.

We have a unique collection of postcards with panoramas of Jewish towns and postcards for Jewish holidays or events in Jewish history. We have about a thousand of them (Moshe Murakhovsky's collection).

We also have a collection of self-published texts, including Yiddish and Hebrew textbooks, articles by Volodymyr (Ze'ev) Jabotinsky and Chaim Nachman Bialik, texts, the magazine *Jews in the USSR*, and so on.

Another block is a unique collection of old photographs. We have more than four thousand pre-revolutionary ones alone! These photographs have preserved not only the vanished world. In those days, photographs were mostly taken in special studios, and on the back of each photo there is a logo of a very interesting design — the photographer's copyright. Probably, in the Jewish environment, for example, in Berdychiv, Lutsk, or Odesa, photographers were also mostly Jews. The photographs we have in our possession contain more than a hundred various spectacular, funny, pretentious, but certainly interesting logos of different photographers. In other words, even the back of old photos gives occasion to a separate exhibition!

A separate section is devoted to letters from and to the front, materials related to the evacuation, and miraculously preserved ration cards from different periods of the Soviet era. Unfortunately, the history of this period is mostly reflected in official documents, either Soviet or German. Both are full of lies.

One day, a lady from the museum of World War II history called me and told me this strange story: when the Germans occupied Kamianets-Podilsky, they collected letters from all the mailboxes in the city and took them to Germany. Apparently, they hoped to get some information. However, this did not happen, and in the 2000s the museum received back the bags that had not been opened for many years. The museum staff read and printed these letters, and in some cases the descendants of the addressees were found. Some of the letters were in Yiddish, and we were asked to read them. While working with the letters, we received yet another proof that the boundary between life and death is not so obvious for material media.

I would also like to tell you about our theatre collection, which covers the most fruitful period of Jewish theatre development from the late 1920s to the 1950s. There were about 70 Jewish theatres in Ukraine at that time. Of course, not all of them were professional; most were amateur theatres. The imprints of each of them have remained and are preserved in the Ukrainian Theatre Museum, but we also have some of them. The documents include programmes of performances, numerous photographs, unique posters, memoirs of participants, and recordings of performances by the theatre's actors. These are, first of all, materials about the Ukrainian State Jewish Theatre (GOSET), which was born in Kharkiv, worked for some time in Kyiv, and ended its existence in the 1950s in Chernivtsi, when an all-out attack on the Jewish community began. We have a unique theatre programme from 1950, printed on tissue paper — there was no other. This is the last document about the activities of a brilliant and long-suffering theatre.

We published *The Stolen Muse* (2003) by the last director of the Ukrainian GOSET, Moisei Loiev, which not only describes in detail and vividly the activities of the theatre, which was driven more and more every year into the Procrustean bed of socialist realism, but also lists the names of all the directors, artists, and actors of the theatre from the first days of its creation (more than 100 people), and carefully selects their photographs and images of scenes from performances. As a thank for publishing the book, Loiev gave us an invaluable gift—a collection of his theatre posters.

Years later, the children and grandchildren of the GOSET actors came to the book's presentation in Jerusalem and donated many materials from their home archives, including an amazing diary in Yiddish by the theatre's actor Dmitry Jabotinsky, which became one of the documents on the history of the theatre kept in our Centre.

Our archives also contain documents on the history of Jewish cinema, which were handed over to us by Yury Morozov, a well-known researcher and participant in the contemporary film process. Over the years, he and Tetiana Derevianko have been collecting these materials, which tell the story of the beginning of cinema in Odesa, from silent films to Yiddish films. This collection contains more than a thousand documents and photographs, invitations and posters, and most importantly, preserved copies of films, that have now been digitised. They are extremely valuable testimonies of the time. Many of them are unique.

In 2004 we published the book *Jewish Filmmakers in Ukraine. 1910-1945*, designed by Pavlo (Pinchas) Fishel. The book is so brilliantly designed that Yury Morozov joked when he saw the layout: 'I used to think that this book would be read, but now I see that it will be watched!' The book has indeed become an aesthetic sensation in post-Soviet Judaica and has won several prestigious awards.

Jewish cinema—what does it mean?
Perhaps at different stages of its development it meant different things. In the early days of cinema, both in the world and in our lands, many films were produced, both silent and dubbed in Yiddish. Jewish communities embraced the invention of cinema as a learning tool that could be used to recreate Torah stories or some version of the Talmud. Since most Jews still spoke Yiddish in the early twentieth century, many films were produced in that language and then dubbed into other languages as needed.

Over time, 'Jewish cinema' has come to be used to refer to films that in one way or another recreate the pages of Jewish history and culture. Jewish film festivals are held in many countries around the world, either to screen new films or to retrospectively screen old ones for interested audiences. There are many masterpieces among the films, such as *Dibbuk* (directed by Mikhail Vashinsky, 1937) or *Jewish Happiness* (directed by Alexei Granovsky, 1925), starring the prominent actor and director Solomon Michoels and written by Isaac Babel based on the stories of Sholem Aleichem.

We have shown *Jewish Happiness* several times. Once, to the accompaniment of a tapeur (an improvisational pianist), and then with the *Pushkin Klezmer Band*. Those were famous evenings, and we were able to feel how these films were perceived by the audience in the early twentieth century. In the West, by the way, it is customary to organise such screenings even with the participation of symphony orchestras.

We had a positive experience of organising the Hanukkah Film Festival in 2000 with the participation of German, Polish and Ukrainian cinematographers, but in the following years we were unable to raise organisational and financial resources.

Does your Centre have any experience of making films?
I have twice acted as a scientific consultant for films. The first time was when I advised Roman Shirman and screenwriter Zinaida Furmanova on the film *And a New Day Will Come* (1994). In my opinion, this is a good film about the drama of Ukrainian-Jewish relations in history and the search for understanding between peoples in modern times. Roman Shirman is one of the most interesting masters of documentary cinema. I love this film, as well as his other film, about Sergei Parajanov, *A Dangerously Free Man* (2004). It is not often that filmmakers manage to present a person whom the world 'chased but did not catch' in such a convincing and artistic way.

The second film is *Spell Your Name* (2006). The Shoah Foundation at the University of Southern California initiated the creation of films based on the memories of Shoah survivors around the world. When they were looking for potential directors, they asked me about it, and I recommended Serhiy Bukovsky and Roman Shirman. They chose Serhiy. He is an experienced filmmaker, but the topic of the Holocaust was new to him. We helped him to get acquainted with books and memoirs from our archives, with our film library, which contains about 200 films, including Claude Lanzmann's *Shoah*, which undoubtedly influenced the style of Bukovsky's film. Then Serhiy and Vita, his wife and also the administrator of most of his films, travelled to San Francisco to select the materials for the film. Eighty films were selected out of hundreds of films they watched. If I'm not mistaken, up to ten of films were selected, but what films! And then there was the painstaking work of the master and a wonderful team of his associates — cameramen, sound engineers, editors... Finally, the film is finished. Serhiy presents the first screening to his colleagues and we see that the film is a success — it is probably one of the strongest films in this category. Then we have to coordinate with the customers: on the one hand, Victor Pinchuk, who initiated the film from the Ukrainian side, and on the other hand, the American staff of the Shoah Foundation. For several months, Serhiy was accused by both sides. Pinchuk accused him of not showing enough Babyn Yar in the film, because he had commissioned a film about Babyn Yar. The Americans suspected that the film had anti-Semitic motives, because in one of the scenes, the Shoah survivor tells about his childhood and a joke he and his friend played on their grandfather when they were children — they put lard on his beard.

Serhiy was very worried about this, and at one stage of the film's production he jokingly said: 'Give me a certificate that I am not an anti-Semite, after all, you are the director of the Centre for Jewish Studies.' When I told this story in the presence of Ivan Dziuba a few years later, he asked for such a certificate, too. So when I retire and have something to earn, I will issue certificates.

The exhausting dialogues with the customers, on whom the fate of the film depended, lasted almost two months. The director was nervous and ready to abandon the film, but he didn't want to change anything. As a result, the film turned out to be coherent and powerful.

When the film was shown to Steven Spielberg, he said that he hadn't seen a documentary of this power for a long time. Then he said it publicly. As soon as the master's opinion was made public, everyone started talking about the film as a great success for Serhiy Bukovsky and his team. The film premiered at the Zhovtnevy Palace with the participation of the then President of Ukraine Viktor Yushchenko, the Chairman of the Verkhovna Rada Volodymyr Lytvyn and other high-ranking officials. Spielberg himself came to the premiere with his father, who was born in Ukraine. The premiere was a real celebration.

I also joined the work on a number of films with Tamara Boyko, a television film director. I played various roles, mostly as the initiator of certain films. Sometimes I told about the heroes, other times I helped to form a circle of experts and select video materials. These are the films about the heroes of our publications — Olga Rapay-Markish, Oleksa Zakharchuk, Mykhailyna Kotsiubynska, and Roman Korohodsky — that were shown on the *Kultura* TV channel in 2014-2016.

There are legends about your audio archive. How did the idea to create it come about?
At a certain stage, we realised that our parents had left almost no memories of their lives. They didn't keep archives, only a few of them kept diaries, and they were afraid to write about anything but everyday life in their correspondence. The fear of the Soviet era pressed people down. My mother, when asked by a correspondent why she had only one son, replied: "What if there was another war or famine? I wouldn't be able to bear it anymore, let alone a child." And probably many people of her generation could say the same.

Even though it is very late, we have collected about a thousand audio testimonies from older people. On the anniversary of Babyn Yar, 29 September, thousands of people have been gathering on its territory for many years to remember the innocent victims — relatives, friends, and neighbours. In 1989, Ukraine was not yet independent, there were no diplomatic relations with Israel, and the Soviet regime was still living out its last days. I thought that if we had questionnaires like the ones I had seen from Yad Vashem, we could collect the names of the dead. We printed ten thousand of these questionnaires. My children and the children of our friends handed out these questionnaires to everyone who came near Babyn Yar.

During this action, we managed to record about five thousand names of the dead, previously unknown. I remember my daughter coming up to me and asking: "This lady filled out a questionnaire with the names of her children, but she doesn't mention the name of one of them, she says he didn't have a name. I said, 'How can that be?' And the lady replied: 'We haven't had time to name him yet'."

We handed these questionnaires to Yad Vashem and at the same time I wrote a letter to the leadership of this organisation with a proposal to hold similar actions in other places of executions and murders. But, unfortunately, I was not heard. Today we have the opportunity to communicate with the heads of many structures, but back then I did not know the people who run Yad Vashem, and they did not know me.

I would like to continue working on the archives and collect more family materials (not only photographs, documents, but also stories and portraits) about the people killed at Babyn Yar. It's not too late to do this, because many families still have this memory in one way or another. Who were these people? Workers, engineers, musicians, poets, talented children… They were killed, their sacred right to life was taken away.

We continue to collect testimonies of people who died during the war saving Jews. They are not counted among the Righteous Among the Nations because there is no one to testify to their deeds. We are trying to record these stories, both on the basis of archival sources and through oral history.

Back in the 90s, we were partially able to arrange a museum exhibition in the building of the Galician synagogue. There, Shlomo Naiman created the Midrash Zionist learning centre, and the building itself was restored with money from the Sohnut Jewish Agency in Ukraine. We offered to organise an exhibition in the synagogue dedicated to Jewish history and culture in Ukraine. Ten video presentations were created based on the collection of the Centre for Jewish Studies, which could be viewed by simply turning on a computer in the hall. Ten more showcases with collectibles, books, and photographs were installed, as well as an exhibition on the Jewish history of Kyiv. On the second floor, we had a good exhibition on the history of book printing in Ukraine, which we updated with new editions. All of this, however, was subject to the fact that the exhibition in the synagogue was open during certain hours, and the exhibits were covered with cloths during prayer.

In recent years, Jewish museums have been opened in Odesa and Chernivtsi, and the Sholem Aleichem Museum is operating in Kyiv. They all need the documents and books we have collected, and we are happy to cooperate with them. We actively contributed to the creation of the Museum of the Memory of the Jewish People and the Holocaust in Ukraine together with the Ukrainian Institute for Holocaust Studies 'Tkuma' in Dnipro. At the request of the community, I was the author of the concept for this museum. For three years, our Centre developed each of the 52 topics presented in the museum. Today it is the largest Jewish museum in Ukraine, with expositions filled with our collections.

In Mohylianka, where dozens of special courses on Jewish history and culture are taught and where our Centre is located, we have also created several exhibitions. It would only natural to create an exposition on Jewish book printing in the building where Father Alexander Glagolev, the last rector of the theological academy, author of the Hebrew course, and one of the best Bible scholars, lived and taught. But this idea is still waiting to be implemented.

We are constantly preparing films and slideshows that are shown at various events. In this way, we hope to raise our Jewish Atlantis from the abyss of oblivion. They say that history teaches those who are ready to learn.

Is it reasonable to raise the question of creating an ethnographic town-museum now?
As part of one of our conferences, we held a roundtable discussion on the historical heritage and present-day Jewish material culture, where we discussed the creation of a Museum of the History of Jews in Ukraine. Experts in Jewish history, sociology, philosophy, and cultural studies were invited to participate. Many thoughts and ideas were expressed, and almost all the speakers agreed that the museum should be created. But, as in the joke, Itzyk agreed to marry the queen, now the queen has to agree.

One of the directions of work on the creation of such a museum may be the reconstruction, or rather the restoration and supplementation of a traditional Jewish shtetl. We cannot, of course, settle people in such a town again, nor can we restore the Jewish community to the level of its traditional functioning. However, we believe that preserving and passing on folk traditions, architectural and material cultural monuments to posterity is not only a noble but also an important goal.

We are not talking about creating such a museum in the near future. But the work must begin while the original Jewish homes in the shtetls are still standing, while the last ancient stone synagogues (built in the sixteenth and seventeenth centuries) are not destroyed, while people are still alive who can tell us about their past lives and traditions. The longer we delay, the more we will lose.

What is the significance of the shtetl in the history and culture of the Jews of Ukraine and what is the fate of its inhabitants?
Our spiritual leaders came from it, our writers and artists sought inspiration from it, our relatives of the 'great Jewish family' were born, lived, and died in it to become the Jewish people. People from the shtetls became the authors of the Zionist concept, and their efforts helped to create the State of Israel, a country that Jews around the world have dreamed of for thousands of years.

Dozens, if not hundreds, of scholarly monographs have been devoted to the shtetl phenomenon, and I dream that we will publish the most interesting of them. In the works of the giants of Jewish fiction who wrote in Yiddish and Hebrew (Isaac Bashevis-Singer, Shmuel Agnon, Chaim Gradet, Sholem Aleichem), the Jewish town and its inhabitants are always present. This literature is one of the most interesting of the twentieth century. We have yet to discover it in terms of translation into Ukrainian.

In 2013, we co-organised a wonderful expedition to the Jewish towns of Ukraine. It was initiated by Ilya Dvorkin, who once founded the St. Petersburg Jewish University and later emigrated to Israel, where he continues to produce dozens of extremely interesting cultural projects. The route of the expedition ran from Kyiv to Chernivtsi and included the towns of Sharhorod, Bar, Sataniv,

Berdychiv... For the first time, we saw Jewish shtetls where our grandparents and great-grandparents lived for centuries. We saw ruined and dilapidated synagogues (Sharhorod, Sataniv), cemeteries with thousands of *matzevot* (tombstones) with fantastic stone carvings... We also saw abandoned Jewish houses, some of which still have *mezuzahs* (boxes with prayers at the entrance to the house). Sometimes locals brought us Jewish books and candlesticks. Every day we listened to wonderful stories about Jewish traditions, history, philosophy, and took pictures of each other in front of synagogues and with local goats...

We saw houses with interesting interiors decorated with artistic patterns, where Jewish families used to live. These houses could be bought for a song, but it was unclear what to do with them afterwards. From that trip, in addition to books and mezuzahs, I have a memento of a chair that, according to legend, belonged to a rabbi and which is now kept in our Centre. We brought back many photographs, and the artists who accompanied us made hundreds of drawings, which we later presented at several exhibitions. The most interesting of them are the works by Viktor Hukailo, which made up the cycle *The Disappearing Shtetl*.

Today, there is practically no Jewish population left in the shtetls of Vinnytsia, Khmelnytskyi, Kyiv, and Ternopil regions. Most of the Jews died during the Holocaust, and those born after the war left their homes and moved to the United States and Israel, or to large cities in Ukraine and Russia. Thus, Jewish homes, some of which were built in the eighteenth century, are now abandoned and dilapidated.

However, I would like to say a few words about the Ukrainian population of these towns. When you ask old people about Jewish history, about the Jewish residents, they are very happy to talk about synagogues, about craftsmen and traders, about Jewish families with whom they lived for many years. Sometimes it is striking to hear their deep knowledge (and not only from the elderly) of the history and traditional religious life of Jews. Especially striking are meetings with the living Yiddish language, which sounds from the lips of a Ukrainian grandfather when he talks about a Jewish neighbour. Unfortunately, such meetings are becoming less and less frequent, and every year the shtetl phenomenon gradually disappears, leaving only memory — books, films, museums. But much remains to be done to preserve the memory at least in this form.

What would you say about the various attempts to build a museum, or, earlier, a community centre, on the territory of Babyn Yar?
The city, the country, and the world need a centre or museum of Jewish heritage. I was one of the participants in developing the concept of such a centre, the quintessence of which was to be a museum and archive of Jewish history and culture. This was followed by the selection of a site for its construction, which we thought would be near Babyn Yar. This was the opinion of many, including the author of the project, Amos Avgar, and myself.

When the architectural design competition was taking place, there was solid evidence that the site allocated for construction was Babyn Yar. I said that if this was true, I would advocate for another location for the Centre. Jewish law prohibits construction on cemeteries. Opposition to these projects was growing in Ukrainian society, and the organisers simply abandoned them. Over time, a group of international businessmen, whose capital is mostly linked to Russia, proposed their own project for an Eastern Europe Holocaust museum on the territory of Babyn Yar. Again, such a museum cannot be built on this cemetery site. For me, the idea of creating a museum of the Holocaust in Eastern Europe in Kyiv or elsewhere in Ukraine is doubtful: we have few experts on events in Ukraine, and none at all on events in other countries. The problems of the Holocaust are very painful even today, and there is a lot of speculation about them on all sides and in every country. Why bring these problems and contradictions to Ukraine? Only to provoke people.

I think the only right decision can be the project of a museum in Babyn Yar, launched on the initiative of the President of Ukraine Petro Poroshenko, which envisages the creation of a museum on the foundations of the building — the former office of the Jewish cemetery — which has been preserved on this territory. It is to be a museum in memory of all those killed and tortured at Babyn Yar: Jews and Roma, rabbis and priests, communists and members of the Ukrainian resistance movement, the mentally ill, and others.

The German Embassy organised a study tour for a group of people who were involved in the idea of creating a museum in memory of those who died at Babyn Yar to learn about German practices of representing the memory of the Second World War. It was an extremely interesting trip, and I was impressed by many things. First of all, the most documentary representation of Nazi crimes — documents, photographs, videos.

It is noteworthy that this was done in the Berlin Centre for Documentation of the History of Nazism in Germany. The money for the building of the Centre was raised by the city community, not the state. It is hard to imagine that a similar centre or museum dedicated to the crimes of communism could appear in Ukraine in the near future.

The most interesting museums and memorial sites are not those where a lot of money has been invested, but those based on creative ideas. In our experience, these are, for example, the One Street Museum or the Mikhail Bulgakov Museum in Kyiv. I do not lose hope for the creation of a Museum of Jewish Culture in Kyiv. After all, such museums exist in almost all European countries.

The creation of a Jewish museum in Kyiv is, first and foremost, the responsibility of the state and society. But how do we make it really interesting for people?
It is extremely difficult to arouse the interest of a twenty-first-century person in museum values. Today, there are many more opportunities for obtaining information than, say, 50 years ago: television and the Internet are available to almost everyone. Therefore, making a museum a real cultural centre is a very difficult task. I think that in Ukraine, the National Art Museum of Ukraine, the Bohdan and Varvara Khanenko National Museum of Art, the Taras Shevchenko National Museum, and the National Art Museum in Lviv are developing in this direction. Almost all of them have interesting exhibitions, creative children's programmes and projects. Alongside these museums are the cultural and artistic centre *Master*

Class by Iryna Budanska; the complex of galleries and classrooms, performance and concert halls *Dukat*, headed by Leonid Komskyi; *KalitaArtClub*, headed by Tatiana Kalita, and many others. Today, these museums and centres compete with each other, forming their own circles of viewers and fans. This has never happened before in our lives.

Among the most memorable events of recent years, I can name the performance exhibitions at Mystetskyi Arsenal. It was a curatorial exhibition by Pavel Gudimov, which featured Sergei Parajanov's *Shadows of Forgotten Ancestors* and the 'kitchen' behind its creation, including paintings and graphic works by the film's artist Georgy Yakutovych, author's designs for various scenes of the film, which Parajanov himself made, etc. The exhibition also showcased art from regional museums that was virtually unknown to the general public. The author of the concept is Dmitro Gorbachov. Before that, there was an extremely interesting exhibition of photographs by Petro Honchar with the simple title 'Windows'. These were images of windows from towns and villages in most regions of Ukraine: different and eloquent, perhaps, like the people who live or lived behind those windows.

And what a wonderful discovery was the exhibition of artworks from the 'special storage' of the National Art Museum of Ukraine — world-class masterpieces that were hidden in the museum's basements (thank God and people, they were not destroyed). It was the Bolshevik leaders who, like the Nazi leaders in their time, dictated their primitive tastes to artists, upholding the canons of socialist realism, which they used to kill everything that did not fall within these canons. I dream that in the future we will organise an exhibition about art that was hated by totalitarian regimes. In Germany, it was called 'degenerate art'. Time has set its priorities, and the names of great artists like Bogomazov[34] and Malevich[35] live on in the current art world, while those promoted by Hitler and Stalin have long been forgotten.

---

34 Ukrainian painter, cubo-futurist, modern art theoretician and is recognised as one of the key figures of the Ukrainian avant-garde scene.
35 Avant-garde artist and art theorist, whose pioneering work and writing influenced the development of abstract art in the 20th century.

Among the many museums I have visited, I consider the Jewish Museum in Berlin to be one of the best, with the best experts from different countries working on the concept and creation of the museum for many years. And most importantly, the target audience was very precisely defined: the museum is open to all people who, regardless of nationality, want to learn about Jewish civilisation. The values of the Jewish world are well shown: traditions, the education system, and symbols of faith. And it is done with the help of modern means. For example, in just seven minutes, the video provides basic information about the architecture of synagogues and why they look more like the temples of their host countries than each other. In the museum, you can also learn about the main elements of interiors, which were necessarily observed: *Aron Kodesh* — a cabinet for storing a Torah scroll, *bima* — a raised platform for reading Torah... A Jewish school corner consisting of several desks with photographs of students of Jewish German schools in the 20s and 30s and Yiddish notebooks with notes on geography and mathematics are presented. The history of synagogue objects, such as *yadas* or *mezuzahs*, which are obligatory at the entrance to a Jewish home, is conveyed through different artistic solutions for these objects. And each of them is self-sufficient and at the same time plays its role in the performance, into which a guided tour for the visitor is transformed.

The museum is visited by about a million people a year. It has special corners where children can learn the Hebrew alphabet and play with traditional toys... There are not many original items in the museum, but the metaphors and images of the exhibition create a much stronger impression than a whole series of 'originals'. And they are what make this museum unique.

At one time, the exhibition 'Artists of the Kultur-Liga', in the organisation of which the Centre and you personally took part, caused a significant public and scientific response. How would you describe this phenomenon?
The *Kultur-Liga* began its activities with the assistance of the Ministry of Jewish Affairs, which was established under the government of the Ukrainian People's Republic as part of the national cultural

autonomy, and functioned until the first years of Soviet rule. Jewish education, enlightenment, book publishing, art exhibitions, and theatres were the main activities of this association. However, a special phenomenon of the Kyiv branch of the *Kultur-Liga* was its artistic section.

Today, few people remember that Mark Epstein, Sarah Schorr, Solomon Nikritin, Isakhar-Ber Rybak, Alexander Tishler, Joseph Tchaikov, Abram Manevich, and many other world-class artists worked in Kyiv between 1918 and early 1920s. For various reasons, only a small part of what they created has survived to this day. Most of them are paintings and graphics, including prints. Even the published books are subject to sad statistics — out of the two thousand copies published, only five or ten have survived to the 21st century. However, the sculpture suffered the most. Now it can be seen only in photographs, but they also testify to the very high level of artists who worked in this field. For example, Tchaikov and Epstein deserve to be mentioned on a par with Jacques Lipshitz and Oleksandr Archipenko. But, unfortunately, the work of these artists is almost unknown to the general public...

Hillel Kazovsky wrote about the activities of the *Kultur-Liga* in his texts, and he brought one of the brightest pages of Jewish culture back into the history of Jewish culture. After the publication of his book *Artists of the Kultur-Liga* (2003), he and I decided to hold an exhibition of paintings, drawings, and sculptures by the artists of the association at the National Art Museum of Ukraine. The exhibition was opened in December 2007. About 150 works, many of which were exhibited for the first time, were shown in the best museum in the country. The works were gathered from the storerooms of the National and regional museums of Ukraine, the Paris and Moscow Jewish Museums, and private collections in Ukraine and Israel. We exhibited paintings, books, Kyiv photographs of the time, and theatre sets.

It was not just an exhibition, but a performance that spoke about time. There were computers in the halls that showed book editions of the *Kultur-Liga* and films about the artists. Photographs of Joseph Tchaikov's brilliant sculptures were hanging from the ceiling, as time had not preserved the originals. However, if it was possible to recreate the bas-reliefs from the descriptions and photographs, we did so, and they were also included in the exhibition in Victor Hukailo's reconstructions.

Hundreds of people came to the opening. First of all, the visitors were greeted by photographic portraits of the artists of that time — smart, bright, free people — who had not yet experienced the tragedies of the following decades. The exhibition was a success and was recognised as the best of that year's museum exhibitions, despite the fact that the 'competitors' were worthy, including an exhibition of Pablo Picasso's graphics.

So, by collecting and publishing this heritage, we have done a good deed — a *mitzvah*, as the Jews say. Prof. Myroslav Popovych said: 'We will correct the previously written history of Ukrainian art. There is no way around the *Kultur-Liga* — it is a world-class phenomenon.'

Then we prepared and published an extremely interesting exhibition catalogue with texts about the era and artists in Ukrainian and English, as well as *Kultur-Liga* programme documents (translated from Yiddish), biographies of the artists, academic descriptions of the works, and an album dedicated to *Kultur-Liga* book graphics. There are rare publications from 1918-1924 that are impossible to find even on the world antiquarian market. For example, a collection of poems by David Hofstein with illustrations by Marc Chagall, published in Kyiv in 1922, or books with drawings by Marc Epstein... Both catalogues were designed by Pavlo (Pinchas) Fishel.

What can you say about contemporary art-Judaica?
Almost throughout all the years of our activity, we have been organising exhibitions of talented artists who, in their works, develop the theme of Jewish history and culture in one way or another. A special place among them belongs to the exhibition 'Nisayon. The Jewish Theme in the Works of Contemporary Ukrainian Artists,' which we, together with its curator Ola Petrova, held at the Ukrainian House in 1993. This exhibition is to some extent significant because it was the first to declare contemporary art-Judaica as a phenomenon.

Individual exhibitions of works by artists who are no longer alive (Mikhail Weinstein, Zinovy Tolkachev), or who have emigrated (Mikhail Gleyzer, David Myretsky, Boris Lekar), and those who are currently active in Ukraine (Pavel (Pinchas) Fishel, Viktor Hukailo, Irina Klimova, Lyubov Rappoport, Elena Agamyan, Matvey Weisberg, Alexander Roytburd) are also valuable. We publish their catalogues, including the magnificent album *Kyiv Collection. Jewish Themes in the Works of Ukrainian Artists from the 1950s to the Present* (2015), compiled by Diana Klochko and designed by Pavlo (Pinchas) Fishel. In addition, to present their work more widely, we created a special website called *Kyiv Collection* (the name was suggested by Lyubov Rappoport). The site allows us to present the artists' work in a very thorough way: exhibitions of their works — sculpture, graphics, painting — texts and photographs, films about their work. For me, this is a very important project, which argues that today's art-Judaica in Ukraine is no less interesting than it was in the early 20th century, and therefore requires the attention of the artistic community and society.

We are not able to buy works of art, but many artists donate their works to us. Our collection includes illustrations to Leonid Pervomaisky's poems and posters to mark the 50th anniversary of the Babyn Yar massacre by Ada Rybachuk and Volodymyr Melnychenko, illustrations to Isaak Babel's stories by David Myretsky, illustrations to texts by Janusz Korczak and Stanislaw Jerzy Lec by Viktor Hukaylo, graphics by Lyubov Rappoport and Iryna Klimova, works by Pavlo (Pinchas) Fishel and Yakym Levych, numerous sculptures by Olga Rapay-Markish, whose archive we keep, and others. These are the artists whose names will still sound in the world like the names of their predecessors who talentedly reflected their time.

While collecting Jewish heritage, you do not forget about the present, and you take an active part in Jewish and Ukrainian cultural life. Are you interested in social and political life?
Very much so! For many years, we have been studying the demographics and sociology of the Jewish community, monitoring

anti-Semitism and countering it, preparing analytical materials, researching international experience, legal acts of the UN, OSCE, and Council of Europe. Now these issues are being dealt with more professionally by a new generation of people led by Vyacheslav Likhachev.

In addition to leading the Centre, I have many public roles. I'll name only the most important ones for me. I am a member of the presidium of the Ukrainian branch of PEN International. Together with my colleagues—Ola Hnatiuk, Mykola Riabchuk, Yevhen Zakharov, Andriy Kurkov and others—we have restored and significantly intensified its activities. This includes the establishment of PEN Ukraine's prizes: the Yury Shevelov Prize for the best essay and the Vasyl Stus Prize for contribution to culture. The establishment of the Yury Shevelov Prize, initiated by Ola Hnatiuk, was our asymmetrical response to the vandals' smashing of a plaque in Kharkiv in honour of the Ukrainian scientist, one of the most famous in the world. Over the years, the prize has been awarded to reputable Ukrainian intellectuals: Taras Prokhasko, Kost Moskalets, Oleksandr Boichenko, Volodymyr Yermolenko, Vakhtang Kebuladze, and Andriy Lyubka. The restored Vasyl Stus Prize was awarded to Oleksandra Koval, the first publisher of Vasyl Stus's works in independent Ukraine and organiser of the Lviv Book Forum since 2004, and to the famous poet and prose writer Serhiy Zhadan.

Another role I have as a conceptualiser and project manager is the publication of the *Library of Resistance, Library of Hope* and *Cultural Figures* book series. I'm not going to talk about other roles, but I have some more. Do you know what a bore is? This is someone who is asked: 'How are you?' and he takes you by the button and tells you a long story. I'd better stop here.

And yet, what's next? What are your plans for the future?
I honestly admit that I have a lot of plans. Stanisław Jerzy Lec wrote: 'Throw your plans to your enemies and let them die trying to implement them.' I won't throw, and what I can, I will do it. But, of course, not alone, but with my friends, colleagues and family.

5. Ukrainians and Jews

You are a person who has perhaps the best and deepest understanding of Ukrainian-Jewish relations in Ukraine. They were both complicated and difficult throughout the course of history. In your opinion, to what extent has the Jewish culture which developed on the lands of contemporary Ukraine, become a fully-fledged part of contemporary Ukrainian culture?
I think we still cannot say today that even Ukrainian culture itself is genuinely Ukrainian. Despite all the years of more or less free development there are still a lot of texts and stories that we do not know.

Soviet stereotypes still prevail in public discourse. As for intellectuals, I would say that those intellectuals who are focused on studying Ukrainian history and culture know approximately eighty percent of what one should know. Or maybe even less.

As to Jewish culture, the situation is even worse. Jewish culture has existed and developed in these lands for centuries. Many people who later became renowned throughout the world were born and lived here. For instance, Shmuel Yosef Agnon, a Nobel Prize Winner; but Agnon's works have never been translated into Ukrainian.

We [*Center for the Studies of History and Culture of East European Jewry and the Dukh i Litera Publishing House – Ed.*] wanted to translate his texts, but we are only just beginning to translate some of his stories. Agnon is an extremely difficult writer. He is one of the most difficult authors of the 20th century, because the fabric of his writing is very much linked to Biblical texts. A translator has to know these texts perfectly, and there is still no such person either in the Ukrainian or in the Jewish culture on our land.

We started from scratch approximately thirty years ago. During this period, we have published nearly one hundred books on Jewish studies. Yet, what does "one hundred books" mean when there are hundreds of thousands of them in developed countries?

We face a challenge every time we have to select the best one, because we are not able to publish a dozen or a hundred books about a specific subject or a specific author, as we can publish only one.

Today, we have a small group of people—several dozens in all of Ukraine—who know languages, who are immersed in Jewish-Ukrainian culture and history. However, in order to dig into the culture of the past centuries, we need hundreds and hundreds of people. It's only in recent years that we began receiving some state support to do this job. Before that, there was nothing.

Let's talk about the major figures in Jewish-Ukrainian culture, the representatives of the Jewish culture who are connected to contemporary Ukrainian lands. For instance, I can think about Paul Celan, one of the biggest German-speaking poets of the 20th century who was born in Chernivtsi/Czernowitz. Or Joseph Roth, the author of one of the best novels about the end of the Austro-Hungarian Empire, who was born in Brody. Who else would you name?
I would absolutely mention Volodymyr Ze'ev-Jabotinsky.

I would also name the figures from the period of the Ukrainian People's Republic [1917-1921 – Ed.]. There was a phenomenon called the Kultur Liga (Culture League), which was, in fact, the ministry for Jewish rights.

Even the banknotes of the Ukrainian People's Republic had an inscription in Yiddish, among other languages.
Yes, and that era was very interesting. It was very short but extremely intense. The Culture League dealt with libraries and schools, but there was also an artists' club. In that period (1918-1924) the club's members included Marc Chagall, El Lissitzky, Robert Falk, Mark Ep-stein, Sarra Shor, Abraham Manievich. All of them became world famous later.

These are world-class phenomena, and people have to know about them. Do you remember how anti-Ukrainian or anti-Semitic texts were promoted in the Soviet era? Do you know how many anti-Zionist and anti-Semitic books were published in the Soviet Union? Four hundred, Can you imagine? And we are happy that we have published one book on a specific topic, and discovered a phenomenon thanks to this book.

How strong was anti-Semitism in the Soviet Union, especially after World War II? Before the war a lot of Jewish organizations participated in the revolutionary movement, but after the war anti-Semitism began to thrive gradually in the USSR. To what extent did you feel it?
There are stereotypes and Soviet clichés linked to this topic. In fact, before the [1917] revolution, Jews in the Russian Empire voted for religious parties, for Zionist parties. Very few of them voted for the social democratic or communist parties.

Then there was a wave of pogroms, and a lot of Jews were killed. Of course, Jews were not the only ones to be killed because violence was very widespread at that time; there were gangs that aligned themselves once with the Whites, then with the army of the Ukrainian People's Republic, and then with the Reds. It was the chaos of hunger and armed violence.

In those years of the Civil War [*late 1910s – early 1920s*], the Bolsheviks (although their gangs also participated in pogroms) were the most consistent in their efforts to end that spiral of pogroms. They did this not because they treated Jews so well, but because they wanted to master the situation and lead the country.

The Bolsheviks managed to do this, although they used the cruelest methods, and we know it. At that time, a lot of people (Ukrainians, Jews, Russians) joined the Bolsheviks. Others hid for some time, but they faced progressive restrictions of their rights and, finally, extermination.

At that time, there was no ideology of anti-Semitism in the USSR, it is true. Yet it was present in people's minds, it had never disappeared.

Do you mean the pre-war period?
Yes. The Bolsheviks were trying to play the international card. But they were playing it in a specific way, prohibiting the Hebrew language and, thus, Judaism as religion: Judaism cannot live without the language. The same happened with the Ukrainian community

when the Bolsheviks went about destroying churches, when they melted church crosses to make cannons. That madness was not national at that time, it was social.

National tragedies began with the Famine of 1932-33. These were already national extermination campaigns, because the empire understood that independent peasants showed the greatest level of resistance to it, and, quite consistently, the empire began to use these barbaric campaigns against peasants. First, the revolution chose various social groups, other classes as its targets. Then there was the Famine, which was, objectively speaking, a fight against Ukrainians.

Later, before World War II, there were socially motivated trials once again, repressions against the military, but not only them. The communists started exterminating their own people, those who knew the truth about what was happening.

After the war, nationally motivated trials — anti-Semitic, anti-Ukrainian — started again. After the war anti-Semitism became horrible because it was organized by the state. First it was soft when the USSR began to cooperate with Hitler (1939-1941); during that period there was silence about all the tragedies involving the Jews that were happening in Europe. The party disoriented citizens and did nothing to protect these groups of citizens later on, when the war broke out. The USSR cared first of all about its factories, so only factories were evacuated, and those who moved with the factories. Others were left behind.

The trials of the late 1940s — the fight against the Jewish Anti-Fascist Committee, the Doctors' plot case — were terrible campaigns aimed at destroying the Jewish intelligentsia. There was a plan to deport Jews as a community to Siberia.

Why did all of this happen? The Soviet Union defeated a huge anti-Semitic power, and instead it became anti-Semitic itself. One of the explanations that I find is that Israel began to drift more towards the US and the West. Another explanation is that Russian

nationalism in the Soviet Union had triumphed. But how would you explain it?

There are several factors. One of them is that Stalin had to exterminate someone all the time so as to keep the country living in fear. The time had finally come for the Jews.

Why the Jews? First, the communist party was fighting against the Jewish Anti-Fascist Committee because these people had huge connections in America and huge influence. During World War II they went to America and collected big money for Soviet weapons.

Similarly, the USSR sent to Siberia those people who were in Western countries during World War II, especially officers. Those officers had seen the West and knew how people could live decently, so they were immediately sent to the camps.

Why did they fight doctors? This, I think, was Stalin's idiosyncrasy. He was afraid of everything. At some stage, he was afraid of the doctors near him—and there were a lot of Jewish doctors and professors among them.

For me, it is obvious that Stalin felt he had to destroy one community after another in order not to let any resistance emerge.

Similarly, after the war there was a fight against Ukrainian "nationalism". I put the word "nationalism" in quotation marks, of course, because everyone who spoke Ukrainian and refused to write an ode for Stalin every day was said to be a "nationalist".

The Soviet regime also created a legend about the disloyalty of Crimean Tatars. There were just as many heroes [*of the fight against Nazism — Ed.*] and Soviet Army soldiers among the Crimean Tatars than among other ethnic groups. There was, perhaps, an even bigger proportion of those people compared to the proportion in other groups. But they were made scapegoats. Stalin was clearing the space in Crimea and the Caucasus to continue the war in the Middle East. He was halted only by American nuclear weapons. He had the strongest army in Europe, which had drunk its fill of blood and stopped only when the Americans became stronger.

Let's talk about Ukrainian national movements and their impact on Ukrainian-Jewish relations. The tragic paradox is that what

Ukrainians see as liberation movements frequently meant tragedies, pogroms, violence for the Jewish community.
Do you mean the Bohdan Khmelnytsky period?

Khmelnytsky, *Haidamaky,* *Koliivshchyna,* **Petliura and others. For instance, a lot of people accused Petliura of anti-Jewish pogroms, although there are documents confirming that he tried to stop them. We know that the assassination of Petliura [Petliura was killed in Paris by Samuel Schwartzbard in 1926 — Ed.] was accompanied by the message that it was the revenge of the Jewish community; but the murderer could also be an KVD agent. Yet if we look at it from a wider angle — how do we interpret this today? The Ukrainian liberation movement and the Jewish community very often went one against the other, and the Jewish community suffered very often from Ukrainian movements.**

Liberation movements were tragic for everyone who stood on their paths. The Poles were killed no less frequently than the Jews. The Jews were a literate nation and a stateless community, so those tragedies were interpreted and articulated in a serious manner. Such phenomena have very simple laws: during such wars Strangers and Others are always killed. But those who were not Strangers, and belonged to the same community, were also killed — but perhaps did not have the opportunity to talk about it.

I don't know if you read an article written by Vadym Skurativskyi [*a Ukrainian intellectual, historian, and art critic — Ed.*] about Taras Shevchenko. He has a brilliant statement that Shevchenko was the first person in world culture who vocalized the largest pains of those people who had no words to express their feelings. Before him, there were people like Byron who could be sent to prison for a short time, and then write a poem about his experience. Instead, Shevchenko went through all the stages of humiliation, imprisonment, exile and sufferings, and he voiced them as nobody had done earlier, which made his voice so strong in world culture. In his article, Skurativskyi used a metaphor of the residents of African tribes who, when experiencing hard times, came together and just howled together.

In the 1920s gangs robbed Ukrainian villages as well, and killed members of the civilian population. But often this remained unexpressed, and there were no words or witnesses to share those stories.

It is important to conceptualize the problem of statelessness. There is no coincidence that the biggest victims of World War II were Jews because of the "specific" policy of Nazism. But Ukrainians were big victims too, because they were stateless as well. All victims of the first years of war were, to a large extent, people from Western territories—Ukrainians, Belarusians, etc. Later, the Soviet army was victorious and began reconquering those lands, but during the first years of the war it was almost destroyed, and out of a five-million army almost four million were captured and made prisoners. The Germans did not know what to do with such a large number of people.

That is why I believe that statelessness means victimhood.

You mentioned Petliura. In the past, together with Roman Korogodsky, we published a book called *Field of Despair, Field of Hope*. There was an article in it about a person belonging to Petliura's entourage who was responsible for preventing pogroms. They really did try to stop pogroms, and pogrom participants were executed.

However, at the latter stages Petliura did not have his own army; it broke down into groups of independent armies or large divisions. He was losing one squadron after another because his people joined the Bolsheviks or others, and he was no longer able to contain them.

That was his fault. Yet this is a bit different fault than one of organizing pogroms. Petliura was an intellectual, and he tried to stop violence in any form, including pogroms.

With regard to Petliura's murder in Paris, I could say that, like in many other similar historical cases, we will not have the evidence of, say, an order from Stalin to kill Petliura. The Russian archives will be closed for a very long time, perhaps until the end of this empire. Yet there is no doubt that during that time the Soviet secret services were killing one opponent after another of the regime, who were hiding in Europe. Petliura was one of them. It is very probable that he was killed by the Soviet secret service.

I don't know if you know an artist, Hlushchenko, who was a Soviet intelligence officer and a correspondent at the Petliura trial. At that time, the Soviet government provided only documents it wanted to provide for the trial. It was in the mid-1930s, and we know which terrible trials began in the USSR from the late 1920s — in 1929, 1930, 1933.

Let's talk about the Holocaust. I think this issue is still not duly researched in Ukraine. We cannot answer the questions as to what extent Ukrainians collaborated during the Holocaust, and to what extent did Ukrainians resist the Holocaust. What can you say about this?
Indeed, this issue is almost not studied — like very many other aspects of Ukrainian history. A genuine history of World War II in Ukraine] is only now emerging. These are the first books written by Vladyslav Hrynevych, Yaroslav Hrytsak, Olena Stiazhkina, Tamara Vronska. Before them, we had only Soviet legends. Everything in them was lies.

The topic of rescuing the Jews was also taboo in the Soviet Union. Commemoration of the executions in Babyn Yar was prohibited and, therefore, investigations only began when there was almost nobody left who could say what happened back then.

The number of Ukrainians who rescued Jews and are called the Righteous Among the Nations is rather high. However, saving the Jews caused unwanted associations [in the Soviet era] and trying to avoid the need to give explanations to the authorities, people were afraid to talk, and were scared that their neighbors would report them.

If reported, then — unlike what was going on in Western Europe — they would be killed. It was not just persons who rescued the Jews or helped them would be killed, but their entire families.

Adam Michnik once wrote, *I don't know what I would do if I had a wife and a child during the war and they the Jews would come to me and ask for shelter. But the fact that there were people who saved others – this, he said, is the sign of God's presence on Earth.* I think these are really great words.

Ola Hnatiuk, in her book *Courage and Fear* showed, using materials from Western Ukraine during the double Soviet and Nazi occupation, that there were a lot of stories of mutual rescue and solidarity among Ukrainians, Jews, and Poles. But in Western literature we can constantly find the stereotypes that Ukrainians were inclined towards collaborating—for instance, that the Ukrainians worked for police and helped to kill Jews.

I avoid the word "collaborator". Collaborators are traitors. Whom did Western Ukrainians (or Poles, or people from the Baltic States) betray when the Soviets came to them? How could they betray the Soviets that destroyed their intelligentsia?

With regard to cooperating with the Germans: people from all nations cooperated with the Germans. [In Ukrainian lands], more than 80% of residents remained in the occupied territories. How could they survive? There were different forms of cooperation. In our publishing house, we published a book by Olena Stiazhkina [*The Stigma of Occupation. Soviet Women in Self-Awareness of the 1940s – Ed.*] about women during the war. It contains different stories. One is about a Soviet patriot who wanted to die but win in the war. Another is about a Ukrainian patriot who tried to save her family, nation, and everything she could. The third is about a person who wanted to survive, and she worked at a sausage factory. Thanks to that work, she was able to save a lot of people who were not sent to Germany and were not exterminated. Later, when she was arrested by the Soviet regime and sent to Siberia, people defended her. They wrote, "She saved us". And they were able to get her brought back [from the Soviet camps], which was an exception, a one in a thousand case.

So there were all types of situations. The war had different stages, and we know it. At the initial stages, some Ukrainian forces were pro-fascist, and some were liberal—but this was the same in all other countries as well. The Ukrainians hoped that after the Soviet occupation they would be liberated by the Germans, and they would be able to create an independent state. However, the Germans did not need this. This Ukrainian movement, therefore, very quickly began to fight both the Soviets and the Germans. There were instances of helping the Germans and of fighting against the Germans. Similarly, there was assistance for Soviet forces and of resistance against them — when Soviet forces repressed the Ukrainians, the Jews, and the Poles back in the first years of their occupation, in 1939-1941. All of this requires careful research.

In 1991 [*the year when the USSR collapsed – Ed.*] together with Ivan Dziuba [*a Ukrainian dissident and writer – Ed.*] we organized a conference [on Ukrainian-Jewish relations], and it had a huge effect. I can quote Yevhen Sverstiuk [*a Ukrainian dissident and writer – Ed.*] who wrote, "For the first time, children of Ukraine and children of Israel sat down together to talk, to clean these stables that no-one had cleaned for centuries, which accumulated legends about Ukrainians who hanged the Jews, and Jews who kept the keys to a church.

The only thing missing in those legends is the truth".

Then we had an interesting presentation by a historian, Yaroslav Dashkevych, who tried to show various stages of the coexistence of Jews and Ukrainians. In his words, if the Jews had felt so bad living on these lands, one third of all the European Jews would not have lived in this territory. Now we are gradually discovering some humane forms of coexistence between the Ukrainians and the Jews.

A wonderful book written by Johanan Petrovsky was published recently about life in shtetls [*Jewish towns in Central-Eastern Europe – Ed.*]. This is not a story about how shtetls struggled for their survival, but about a period that came before that difficult time. When Russia capitalized on the part that had earlier belonged to the Polish-Lithuanian state, it gave concessions to Polish magnates. These magnates invited Jews, who acted as catalyzers of development in big and small towns.

Was this in the 19th century?
Yes, it was in the early 19th century. Petrovsky had access to archives and discovered fantastic materials. For example, he discovered evidence about joint Polish-Ukrainian-Jewish gangs, "counterfeiters", but also about all the other legal social structures, which had not yet been suppressed.

At later stages, when the Russian authorities began to "tighten the screws", everything was ruined, and there was nothing to hold on to for survival. But before that, those communities cooperated in a normal way. "Normal" has both a positive and a negative sense.

They cooperated but they also fought, though this was not a fight on national grounds.

The level of anti-Semitism in Ukraine is currently very low. After the Maidan [in 2013-2014], anti-Semitism-based crimes have been virtually absent. One can say that Ukraine is one of the least anti-Semitic countries. We are sitting now in the office of Yosyf Zisels [Ukrainian-Jewish dissident, co-president of the Association of Jewish Organizations and Communities of Ukraine (VAAD)]. He describes very well how Ukrainian and Jewish dissidents met each other in Soviet camps. Was this the beginning of reconciliation?
I would not say "reconciliation", but rather "mutual understanding".

Can we say that it was the Ukrainian-Jewish dissident movement that led to this understanding?
I think that the dissident movement played a positive role in the entire "healing" of Ukrainian society. Before that, we had Soviet stereotypes. Dissidents provided a breath of "fresh air": European traditions, traditions of respect for the law, for a human being, and for religion.

Of course, dissidents played their role in it.

It's another matter that all of this was a gradual process, and almost no-one knew about their [Ukrainian-Jewish] cooperation. It was only in the years that followed, with *Rukh* [*literally, "Movement", a Ukrainian national movement founded in the late 1980s – Ed.*], with Chornovil, Sverstiuk, Zisels, Gluzman, that we learnt a lot more than we knew before. Yet, it is important to remember that actions of solidarity between the Ukrainian and Jewish intelligentsia during the Soviet era were numerous. When anti-Semitic manifestations appeared, provoked by the authorities, instigated by the KGB, or someone did something individually, there was always a response from Sverstiuk, or Marynovych, or Antoniuk [*Ukrainian dissidents – Ed.*].

Similarly, we held many actions of solidarity when Ukrainians were groundlessly or provocatively accused of anti-Semitism.

Yet, it's not only this that's important. The main point is that after the "Soviet Wall" collapsed (there was not only the Berlin Wall, there was the Soviet Wall as well), and all this Soviet madness came to an end, world culture opened up to us. During the Soviet era, we knew nothing about democratic movies, tolerant movies or movies about Jewish destinies, or about the Holocaust, or human solidarity in general. We knew the Soviet communist ideologemes that had been pounded into our heads. The specific trait of Soviet propaganda was that it emphasized negative things. It darkened the positive sides of joint histories of different countries or different nations. I think that Soviet propagandists had their own kind of "divide and rule" game, and they played it quite successfully. According to them, the Ukrainians had always been nationalists, and the Jews had always been Zionists; both these words had negative connotations.

During the Maidan in 2013-2014, a new meme was created, *Zhydo-Banderites* [Jewish Bandera supporters]. It is very paradoxical, because Bandera's ideology in the 1930s had elements from the far-right movements of that time, including fascism, with their anti-Semitic aspect. How should we look at this aspect today?

The same terms work differently in different contexts. I think that the victory of this term, *Zhydo-Banderite*, is in the fact that it has removed pre-existing stereotypes, as it destroyed the pejorative meaning of the word *zhyd* [*one of the names for Jews, that got pejorative connotations in the 20th century – Ed.*]. It is important to remember that a Zhydo-Banderite is a self-appointed name of the Jewish intelligentsia which associated itself with the Maidan movement, which was part of the Maidan.

The same has happened now, for instance, in relations between Israel and Germany. There is no-one who brought more grief to the Jewish people than the Nazis. Yet today, Germany and Israel have normal relations, a constructive approach and support. I think that Ukrainian-Jewish relations are now at this constructive stage in our country. And I believe that this is the achievement of those people who we have already mentioned, and many others who we have not been mentioned here.

We recently published a book by Yurii Skira about how Jews were saved in the Stoudios Charter monasteries. For some reasons, Ukrainians did not talk about this for so many years. However, along with the tragic pages of history there were heroic pages as well. We know Schindler's list, we know Polish, Dutch, and Danish stories. Now we also know some Ukrainian stories.

The first book about it appeared three months ago. It is about an extraordinary, heroic deed: Jewish children (and not only children) were hidden in monasteries, and the whole community and an entire branch of the Christian church was involved in this process. Now I want to find someone who could make a documentary about it, and translate this book into English. For ten years, I was looking for someone who could write this book—and finally I found this person: the book was written by a young 26-year-old scholar from the Ukrainian Catholic University, Yurii Skira. Together with a priest, he visited those people who are very old now, and who told these stories to them. They would have not talked without a priest [*the book by Yuri Skira is called* "Those Who Were Called: Monks of Stoudios Charter and the Holocaust"—Ed.].

We recently published another book, it's called Silence Speaks. The problem is that first of all those people who survived the Holocaust wanted to talk, but no-one wanted to listen to them because of fear. This was just after the war. And then they locked themselves up and fell silent because they were afraid. At a certain moment in time, many of those who found strength in themselves to share their stories committed suicide because it was extremely difficult to experience all that again...

There is another very tragic event in Ukrainian history of the 20th century—the *Holodomor* [Artificial Famine] of 1932-1933. In Ukraine, it is often called the *Ukrainian Holocaust*, and there is even a multi-volume publication that collected personal stories about the Holodomor with this title. I do not think this is a good title—but still, do you think that these two events can be compared, and do you think that Nazism and Stalinism were in some ways close?

Yehen Sverstiuk once said very correctly that if the world had not turned away from the Holodomor, if it had not turned a blind eye to what was happening in Ukraine in the 1930s, then perhaps the Holocaust would have never happened. The Holodomor was a warning to humanity, but humanity buried its head in the sand. And I think that Sverstiuk is right. Had the world's attention been focused on the Holodomor tragedy organized by Stalin's regime, maybe they would have found the levers that would have helped to contain other totalitarian regimes at a later stage. In any case, they would have been able to better unite the efforts of democratic forces.

Yet, every tragedy happens in its own way. Tragedies, as joys, are all unique. Both the Holodomor and the Holocaust were terrible, and both tragedies should be known, remembered, and studied. We should be strong enough to fight it, because we cannot live our entire lives with this tragedy, with such hard feelings. Memory should be full of light as people say—we should remember, but move on.

Why is there constant talk about Bandera? Why don't people talk about Stalin? Stalin has the blood of millions of people of all ethnic origins on his hands. Yet he is glorified by some people today, and for some people—in Russia, and not only there—he is a hero. Instead, people are talking about Bandera, whose role is much smaller. And what about Zhukov? What about Sudoplatov? This list can be contin-ued. Not only in the Russian context, but also in the Ukrainian and Jewish contexts, there are a lot of people who deserve to be condemned.

But there is a set of stereotypes that frame human thinking and I believe that, to a large extent, these stereotypes are still the remnants of Stalinist propaganda.

How would you describe the Jewish movement in Ukraine today?
I think it is very difficult to analyze it today, because the Jewish community is no longer as important, as influential and organized as it used to be. In the past, Ukrainian parties and Jewish parties, Ukrainian communities and Jewish communities were well-structured, in one way or another. They are no longer like that. Today, there are perhaps a dozen Jewish organizations that exist nominally in Ukraine, of which 90% are absolutely fictitious, there is nothing behind them. They are used by some oligarchs of Jewish origin who need to show at some moment in time that they are Jewish leaders. So they bring old Jews from different places, and they have a one-day gathering to adopt a decision, because the community, as such, practically does not exist.

Perhaps the only exception is VAAD Ukraine, which is headed by Yosyf Zisels, but this association does not represent the interests of all Jews either. The integral community is, by and large, no longer around.

There are simply fewer people left.
Yes, of course. There are individual communities and small groups that work. And we are one of them.

6. On Cultural Shifts

We didn't notice how much we had changed. How our museums have become qualitatively different, and they are headed by responsible professionals, large-scale personalities—Taras Vozniak, Yulia Lytvynets[1], Dmytro Stus, Oleksandr Roitburd[2], Petro Honchar[3]. Ukrainian cinema has been revived, and as in the days of Parajanov, Balayan, and Muratova, it has become a part of the cultural life of the country and the world. Akhtem Seitablaev's *Cyborgs*, Serhiy Loznitsa's films, and the documentaries by Serhiy Bukovsky and Roman Shyrman have become an important part of Ukrainian contemporary culture. How has the network of Ukrainian theatres expanded—there are about 50 in Kyiv alone. How did performances appear where everything—from the direction to the acting—is at a very high level. I'm talking about *Morituri te salutant* on the small stage of the Franko Theatre directed by Bohomazov, about the performances of the DAKH Theatre by Vlad Troitsky, and more. In Kyiv, dozens of public and private cultural institutions compete every day, especially on weekends, such as the Arsenal and the M17 Gallery, Master Class and the Kalita Art Centre, Isolation and Dukat. They offer exhibitions, concerts, workshops, and lectures.

Fantastic changes have also taken place in the area I am involved in and know best—the country's book market. We have a completely new library of philosophical literature, headed by the *Dictionary of Untranslatables*, a world intellectual bestseller published in Ukrainian by Kostiantyn Sigov and Andriy Vasylchenko. This library is adorned with books by Andriy Baumeister, Vo-

---

[1] Ukrainian art historian, researcher, director of the National Art Museum of Ukraine.
[2] A participant of the Ukrainian New Wave and co-founder of the theory of the Ukrainian Transavantgard. He worked as a painter and installation artist, among other things with video and photo projects. Director of the Odesa Art Museum (2018-2021).
[3] Ukrainian monumentalist, painter, and museologist, and the Director General of the Ivan Honchar Museum (since 1993).

lodymyr Yermolenko, and Oleh Khoma, written by them or translated from various languages under their editorship. We have a new historical library that represents world and national history, an alternative to the Soviet and Russian lies that have been fed to generations of our grandparents, parents, and us for a long time. We read books by Natalia Yakovenko, Yaroslav Hrytsak, Tamara Vronska, Serhiy Plokhiy, Timothy Snyder, David Sutter and many others.

Judaic studies have been revived: three universities have master's programmes. In our Centre for Jewish Studies at NaUKMA alone, we have published more than 100 books (unfortunately, there are not many competitors). We have held about 30 academic conferences and more than 60 artistic, historical, and cultural exhibitions. A separate victory is the Ukrainian children's book, which is one of the most interesting in Europe today. Some of these books have hundreds of thousands of copies. This is a synthesis of texts and videos that have never existed before.

Our achievements are no longer just individual books, but entire libraries: translations of humanitarian books supported by the Renaissance Foundation; European philosophy (projects of the Institute of Philosophy and the *Dukh i Litera* publishing house), Polish literature and journalism; the library of Judaic studies; the "Resistance and Hope" and "Cultural Figures" libraries; the Nobel laureates library. I have not mentioned all of them, even not all of those I know. But I emphasise that I am talking about libraries as collections of books. We see considerable changes in other areas of humanities as well.

And what opportunities for study and internships young scientists and students have now! They can't even imagine that their parents had to get permission from the party committee to study abroad, and then a visa from the authorities to leave the country.

The situation has also changed dramatically in the language sphere. While Russian-language texts used to dominate, and were responded to by "masters" from Moscow and St Petersburg, now, especially with the outbreak of the Russian-Ukrainian war, this information channel has virtually ceased to exist. Ukrainian-language humanities and Ukrainian literature dominate. If I, as a publisher, receive a good text written in Russian, I look for translators into Ukrainian to make it heard. We often refuse to publish texts, even good ones, in Russian—not us ourselves, but the buyers.

It's important for me to say all this because we need to compare our present with what we had yesterday, and only then with what exists in Berlin, Paris or New York. That's right, not vice versa. We cannot jump over that Soviet-Russian gap, we can only get out of it, sometimes crawl out, and even then with great effort.

Having mentioned the victories, I would like to focus on the challenges that need to be addressed.

We do not have our finger on the pulse of global humanitarian thought, because we translate a relatively small number of books that are needed by educated communities. We have not learned how to effectively disseminate modern concepts and books, and the distance from a small group of intellectuals to the wider public is prohibitively long. We have minimal volumes of electronic versions of non-fiction—it practically does not exist. The problem requires systematic reflection. We are only taking our first steps abroad, distributing Ukrainian books. It is difficult to build chains between us and our partners in the world, but it is absolutely necessary. But the main problem is not communication. If we make the world interested in our extraordinary experience and creative ideas, the world will hear us!

I will try to outline ways to solve some of these problems. First of all, no one but us can solve them. But how do we solve them?

We need to clearly define the problem as a managerial task. Let's remember Stanislaw Jerzy Lec: it is easier to hide your thoughts when they are not put into words. So, we need to clearly answer the question of how to keep our finger on the pulse of the world's humanities. To do this, we need to unite a group of intellectuals (philosophers, historians, geopolitical experts, etc.) who will collect a database of texts that need to be translated and disseminated. It is necessary to calculate the resources needed for this: finances, specialists, publishing houses, and determine where to find them. There are many resources available—you need to look for them in international and domestic funds, contact philanthropists, etc. Recently, government agencies have begun to work quite effectively in this area—the Book Institute, the Ukrainian Cultural Foundation, and the Ministry of Information. Responsible business has also emerged—philanthropists are lending their shoulders to important projects. I have dozens of confirmations of this in our experience alone. Someone or a group of people has to take responsibility for solving the problem. It is very important how many people are willing to take this responsibility. Independent civil society organisations play an important role: PEN Ukraine is implementing project after project, while the post-Soviet Writers' Union, with its incurable Soviet genes, continues to have endless internal conflicts. This moment—personal responsibility—is crucial: if we feel responsible for the country's problems, we have to do it. If not, we are doomed to failure. We need to create powerful intellectual centres that will formulate and dictate to society and the authorities a list and hierarchy of problems that need to be solved jointly. To some extent, the activities of the Club of Rome can serve as an analogue.

I don't have a ready-made recipe for how to form such intellectual centres, but I am absolutely sure that they are essential. I am ready to get involved in the creation of one of these centres, clearly understanding that the key roles here should belong to our children—more energetic, more educated, etc. The leading role in the implementation of this idea should be played by individuals who feel responsible for themselves, for the fate of their children, for the fate of the country, and for the memory of their great predecessors.

The Maidan did not end in 2014. The humanitarian development of Ukraine is one of our Maidans today, and the drama is no less than it was then. The war is going on not only in the East of Ukraine. We have our own battlefield, which is perhaps safer, but no less responsible. We have passed a honorable way in recent years, and what we have done allows us to speak of Ukraine as one of the centres of freedom and democracy in the modern world.

The solidarity of Ukrainian intellectuals, proven in many cases, is our potential. It needs to be consolidated in an adequate, organisational way, understanding the importance of this step. This is solidarity with each other and solidarity with democratic civilised forces in the world—with those for whom the ethical values of the Judeo-Christian civilisation are the guiding lights of life, for whom human rights and the legal culture of the civilised world are not empty words but absolute values.

7. "Despite the pain, find some ways of survival"
Leonid Finberg on Books Published During the War

Leonid Finberg, the editor-in-chief of Dukh i Litera, talks about the landmark publications of this publishing house where the experience of confronting aggressors and experiencing trauma, restoring justice and rebuilding from the ruins in the context of the past and present are interpreted. The conversation was hosted by Vlada Davydenko.

The full version of the conversation is available on Soundcloud, Apple Podcasts, Spotify, or YouTube.

Vlada Davydenko: The books recently published by Dukh i Litera deal with topics that are important for every Ukrainian in one way or another, because these books, in particular, illustrate many historical parallels between today's events and what happened in the last century. Mr Finberg, please tell us more about the book by Williamson Murray and Ellan Millet "The War That Had to Be Won. The Second World War: Strategies, Battles, Decisions". How did you come up with the idea to publish it?

Leonid Finberg: We know the Soviet practice where books were published selectively and were ideologically influenced. That is why most of the books that were published about the Second World War in the Soviet Union, particularly in Ukraine, were about the Soviet-German war, about the events of 1941-1945. Not only were such books very biased, highly censored, and therefore quite specific and untruthful, but there were practically no books about any other events of the Second World War, except for a few memoirs published in the Soviet Union in Russian.

And so one of the problems that we, as publishers, faced was the need to prepare and publish a book, or rather a series of books, that would tell readers about all the events of the Second World War. So, we wanted to present the historical truth about those years. We asked our experts what books they could recommend to us, and we settled on this book by Murray and Millet. In my opinion, the book is brilliant. In fact, it is an encyclopaedia of the events of those times. The bibliography alone is worth a lot—hundreds and hundreds of titles! The book shows the events of the Second World War throughout its duration, on virtually all of its fronts. To a certain extent, it can be considered a guide for those who want to understand what happened then in order to be able to extrapolate that experience to the present day. We handed over copies to Ukraine's top military commanders—they also need such books.

V.D: Let's talk about the book by Oleksandr Potekhin and Yuriy Klymenko *Geopolitics vs. Security: Allied Deterrence of Aggression in Europe in the Twentieth and Early Twenty-First Centuries*. The book can be considered extremely relevant for the military, politicians, diplomats and anyone interested in the question "Why should Ukraine join NATO?". Please share your thoughts on this publication.

L.F.: I have known one of the authors of this book, Oleksandr Potekhin, for many years. He used to be a counsellor at the Ukrainian Embassy in the United States and is one of those who knows geopolitics best. When Oleksandr offered his manuscript to our publishing house, I gladly accepted his offer. It is obvious to everyone that humanity today is unable to ensure peace and security on Earth. It was the case during the First World War, it was the case during the Second World War, and we are seeing the same thing in the following decades. This became especially clear against the backdrop of Russia's aggression against Georgia and later against Ukraine. The world seemed to stand still, unable to respond to these blatant violations of international law. So, the problem, which the authors have studied in some detail, is that in international politics, the self-interests of each country or, more broadly, each group of countries have outweighed, by and large, the most important problem—the problem of the security of humanity, and perhaps even civilisation.

I think that today's solidarity of the entire civilised world with Ukraine is a tactical reaction to what is happening. In fact, I would like to hope that after our victory, after this war, humanity will take a more responsible attitude to the problem of global security, to the problem of further life on the planet. I highly recommend this book to anyone interested in these issues. I am sure that it can be important not only for Ukrainian readers, but also for foreign ones. We talked to Prof. Potekhin about preparing an English-language version of this book, and he is working on it.

V.D.: I propose to discuss another large-scale publication of this year — the book *The Marshall Plan* by Benn Steele. How can this book be useful in the context of the current Russian-Ukrainian war?

L.F.: We have long heard the words "Marshall Plan". We know that it was a system of assistance to Europe after the defeat of Nazism so that it would not be revived, so that Germany would follow a more or less democratic path and no longer threaten humanity. But apart from this general information, we know very little in detail. That is why it was very important for us to tell in detail what the essence of the Marshall Plan was, how it was prepared, how it was implemented, and how effective it was.

I am confident that the book will arouse considerable interest in various segments of Ukrainian society, because we all hope for the defeat of Russia and that international structures will help solve our problems. The number of destroyed towns and villages in Ukraine is huge, the economy is disrupted, and there are significant demographic problems. We will be able to rise from the ruins and rebuild the country, largely relying on the strong international solidarity of democratic countries, primarily the United States, Britain, Germany... Therefore, this plan, as well as similar plans, will be very important for us.

V.D.: One of the most powerful publications of this year is Dan Porat's book *Bitter Reckoning*. Since 1950, the state of Israel has persecuted and imprisoned dozens of those who served as "kapos" in the camps or as police in the ghettos. *Bitter Reckoning* invites us to rethink the ideas of complicity and justice and to reflect on what it means to be a victim in extraordinary circumstances. How would you rate this book?

L.F: I think it is extremely important. We are already facing problems of collaboration, and they will be significant for society after our victory. These problems are very delicate, so the experience of Israel, namely the trials of Jewish policemen who worked in the ghettos and camps, is extremely valuable. There were representatives of the ghetto and camp administrations who tried to help those who were imprisoned, who lived there, if you can call this experience life. But there were also people who zealously carried out the Nazis' orders and abused their fellow Jews. The drama of these situations was frightening. People — whether managers or police officers who worked there — had to solve problems that were beyond the limits of the normal human psyche. For example, who should be sent to executions first (and they understood that they were sending people to execution), whether it was possible to save someone's life or whether it was completely impossible. People behaved very differently in these situations.

On the one hand, it seemed that everything was black, and on the other hand, that the guilt of the Nazis was so great that no one else should be blamed. But a state governed by the rule of law, which Israel was and to some extent still is, organised these processes, analysed the behaviour of each of the people whose collaboration with the Germans was known, and tried to separate shameful behaviour from the actions of those who behaved more or less humanely. This experience is unique, and I am very pleased that we will share it with Ukrainian readers. Unfortunately, we have to solve similar problems.

V.D.: Please tell us about the publication of the book by Minka and Martin Straube *Trauma Counselling: A Handbook for Therapists, Victims and Their Relatives*. What is the idea behind this book and how can it be useful in modern Ukraine?

L.F.: It is the most difficult to talk about this book because we are just starting to work with it, negotiating with the authors. Their texts were recommended by our friends who have been working with them for a long time as psychology consultants. According to the stories of their colleagues, the authors have summarised the experience of tragedies in almost 20 countries — those where military conflicts took place and where many people—military, civilians, children, women—suffered. All the types of traumas that were described there are present in Ukraine now, so this experience is very important for us in order to better help people who have experienced these traumas, to help society. It is important that traumas do not turn into hatred of each other. We must, despite the tragedy of these events, despite the pain that these events cause, find some ways to survive. From this point of view, this book and the recommendations of those people who have summarised the experience of other countries are extremely important. The book has not yet been published in German. We are asking the author to give us the opportunity to work on the Ukrainian translation in parallel with the German publishers, arguing that it is more important to us than to them. Europeans, including the Germans, live in a more or less calm society, while in our country the drama is off the charts.

V.D.: The last topic I would like to address today is children's books. At the end of last year, the *Dukh i Litera* publishing house, together with the *Mamino* publishing house and with the support of the Goethe-Institut, launched the *Let's read* children's digital library project. One of the books in this project, *The Incredible Stories of Buchyk the Cat*, has already been released in paperback. Please tell us more about the idea of the children's library, future projects, and where children can meet the red cat from the heroic town of Bucha?

L.F.: This project came about a few years ago when my grandchildren (and I'm a rich man: I have six of them) said: "Why do you publish books only for adults! What about us?" That's when we started our children's projects. The idea of books that will be available to Ukrainian children wherever they are was suggested to us by the project of the American Jewish family Grinspoon, which has existed in the world for about 30 years. The family donated their wealth so that every child aged 6 to 12 could receive books on Jewish history and Judaism personally at home if they wanted. The project was launched in the United States, but today it operates in 14 countries. About 300,000 books of the so-called *Pajama Library* are published every month. Children receive them free of charge: if you are interested, you can subscribe and receive these publications. About 70 books of the library have been published in Ukraine in recent years (and each country has different editions). These books are great in content, well illustrated — the best authors and artists from many countries have been involved in this project. I am very glad that we, as the *Dukh i Litera* publishing house, are publishing these wonderful books.

This idea suggested to us that in our situation, when many Ukrainian children are scattered around the world, far from their homes, we also need to give them books in Ukrainian — fairy tales, author's texts, riddles and much more. We decided to do this in an electronic format, as we cannot print hundreds of thousands of paper books. We have implemented our idea. This project has been running for about 5 months and has thousands of readers. At one stage, a book by Olena Finberg became a hit of this project. This is a "translation from cat language into Ukrainian" — *Incredible Stories of Buchyk the Cat*. The book contains stories about the participation of cats, dogs and mice in helping Ukrainian soldiers. Now we have published the second book, in which Buchyk the cat and his owner have come to the city of Lviv, where they help the wounded and also help to preserve artworks in the city's museums. I know a big secret — the third book has already been written. But it will remain an intrigue, I won't tell you about it.

The third book about the adventures of Buchyk the cat and his owner in London, where the Ukrainian military is studying, has been published. In my opinion, the book very well describes the basics of law and democracy on the example of Britain. The author has managed to create a dynamic detective story that shows the solidarity of both humans and cats in the fight against the barbarians of our time. The characters of the book include the Cheshire Cat and Sherlock Holmes and other characters known to children.

The book about Buchyk is quite successful. It is well illustrated by Ms Valentyna Yesypova-Levych. Read it! I think children should know about the war, but at a level where they can withstand it psychologically. According to children's psychologists, our books, including the one about Buchyk, are among the best in contemporary war literature.

We published two books in pocket-sized format with covers of military uniforms, namely Taras Shevchenko's Kobzar and a book of poetry by Vasyl Stus. The foreword to *Kobzar* was written by the First Deputy Commander-in-Chief of the Armed Forces of Ukraine, General Zabrodsky. We distribute both books widely among the military. Especially in hospitals, psychological rehabilitation centers, etc. We get fantastic feedback when a soldier reads Shevchenko's poems from Bakhmut during the shelling of that city.

Another military book is a book prepared by Khrystyna Parubiy and Iryna Berlyand about Ukrainian women who are involved in the resistance to Russian military aggression. The book is based on a TV interview conducted by Khrystyna Parubiy on the Espresso TV channel. The book tells the story of Ukrainian women who are confronting the Russians alongside men: snipers, military communications officers, etc. They fulfill different roles, sometimes as privates, sometimes as commanders. Their stories are extremely powerful, and they realize that in order to defeat the enemy, everyone must prepare. There are many unusual things in these texts: the ambiguous perception of women in male military teams, certain difficulties of war, which are often felt even more by women than by men, and much more. But the main thing is that the enemy must be defeated despite this.

We continue to work on books in this series, and we plan to publish books about the fight against collaborators in Europe after World War II, about rebuilding cities that were destroyed by the Nazis (as racists are destroying our cities today), and about prostration in society after World War II (the Polish experience). Ours was even more terrible, but it was not recorded-Soviet people were afraid to write, because they faced terrible punishments from the Soviet authorities, and they needed it to develop their myth of the war-the "myth of the victor," and they were not interested in the truth of the war with its many victims. We are thinking about other topics caused by the war, and these are our priorities today.

8. *Philisophical and Sociological Tought* in the Late 80s and Early 90s of the Last Century

Leonid FINBERG, a sociologist, public figure, editor-in-chief of the *Dukh i Litera* Publishing House, director of the Centre for Research on the History and Culture of Eastern European Jewry at the National University of Kyiv-Mohyla Academy, editor-in-chief of the *Yehupets* almanac, co-editor of the *Dukh i Litera* journal (since 1997), and a member of the editorial board of the *Philosophical and Sociological Thought* journal in the 1990s.

It was a great time when, after decades of all kinds of restrictions, we became free. The late 1980s saw the formation of most of the civic organisations and associations that were destined to radically change the situation in the country in modern times. First of all, we are talking about parties and movements: The People's Movement of Ukraine (Rukh), the Greens, the Ukrainian Republican Party, etc. In the same years, religious communities, youth associations, and independent artistic centres emerged, which were impossible in Soviet times. New newspapers and magazines were launched, existing ones were radically changed, and the first private publishing houses appeared.

Philosophical and Sociological Thought journal also underwent a radical change in the late 1980s. The promoter of these changes was the creation of the Editorial Council, which began to work together with the full-time editorial staff and editorial board, which included Stepan Kosharny, Svitlana Ivashchenko, Yuriy Pryliuk, Volodymyr Zhmyr, Natalia Vyatkina, Yevhen Holovakha, Viacheslav Nedashkivsky, and others. The Council included, among others, Iryna Bekeshkina, Vitaliy Kryukov, Vasyl Lisovy, Serhiy Moskvin, Natalia Panina, Vadym Skurativsky, Kostyantyn Sigov, Danylo Yanevsky, Leonid Finberg and others. The Council included, among others, Iryna Bekeshkina, Vitalii Kriukov, Vasyl Lisovy, Serhii Moskvin, Natalia Panina, Vadym Skurativsky, Kostiantyn Sigov,

Danylo Yanevsky, Leonid Finberg, and others. Since 1989, the journal has published many texts from scholars from different countries, many more than before. This is due to scholars who have already worked abroad. Most of the texts were offered by Konstantin Sigov, who organised, in fact, the French "portal" of the journal. Our authors included, for example, professors Paul Ricoeur, Emanuel Levinas, and Georges Nivat. The thematic range of socially oriented publications and previously banned historical texts expanded significantly, which radically changed the nature of the publication. My speciality in the magazine were expert surveys, of which we managed to conduct quite a few over the years. I would like to remind you of them, because many of those surveys deserve to be mentioned and analysed even after almost 30 years.

***

One of the first such surveys was conducted in the second half of 1989. It was entitled "Prospects and Dead Ends of Perestroika" and included a number of questions, including the following: the hierarchy of problems in society; environmental problems in the world and the USSR in the late 1980s; national relations (as the events of Lithuania, Georgia, etc. were still fresh); the laws of history and significant historical events; trends in the formation of civil society; the threats of bureaucracy and ochlocracy; the impact of general trends in human development on what was happening in the USSR, etc. About 30 leading scholars of the Soviet Union at the time responded to this questionnaire in detail. Among them were leading Ukrainian philosophers and historians, such as Serhiy Krymsky, Vadym Skurativsky, Vasyl Lisovy, Moscow intellectuals, such as philosopher Yuliy Schrader, sociologist Viktoria Chalikova, philosopher and theologian Grigoriy Pomerants, philosopher Serhiy Batishchev, philosopher Anatoliy Akhutin, Lithuanian sociologist J. Minkevicius, sociologist Larisa Lisyutkina, and others. The answers to this questionnaire were published in three issues of the journal in 1990. I do not have the space in this article to quote the answers to the questionnaire in detail. However, almost 30 years later, I read them with great interest, because much of what we heard then remains relevant today. I will not resist quoting only two short quotations from Grigoriy Pomerants's answer to the questionnaire:

> "The most dangerous event for human existence on Earth in the twentieth century was an unprecedented 'release' of the totalitarian spirit (the roots of which are unknown), a kind of thermonuclear explosion that swept the entire world in the twentieth century. Our side was almost at its epicentre. Totalitarian ideologies and regimes lead to a catastrophe of catastrophes: to the destruction of human qualities... to the degradation of man—spiritual and physical. Under their influence, uncontrollable elemental forces of man and nature break out into the world. Totalitarianism feeds on the magical power of abstractions over the human soul. Everything individual, special—in culture, in nature—is destroyed by its devastatingly monolithic unity. It promotes contempt for the individual and creates a distrust of the individual in himself, his reason, his conscience. Totalitarianism feeds on the deep human desire to voluntarily surrender to the power of nameless and faceless "communities"—racial or class, soil or technical, mystical or state. This is the main thing. And the anger of the masses and the paranoia of the leaders, world wars and domestic concentration camps, genocide, nuclear weapons, ecological catastrophe, moral and genetic degeneration of man—all these are consequences, results."

And more:

> "I consider the most auspicious event of the twentieth century to be what might be called the discovery of the world—in space and time—as an event. I do not mean simply the discovery that the space of our existence is finite, that what happens anywhere in the world is now of universal significance. What is more significant is the emergence of a new self-awareness of man as a co-participant, an interlocutor in the world-historical task of unravelling existence; the discovery of the world in this sense is the discovery of the universal significance of the original other—of another person, another culture, another experience of being."

To be honest, I would like to quote and quote my correspondents, because not only then, but also later, it was not often possible to collect the opinions of stars of philosophical and sociological thought of this level. I am happy to refer today's reader to those texts. In a sense, the historical time of these almost 30 years is not even minutes, but seconds of human history. Very little of what was said then has become outdated.

The next publication of the journal of those years, which has not lost its relevance today, is the proceedings of the Conference on Ukrainian-Jewish Relations held in Jerusalem in 1993. The participants of the forum from the Ukrainian side were: Yaroslav Dashkevych and Oksana Zabuzhko, Myron Petrovsky and Leonid Plyushch, Kostiantyn Sigov and Roman Zvarych, Myroslav Popovych and Ivan Khymka, Vadym Skurativsky and Martin Feller... Israeli scholars were represented by professors Mordechai Altshuller, Naftali Prat, Grigoriy Ostrovsky, Wolf Moskovich, and others. This conference continued the dialogue initiated in Ukraine in 1991 by Ivan Dziuba, whose materials were published in the journal *Svit* (a publication of the People's Movement of Ukraine, 1992, No. 3-4). When publishing the materials of the Israeli conference, I wrote:

> "...We would like to draw the reader's attention to the fact that at our stage a civilised, cultural dialogue between Ukrainian and Jewish intellectuals is ongoing. Of course, such a dialogue was virtually impossible in the Soviet Union—in those difficult decades, only a few diaspora scholars and prisoners of conscience did their best to maintain the broken threads of truthful conversation around a topic that was forbidden to touch upon in our country. With the first breaths of free air, we suddenly realised how much we had to research, study, and negotiate. After all, as long as the lips of honest intellectuals were sealed, semi-intellectuals, specialists in falsification and slander, were given the right to vote at the master's command "bark!". How many books, articles, and dissertations full of bias, cynicism, and duplicity have accumulated! What the party ideologues have fully demonstrated their talent and skill at is exposing fictitious lies and inciting hatred. And even a systematic hatred—first towards "class enemies", then towards different segments of society—believers, intellectuals, and then towards entire nations in turn (or even out of turn, as we know well, in particular, from the Bolsheviks' anti-Ukrainian and anti-Semitic campaigns). Each of the campaigns had vigilant overseers and well-trained ideological servants who, over many years of methodological and methodical im-

provement, created a cunning weave of theories of suspicion, poison-soaked thoughts about the inferiority and disloyalty of Ukrainian, Jewish, Belarusian, Armenian, Tatar or other peoples. It made it easier for the authorities to keep everyone in their grip."

And further:

"This conference raised very important questions about the history of peoples and their relations. But the delicacy, friendliness, and scientific balance of the speeches showed how strongly we are united by humanistic values, and that there is no spirit of confrontation in the face of any differences in opinion. This, perhaps, is the difference between a dialogue of true bearers of culture and the attacks of a lumpenised, primitive element with a crowd instinct."

And in conclusion:

"...Either society will listen to the voice of the humanistic intelligentsia and build a civilised, democratic, free Ukraine, or populist xenophobes will prevail, who will take advantage of the difficulties of the times and bring us—God forbid!—to discord and disaster."

Again, I refer the reader to the proceedings of this conference (*Philosophical and Sociological Thought*, 1994, Nos. 1-2, 5-6). For today's reader, I will give only the titles of the main reports:

- Yaroslav Dashkevych, "The Main Problems of Modern Research on the History of Jewish-Ukrainian Relations."
- Oksana Zabuzhko, "Jewry as a Carrier of the National Idea in the Reception of Ukrainian Literature of the Early Twentieth Century."
- Kostiantyn Sigov, "Buber and Chizhevsky: Towards an Analysis of the Utopia 'I—YOU'";
- Roman Zvarych "Zionism and Ukrainian Nationalism: Historical, Political, and Philosophical Parallels";
- Taras Vozniak "The Revival of the State and the Human: An Aspect of the Promised Land and Salvation".

One of the most important speeches at the conference was delivered by Yaroslav Dashkevych. It was programmatic in nature, both in terms of research that will help us understand the past and the need for cooperation between the Ukrainian and Jewish academic and civic communities for the future. Prof. Dashkevych drew attention to the deformation of the main trends in research on Ukrainian-Jewish relations, which are influenced by several stereotypes:

> "Several stereotypes have influenced the deformation of the main trends in research (and, unfortunately, often still do): 1) the thesis about the eternal and almost irrational anti-Semitism of Ukrainians; 2) the refusal to recognise the status of the subject of history for Jews, turning them exclusively into an object (the hammer and anvil theory); 3) the scapegoat theory. The negative, stereotypical aspects of the study are exacerbated by the neglect of a number of objective circumstances: a) the attempt to mechanically equate the persecution of Jews in Ukraine with the pogroms and deportations that took place in Western Europe (e.g., Spain, Germany), where power was in the hands of the autochthonous ruling nations; in Ukraine, for centuries, the real power was in the hands of foreign dominant nations of the invading states (Poland, Russia); Ukrainians—by applying the geographical principle—are attributed to many of these discriminatory actions on the territory of Ukraine, the implementation of which depended solely on non-Ukrainian dominant nations; b) Ignoring the fact that Ukraine during these same 360 years was the scene of a fierce national liberation struggle of the enslaved Ukrainian nation, which created a situation completely different from Western European conditions, where Jews did not have to take a position on enslaved nations; c) failure to take into account the processes that in Western Europe led to the gradual formation of rule-of-law states, while in Ukraine in the early twentieth century lawlessness, discrimination, and persecution prevailed, primarily against the Ukrainian population, but also against other dominant ethnic groups; d) a definite exaggeration of the degree of persecution of Jews in Ukraine—if such statements were true, then almost a third of the world's Jews would not have gathered here in the early twentieth century—a population characterised by its mobility, which for centuries could freely migrate to countries favourable to Jews; migration flows from Ukraine, although fluctuating, never reached a catastrophic level at that time; e) silence about the fact that interethnic relations were formed differently in different parts of the territory of Ukraine; attempts to generalise the manifestations of conflicts of a certain period of time or a certain limited territory

as characteristic of the whole of Ukraine, the whole Ukrainian nation, and a number of centuries."

In my opinion, the report by Oksana Zabuzhko was also extremely interesting, as she analysed in great detail and thoroughly how Ukrainian intellectuals comprehended the stages of their nation-building, largely by analysing Jewish history as a universal model.

Not being able to paraphrase the texts of the reports in detail, I will cite only a few quotes.

> "It is a fact that in Ukraine, Ukrainians do not know Jewish history and culture, and Jews do not know Ukrainian history and culture. Worse, Jews in Ukraine do not know their own culture, and Ukrainians do not know theirs. On such a basis, it is hard to expect anything other than myths, mostly positive about themselves and negative about others. Perhaps this is the central reason for mutually chauvinistic mythologies" (Leonid Plyushch).

> "Both peoples, especially their national movements, have drawn their inner strength from the suffering caused by mass genocide: for Jews, it was the mass destruction of their nation during World War II, the Holocaust; for Ukrainians, the Holodomor, artificially created in 1932-1933. These events burned the historical memory of Jewish and Ukrainian nationalists, and the pain was so searing that it left a lifelong scar on the mentality of both peoples, who concluded that only their own independent state would prevent such catastrophes from happening again in the future" (Roman Zvarych).

> "Thus, Israel-the-people and Israel-the-Promised-Land as the subject and object of the oath to the Lord are concepts much more fundamental and therefore more enduring than Israel-the-territory, Israel-the-state. And no amount of destruction of the Temple, Jerusalem, or the state has destroyed Israel as a people who swore an oath to God, nor has it cancelled its oath to return the people to the Promised Land" (Taras Wozniak).

***

Another expert survey I would like to talk about was called "New Ukraine – Where to Go?". It was one of the first attempts by

Ukrainian intellectuals to reflect on the prospects for independence. Les Taniuk, Vasyl Lisovy, Volodymyr Kulyk, Volodymyr Polokhalo, Taras Voznyak, Mykola Riabchuk, Vadym Skurativsky, Myroslav Marynovych, Yevhen Holovakha, Oleksiy Haran... answered our questionnaire. Out of necessity, I will quote myself, a fragment of the preface to the questionnaire:

> "In recent years, the middle and younger generations have felt the breath of history next to them for the first time in their lives. Older people felt it in 1917 and 1941-1945. In other times, the reinforced concrete walls of totalitarianism have fenced off the development of the world from us, and us from it. And today, next to us, through us, CLIO is walking. Like a house of cards, a huge communist utopia has collapsed before our eyes almost instantly. The countries of Eastern Europe are crawling out from under its rubble, no longer propped up by tanks and missiles, and the peoples of Ukraine and the Baltic States, Russia and Kazakhstan, Belarus and Moldova, racing each other, are throwing off the shackles of socialism. We hope that those who were lucky enough to be rescued will learn these lessons from history to some extent. But history seems to be a little easier — it is more difficult to comprehend the massive social processes. At the same time, almost all of Eastern Europe is undergoing a radical change in political, economic, psychological and other structures. How to maintain at least some stability? How to understand the patterns of these processes to some extent and develop adequate political solutions? What knowledge can we rely on when the degree of knowledge is too modest? Of course, over the years, scientists will diagnose, classify and define everything."

Here are some of the questions in the questionnaire:

- Ukraine's independence has been declared. There is no doubt that the path to real statehood cannot be overcome in one day. What do you think is the most important thing on this path? What stages will we have to go through? What conditions could facilitate positive processes and what could hinder them?
- The historical experience of the people — what is the most important thing in it today, what promotes freedom and what drives it into a yoke? Do we have freedom of choice, and what are its limits?

- We have named a number of factors that determine our future. Maybe you think something else is important? What is it?

As with previous surveys, I suggest reading the original answers to our expert questionnaire. I will only say that many of the problems we face today were foreseen by our experts. For example, Les Taniuk drew attention to the need to change the pantheon of Ukrainian culture, in which Hryhoriy Skovoroda, Mykola Khvylovy, Les Kurbas and many other cultural giants should have taken a prominent place. Vasyl Lisovy wrote about the threats facing Ukrainians from our neighbours, imperial Russia:

> "People and nations should think more about the historical perspective of their existence, look at themselves from the point of view of eternity, so that disputes over 'interests', 'advantages', 'borders', 'fleets', 'territories', etc. do not undermine more fundamental and eternal values—the value of human life, physical and moral health. So that the hope of a child born into the world to live and create as a biologically and mentally complete being is not crossed out by the insane world of adults who are ready to destroy the fundamental and eternal for something temporary and secondary."

This was one of the first publications of the Ukrainian philosopher and dissident, who had been released from the Gulag only a few years before.

> One of the best political scientists of the time, Volodymyr Polokhalo, wrote: "...What kind of state [Ukraine] this will be—authoritarian, totalitarian or democratic—depends on many, mainly internal, factors. Later, in answering other questions, I will touch upon some of them. For now, I will only note in general that building a democratic state is a more difficult task, and unfortunately, it has a lower probability of success than the other types mentioned. In any case, the transition period from the Soviet-style totalitarian society that still exists in Ukraine to a civil, democratic one will, in my opinion, last at least 20 years."

Even then, as he did for many years afterwards, Mykola Riabchuk paid attention to the self-identification of Ukrainians. He wrote:

> "The reality is what you can hear in any eastern or southern Ukrainian city: "We are not Russians or Ukrainians, we are Odessans" (the variant is "Donbassians", "Cossacks", "Kharkivians", "Kyivans", etc., etc.) or in a village: "And if one asks them: "What nation are you people?", they answer: "Who knows... We are local... Orthodox..." (Ostap Vyshnia, The Chukhrainians). In addition to this "Chukhrainian" ethnic group, we also have a considerable number of people who quite clearly consider themselves Russian, Polish, Jewish, Hungarian, or, in extreme cases, "Soviet", but not Ukrainian... So, the most important thing on the way to real statehood is to complete the formation of the Ukrainian nation as a certain psychological and political integrity, to turn the population into a people, that is, to transform a rather inert and amorphous mass into a developed civil society united not so much by a common past and present as by a common future—a convincing and attractive project of living together."

In conclusion, I will quote Vadym Skurativsky on the importance of human freedom and our economic preferences:

> "In its independence projects, Ukraine should proceed not from the interests of the 'peoples of Ukraine', 'non-indigenous nationality' or 'minorities', but from a separate legal, absolutely sovereign personality, from its inalienable rights. It is this direction in Ukrainian public life that will lead to its non-violent and 'precipitous' Ukrainisation... We are all, in fact, the grandchildren of Karl Marx, with his deadly hatred of market institutions and private property. But let us finally understand that the world has not yet developed a serious and effective alternative to the European way of doing business, which is now so inaccurately called 'capitalism'. So, let us become children of Adam Smith with his pathos of the absolute economic independent man. Let's leave Marx to analyse the socio-historical landscapes of the last century that gave rise to him."

***

At some point, the journal acquired a subsidiary, the newspaper *Ukrainian Observer*, with Natalia Vyatkina as its editor-in-chief. I will not characterise this publication. That is for Ms Vyatkina to do. I will only say that an intellectual newspaper, unusual both for those times and for ours, has taken a prominent place in the cultural space of the country.

Now I will describe the members of our editorial board. **Yuriy Prylyuk** is the editor-in-chief of the journal. He was a good manager and a man who could see several steps ahead. Yuriy was one of the first to organise an independent publishing house called *Abris*. I remember that he was looking for a name for the publishing house in my presence in the following way: he opened a dictionary and suggested choosing something that started with the letter "A" in order to be the first in any list of publishing houses. I was not involved in the activities of this publishing house. Others will tell you more about it. However, I remember one of the first publications — graphic panoramas of Kyiv, and later Podil, prepared by the artist Mykhailo Biletsky. They became the first souvenir graphic works of independent Ukraine. Yuriy Prylyuk was also one of those who created the first independent banks, and the *Abris* publishing house offered services in publishing Ukrainian securities. Yuriy Prylyuk was one of those managers who delegated many of their powers to employees and partners. His deputy, **Volodymyr Zhmyr**, performed almost all the technical work on the production of each issue of the journal.

Volodymyr meticulously and professionally organised the technological processes of editing, layout, proofreading, translation, and then printing the journals from month to month, year after year. At that time, they were published simultaneously in Ukrainian and Russian versions. I remember that once, when I was preparing another expert study and handed over the materials to Volodymyr, he told me that it was imperative that each article should have a photo of the author. Several dozen authors, including foreign ones, took part in my survey, and it was almost impossible to get photos of all of them. These were still the years before the Internet, and telephone contacts with foreign countries were expensive and virtually inaccessible. I explained this to Volodymyr, but he insisted: "Even though we are friends, I can't do anything about it, just look for the photos." In a hopeless situation, I resorted to falsification. Instead of a portrait of John-Paul Himka, I took a photograph of Sergei Naboka, and instead of a portrait of Harold Aster, I took a photograph of my father. When I handed them to Volodymyr, he said to me: "You see, I found everything, and I said it was impossible!" About 20 years later, when we met John-Paul Himka, he said that he knew about the publication and was grateful for it, but that he did not look like himself in the photo. So I told him the story and we laughed together. Sergei Naboka knew about everything in advance, so he was a conscious "accomplice" to my crime.

And now a little about the other members of our team.

Danylo Yanevsky is a brilliant historian to whom I owe my first private (for me personally!) lectures on Ukrainian history. We walked the streets of Kyiv, and he talked about the beginnings of Ukrainian statehood, Stalin's repressions, and the figures of Ukrainian history and culture. For me, a person of technical knowledge and self-education, these were royal gifts. I would also like to mention my editor, Ms **Larysa Malishevska**. It was to her that I gave my first text, which was supposedly written in Ukrainian. She revised it almost beyond recognition. When I asked if I could check and review both versions, mine and hers, she advised me to work better with the version she suggested and if I had any questions, she would be happy to answer them. I didn't have any questions. I am very grateful to her for this and other Ukrainian lessons.

I am also grateful to **Yevhen Holovakha** and **Natalia Panina**, professional sociologists who were kind enough to take part in my expert surveys and often gave me important advice. I should also mention **Myroslav Popovych**, the undisputed leader of our team. He had even a leader armchair, while we all sat on chairs. Myroslav Volodymyrovych led our discussions and debates delicately, with maximum attention to each proposal, each topic, each participant. At the same time, he always told some stories about his communication with the leading philosophers of the 70s to 90s: Pavel Kopnin, Ewald Ilyenkov, Henrikh Batishchev, and others. Myroslav Volodymyrovych also spoke about the repressions against the Institute's staff in the late 40s and 50s. One by one, they disappeared, and one day only a cleaner came to work.

Friendly feasts were an obligatory part of our gatherings. I remember that at one of them, Myroslav Volodymyrovych suggested that we drink bruderschaft and become first-name terms. It was not easy for me, given the age gap between us. However, I had no choice, and eventually we switched to first names.

I would like to recall one more episode. It was a holiday, and we were already a little drunk. Myroslav Volodymyrovych knew that at that time I was already creating a centre for the study of Judaism, and he knew about my interest in Jewish history and culture. And then, coming up to me, he sang a song in Yiddish.

- "How do you know that?" I asked.
- "Do you think I wasn't a *shabbos goy*?"[1] Myroslav replied.

I recall how the whole country was waiting for a dialogue between Leonid Kravchuk and Myroslav Popovych, who was delegated by the Rukh on the eve of Ukraine's independence. We gathered together as an editorial council and, to the best of our ability, predicted questions and answers for the meeting, which was watched by the whole country. I can't say that we got a lot of it right, but it was certainly useful.

***

Late 80s — early. 90s was the period of formation of the democratic electoral system. Back in 1989, elections to the Congress of People's Deputies of the USSR (before independence) were held. We were all involved in these processes, and today it is hard to imagine that everything was happening for the first time: the formation of candidates' programmes, the organisation of the election campaign, the preparation and printing of the first leaflets and programmes of activities of candidates for deputies, etc. After a while, we celebrated our first victories: our candidates Yuriy Shcherbak, Serhiy Ryabchenko and others (independent!) became deputies. They subsequently joined the democratic part of the all-Union Parliament. The new representatives of the people and we, those who

---

1   A *shabbos goy* was a non-Jew who was hired by Jews to work on the Sabbath when they were unable to perform certain types of work themselves.

helped them, knew very little about how to organise their work. Let me recall a few episodes along the way.

On the basis of the *Philosophical and Sociological Thought*, we created a Deputies' Club, which began preparing expert texts for deputies and draft laws. Over time, the mechanism of full-time assistants to MPs and special structures of the Verkhovna Rada for these processes emerged, and at that time we were the first, of course, semi-professionals. My archive contains the draft laws we prepared; I will give the names and authors of some of them here:

1. Serhiy Moskvin: assessment of draft laws "General Principles of Restructuring the Management of the Economic and Social Spheres...", "On Product Quality and Consumer Protection", "On Property in the USSR", "On the Socialist Enterprise", "On the Rights of State Tax Inspections", etc. A total of about 20 assessments.
2. Vitalii Kriukov: comments and remarks on the draft laws "On the Status of Judges in the USSR", "On the Procedure for the Publication and Entry into Force of Laws Adopted by the Congress of People's Deputies of the USSR, the Verkhovna Rada and its Bodies", "On Employment", etc.
3. Leonid Finberg: "On the Fundamentals of Criminal Legislation", "On the Legal Regime of the State of Emergency", "On the Electoral System and Elections in the Ukrainian SSR" (co-authored), etc.

In addition to laws, we also set out to draft the country's Constitution. "We" — this sounds half-truthful, because this project was proposed by Vitalii Kriukov, and we, other members of the Deputies' Club expert group, took part in its discussion. Given that only Vitalii was a lawyer, our amendments were mostly not fundamental. Nevertheless, the project was one of those discussed in society. The activities of this club were a good school for us and important for people's deputies.

Let me recall another episode that was to some extent a continuation of this practice, at least for me. The writer and public figure Yuriy Shcherbak was then elected as a people's deputy by the residents of Kyiv. According to the law, people's deputies had to open offices to communicate with voters. Yuriy Mykolayovych opened such an office. He invited me to the first meeting with those who wanted to talk to him (I was one of the organisers of his election campaign and we had known each other for decades before). And so the deputy's reception began, with people coming in one after another, most of whom were clearly inadequate: either unable to articulate what they wanted from the deputy or behaving aggressively... It took several hours for this "performance" to end. Yuriy Mykolayovych and I are looking at each other and trying to comprehend this unusual experience. I said: "Yuriy, I'll call my friend who works in the 'letters from workers' department of a workers' newspaper, maybe she can tell us something." And I did. She told me: "All of us who work with the public have lists of the inadequate and crazy in the city, who appeal to everyone they can appeal to." Then, of course, we followed this advice, and the next meetings were a little easier.

Finally, I would like to conclude these memories with the hope that we, the participants in those events, those who still have different active roles today, will come together and tell the story of those tumultuous years in a much more adequate and complete way. Those were the times when magazines and newspapers played no less of a role in the life of societies than the Internet and all its mass media modifications do today. I think that the *Philosophical and Sociological Thought* of the late 80s and the first half of the 90s played a positive role and contributed to the preservation of a certain amount of personal freedom in Ukraine and the establishment of democratic trends and civil society.

II
Articles, Speeches, Opinion Polls

9. "Orange Prowess" (Expert opinions)

The following respondents answered the questionnaire: Taras Voznyak, Olya Hnatiuk, Yevhen Zakharov, Joseph Zissels, Oleksandr Irvanets, Vakhtang Kipiani, Mykhaylyna Kotsiubynska, Myroslav Marynovych, Oleksandr Paskhaver, Yevhen Rashkovsky, Vsevolod Rechytsky, Yevhen Sverstiuk, Dmytro Stus, and Fr Mykhailo Shpolyansky.

Introduction

This text is a compilation of answers to the questions posed by the *Dukh i Litera* magazine about the causes, phenomenon, and possible consequences of the Ukrainian Revolution of 2004. The experts are well-known people in Ukraine: lawyers, journalists, publicists, historians, public figures... Most of the authors of the texts are people who welcomed the revolution, and were partly active participants in it. This does not prevent them from being critical in their reflections on the events, up to Vakhtang Kipiani's conclusion: if the new government does not meet the expectations of the Maidan, we will be able to go to Khreshchatyk again and tell it: "Get out!"

Unfortunately, the voices of the opponents of the Orange Revolution are difficult to gather. A real dialogue between the intellectuals of the East and West of Ukraine, I hope, is yet to come. Perhaps later, this much-needed work (see Fr Mykhailo Shpolyansky) will be done. The text presents subjective perceptions of the events of the revolution, ranging from questions to the choice of experts. I think that an objective picture of events is formed from a set of such subjective reflections, somewhere in infinity. According to the well-known formula of historians: the further we are from the Middle Ages, the Renaissance and other eras, the more we know about these periods of human life. However, contemporaries also want to understand what is happening. This text is one of such attempts to understand the events of Ukraine's recent history...

1. At the end of 2004, when assessing the Orange Revolution, the world started talking about a new Ukraine. What do you see as this newness? What are its signs? How long do you think the changes will last? What are the economic, social, and ideological foundations of these changes?

Yevhen Zakharov, human rights activist (Kharkiv)
In my opinion, what happened was natural, and the world, which started talking about the new Ukraine, simply did not notice and did not take it into account before. The Ukrainian people, who, on the one hand, despite all the famines, wars and persecution, retained their will to become independent, and on the other hand, who gained it in 1991 as a result of the collapse of the Soviet communist empire, were not at all ready for it. Ukrainian democracy, weakened by repressions, failed to turn the tide, and Soviet-style post-communism prevailed in the country, resulting in the impoverishment of the general population, the enrichment of a small handful of former party and Komsomol *nomenklatura*, and a major spiritual, social, and economic crisis. At the same time, the general vector of development of Ukrainian society, despite all the talk of multi-vectorism, was Euro-Atlantic, but it had to grow and mature to it. A critical mass of socially active people had to be formed who would feel the priority of European values and could convince the majority of the public of their superiority.

The country's economic decline halted in late 1999, and with Viktor Yushchenko at the helm of the government, there were gradual signs of improvement in many areas. Even the mood of society changed in a very short time and became more optimistic. The case of Georgiy Gongadze and the tapes of Major Mykola Melnychenko, as well as the actions of the Committee "Ukraine without Kuchma", accelerated the process of confrontation between the government and the people and its institutionalisation in the political sphere. After the resignation of Viktor Yushchenko's government, it became clear that a political opposition had emerged that had every chance of changing the course of events in the country. This happened in two stages: first, in the 2002 parliamentary elections, when victory was stolen from the opposition, and then in the presidential race. The latter election campaign was marked by a confrontation between the power of the government and the power of the people, who found the inspiration and courage to overcome the government. The basis of this victory was the emergence of two fearless generations, devoid of inferiority complexes and endowed with a modern worldview, the strengthening of small and medium-sized businesses, the country's openness, massive travel abroad by Ukrainians, the growing maturity of mass consciousness and readiness for change, and the strengthening of civil society.

So, the new Ukraine was not new at all. The events of September-December 2004 were to be expected, but it was hard to foresee the scale of the events, the hundreds of thousands of people on the Maidans, especially in Kyiv. I think that the main driving force that brought people to the streets was hatred of the government, which had so brutally and shamelessly imposed its scenario on people — there was no longer any possibility of tolerating Leonid Kuchma's regime. Moreover, the man who was to replace him, Viktor Yushchenko, aroused great sympathy and trust. I was convinced that the nomination of Viktor Yanukovych as a presidential candidate was just a way to beat the opposition and keep Kuchma in office for another term. I was convinced that Yanukovych would not win the election, and the only question for me was whether Yushchenko would win now or whether he would win later, because it was difficult to assess a priori the willingness of the government to go all the way in its desire to stay and the willingness of the people not to be fooled again.

As for the duration of the changes, I think they are inevitable, unless there is a strong external influence that will hinder social progress. This does not mean that the development will be exclusively positive. There will be crises, defeats, scandals, disappointments... However, the general Euro-Atlantic vector of modernisation will remain.

Taras Vozniak, writer (Lviv)
The novelty of Ukraine after the Orange Revolution is that for the first time the mechanisms of civil society have started to work in

full force. First of all, this concerns such a civil institution as elections. Are these the first relatively free elections in Ukraine? No. There were similar or almost similar elections and referendums in the early 90s, before the regime of Leonid Kuchma. However, the relative freedom of choice then was due to the confusion and demoralisation of the post-Soviet *nomenklatura*. At that time, the oligarchy had not yet been formed and could not significantly influence the course of the elections. Therefore, the elections were relatively free. In contrast, during the Orange Revolution, civil society institutions broke the stiff resistance of oligarchic structures. In general, the 2004 revolution was driven by the middle class, which has grown imperceptibly over the past decade. It became the basis for civil society institutions. Thus, Ukrainian society, in terms of its structure, has begun to approach the structures of Central European countries. In spite of all this, Ukrainian society is slowly moving away from the glaring imbalance in the distribution of the national product that emerged during the presidency of Leonid Kuchma, when an extremely small social stratum controlled the lion's share of the national product. The more balanced the property structure of society becomes, the more stable it will be. I believe that this is what can guarantee Ukraine's further development. How stable the progress will be will also depend on whether these processes of equalisation in society are completed.

Mykhailyna Kotsiubynska, writer (Kyiv)
First of all, the novelty is that the world has finally separated Ukraine from Russia in its mind and realised that it is not somewhere on the Balearic Islands, but in the centre of Europe, and that European values are not alien to it. I think the biggest novelty was the powerful moral potential of the Orange Revolution. Not purely socio-economic motivations, but the universal dominance of these events. The world saw the face of the Maidan, had the opportunity to look into its eyes — and they were good eyes, indeed. Intelligent, lively, with a spark of healthy irony, capable of flashing with righteous anger and moistening with tears in the most sacred moments. And this face, illuminated by an orange flash, became the face of Ukraine. Will it last for long? I would like to hope so. It depends on

further developments, on how far we manage to avoid painful falls, both economic and moral. But this face has already been recorded in the annals of history. It is the face of a nation, albeit an underformed one, burdened by past negativity, but no longer an "embryonic" one (to recall Stus's formula "eternally embryonic Ukraine").

Joseph Zissels, human rights activist (Kyiv)
The novelty of Ukraine for the world is the discovery of Ukraine as a subject of history and world politics. Apart from a few specialists, the world knew almost nothing about Ukraine. Ukraine was a peripheral fragment of an obscure post-Soviet space that was seen as more of an uncertainty than a threat. All the remnants of its former greatness, including its natural resources, had gone to Russia.

For me, the novelty of Ukraine consists primarily of two factors: irrational and rational.

Ukraine surprised the whole world and, first of all, itself with an unexpectedly powerful surge of energy of its people—"passionarity".

One can try to explain this irrational circumstance, but these explanations will not add to understanding. Both the government and the opposition were preparing for the elections as well as they could, knowing almost everything about each other: human and material resources, organisational capabilities, contingency plans... No one counted on passionarity—precisely because of its irrationality. Some counted on a miracle, but these were abstract dreams.

"Passionarity" cannot be organised and cannot be fought against. It comes out of nowhere and disappears into nowhere. It can probably be provoked, but no one knows how or with what. And those who eventually unknowingly provoke it, not only do not set themselves such a goal, but also try to avoid it in every possible way.

A nation that has been visited by "passionarity" suddenly jumps to the first league of the world championship, and then it depends only on the people themselves and their new elite whether they will stay at this level and in what role.

At first and afterwards, everything is more or less clear, but the very moment of transition is a "zero-transportation", that is, a "miracle" that is often, perhaps almost always, expected, but which, in the end, occurs according to unknown laws.

The rational factor of Ukraine's novelty, in my opinion, lies primarily in the fact that over the past two decades, Ukraine has formed significant masses of citizens (several million each), who, together with the most nationally conscious and national-democratically organised group of the older generation, created both Yushchenko's electorate and the main human resource of the Orange Revolution. We are talking about people of a new (for Ukraine) mentality or identity, which can be conditionally called "European", in contrast to another mental group, which can, conditionally, be called "Eurasian".

When political scientists talk about the creation of a political nation or something similar, this terminology does not explain anything, but rather hides a fog of meaning behind recognisable labels.

The first group of the new identity is a significant part of the younger generation of Ukrainian citizens whose mental formation took place in the 1990s with the collapse of the communist imperial system. This generation was formed not thanks to, but rather in spite of, the previous government, which, fortunately, left this generation to its own devices. A significant part of this generation owes nothing to the authorities: neither beliefs, nor education (which was mainly obtained at the expense of the family), nor employment (mostly in commercial and foreign structures). Unlike the "oligarchs" and their teams, who owed everything to the authorities and therefore defended them, the new generation wanted to live in a world where the rules of the game did not change every day depending only on which leg the "guarantor" or his cronies stood on; where success in life and prosperity were not achieved through proximity to the President and demonstration of loyalty, but through education, hard work and active civic position.

The second group includes millions of Ukrainian workers who have travelled to civilised countries to work, and their families. The principle is the same: they owe nothing to the government—neither material well-being nor elements of a new mentality acquired during their "business trips abroad".

All of the above-mentioned groups constitute a qualitatively new and, most importantly, mass reality in Ukraine and are the prototype of its future middle class, an analogue of the "third estate" — the main organising force during the French Revolution.

Vsevolod Rechytskyi, human rights activist (Kharkiv)
I think that the new Ukraine is a society that has suddenly become ahead of its time. Almost none of the intelligentsia — the minds of the nation — seriously expected or foresaw the revolutionary events. When Viktor Yushchenko said that the street could "speak", it was perceived almost as a rhetorical figure, nothing more. That is why the old government did virtually nothing to prevent the revolution.

Of course, the revolution had certain economic, historical and ideological preconditions. But I think that the main driving force behind the events was simply the emotional fatigue of society and individuals from a life that no longer met the organic needs of a healthy, active person. There was an obvious lack of freedom, prospects for personal development, a lot of political hypocrisy and outright boredom in the cultural sphere.

It is precisely because the basis of the revolution was emotional that I do not believe in the possibility of any reaction (degradation) of society to the previous state. The emotional state is indeed a river that cannot be stepped into twice. On the other hand, I am afraid of another spread of illusions in Ukraine about the arrival of a "good government". The state is a necessary evil that must be operated according to certain rules. The American founding fathers understood this well and created a constitutional system for their country devoid of "sentimentality". Ukraine should do something similar now.

Ola Hnatiuk, writer (Poland)
The new Ukraine is a country in which society has become a subject rather than an object of politics. In my opinion, it is no longer possible to return to the old regime, the old style of government. Among the economic factors, I would single out the revolt of the middle class. Although it is said that the middle class does not exist

in Ukraine, it does exist—to the extent that it was possible. The attempt to subjugate these people to state-mafia (or vice versa) structures, the rise of the "Donetsk people", led to the fact that these people had nothing to lose. So, they made their bet. But in doing so, they joined "something bigger than them". I would like to draw attention to another phenomenon that is not as large, but nevertheless significant for the future of Ukraine. Ukrainian citizens who are temporarily outside of Ukraine (sometimes "temporarily" turns into "durably", although few say "permanently") joined this rebellion. They have almost unanimously voted against this government, this system of rule, this economy, which forces them to look for work abroad, leaving their families and their education in Ukraine, and to travel "for bread". These people want to come back to Ukraine, they want their money (millions of euros on a national scale) invested in rebuilding their homes, in education for their children, in the health of their parents who look after their children, to give them a certain future. This is my experience of communication.

When it comes to the historical factors that influenced the events, the most obvious is the Ukrainian experience of democracy: at the present stage (the awakening of the sprouts of civil society in the 1990s) and in the interwar period in the regions of Western Ukraine, in particular in Galicia and Volyn. As it turned out, young people played a considerable role, which significantly differs the situation in Ukraine from that in Russia, where very few representatives of the older generation are carriers of democratic experience.

Fr. Mykhailo Shpolyansky, writer (Mykolaiv)

> "...suffering produces perseverance; perseverance, character; and character, hope. And hope does not put us to shame, because God's love has been poured out into our hearts through the Holy Spirit, who has been given to us." Rom. 5. 3–5

Understanding the legitimacy and even the need for different approaches to assessing the events that have taken place, I will immediately outline my position: for me, the main significance of the Orange Revolution lies not in the political, economic or even social sphere, but in the spiritual one. For me, the ideals of Eurocentrism, which are being discussed a lot these days, are very relative. There is an attractive side to them: Europe of "holy stones", cultural and spiritual traditions, Europe of the self-worthy individual, Europe of unity in diversity. But there is also something unacceptable, which we will not discuss in detail now (however, it is mostly the mental expansion of the New World). However, it was not the issue of the vector of foreign-policy sympathies that caused the events in Ukraine. I am convinced that the main discovery of the Orange Revolution belongs to the spiritual sphere. The Lord visited His people. Not in religious reflections and reminiscences, but in a living manifestation of the Power and Spirit. That is why I can only speak of the only "centrism" that makes sense — spiritual Ukraine-centrism.

I perceive what happened as a miracle of God. When analysing various aspects of the events of the recent past and present, it is impossible not to see that not everything coincides with the ideal. And yet, what the participants in the events experienced cannot be wiped out of our hearts and memories. God is love. Love in Christ is not passion, but willingness: " Greater love has no one than this: to lay down one's life for one's friends." (John 15:13). Peace is not passivity, but the absence of any anger or aggression (characteristically, counter-aggressive movements were channeled into humour). Joy is not a tasty sybaritism, but a creative energy that multiplies strength. Mercy is not metered charity, but complete selflessness, so that "men... have one heart and one soul... and have all things in common" (Acts 4:32). Freedom in Christ is not the rampaging of the crowd, the "Russian revolt" (and not only Russian — what a contrast — the March events in Kyrgyzstan!), but unity in the Spirit, "and where the Spirit of the Lord is, there is freedom" (2 Cor. 3:17)

And the Lord spoke in the words of Isaiah the prophet: "The Spirit of the Lord is on me, because he has anointed me to proclaim good news to the poor. He has sent me to proclaim freedom for the prisoners and recovery of sight for the blind, to set the oppressed free, to proclaim the year of the Lord's favor."

We all felt it — the Lord was with His people on the Maidan:

> "For I was hungry and you gave me something to eat, I was thirsty and you gave me something to drink, I was a stranger and you invited me in, I needed clothes and you clothed me, I was sick and you looked after me, I was in prison and you came to visit me... Whatever you did for one of the least of these brothers and sisters of mine, you did for me." (Matthew 25:35, 36, 40).

Of course, one could say that all of these are too artificial parallels of the sublime and the profane, but... The parallel reveals the general direction of events, and this is enough. Besides, let us ask: can the presence of God be something profane? Another thing is that some people feel the presence of God, while others do not. But this has always been the case in religious life...

I will always remember the words of a simple woman on the street near the Presidential Administration at a tense moment of the blockade: "Father, isn't it true that such love between people can only exist in paradise?" True love, peacefulness, selflessness, mutual respect, unity — what could give all this to the community that we used to call a crowd? What else but the gracious cover of Heaven? People rose "above themselves". The absence of drunkenness and swearing, the reduction in crime and disease are also evidence, albeit of the opposite. Evidence of God's visitation. It is also evidence that the people accepted this visitation and did not pass it by. And this is a special miracle in our world of things and consumerism. This is synergy. This is the birth of the soul of the all-Ukrainian nation.

The now commonplace idea of the birth of a nation on the country's "maidans" has a special meaning for me: I see this birth not in "interests" but in spirit. The millennia of the moving mosaic of the body-soul-spirit of the people, the East-West coordinate and the point of the European axis, the durability and impermanence, the greatness and the fall — this is the history of Ukraine and its people. And here is the result by the third millennium — disparate and almost antagonistic fragments.

And then the Lord visited His people. Thanks to the grace of God, the Maidan became a melting pot in which fragments became united and a nation was born.

"A woman giving birth to a child has pain because her time has come; but when her baby is born she forgets the anguish because of her joy that a child is born into the world." (John 16:21).

Yes, all of this is pure idealism. But let's not forget that idealism as an idea is a philosophical justification for religion. And so, in this context, it should be spoken in this way. However, idealism does not negate sobriety. But this is a completely different story...

The Church assumes that a nation, like every person, is a spiritually holistic phenomenon, with its own Guardian Angel. And a nation, like a person, can be led by its Angel, or it can forget about it, and leave it. This is the highest freedom — the freedom to choose the Good, the freedom to be faithful to God. What will happen to us? It depends on each of us, and it is in this, in our future, that we are ultimately responsible to the Creator. And we can only hope for the celebration of the common Good (in order not to succumb to the illusion of chiliasm, let us make significant allowances for the empiricism of political life), and for the preservation of the Gift in the national dimension...

Vakhtang Kipiani, journalist (Kyiv)
The phenomenon called the Orange Revolution, in my opinion, can already be considered separately from its direct political consequences. The very fact of such fantastic changes in terms of emotional intensity and human scale in a country that was believed to be devoid of civil society, strong political parties, a real middle class, and a tradition of street-based solutions to political crises allows us to define these 17 days of autumn and winter 2004 as a democratic revolution. A classical "velvet" bourgeois-democratic revolution, modelled on the Eastern European nations. Of course, with some Ukrainian specifics.

Through the joint efforts of the people and the Ukrainian opposition of the time, the Turkic word "Maidan" entered the world lexicon as a symbol of peaceful resistance to a corrupt, anti-democratic system.

When I was at university, I had to study the history of Indian non-violent resistance to British colonialism, and I remember the word *satyagraha*. Literally translated from Sanskrit, it means "steadfastness in truth". Gandhi's doctrine included a combination of mass actions — rallies, demonstrations, pickets, strikes, boycotts — and more radical measures such as refusal to pay taxes (in our case, this can be compared to the transition of some police officers and tax officials to the "side of the people" and statements by some heads of local administrations that they would implement the resolutions of the National Rescue Committees rather than the Presidential Administration led byMedvedchuk).

Thus, our revolution can (and should!) be included in world textbooks as an example of a new form of non-aggressive resistance (standing on the square for many days).

At the same time, it is difficult to talk about a "new Ukraine" that allegedly emerged as a result of these events. The Orange Revolution was not a revolution in the full sense of the word. It has not yet brought tangible irreversible changes not only to the "basic" but also to the "superstructure" spheres of society.

For example, the ideology of renewal of the Ukrainian government's personnel can only be welcomed. But! As before, the process of rotation rather than lustration is being carried out according to criteria that are completely opaque and not defined in advance. For example, it is unclear what motives the new President Viktor Yushchenko has when he brings the "new-old" Prosecutor General Svyatoslav Piskun closer to him and demonstrates his trust in him. If he is an indispensable "professional", then that is what should be said. If he is a "patriot", then society should know about at least some examples of his active civic patriotism. If he is just a "terminator" who has to clear a place in the sun from the vestiges of the past, then this should also be said. Out loud.

Obviously, changes in Ukraine will take place according to the well-known Lenin's algorithm "one step forward, two steps back", which has been turned upside down. In other words, progress seems to be being made (at least on an emotional level), but we are constantly faced with relapses of "Kuchmaism" in various areas. These relapses are a "step backwards". There is a danger that when these small steps are too many, a "Reconquista" may begin — the current "opposition" regaining its lost ground. First, in politics (as the next elections to the Verkhovna Rada and local authorities are coming up), and then—"further everywhere"...

Myroslav Marynovych, writer (Lviv)
Let me start with an external observation. Before the events mentioned above, Ukraine only complained that the world did not understand it and tried to arouse its pity. The world, accordingly, considered Ukraine a failure and shunned it even more. On the Maidan, Ukraine took charge of its own destiny for the first time, and the world instantly recognised it. In my opinion, all Ukrainians should get this well into their heads.

If we talk about things of substance, the level of deep popular democracy was a real discovery for both the world and Ukraine itself. Unlike in the 1990s, Ukraine was no longer striving for exotic freedom and democracy without understanding what it meant. Now it clearly understood that it wanted fair and just elections, freedom of speech and press, indiscriminate application of the law, freedom of enterprise, freedom of creativity, etc. Despite Leonid Kuchma's attempts to rape democracy and introduce a new (CIS, i.e. quasi-Soviet) style of governance, 13 years of even limited democracy have not been in vain: the people (especially young people) have accumulated a lively and practical understanding of how democracy should work.

The second discovery is the willingness of the people to make certain sacrifices to establish moral principles. The latter were no longer principles that were mentioned only on Sundays in churches (or on Saturdays in synagogues, or on Fridays in mosques). These principles were no longer just something to lean on. For the first time in many years, it became obvious that they could bring about a win, that morality was not a consolation for weak and helpless losers. Ukraine won by believing in the principles that have long been perceived with postmodern scepticism in much of Western society. And it turned out that the revival of moral principles in the functioning of state and social structures can become a passionate and unifying idea for all regions of Ukraine.

However, with success always comes a new danger. In their history, Ukrainians have shown the capacity for solidarity in rebellion before. With the solidarity in daily routine creative work was much worse. The near future will show whether we will be able to resist losing heart, disappointed in the recent struggles after their first steps, and not give up as usual, saying: "They're all the same, so I'm going back to my cosy little house on the edge."

Oleksandr Irvanets, writer (Kyiv)
"New Ukraine" is a very cute stamp, especially for the West. Of course, we have really renewed ourselves. But these changes are still hardly irreversible. We should beware of the disappointment that may come to society after a certain period of time in office of the new government and president, and the rollback in public consciousness as an inevitable and natural consequence of this disappointment. One of the journalists cited Moscow in 1991 as an example: there, too, old ladies brought pancakes and pies to the defenders of the White House, and today they unanimously praise the President and collect signatures for his third and subsequent terms. I would like to be wrong and see the opposite on the example of Kyiv. A certain figure told us, indeed: "Ukraine is not Russia".

Dmytro Stus, writer (Kyiv)
Ukraine, or rather Kyiv itself, has been in turmoil for a long time. Society has stabilised a little, people's financial situation has improved somewhat, and many Kyivans, just like in the 1980s, have been able to worry about something other than earning their daily bread.

And when people's attention turned to public affairs again, most of them immediately realised with regret the complete failure of politicians of all kinds to protect the achievements of the democratisation period. Corruption, disrespect for the opinion of citizens, the absence of obvious signs of civil society, complete arbitrariness of officials and the bureaucracy... All this was irritating. And the irritation was so strong that Kyiv residents (and the fact that no mass movement of people was seen in other cities seems to be a given) took to the streets. The mass movement—the biggest and only feature of the Orange Weeks — was so significant that it drew attention to Ukraine even from Europe, which had always been indifferent to us, and which seemed to be as frightened as our politicians: no one expected this.

Unfortunately, no changes have been seen so far, except for new people in the old government offices. The declarations of "honesty" and "decency" of the "new-old" do not convince me personally. The only positive thing is the fact that one gangster team has been replaced by another. Time will tell which one. I personally, at least, am convinced that unless society exerts constant pressure on its government, even the best and most honest one, we should not expect anything good.

Yevhen Sverstiuk, writer (Kyiv)
First of all, this is a question to the world: what does it see as novelty? I think that we have regained our faith in ourselves and discovered the reality of our strength in confronting the evil that has been organised and legalised.

Oleksandr Paskhaver, economist (Kyiv)
The Orange Revolution is an important stage in the historical maturation of Ukraine. This is a leap of development that has a huge potential in the formation of a political nation, capitalist economy and liberal democracy. The seriousness of the changes is confirmed by the replacement of the power stratum, which happens dramatically. But so far we only see potential. Not months, but perhaps years will give an idea of how Ukraine realizes this potential: calmly, systematically, purposefully, or bloodily and contradictorily. The risks of turning victory into defeat, as has happened many times in Ukrainian history, are enormous. First of all, due to the absence of an elite as a stratum of citizens, which grew naturally, and was not appointed by circumstances, prepared and brought up in appropriate traditions, with awareness of its mission.

The main driving force of the Orange Revolution was a stratum of millions of citizens who provided for themselves, who grew and financially strengthened over the past five years. The state machine controlled by the oligarchs, corrupt and stagnant, prevented them from growing. This new bourgeoisie, the upper layer of the emerging middle class, needed the Law and freedom of activity. Their interests coincided with the European-oriented values of the population of the west and partly the center of Ukraine, with the protest moods of young people. Protest moods were aggravated by fear of criminalization of the old government.

The main risk of the current moment in the behavior of the new government is the possibility of transferring the methods of revolutionary opposition to the technologies of public administration and reform. Expediency instead of legality, pressure instead of consistency — this is a direct path to failure.

2. Were these days a moment of truth for the Ukrainian nation? To what extent did the revolution pave the way to Europe and move away from the space of prisons and Gulags? How do you assess our European potential?

Vakhtang Kipiani, journalist (Kyiv)

The days of the Orange Revolution turned out to be the highest rise of the Ukrainian people over the past few centuries. The significance of these days, in my opinion, is higher than the events of August 1991, when the independence of Ukraine was proclaimed. After all, the Act of Proclamation of Independence was a choice (in half with fear!) of the political elite at the request of the national-democratic minority, it was a compromise that did not give us the opportunity to become the second Lithuania or Poland.

Now we have become witnesses and participants in the mass popular movement for our own dignity. I already had to write that over the past decade we have constantly forgiven Leonid Kuchma and his entourage everything, from the *Krivorozhstal* plunder to (unfortunately, this is true) the murder of journalist Georgy Gongadze. But this time the most active and modern part of society exploded, because they tried to impose on us not just the role of the "southwestern underbelly" of Russia, but also the role of extras in this theater of the absurd. If Ukrainians had not rebelled against the "proposal" to elect a twice convicted as president, there would hardly have been any sense in the further existence of such a nation... This, in my opinion, was the "orange" moment of truth.

And this is against the background of what is now happening in Russia, Belarus, post-Soviet Central Asia, Azerbaijan, Armenia and Moldova—a terrible narrowing of democratic freedoms, the authoritarianism of political regimes and the complete alienation of the peoples of these countries from any, even ephemeral, influence on the adoption of the most important decisions. It was different in our Maidan and around it. This was the first experience of combining the interests of the political class (both the opposition and the authorities) with the interests and views of the very broad masses of the people—from "tops" to "roots." The social influence of Kyiv businessmen and Lviv intellectuals was in the days of the revolution almost equal to the voice of a peasant woman from Poltava region or a student from Kharkiv.

The Europeanness of Ukraine and Ukrainians is a great and eternal topic that deserves a separate discussion. In short, we are Europeans. But geographically rather than psychologically. Soviet, "cut off" from the rest of the world mentality remains strong. Stronger, at least, than our own attempts to move "away from Moscow" and "forward to a psychological Europe."

Objectively speaking, the processes of desovietization, deKGBization, decuchmization in Ukraine, provided their implementation, should bring us closer to the traditions of the Old World. It can be assumed that the vector of attraction of the "European" Yushchenko to the West may be weaker than the direction of action of the "anti-European" Putin. And then we can become for Europe a kind of "South Korea" against the background of Russia—"DPRK." They will be forced to support us, because, anyway, we are and will soon be a balance for that "Upper Volta with nuclear missiles." It is in this sense that we will be "Europeans."

The real path to European structures is much more complicated than the implementation of certain points in declarations and memorandums. There will be many disappointments. In particular, the readiness of the political leaders of the nation for self-restraint and self-sacrifice causes skepticism right away.

Oleksandr Irvanets, writer (Kyiv)

In those two weeks of standing on the Maidan, our "European potential" was perhaps the highest in Europe — higher than the French, Germans and Poles — without jokes. How polite Maidan was, how well people behaved! No rudeness, no ill-will or insincerity. Personally, it seemed to me in those days that it was God who finally turned His eyes to Ukraine, and until He takes His eyes from us, people do everything right. If only all of us remained in his sight as long as possible... But, perhaps, God has other troubles, other peoples and countries. Therefore, it is important that all of us remain in the new conditions as they were in those days.

Mykhailyna Kotsyubynska, writer (Kyiv)

Yes, undoubtedly, these days became a moment of truth, a powerful effort to escape from the post-Soviet spiritual space. Already in the figures of two candidates two directions of development were personified, these two civilizational models — socio-economic, cultural-national, moral-psychological. On the one hand — continuation and perpetuation in different dimensions of our post-Soviet, post-colonial status. As caustic Oleksandr Irvanets predicted, "following such people we will reach Europe through Mongolia and Korea..." On the other hand — organic, conscious cultivation of oneself in Europe and Europe in oneself. I assess our European potential reassuringly. But this does not mean that we are ready to integrate instantly into modern European political and economic parameters. Such a situation must be prepared gradually and nurtured on the basis of significant internal transformations that are needed not so much by Europe as, first of all, by ourselves. And here, in Ukraine, — this is evidenced by history, culture, psychological type — "Europe" has always been and is present. We are not the "natives" who need to start from scratch.

10. "Maidan. Testimonies" (Foreword to the book)

Maidan is a significant event of modern Ukrainian history, which marked the civilizational choice of people and country. And this choice is European values: freedoms and human rights, the rule of law and guarantees of minority rights in the relationship between society and government. The alternative to this is well known to our people—the destruction or desecration of national culture, the absence of the state as an institution that should stand in defense of its citizens, many victims and crippled destinies.

We know that slaves do not rebel. In defense of rights and dignity stand up people for whom freedom is a value. Maidan became an arena of confrontation between the people and the corrupt power of villains, for whom neither the citizen nor the interests of the nation were priorities.

The victory of the Maidan was paid for with the most precious thing—the lives of hundreds of the best sons and daughters of the nation, and thousands of wounded. This is a high price to pay, but unfortunately, in the history of mankind, it never happens otherwise.

We have won this stage of the difficult road to freedom and dignity. But we must fight for freedom and dignity every day—there are no other ways.

In their testimonies participants'record the events and reflect on the Maidan phenomenon. We have collected these texts and present them to the readers.

***

Risking their lives in the name of dignity and freedom, people defended their beliefs—"resisted in spirit". This was the motivation for their actions. The Maidan hoped that the authorities would listen to the hundreds of thousands and millions of voices that united for change, but this did not happen. At the beginning of the events, there was a peaceful protest and a desire to find a solution in a constitutional way. However, very quickly, the authorities showed that they ignored their opponents and preferred to rely on the use of force to suppress peaceful protest. The response of the Maidan was mass participation, and when the authorities used weapons, courageous defence of their righteousness. "Everyone who came to the Maidan added a guarantee of security," everyone understood this. Sometimes tens or hundreds of thousands of people gathered. However, at night or in moments of direct confrontation with armed security guards, the defence was held by the bravest—truly heroes. The choice was not an easy one. "The hardest decision to make was to leave everything you have and go there," said one of the combatants. "I understood that I could die at any moment," another participant, a woman, shares her experience. They told us— each in their own way—how they overcame their fear. At the same time, they claimed that "Maidan was the calmest place", because the further away from the events, the scarier it was. Positions of dignity were formulated: "When the boys were killed, when the youngest were killed, we no longer had the right not to go into battle." Many Maidan people tried to do everything they could to prevent bloodshed. But the government, which was behaving more and more aggressively, did not engage in dialogue with the people, and did not leave them any chance. People told us how they could not bring themselves to throw Molotov cocktails or paving stones. Some were unable to cross this barrier, while others took up arms in the face of a deadlock—either defeat and humiliation or victory.

While at the beginning of the Maidan the barricades were more symbolic and the dialogues peaceful and non-violent, in January and later, real armed clashes took place. The authorities were not making any concessions, and it was becoming increasingly clear that there would be no peaceful resolution to the conflict: "People started throwing Molotov cocktails out of hopelessness—no one heard them on the other side." Radicalisation, including among the Maidan participants, was growing, and there was no way around it.

In January and February 2014, the most dramatic and tragic events took place. *Berkut* officers and other 'special forces' started shooting—first with rubber bullets, and then with live ammunition. As if on a hunt, they were aiming at people's eyes and noses, and there were no barriers for them—they killed journalists and medics alike. "The combatants were getting wounded one by one," said a centurion from the Maidan Self-Defence. The dead were already counted in dozens. The Maidan's response was adequate—weapons were used against the government guards. The expectations of the special forces that they would kill with impunity did not come true. And when fighters started shooting at them, the security forces first retreated and then scattered. This is how Maidan defeated its opponents not only spiritually but also militarily.

***

A large part of the book's evidence constitute the accounts of the events by members of the Self-Defence. It is difficult to overestimate their role in the victory of the Maidan—they were the ones who bore the brunt of the confrontation, they were the ones who suffered the most, it was they who had the hardest time. Here are just a few quotes from the testimony of one of the fighters, Taras Tym: "When the first victims appeared on our side, when those captures and beatings began (not deaths yet, just such brutal things that people were stripped naked, forced to run in such an appearance, beaten), then you could see how people were not only getting angry, but becoming tougher—'yes, we are in a fight, and we will fight to the last, because the truth is on our side'."

"There was a wall of wooden shields on the front line all the time, and it was the hardest thing to stand there and just hold back the shots and grenades with those wooden shields, and under a constant stream of water from a water cannon."

***

Perhaps one of the most surprising phenomena of the Maidan was its self-organisation. Specialised, efficient groups covered a huge range of Maidan needs. People created an infrastructure of resistance—at different stages, it was tent cities, barricades, mobile medical teams, field medical stations and underground hospitals. Groups were formed to protect the wounded in hospitals and supply them with medicines. Volunteers supplied firewood to the Maidan during the bitter cold, made homemade weapons, shields and bulletproof vests—the list is very long. An information support for Maidan was provided—hundreds of journalists covered the events and countered the state's lies, the online community informed the world about the events of Maidan in dozens of languages, and lawyers organised legal defence for the arrested participants. The Maidan kitchens fed tens of thousands of people every day for almost three months of confrontation.

A very important factor in the events was Automaidan, whose role in providing resources, rescuing the wounded, and organising pressure on the authorities cannot be overestimated. There were also think tanks that tried to help Maidan leaders formulate action strategies, predict the stages of confrontation with the authorities and the appropriate actions of the Maidan community.

Certain business communities also played an important role: they—mostly small and medium-sized businesses—provided the Maidan with resources: infrastructure, medical equipment, expensive medicines, etc. The people who usurped power outraged everyone, and so citizens joined forces to fight them.

"People came, saw what was needed, and did it," our respondents say. "In this revolution, everyone fulfilled their mission and played their role," almost everyone says. There were many educated, creative people on the Maidan who set a certain style of fighting the system. "We supported non-violent resistance in all possible ways," Andriy Meakovsky shares his experience. Performances and artistic events by musicians, poets, artists, and designers took place on and around Maidan. The Open University of Maidan was operating, and hundreds of brilliant lectures were delivered. The Maidan Library functioned in the Ukrainian House, and books were very popular during the peaceful stages.

Some of the testimonies in this book tell about the art of the Maidan: icons painted in those days and blessed by priests, drawings on helmets and shields. Hundreds and thousands of eloquent photographs depict the faces of the participants in this truly historic event. It is impossible to describe the role of all the groups that took part in the Maidan in a short preface. But some of them, in particular, doctors and priests, must be mentioned.

***

The need for medical care for Maidan participants was enormous. In times of peace, it was necessary to help the sick, because it was not easy to withstand the cold. But very soon, people started to appear who had been beaten by security guards and government servants—Berkut officers and *titushky*. Emergency medical teams were set up on Maidan, and later medical stations, which gradually grew into hospitals. The authorities also tried to put pressure on Maidan through hospitals—Maidan protesters were denied medical care, the wounded were abducted or classified as criminals and imprisoned. The Maidan responded by creating its own network of medical aid centres, organising groups for the safe transportation of the wounded, and providing security at hospitals. But the most dramatic events took place when the government forces started shooting at people. Doctors carried the wounded under fire and often became targets for the killers themselves. The courage of the medical workers was impressive, although doctors often stressed that they were apolitical. But in response to the aggression of the authorities, they came to the Maidan as professionals and as citizens. True to their Hippocratic oath, they helped not only the demonstrators but also the soldiers of the internal troops. "It was the time of surgeons," said the Maidan doctors. They testified: "We stitched up wounds not only on tables, but also on chairs and on the floor", "we resuscitated people on the sidewalks". I think that these pages of events will be described in more detail over time.

***

People understood their position as a fight on the side of Good," says Father Vasyl Rudeiko. And dozens, hundreds of priests of all churches, as well as rabbis and muftis, were in solidarity with their people. "The fact that the liturgy was celebrated there sanctified the sacrifice not only of those people who were on the Maidan, but of millions of people throughout Ukraine," says Father Mykhailo Dymyd. "Thanks to the liturgies, this sacrifice was ennobled, and this is important.

"We have no right to remain silent when God's commandments are violated," said Father Bohdan Ogulchansky. The priests blessed people who defended biblical values, confessed believers, and supported people with words in moments of despair and discouragement: "And it is very important that the priests were next to people who were falling victims, who needed to close their eyes and who needed to be prayed over."

The Maidan united believers of different religions. Representatives of almost all religious communities testified to this. Will it be possible to maintain this height of spirit? But even today it is clear that the Maidan was an arena of humanity, faith and hope, and the role of clergy who helped their faithful is worthy of respect, reflection and emulation.

***

Characteristically, the Kyiv Maidan community united people from all over the country — it was not a regional resistance. All those who shared the Maidan's choice stood up to defend freedom: Galicians, Bukovinians, residents of the South and East of Ukraine. Witnesses point to the significant involvement of women in the resistance ("We women did not just make sandwiches"), the participation of young people in the fateful events ("He asked me if I was 18. I said I was"), the role of older people, especially Kyiv residents, and the Maidan's ethic of solidarity ("Let's unite because we are worth it!").

***

The Maidan spoke both Ukrainian and Russian, and it was a bilingualism of understanding, not discord. The events of those days destroyed the stereotypical characteristics of Ukrainians ("it's no concern of mine"), and the people rose up and defended themselves and their descendants. The hope for a better future, albeit very cautiously, is often voiced in testimonies: "the city will become kinder" or "the country is poor, but it is already different".

***

I can't tell you everything, but almost everything is in the testimonies of our respondents, the participants of the Maidan. I am sure that their texts will be read, re-read and studied by our descendants. And this is despite the subjectivity of the stories, their fragmentation and emotionality (how else!), and perhaps excessive hopes for the future. But these are the peculiarities of the oral history genre. We recorded more than 300 memoirs — only a part of them is included in the book. The texts were transcribed and edited. We faced a rather difficult task: on the one hand, to preserve the authenticity of the stories, and on the other hand, to make the texts accessible to a potential reader. We have left out of the book the unsubstantiated judgements of respondents who recounted what they did not see. We also left out emotional accusations against other participants in the events. We tried to recreate the chronology of the Maidan, its geography, and the roles of different communities and people. That is why, when collecting testimonies, we quoted the number of respondents from different groups. We deliberately did not interview the leaders — we tried to hear from those "ordinary" history makers. Whether we succeeded in becoming chroniclers of witnesses and events will be judged by our readers. We tried to do our job responsibly and professionally.

We perceive the preparation and publication of the *Maidan Testimonies Book* as part of the great work being done by other participants in the events — witnesses and researchers of modern Ukrainian history. Only by working together can we document those fateful days as accurately as possible for future generations. Finally, I would like to thank all my colleagues whose names appear in the book. Without the daily work of more than a hundred people for almost two years, this project would never have been possible.

We dedicate this book to the memory of those who gave their lives for the future of Ukraine.

11. Selected Characteristics of the Soviet Totalitarian Abyss

1. For totalitarianism, a person is not a value, but a tool. Tens of millions of compatriots were sacrificed to the system that was being born. To this day, researchers are still deciding how many victims there were—40 million, 60 million? Perhaps only historians of the next generations will be able to give an adequate figure. "Cog man", "soldier of the party", "we will pay any price"—these are well-known quotes. In the Soviet Union, where life on the outside was not often different from being in the Gulag, people were not necessarily taken deprived of their lives. But without exception, everyone was deprived of their property. The Holodomor of 1932-1933 was one of the last bastions taken by the state in its struggle for the disenfranchisement of citizens. It was the expropriation of the last piece of bread, " so that people have nothing". Everyone had to become proletarians—economic and spiritual. A person was created who was unable (had no opportunities) to rely on himself or herself—only to ask the state. Hence the infantilism of contemporaries who have been expecting salaries, benefits, and cheap sausage from the new state for ten years instead of taking responsibility for their own destiny. (It is in Poland and Lithuania that citizens are returned their property, in Ukraine it is almost impossible). The builders of communism ensured absolute human disenfranchisement: the immensity of the Gulag, a developed system of repression from which no one was protected.

Just one example. Ukrainian dissidents Semen Gluzman and Mykola Horbal, who tried to resist the system during the "vegetarian years" (Anna Akhmatova's phrase), tried hopelessly to fight for the right to dispose of their bodies after death. According to the Gulag's instructions, the victims were buried with only numbers assigned to them. A separate subsystem of this disenfranchisement was the system of searching for — or rather creating — enemies in the history of Soviet totalitarianism. Alexander Solzhenitsyn's *The Gu-*

lag Archipelago chronicles those events. This practice has been entrenched for a long time: the structure of the state includes repressive law, repressive bodies and a system of informers; institutions of prisons, camps, pre-trial detention cells. The conditions of lawlessness in them hardly change. Only in recent years has Ukraine, under pressure from the European community, taken the first steps to change its penal system.

A person in Ukraine today is still not protected by law or the judicial system, and there are thousands of signals of this. Only the lawlessness has become different. Examples can be found almost daily in almost all Ukrainian media.

2. Under totalitarianism, individual behaviour was almost completely impossible. The system inspired obedience, the postulate of "living like everyone else". This was achieved by creating an atmosphere of fear, on the one hand, and, on the other hand, by educating *mankurts*—people without memory—as "true Soviet patriots". The system demanded unification of thoughts, behaviour, clothing...

Personality was an additional risk factor. In their sociological study *Generation 1917*, Novosibirsk sociologists concluded that it was not the smart who survived—they were killed in numerous gulags, nor the strong—they were killed by the war. It was more often the outsiders who survived—janitors, unskilled workers, etc.

A dissident challenge to the system was an attempt to talk to the executioner. The price of dialogue was usually life. Thousands of Ukrainian dissidents (only some of them are known) became victims of torture chambers. The story of their lives has not yet been written. Only the first publications have appeared: documents, diaries, correspondence. This is perhaps the greatest treasure of the nation at the turn of the millennium.

Will the value of the individual be restored? The system is changing very slowly: The Cheka and the NKVD have been replaced in recent Ukrainian years by the prosecutor's office and the tax inspectorate, which are certainly milder. As Stanislaw Jerzy Lec said: if a cannibal eats with a fork and knife, is this progress? I don't know, time will tell.

3. A distorted spiritual field: the extermination of faith and religion (we write the history of the church and synagogue in the 1940s to 1970s based on denunciations by clergymen and commissioners for religious affairs); forbidden culture: the barbed wire and the Berlin Wall left the Soviet person with specific texts. There was neither the Bible nor culture among them—only propaganda, which is no longer remembered today. Classical Soviet books by Fyodor Gladkov and Alexander Fadeev had new editions every year. This spiritual field included a specific history of mankind that began in 1917, and it had sacred spaces of Moscow as the Third Rome (there will be no fourth!) and revolutionary Petrograd. Imperialism was the dominant value (even in the late 1980s, the majority of the population associated themselves with the USSR rather than Ukraine or Kazakhstan, although this was not the case in Estonia).

The system destroyed the foundations of the Judeo-Christian tradition, especially ethics, by imposing "in the name of great goals" denunciation, principles of collective responsibility, etc. (I still remember the article of the Criminal Code on "non- denunciation "). The spiritual descendants of Pavlik Morozov shaped many generations of Soviet people.

The defensive reaction of people was doublethink: "They think we are paid, and we will pretend to work". Another side of this phenomenon was the fear of independent thinking. It was replaced by other people's (party) recommendations for life. Let's recall the collective condemnation of linguistic theories, cosmopolitans, etc. by workers. How to stop this virtual reality? How can we expect a quick return to universal values after this? I don't know any recipes. I only know about the enormous length of this path. The first steps have been made, but not so long ago I saw a demonstration by the Ukrainian Orthodox Church of the Moscow Patriarchate with the slogan: "The Pope is the executioner of the Ukrainian people."

The information space was a field for listening to orders — "recommendations" from the authorities. It was fundamentally monological and excluded any space for dialogue. All of Joseph Goebbels's recommendations on propaganda were taken into account and assimilated. It was a metaphorical field with its own type signs:

"Glory to the CPSU" and "The plans of the party are the plans of the people", etc. It was informing without negative information about the events in the country (remember Chernobyl). Verbal information was more important than real information. This was in the face of numerous falsifications of history, when all previous versions of events disappeared from libraries and were banned from private collections.

The totalitarian system did not develop the humanities and social sciences. Only a tiny part of the budget of the Academy of Sciences of Ukraine was allocated for history and philosophy, law and literature, art and archeology. As researchers of this period wrote: the word was dead, because it was allowed only in propaganda texts and literature of socialist realism. Social science and humanitarian texts of that period are impossible to read today. They have already taken their place in the dustbin of history and are interesting only to researchers who analyse that pathology (there are, of course, exceptions, but they only confirm the rule).

Language was becoming a barbed wire (Dashevsky). It will take us a long time to get rid of it. I think that at least a few generations will still reflect that wire. After all, language is one of the most conservative memory systems.

It is very difficult to get out of that "pit" (Andrei Platonov): the official media are still Soviet in nature. The coverage of the "cassette scandal" is traditional Soviet and post-Soviet falsifications, lies, distortions of facts, etc. Go to the libraries: in the district centres, the latest books are Soviet. The decade of new life, new texts, new ideas seems to have never happened. It's only in Kyiv, in Lviv something has changed. In Melitopol or Zhmerynka, people hardly know about it. The index of citations by humanities and social scientists is still headed by Karl Marx, Friedrich Engels, and Vladimir Lenin. (However, young people say: "Karl Mars and Friedrich Snickers" — it's good that these gentlemen are no longer their authorities). These are semi-random examples from an almost endless series.

Some conclusions:

- Post-communist societies largely retain features of the past, because even its denial includes features of its predecessor.
- Negativism is a necessary feature of change ("Down with the CPSU" and "Ukraine without Kuchma", etc.), but serious change requires decades of painstaking work, which is only just beginning. We declare our commitment to democracy, but we do not know what it is. "How do those who have never seen freedom recognise it?" (Stanisław Jerzy Lec).

The scale of the changes is such that there will be enough work for more than one generation. And in the coming years and decades, many more people will mostly be looking for themselves in the remnants of the distribution economy and *nomenclatura*-based personnel policy.

There will be no miracle of rapid construction of "Western civilisation". There will be (optimistically) a very difficult path of development. In which direction? I don't know! What's left? To do our hopeless job: to build, to unite, to produce ideas, to publish books, to have children... And hope for the best.

12. Preface to the Issue of the Almanac *Yegupets* Dedicated to Yiddish Culture

I congratulate our readers, because for the first time a special issue of the *Yegupets* almanac is dedicated to the texts of Yiddish culture. Today, translations of Yiddish texts into Ukrainian are one of the main priorities of the Center for Jewish Studies.

The point is that Jewish culture in Yiddish and Hebrew at the beginning of the 20th century or even at the end of the 19th century was one of the most powerful cultures of that time in Europe. It is hard to imagine today that back then not only Yiddish was translated into different languages, but many masterpieces of world culture were translated into Yiddish. Myron Petrovsky said that Hitler killed readers of Jewish literature while Stalin—its writers. The Holocaust and repressions took many lives. Only with *perestroika*, when the more or less free existence of communities in the post-Soviet space began, did the structures of Jewish life begin to form. We understood—it is very important to preserve this culture that has existed for centuries. To publish Yiddish texts in a country in which almost no one spoke this language at the end of the last century did not make sense. Therefore, one of the priorities for us was the retransmission of prose, poetry, art texts in translations from Yiddish into those languages in which both the Jewish and Ukrainian communities communicate. We started a Yiddish translation school, and today seven or eight people translate book by book. Books are sold out, and this means that there is interest in these texts.

We also try to present to the reader texts of Jewish culture written in other languages. They also depict the life of Jews of different times. Some of them are written in English, in particular, texts by Bashevis Singer, some—in German, as texts of the Bukovinian school of Jewish writers: Paul Celan, Rosa Auslander and others.

In the late 1990s and early 2000s, we collected archives of Jewish writers who lived in Ukraine. They were kept in their families. They were given to us quite easily, because the children of these writers did not speak Yiddish. Parents did not teach children Yiddish — the command and use of this language led to accusations of Zionism, just as consistent use of Ukrainian led to accusations of Ukrainian bourgeois nationalism. Those were the days.

We have a unique collection of hundreds of thousands of documents, including manuscripts of works, correspondence, photographs, private documents of Jewish writers. Our archives contain texts by Matvey Talalaevsky, Nathan Zabara, Alexander Lizen, Ihil Falikman, Dora Khaykina, Ryva Balyasnaya, Itsik Kipnis, Mikhail Pinchevsky, Joseph Buchbinder... There are researchers of Jewish culture of the twentieth century in the world, but there are not so many places where documents would be stored, especially those belonging to the post-war period.

Most of the writers went through the war, were war correspondents, passed the Gulag. Some kept their papers. One of these archives, the largest in our collection — the documents of Matvey Talalaevsky. In it, in particular, his correspondence with his wife was preserved, to whom he wrote from the front almost every day, and he passed a difficult path from Stalingrad to Prague. A unique part of this archive are scenarios of Soviet holidays, which were compiled by Matvey Talalaevsky and his colleagues, employees of the camp culture-educational unit, for traditional celebrations of May Day or November 7. Many other materials from the period when the writer returned from the camp and was rehabilitated have been preserved. He translated Janusz Korczak, wrote poems and scripts for Ukrainian theaters.

Archival manuscripts require careful study: in Soviet times, under conditions of total censorship, they were printed with cuts. Some, also censored, were printed only in Yiddish. In addition, the authors were limited by self-censorship. These circumstances left their mark not only on Jewish literature, but also on Russian and Ukrainian, too. Real texts began to appear only in the 1970s and 1980s, and not all writers survived to this day.

The greatest interest attracts the correspondence of Jewish writers, where, using metaphorical language, referring to sources known to them, they felt more free. In addition to correspondence, there are some interesting texts that I want to mention individually. This is the manuscript of Nathan Zabara's famous novel *The Wheel Turns*, with all the preparatory materials for it, as well as the diaries of Joseph Buchbinder about the Gulag written in Yiddish. These materials need to work and work on. Gradually we do this.

I am very glad that we managed to publish several books translated from Yiddish. The first book was *Tevye the Milkman* by Sholem Aleichem without cuts (2017), the second was the first translation into Ukrainian of the Avrom Sutskever's book *From the Vilnius ghetto. Green aquarium. Stories* (2020), the third is the first translation into Ukrainian of Joseph Buchbinder's memoirs *Emmanuel Narrates: Pages of the Life of a Jewish Writer* (2021). I am very pleased that researchers from other countries are involved in working on texts from our archives. Joint projects are born. We are talking about the University of Toronto with Anna Sternschis, and Bar-Ilan University with Ber Kotlerman...

In parallel, we try to translate classical Jewish literature of those times. Bashevis Singer became a Nobel laureate in 1978, and his will contains a stipulation that his texts be published in English translations, because he originally wrote them in Yiddish and then revised them to make them available not only in Jewish communities. We published in Ukrainian his novels *Slave* and *Shosha* (translation by Yaroslava Strikha). We have translated and continue to translate texts by Bruno Schulz, Janusz Korczak, Shmuel Yosef Agnon, Isaac Babel...

At some stage, we realized that the Ukrainian readers did not have the opportunity to get acquainted with the work of these brilliant writers whom Europe knows, so they need anthologies of Jewish literature. Today there is such an opportunity: we have published a book *American Jewish Fiction. A Century of Stories* (translated from English by Alexander Butsenko, Daria Litoshenko, Natalia Komarova). It presents selected works by Avrom Kagan, Anzi Jezerska, Isaac Bashevis Singer, Saul Bellow, Grace Paley, Tilly Olsen, Bernard Malamud, Philip Roth and others. We also published the book *Mahogany Box: Jewish Prose of Eastern Europe in the Second Half of the 19th – 20th Centuries* (transl. by Mykola Zerov, Oleksandr Hera, Oleksandra Uralova, Oleksandr Irvanets, Yurko Prokhasko and others), which contains translations of works by Yitzhok-Leib Perets, Sholem Aleichem Janusz Korczak, Shmuel Josef Agnon, Bruno Schulz, Isaac Babel, Itzik Kipnis, Itzik Manger, Isaac Bashevis Singer, Deborah Vogel, Avrom Sutzkever. Now we are working on the book *Jewish Theme of Ukrainian Literature* (compiled by Christina Semerin). These are also extremely interesting texts that were either previously hushed up or are little known.

Not only literary works were created in the Yiddish language — there was also cinema. The films of the Odessa Film Studio were preserved thanks to the researchers Yuri Morozov and Tatyana Derevyanko, who wrote a book about the Jewish cinema of Ukraine, about unique films that are not found anywhere else in the world. During specially organized events that gather hundreds of people, we talk about these films, present them accompanied by a pianist or klezmer orchestra. This is generally the trend of modern European culture — to take films of the beginning of the 20th century, which need to be restored, and to demonstrate them accompanied by orchestras. Once I happened to be at such a show, which was organized by the European Union, with a symphony orchestra accompaniment. The film of the early twentieth century traveled to Europe. We have the opportunity to show such films at our festivals. With God's help we will win and do it further.

Another layer of culture in the Yiddish language is the Jewish theater. We have published several books on the history of the Jewish theater. The very first is the story told by Moses Loev, the last director of the Ukrainian GOSET that completed his existence in Chernivtsi, and before that he worked in Kyiv. Loev, a picky researcher, found portraits of all the actors, directors and artists of this theater. The theater ceased to exist during the anti-Semitic processes of the post-war years. The second book is Irina Meleshkina's *Wandering Stars in Ukraine. Pages of the History of the Jewish Theater* about almost a hundred theaters that existed in the country. Of course, theaters had different levels, some were professional, others were workers', but there were. Workers' theaters became a common form of activity of semi-educated people of the 1920s-1930s, not indifferent to Jewish culture. Gradually, these theaters were closed.

Characteristically, many of them, as Anna Shternshis says, began with theatrical performances of trials of Judaism, yeshivas, rabbis. Then these allegedly public courts often became a reality — in those days people were condemned very cruelly. I am glad that we managed to collect these materials, largely in partnership with the Museum of Theater, Music and Cinema of Ukraine and Israeli researcher Hillel Kazovsky. We organized a wonderful joint exhibition, which was open to visitors for almost three months. A wonderful Jewish art calendar was also published for this exhibition (artist Pinchas Fischel). In this way the world learned about such a page in the history of Yiddish culture.

Another page was opened to us by Hillel Kazovsky. The point is that at the time of Hrushevsky, and then Skoropadsky in Kyiv, the association *Kultur-Liga* worked, which took care of libraries, schools, and published books. It was funded by Ukrainian governments. The artists who worked on those books later became world famous. Almost no one knows that David Hofstein's book with illustrations by Marc Chagall, books with illustrations by Sarah Shore, Mark Epstein were published in Kyiv at that time. Solomon Nikritin, Isaak Rabinovich, Abram Manevich worked fruitfully. Exhibitions were held, a Jewish Museum in Kyiv was created. The fate of this museum is unknown, but from brief information published in contemporary newspapers, we know that there were exhibited works by Picasso and other world-class masters. Artists who worked in Ukraine were subjected to various forms of repression, many managed to emigrate and became great artists of France, Germany or other countries. Those who stayed here were forced to choose the style of socialist realism.

I spoke about the main blocks of Yiddish culture that existed on our lands. We want to preserve them. It took us years to build a team that knows the language and knows how to work. I am convinced that much more work is needed to ensure that the great Yiddish culture that existed on the territory of Ukraine is retransmitted and becomes part of Ukrainian culture. We continue our work as best we can. One of our platforms is the *Yegupets* almanac, where we publish relevant texts. This issue, as I said, is entirely devoted to Yiddish culture.

13. Ukrainian Intellectuals on Ukrainian-Jewish Relations

Rethinking one's own history has become a dominant intellectual process in all countries of the former Soviet bloc. The interpretations of history imposed by the totalitarian system could not withstand the breath of freedom. And there were many reasons for this. First, the true Soviet orthodox ideologues had long since completed their earthly journey by the end of the 1980s and 1990s; second, the authors of *samizdat* and reformers of the system had by then seriously shaken the ideological monolith of Leninism-Stalinism; and finally, the windows opened at the end of the century for the theories of Western scholars finally destroyed Soviet ideologemes.

Under the new historical conditions, new economic, legal and social structures were built, and new ideologies were formed. New interpretations of the national past emerged, competing with each other and gaining supporters. One of the most prominent ideological trends in the rethinking of Ukrainian history was the writing by Ukrainian intellectuals about Jews on the territory of Ukraine and Ukrainian-Jewish relations.

The well-known Ukrainian intellectual Ivan Dziuba justified the need to understand Ukrainian-Jewish relations in this way: "...This is a historically complex topic, burdened by heavy memories. And at the same time, it is a topic that has been tacitly banned for several decades. It was avoided for various reasons—political, ideological, and psychological. Officials and authorities had their own reasons for this, far removed from the interests of both the Ukrainian and Jewish peoples. A part of the public, which sincerely and benevolently sought mutual understanding, also avoided sensitive issues, fearing that discussing them could cause negative emotions. But the experience of our history shows that any silence, even with the best of intentions, eventually turns out to be harmful and hinders mutual understanding... We can and should talk about everything. And this will only benefit us all, but on one condition—if we tell the truth with an open heart. With a sincere desire to achieve mutual understanding, to prevent the recurrence of evil. And to take with us into the future the best that was between us...". And further: "We need a dialogue between Ukrainian and Jewish intellectuals. We need constant communication at a high level of competence and morality. Over the past decades there has been no such dialogue: the space of the devastated spirit has been filled with myths, stereotypes, and anecdotes..."[1] Where to start? We had to find an answer to this question. We started with the analysis of national myths, with the recording and comprehension of everyday consciousness, with a critical analysis of texts by national historians.

Leonid Plyushch, an Ukrainian intellectual and dissident who has lived in France for a long time, wrote: "The anti-Semitic myth in Ukraine is not much different from the general anti-Semitic myth. In general, it has less mysticism, and in particular, there is no mysticism of the 'Zionist conspiracy', but more socio-national elements (Jews are exploiters, loyal supporters of the dominant nation, party, government; Ukrainophobes)." And further: "The anti-Ukrainian myth is based on the actual and falsified history of the national liberation struggle: The Second World War with its Ukrainian policemen, the pogroms of the Koliyivshchyna and... Khmelnytsky uprising entered the religious consciousness of modern Judaism. The Koliyivshchyna superimposed itself on this collective trauma and also provoked a religious response in the form of 'Hasidism,' an amazing Judeo-Slavic mysticism. All subsequent events were superimposed on this deep trauma, in which the Ukrainian played a mystical role comparable to the apostate Jews in Christian folklore... "[2]

Leonid Plyushch emphasises the degree of prejudice, the depth of hostile stereotypes. It becomes clear that we are dealing

---

1 I. Dziuba, Introduction // *Svit. Journal of the People's Movement of Ukraine*. Special issue. Materials of the international scientific conference *Problems of Ukrainian-Jewish relations*. K.: Svit, 1991. No. 3-4. p. 1.
2 L. Plyushch, The role of chauvinistic mythology in interethnic relations // *Svit. Journal of the People's Movement of Ukraine*. Special issue. Materials of the international scientific conference *Problems of Ukrainian-Jewish relations*. K.: Svit, 1991. No. 3-4. p. 4.

with a problem of such proportions that, even under the most favourable circumstances, cannot be resolved within the lifetime of one or two generations.

The disproportionality of the desire to overcome negative prejudices in the relations between the Ukrainian and Jewish peoples with the capabilities of intellectuals is probably one of the dominant characteristics of the problem. However, awareness of the fact that this is a long journey, not an one-time action, helps everyone to see their place, their niche in the process of rethinking and transformation. Ivan Dziuba, already mentioned above, suggests that we should reflect on the contribution of Jews to both the history and modernity of humanity and Ukrainian history and culture. He writes: "I am referring not only to famous scientists, composers, and artists (many of whom are from Ukraine). I am also referring to the contribution of the Jewish mind, spiritual genius, to the creation of universal ideas, concepts, moral norms, and models of existence. I will name some of these ideas: the idea of guilt and repentance, the idea of primogeniture, both literally and metaphorically with a deep moral and disciplinary meaning; the idea of pilgrimage."[3]

These thoughts, which have long been part of the history of Jewish thought, are voiced for the first time in Ukrainian. Also for the first time, Ivan Dziuba offers Ukrainian and Jewish readers a chance to reflect on the contribution of Jews "to economic life, technical culture, jurisprudence, journalism, religious thought, and so on. And in these areas such prominent personalities as Avram Ovrucher, Mordechai Chornobyl, Moses Oks, Pasmanik, Ilya Orshansky, Osip Pergament, Lev Pinsker, Avram Peretz, Veniamin Portugalov, Samson Ostropoler, Naum Bogoraz, and others proved themselves — and that only in the 19th century alone!"[4]

A very interesting facet of our topic is the comprehension of Jewish civilisation by Ukrainian intellectuals. And there are undoubted achievements on this path today. The monograph by the

---

[3] I. Dziuba, Introduction // *Svit. Journal of the People's Movement of Ukraine*. Special issue. Materials of the international scientific conference *Problems of Ukrainian-Jewish relations*. K.: Svit, 1991. No. 3-4. p. 3.

[4] Ibid., p. 2.

famous Ukrainian cultural critic Vadym Skurativsky on the authorship of the *Protocols of the Elders of Zion* is surprisingly interesting. In a brilliant study, he convincingly proves to the reader that the author of the tragically famous forgery, one of the most popular books of the 20th century, was Matvey Golovinsky. A comparison of the texts of the *Protocols* themselves leaves no doubt as to his authorship.

Over the past decade, Ukrainian intellectuals have published dozens of in-depth articles examining various aspects of Ukrainian-Jewish relations. These include philosophical journalism, historical research, sociological analysis of stereotypes in the mass consciousness, and literary texts... What unites them, however, is an attempt to rethink history, a desire to overcome the accumulated barriers that impede mutual understanding between peoples.

The head of PEN Ukraine, writer, long-term prisoner of Soviet prisons and camps, Yevhen Sverstiuk, drew the attention of researchers to the question: what is the causal relationship between the genocide of Ukrainians in 1932 and Jews in 1942? Could there have been 1942 without 1932? "I believe," he writes, "that we are united in the 20th century by one lesson that was not fully realised, which brought our nations to the brink of death. In 1932-1933, a colossal experiment of genocide was organised, when the vast Ukraine was turned into a ghetto, a starvation zone. The morally weakened and drugged world deafened itself with the devil's whistle and did not have the spiritual strength to understand and rush to the rescue. Our dying moans were not listened to. Defending Ukraine then would have meant defending life and defending Europe. "You will see, he will learn from ours," said Osip Mandelstam when Hitler came to power. Less than ten years later, the experience of the Ukrainian genocide was applied to the Jewish people, adjusted for the conditions of war and the nature of the settlements."[5] This topic of the tragic fates of two non-state peoples, Jews and Ukrainians, is studied in the most fundamental way.

---

5   Y. Sverstiuk, In the Egyptian captivity of indifference // *Svit. Journal of the People's Movement of Ukraine*. Special issue. Materials of the international scientific conference *Problems of Ukrainian-Jewish relations*. K.: Svit, 1991. No. 3-4. p.16.

Comprehending Ukrainian-Jewish relations is "a problem of finding mutual understanding between the victims of the historical process, the victims of the creators of empires, the victims of regimes hostile to freedom. A Jew is an eternal dissident, an eternal dissenter. A Ukrainian is an eternal complexed, an eternal object of someone's claims. They are 'homeless'. They are 'not ours'," writes the well-known Ukrainian historian Yaroslav Dashkevych, who was one of the first to study Ukrainian-Jewish relations. "The following methodological (or rather anti-methodological) technique has become widespread in Western historiography: to label everything that happened in Ukraine as 'Ukrainian'. This completely ignores the fact that for centuries in Ukraine, power did not belong to the Ukrainian people. That the conditions of barbaric lawlessness that prevailed in Ukraine were not the result of the activities of the Ukrainian people, but the consequence of actions taken against the Ukrainian people by the occupying power, either in the role of the Polish State or in the role of the Russian Empire... Foreigners have never sought to turn Ukraine into a legal territory because it would interfere with their domination... Inhuman conditions have become the soil that has stimulated bloody ethnic conflicts for centuries."[6]

Yaroslav Dashkevych draws attention to a certain incorrectness of canonised studies of Ukrainian history, "ignoring the fact that Ukraine for the same 360 years was the scene of a fierce national liberation struggle of the enslaved Ukrainian nation, which created a situation that was fundamentally different from Western European conditions, where Jews were not supposed to take a certain position with regard to enslaved peoples; underestimating the fact that social transformations in Western Europe led to the gradual emergence of rule-of-law states, while in Ukraine in the early 20th century "lawlessness, discrimination, and persecution prevailed, primarily against the Ukrainian population, but also against other non-dominant ethnic groups... "[7]

---

6   Y. Dashkevych, Problems of Studying Jewish-Ukrainian Relations (16th — early 20th centuries) // Ibid., p.26.
7   Ibid., p. 26.

Virtually all works on this topic emphasise that, for various reasons, Ukrainian-Jewish relations have not yet been the object of study. Even significant periods of history, such as the Khmelnytsky uprising, the period of the Ukrainian People's Republic, and the national processes of the 19th and 20th centuries, have not been studied. Even the widespread stereotypical mutual prejudice about Jews "with the keys to the church" and Ukrainian collaborators during the Nazi era has not found its researchers (Ivan-Pavlo Khymka).

The version of different models of national survival proposed by Myroslav Marynovych is interesting. "The Jewish and Ukrainian peoples have different models of survival. These models are rigidly determined by history and cannot be changed voluntarily, no matter how well intentioned this attempt may be... Both models of survival are incommensurable: Jews survive in dispersion among foreign nations, Ukrainians survive on their own land. The logic of one model does not follow from the logic of the other, which means that the devil of misunderstanding dances on the border of these two models. Living among alien and often mutually hostile ethnic substrates posed a difficult imperative for Jews: to accurately identify the strongest. Since Ukrainians have often been the weak side throughout their history, it is natural that a persistent stereotype of Jews' hostile attitude towards Ukrainian national interests has developed in the popular consciousness... Until now, the reaction of the Ukrainian side to the disloyal orientation of Jews has not been able to rise above the level of conventional social reflexes: the sad circumstances of national defeat forced us to respond to hostility not by analysing its causes but by retaliating. However, this old problem has an unexpected solution. The best way not to be at odds with Jews who refuse to take the side of the weak is to become strong ourselves."[8]

Over and over again, Ukrainian historians, philosophers, and literary critics have emphasised the need to study the stages of sol-

---

8   M. Marynovych, Jews and Ukrainians: an attempt at a tolerant projection of mutual interests. // *Svit. Journal of the People's Movement of Ukraine*. Special issue. Materials of the international scientific conference *Problems of Ukrainian-Jewish relations*. K.: Svit, 1991. No. 3-4. p.21.

idarity and constructive cooperation between peoples. This includes, of course, the political solidarity of individual parties and movements in the early 20th century, mutual assistance during tragic periods of history, such as the rescue of Jews during the Nazi era, assistance from the *Joint* during the famine, mutual assistance of cultural figures, and so on.

It requires studying the mutual influence of Jews and Ukrainians in the formation of national literatures, language borrowings, and models of relations in peaceful decades and centuries. "For the first time in history, perhaps, the sons of Ukraine and Israel are meeting without intermediaries to begin cleaning the Augean stables. They have not been cleaned for centuries. There are legends about what happened and what did not happen, legends about enmity and unprecedented cruelty, about a Jew with the keys to the church and a Cossack with a rope in his hands. Instead of a horseshoe, stereotypes of a Jewish exploiter and a Ukrainian butcher hang on the stables' doors. The main thing is that there is not a single one of the thousands of facts of normal human cooperation between Ukrainians and Jews in the stables — these facts were simply not recorded...", wrote Yevhen Sverstiuk.[9]

Interesting are the studies by Ukrainian historians who compare the ideologies of the Ukrainian and Jewish liberation movements, Zionism and Ukrainian nationalism. Roman Zvarych points out that these two movements, "Ukrainian and Jewish nationalism, shared the same cultural, social, and political environment, whether it was during the occupation of Ukraine by Austria, Poland, or Russia. And so it is hardly a coincidence that both movements have developed similarities in ideology, political orientation, strategy, and shared worldview." The researcher emphasises that most Ukrainian nationalists and Zionists "...relied on a universal moral principle: all people have the right to national self-determination, independence, sovereignty, and statehood", and further: "in the 20th century, Ukrainians and Jews finally realised that in order

---

9   Y. Sverstiuk, In the Egyptian captivity of indifference. Ibid., p. 13.

for dreams of independence and statehood to become a reality, one must rely solely on one's own strength."[10]

Most of the Ukrainian scholars to whose texts I refer in this article went through the Gulag. Their thoughts and reflections on the Soviet period of Ukrainian-Jewish relations are therefore extremely important.

Yevhen Sverstiuk wrote: "Perhaps never in history have the Ukrainian and Jewish peoples been so opposed as in the 'zone of internationalism'. The peoples have lost the true biblical support that united them as a common sacred book, the Bible. After all, an illiterate Ukrainian peasant or a Jew knew this book from childhood. In this century poisoned by hatred, who knows the Book of Psalms of David, the Book of Proverbs of Solomon, the Book of Moses? But everyone knows the jokes about Abram and Moisha."[11]

Mykola Riabchuk's thoughts complement Yevhen Sverstiuk's brilliant formula: "By its very nature, Soviet society was... deeply xenophobic, militantly intolerant, 'irreconcilable' to any otherness — both in the sphere of production (the infamous 'equalisation') and in the sphere of consumption (the infamous 'equality in poverty'), and, finally, in the ideological sphere, where xenophobia was deliberately fostered both by the image of the 'external enemy' (the 'besieged fortress' syndrome) and the image of the 'internal enemy' (here you have 'spies', 'saboteurs, 'kulaks', and 'bourgeois intellectuals'). .."[12]

Summarising his own and his colleagues' reflections, the renowned Ukrainian philosopher Myroslav Popovych formulated a question that Ukrainian intellectuals are asking themselves: "Four horrific genocides of the Jewish people occurred on the land of Ukraine: during the national liberation struggle (Khmelnytsky uprising) of 1648-1657, the Haydamak uprising (1768), the civil war

---

10 R. Zvarych, Zionism and Ukrainian Nationalism: Historical, Political and Philosophical Parallels // *Philosophical and Sociological Thought*. K., 1994. No. 5-6. pp. 133, 135, 140.
11 Y. Sverstiuk, ibid., p. 14.
12 M. Ryabchuk, Antisemitism and xenophobia // *Svit. Journal of the People's Movement of Ukraine*. Special issue. Materials of the international scientific conference *Problems of Ukrainian-Jewish relations*. K.: Svit, 1991. No. 3-4. p.8.

(1919-1929), and the Holocaust (1941-1944). Am I, as a Ukrainian, responsible for these tragedies? If so, to what extent and in what sense? And what symbolic or real actions can remove historical sin? What, in general, is the nature of historical evil and how can it be prevented from entering our 'today' and 'tomorrow'?"[13]

The logic of these questions necessarily leads to the analysis of anti-Semitism, its manifestations, causes, Ukrainian specificity, and the search for ways to overcome all types of hatred.

The study of models of anti-Semitism proposed by Vasyl Lisovyi proves to be surprisingly fruitful. He distinguishes between: "1) a religious myth as a universal myth that gives a certain interpretation of Judaism and the history of its relationship to Christianity; 2) a conservative myth that revives the archetype of the 'stranger' included as a component of any ethnic culture — that is, it is about the threat posed by a person of another tribe, another race or nation; this myth can be called the myth of xenophobia; 3) political myths, which often combine or overlap with the first two; these myths are very diverse, including the myth of a 'world conspiracy', the myth of the Jews' role in the October 1917 revolution in Russia, etc."[14]

Vasyl Lisovyi's thoughts are developed by Ivan-Pavlo Khymka, a well-known Ukrainian historian from the United States. He is looking for an answer to the question of the lack of understanding of the Jewish tragedy by Ukrainians. In his opinion, the main reasons for this are as follows:

- deep hostility to Jews on the part of a part of the Ukrainian community, which intensified with the penetration of the nationalist worldview and modern anti-Semitic ideology;
- the abnormality of the moral and political environment in which Ukrainians found themselves;

---

13   M. Popovych, Jewish Genocide in Ukraine: History and Lessons // *Philosophical and Sociological Thought*. K., 1994. No. 5-6. p. 160.
14   V. Lisovyi, Mass Consciousness and Antisemitism // *Philosophical and Sociological Thought*. K., 1994. No. 5-6. p. 156.

- the inability to realise the magnitude of the crime committed[15].

The researcher writes about something that other scholars do not often pay attention to: "The Ukrainians themselves were victims of such discrimination and physical violence that to a certain extent they became insensitive to the situation of the Jewish population."[16]

Ivan-Pavlo Khymka turns page after page through the Ukrainian history of the 20th century: the tragedy of the revolution and the Russian occupation (which was called the civil war in Soviet times); the Holodomor of 1932-1933; the deportation and repressions of 1939-1942; and, finally, the Second World War.

Few people know the figure of the Ukrainian population destroyed during these years, and it is horrific — about 12 million. This figure includes all Ukrainian citizens, including 1.5 million Jewish victims of the Holocaust. Of course, Ukrainians died in other ways: as civilians, as soldiers of various armies, and as prisoners of war... The figure of 12 million is impressive!

Khymka writes about this: "Thus, Ukrainians had to live in conditions where mass murder became a terribly commonplace event. From the point of view of their own experience, the mass murder of Jews by the Nazis was not perceived by Ukrainians as something unheard of and abnormal in politics, as it would have been interpreted by other nations living in peace and security."[17]

As we conclude our review of texts by Ukrainian intellectuals on Jewish history and civilisation and Ukrainian-Jewish relations, we turn to questions of the present: what to do with this history? What should we do today to leave the pain of the past to history in the future? In order to move into today and tomorrow together, without forgetting the tragedy of history, but also without allowing the past to prevent contemporaries from building new relationships of mutual understanding and cooperation.

---

15   I.-P. Khymka, The *Krakiwski Visti* about Jews, 1943. A note on the history of Ukrainian-Jewish relations during the Second World War // *Philosophical and Sociological Thought*. K., 1994. No. 5-6. p. 204.
16   Ibid.
17   Ibid.

"It is equally necessary for both Ukrainians and Jews. Even if all Jews go to Israel, this will be necessary not only for Ukraine and Israel, but for every Ukrainian anywhere: not only because we live on the same planet, but also because each of us is a human being, and how can one be a human being without getting rid of mutual scores, grievances, and sins?" Ivan Dziuba wrote.[18]

First, the authors propose replacing the myths of social significance in the minds of both peoples with historical knowledge worthy of free nations of the late 20th and early 21st centuries. "A huge amount of archival materials," writes Yaroslav Dashkevych, "figuratively speaking, tons, if not tens of tons, which are directly and indirectly related to the history of the Jews of Ukraine — to their ethnic history, to their religious history, to the history of Jewish culture, and so on — lie as dead capital... "[19]

Leonid Plyushch, who was well aware of the limited possibilities of education in combating negative myths of mutual perception, draws attention to the historical consciousness of his contemporaries. "It is a fact that in Ukraine, Ukrainians do not know Jewish history, and Jews do not know Ukrainian history. Moreover, Jews in Ukraine do not know their own culture, and Ukrainians do not know theirs. On such a basis, it is difficult to expect anything other than myths, most of them positive about themselves and negative about others. Perhaps this is the central reason for mutually chauvinistic mythologies. In order to understand another culture, you need to know your own. But you can also understand your own only by knowing others," he wrote.[20]

The authors place perhaps the greatest hopes in the new living conditions for both Jews and Ukrainians — life in their respective national states, Ukraine and Israel. "Both states," writes Taras Wozniak, "are still in their infancy. In Ukraine, there is a large Jewish

---

18 I. Dziuba, Introduction // *Svit. Journal of the People's Movement of Ukraine*. Special issue. Materials of the international scientific conference *Problems of Ukrainian-Jewish relations*. K.: Svit, 1991. No. 3-4. p. 3.
19 Y. Dashkevych, Problems of Studying Jewish-Ukrainian Relations (16th — early 20th centuries) // Ibid., p.26.
20 L. Plyushch, The role of chauvinistic mythology in interethnic relations // Ibid., p. 4.

community, and for its part, the modern Jewish culture has simply taken root in the Ukrainian land, much of it was born and formed in Ukraine... Ukrainian content, whether it is called Polish, Russian, or Austrian, will still be a significant dominant of the new Jewish culture. On the other hand, Ukraine should not underestimate the weight and influence of global Jewry, and Israel should not underestimate the size and possible role of Ukraine in Europe and the world. Mutual exchange of experience in state-building would also be fruitful... The problems of reviving native languages are also great."[21]

And finally, he formulates a philosophical, ethnic maxim: "...We must be aware of what both Israel and Ukraine were built on — the universal desire for Salvation. And then it is up to everyone to choose their own. Whether we renounce this path or not, this will be our future destiny. Especially since the warnings of the Holodomor and the Holocaust have already been sounded."[22]

I would like to conclude my review with this text by Taras Wozniak. Of course, it is not complete. However, I think that the main body of ideas has been covered in the review, and I hope that an impartial reader will appreciate the honesty, depth and sensitivity of the texts of the authors presented.

A natural question arises: were there other texts, of other concepts and views, that were aggressive and unfriendly? There certainly were. But their analysis may be the subject of another article. Thank God, there were much fewer such texts, and they are different in terms of their line of thought and ethics. And their authors are not moral authorities in independent Ukraine. All of this allowed me not to include them in this review. After all, I, along with my Ukrainian friends, am concerned with the search for truth and ways of understanding between people and nations.

---

21 T. Voznyak, Revival of the State and Man: the Aspect of the Promised Land and Salvation // Ibid., p. 143.
22 Ibid., p. 143.

14. A Warning from Hannah Arendt

The madness of the twentieth century was so large-scale and impressive that few dared to comprehend it, let alone analyse its components and factors. How could the hitherto unknown mechanisms of humanity's self-destruction be explained? After all, more people died in the two world wars of the century than in all the wars of previous history. How to explain the rapid victorious march of totalitarian regimes in Europe, for whom the murder of millions was no longer an ethical but a technological problem? For the first time in history, the survival of humanity and the preservation of its cultural experience have become the central problem of civilisation.

Of course, scholars, politicians, and cultural figures have tried to comprehend these events. However, for various reasons, there are almost no convincing versions of the European history of the first half of the 20th century. At best, some thinkers managed to comprehend local problems, to analyse certain cells of those cancers. Many of the researchers could not withstand the strain at all — texts of "self-hating spirit", demoralisation, and denial of knowledge multiplied, which, in turn, deepened the crisis of civilisational development.

One of the most convincing intellectual alternatives to this despair and degradation of the spirit in the second half of the 20th century was Hannah Arendt's *The Origins of Totalitarianism*. Step by step, in the tradition of rational cognition, the researcher analyses the European history of the 19th and 20th centuries, identifying ideas and events that led humanity down a road to nowhere.

***

Hannah Arendt begins her study of the origins of totalitarianism in the second half of the 19th century, focusing on the structural changes in the world of that time, analysing its ideological doctrines. Arendt accurately captures those significant changes, events, and ideologies that would eventually have catastrophic consequences for humanity.

First of all, the author draws attention to how anti-monarchical revolutions are gradually changing the self-identification of national communities. The ideas of national solidarity as the solidarity of people of common origin are being established in the public consciousness of European peoples. "The spiritual unity of Christian peoples has given way to a plurality of nations," Hannah Arendt formulates.[1] A new, hitherto unknown type of national feeling is being born, which deifies national communities rather than the individual — God's creation.

Industrialisation, which is becoming one of the most important signs of development, produces "superfluous people" — those thrown out of society. And so, new communities — the crowd, the mob — enter the political arena of public life. These are situational associations of people who stand in solidarity with each other in rejecting the established mechanisms of state and society. The intellectuals of the time sympathised with the crowd in their nationalist theories, arguing that "the voice of the people is the voice of God". Meanwhile, the crowd was undermining the legal foundations of coexistence in an attempt to assert the right of force in the face of lawlessness. Demagogues and provocateurs quickly took over the crowd, channeling the spontaneous activity of the new lumpen against organised society.

Hannah Arendt describes in detail how the new Darwinists, the ideologues of the time, rejecting the values of Judeo-Christian civilisation, build theories of social development as a struggle between classes, races, and nations, analogous to the theory of the struggle between species. To explain this struggle, the first racist theories emerged. With surprising ease, in almost all European countries, they gain more and more supporters, becoming perhaps the most influential ideologies of the turn of the century.

Again, the contradictions of industrialisation and social development give rise to a large number of disenfranchised groups of people who have no place in national states. In their wanderings, they seek refuge, but society shows almost absolute indifference to

---

1   Arendt, H., *The Origins of Totalitarianism* / Transl. from Engl. 2nd ed. K.: Dukh i Litera, 2005, p. 238.

their problems and their place in the human community. In this context, the author analyses in detail the fate of Jewish communions in European countries, their role in interstate relations, in the formation and development of the financial systems of Europe at that time; and then the tragic fate of Jewish communities in Europe, which became victims of the processes of collapse of the continent's system of nation-states. Hannah Arendt convincingly demonstrates the transformation of anti-Semitism from an obscure theory into an influential ideology that later played one of the most terrible roles in the 20th century.

***

The researcher focuses on analysing the problems and contradictions of the beginnings of imperialism.

National capital, which encounters state borders, easily rejects them and involves states and societies in the process of expansion. The economic crisis of overproduction is becoming the most powerful locomotive of this train. With the expansion of capital, state power is of necessity exported. And now the police and the army occupy the highest positions in the hierarchy of power. In the search for ideologies adequate to these states of imperialist development, racist theories with their dichotomy are perhaps the most prestigious: "us—them" (where *they* are secondary, inferior, superfluous, and *we* are the rulers, "carriers of progress" and people of the future). Racist ideologies are confidently occupying a leading place in public opinion, and are being assimilated and propagated by a large corps of Boers—racist bureaucrats who rule colonial Africa by shooting "natives". But the world does not hear these death cries. The world does not notice the murders of millions of Africans as a continuation of the division between *us* and *them*, where the price of division is life.

A new civilisation is being born on the African continent, with racism as its dominant ideology. In it, human life is not a value, and the laws do not apply. The "profit motive" that had previously driven societies' development is easily discarded and replaced by the political arbitrariness of racists.

In this situation, even Christianity, the most influential tradition of Europe in previous centuries, becomes unable to curb the "dangerous distortions of human consciousness," writes Hannah Arendt.[2] And after that, "the stage of history was fully equipped for all possible horrors," the researcher summarises.

The contradictions of the world at the turn of the 19th and 20th centuries culminated in the First World War. It became the key event of the era and determined most of the events of the following decades, if not the fate of the entire 20th century. The time before and after this event "are delimited not as the end of an old period and the beginning of a new one, but as the day before and the day after the explosion," wrote Hannah Arendt.[3]

This war destroyed the respect of nations for laws and customs. Ruthless destruction, chaos and ruin became the values, terrorism and revolutionary fanaticism spread to new groups of the population. Unemployment, with few exceptions, swallowed up entire nations. Vast masses of people almost simultaneously became superfluous to the world, became sacrificial groups of civilisation, not subject to laws and regulations. They became outcasts from the world, and millions of people were handed over to the police. It was as if the world of that time had deliberately collected so many contradictions and pain that it was impossible to resolve and eliminate them within the existing political systems.

Hannah Arendt analyses the structural economic, political and ideological components of the world of the time. She looks into the mechanisms of the spread of cruelty and violence that replaced liberal principles in the building of social life, as the latter proved to be unable to protect people in the new world. The author examines the stages of development of revolutionary fanaticism, as well as the emergence of totalitarian ideologies as myths of mass consciousness that spread at an incredible rate in societies of despair.

Organised violence is gradually replacing the law, and power is concentrated in the hands of the police. The newly emerging leaders gain the leverage to manipulate humanity on an unprecedented

---

2   Arendt, *The Origins of Totalitarianism*, p. 224.
3   Ibid., p. 299.

scale, preferring to have no limits. The corresponding ideological doctrines are created, for which content is no longer a serious problem — an "Orwellian world" is coming.

The new elites, having concentrated the monopoly of power in their hands, try to neglect almost everything: their arbitrariness becomes dominant. Hannah Arendt convincingly argues that an entirely new and unprecedented concept of power emerged in the world at that time. It is characterised by "disregard for direct consequences, not ruthlessness; eradication and neglect of national interests, not nationalism; contempt for utilitarian motives, not the reckless pursuit of self-interest".[4]

The totalitarian world — and it has emerged in a large part of Europe — has since then determined the rules of life in its territories. It considers both territories and new lands to be its own, which it is absorbing at an incredible rate, catastrophically reducing the space of democratic civilisation.

Concentration camp systems are being built — the most consistent institutions of totalitarian regimes. In them, people were separated from the lives of other people and then killed impersonally. The world outside the fences of the concentration camps gradually approached the level of madness inside them. It was becoming clear that totalitarianism sought not so much power over people as a system where people were not needed," Hannah Arendt wrote. Further events are well known: the clash of two totalitarian regimes, the Nazi and the Soviet, which led to the destruction of fascism. Thus, one of the regimes fell. Subsequently, though much later, Soviet totalitarianism also came to an end. The price of these "victories" was the disfigured fates of tens of millions of innocent victims. But is this price final? Hardly.

Totalitarian temptations will haunt humanity for a long time to come. Perhaps for this reason, and for this reason alone, the relevance of Hannah Arendt's The Origins of Totalitarianism cannot be overstated, especially in our country, where every family and every piece of land remembers the horrors that will continue to influence the present and the future for a long time.

---

4   Ibid., p. 469.

***

Hannah Arendt does not study the resistance to totalitarianism; this is a topic for other authors. However, she provides a brilliant philosophical formula for an alternative to Nazism and Stalinism. "Every end in history inevitably contains a new beginning; this beginning is a promise, the only 'news' that the end is capable of producing. Initiating, before it becomes a historical event, is the highest human capacity; in the political sense, it is identical to human freedom. *Initium ut esset homo creatus est* — 'The beginning has been laid, man has been created,' said Augustine. This beginning is ensured by every new birth; it is indeed in every human being."[5]

So, as was often repeated in the twentieth century: "Hope dies last". We live and will continue to live, remembering and understanding the past well.

---

5   Ibid., p. 534.

15. Leonid Finberg's Speech at the Stanislaw Vincenz Prize
For Humanitarian Service and Contribution to the Development of Regions **(26.09.2020)**

Dear colleagues, dear friends!

First of all, I would like to thank the Stanislaw Vincenz Prize Committee for this high honour. I will try to work off it in my future projects.

The impetus for the topic of my speech to you came from the words of one of the best Ukrainian translators, who said in a conversation with me: "This unfortunate Ukrainian literature". I took these words very seriously, because I believe that despite all the problems, Ukrainian literature, and more broadly, Ukrainian culture, has never been on the rise like it has been in recent decades. Today, hundreds of Ukrainian publishing houses annually publish tens of thousands of books of fiction, children's books, books on history, philosophy, cultural studies, etc. For comparison, in the Soviet 70s and 80s, there were many times fewer books, not to mention the quality of the publications. We have writers who are among the world's leading. Suffice it to mention the iconic names of Yuri Andrukhovych, Serhiy Zhadan, and Oksana Zabuzhko. We read world literature in Ukrainian, which we translate from dozens of languages. Only the *Dukh i Litera* publishing house has translations from French, German, Polish, Czech, Lithuanian, Slovak, Japanese, ancient Japanese, Chinese, Hebrew, and Yiddish.

We remember the great Ukrainian translators—Mykola Lukash, Yevhen Popovych, Hryhoriy Kochur, Mykhailo Moskalenko, Mar Pinchevsky, Anatoliy Perepadia, and others—who kept Ukrainian culture on their shoulders when censorship and the grip of socialist realism were crippling and killing writers. Today, however, we have contemporaries of their calibre who have translated into Ukrainian the giants of world culture, such as Umberto

Eco, Bashevis Singer, Paul Celan, Czesław Milosz, Bruno Schulz, and many others. Many of them have been awarded international prizes as the best translators. We have high Ukrainian poetry. Thank God, we have Lina Kostenko, Ihor Kalynets, Marianna Kiyanovska, and Borys Khersonsky with us. I've focused on fiction, but there are also books of the highest quality by Ukrainian historians, philosophers, and cultural critics. The texts of Serhiy Plokhiy, Yaroslav Hrytsak, and Natalia Yakovenko are read in the leading countries of the world. The texts of Olena Stiazhkina, Tamara Vronska, Vladyslav and Liudmyla Hrynevych are next in line... Similarly, texts by philosophers (Volodymyr Yermolenko, Andriy Baumeister) and art historians (Dmytro Horbachov, Vita Susak) can be presented. Ukrainian filmmakers have once again become known to the world. They have won awards at the most authoritative international festivals, including Cannes and Berlin. The names of Roman Balayan, Serhiy Bukovsky, and Akhtem Seitablayev are known all over the world. Our outstanding theatre directors, Vlad Troitsky, Sergei Masloboyshchikov, Dmitry Bogomazov are also well known.

In addition to the works of art I mentioned earlier, in recent decades certain cultural mechanisms have been created that did not exist before. Non-governmental, but no less influential, prizes have been established and become authoritative: the Vasyl Stus, *Ї* magazine, Yuriy Shevelov, Georgiy Gongadze prizes, and a number of others.

In my opinion, it is very important that the Ukrainian PEN Club has taken on a new quality, and its authority allowed us to hold the World PEN Forum in Lviv; the Є bookstores have developed and become a powerful network of Ukrainian book publishers in the country; many electronic publications have been launched and become powerful information sources (*Zbruch*, *Livyi Bereh*, *Ukrainska Pravda*); and high-quality paper magazines are being published (*Ukrainskyi Tyzhden*, *Krayina*, and the newspaper *Den*). These are certainly our achievements. It is very important that we do not underestimate what has been done. First of all, let's compare it with what we had yesterday, and then with what is around us in the world.

Let's ask ourselves, do we know about these achievements of Ukrainian culture? I am afraid that we know much less than we should. This ignorance, multiplied by Soviet stereotypes and enemy propaganda, imposes on us a sense of our inferiority, of our deficiency. I would like to focus here not so much on external influences as on our responsibility for them. If in a country of forty million people we sell up to five hundred copies of our best books a year, then something is wrong with us. I would also like to draw attention to the representation of culture in the information media. It is practically absent on television channels, which mainly report on political news, but take up a lot of space with stories about disasters, murders, etc. There are, of course, exceptions to this rule, such as *Radio Kultura*, but they are very few.

The experience of recent years has reminded us that the share of educated people who share the values of the individual, the importance of an effective legal system in the country, and the value of state independence is not that high (25% in the country). Perhaps in other countries it is not higher, but not all of us have a neighbour that flexes its muscles with nuclear warheads on our borders, and we are building a state after decades of communism and colonial status. In my opinion, we have no other way but to become stronger. We have shown that we can be strong when the authorities irritate us—our Maidans are unprecedented in the European history of recent years. We have demonstrated to the world a non-aggressive, non-vandalistic resistance to the authorities who ignore our civilisational values. At critical moments in history, we have learnt to fight and win, but do we know how to win in non-extreme situations, in everyday life? Yes, of course, it is sometimes more difficult, but it is absolutely necessary. What should we do? "Fit into influential circles," as Stanisław Jerzy Lec, a great Lviv citizen, recommended, or form them, as I propose. We need to create and build influential communities, unite in powerful associations and unions that are independent of the authorities and able to defend their interests. Associations of historians and philosophers, filmmakers, writers, etc. There are many such communities, but they are mostly formal and weak, and they could become powerful and influential. Resources for this can and should be found. The experience of many, including ours, proves that it is possible. The corona virus has shown that large conferences can be held at minimal cost — the zoom is not too expensive. The publication of texts, especially in electronic format, is also real. What is often lacking is initiative, will, and, ultimately, personal responsibility (sorry for the pathos) for the community, culture, nation, for one's future and the future of one's children.

I am not simplifying the situation, I agree with Natalia Sniadenko's words: "We are fixed on failures, shortcomings, miscalculations. We subconsciously expect failure, because the number of injuries in our individual and historical experience significantly exceeds the number of victories and achievements...". This is true, but there is another thing: we are strengthened by an adequate understanding of history, the deepest possible comprehension of the challenges of the present and the prediction of the future. Reflecting on history, let's listen to Vitalii Ponomariov:

"Today, Ukrainians of different ethnic origins are once again defending themselves and the West, which is unable to defend itself, from the darkness from the East... An ancient Cossack sabre points to one of the sources of this strength. The inscription on its blade reads: 'Loyalty to the land and traditions'. It is about the land as historical space in which humanity gradually formed into an ethnic group, and then into a modern nation. The Ukrainian people have been nurturing their land for centuries, building cities on it, constructing temples and fortresses, building houses in teams... On this land, it developed its own and adopted borrowed forms of civic community — a city assembly, a church council, a Cossack circle, a craftsman's workshop, an intellectual circle, and an Orthodox brotherhood. Here, it laid the foundations of its freedom: city self-government, golden noble and Cossack rights and freedoms, university autonomy, and free thinking. The Ukrainian community has defended this land many times against enslavement, deprivation, depersonalisation, against loss of memory, language, and historical subjectness.

The long and continuous stay on this land has shaped the experience of the Ukrainian people's settled life through legends, traditions, values, and culture. This experience is imprinted in its historical memory, encoded in the cultural heritage that defines its difference from others. Under the influence of this experience, the Ukrainian community developed dignity and individualism, a sense of spiritual unity, a desire for freedom and a commitment to privacy, an idea of themselves and their place in the earth's space and in historical time, and the boundaries of their own and others. This experience taught us to defend ourselves, to fight instead of obeying, to die instead of surrendering in the event of an invasion."

Let's realise the enormity of this foundation!

But let me return to the answer to what will help us find the strength to overcome the negative trends and challenges of our time. For me personally, it is important to understand the lives of people who overcame the limits of human capabilities — Taras Shevchenko, Vasyl Stus, Zeev Jabotinsky, Omelian Kovch, Osip Mandelstam, Olgerd Bochkovsky, Yevhen Sverstiuk... They have already been canonised. But there are also our contemporaries whose texts are worth listening to.

I will quote Father Borys Gudziak: "The idea of oneself, of one's place in the earthly space and in historical time, of the boundaries of one's own and others' are very important. Our strength is in relationships. Not just in you or me. It grows between us. It is interpersonal. It is divine and human at the same time. We need to see and understand strength and power as cooperation, as solidarity, as a gift."

We will win, there is no other way!

16. Holocaust. Babyn Yar. Present Day

One of the best books that told the world about the tragedy of the Holodomor in Ukraine in 1932-33 began with the following thought: the destruction of millions of Jews in World War II shook Europe and became a factor in understanding the guilt of twentieth-century civilisation. The famine in Ukraine in the early 1930s, which killed at least 7-8 million Ukrainians, is still unknown to the world, unknown to Ukrainians themselves. I would like to add to this idea a little bit: the world knew about the tragedy of the Jews, but Jews in the former Soviet Union knew little. The ideologues of the Soviet regime did everything possible to prevent the people from knowing their history, because such knowledge would inevitably lead to the search for those responsible for the tragedies. It is clear that in this case, the Communists would have been no better than the Nazis.

So, I will try to tell the Ukrainian reader about the Holocaust, the catastrophe of European Jewry during the Second World War. (For every nation needs to bury its dead, literally and figuratively, by telling about them. After all, it is difficult for people to live without burying them).

***

The Nazi takeover of Germany marked the beginning of massive anti-Semitic actions. In the early stages, it was the restriction of Jews' economic and then civil rights. The reaction to this was the emigration of about 300,000 Jews (60 per cent of the Jewish population of Germany). The rest—200,000—died in concentration camps or were simply murdered in their own homes. The emigration of Jews was complicated by the fact that there was nowhere to go—all countries had emigration quotas. And the Jews were left alone with their tragedy. The world was practically indifferent to this.

On the eve of the Anschluss, 185,000 Jews lived in Austria. 65,000 of them were killed, and the rest emigrated.

Of the 118,000 Czech Jews, 75-80,000 were killed by the Nazis.

In 1938, 450,000 Jews lived in Hungary. After the annexation of Northern Transylvania in 1940, 752,000 Jews found themselves under Hungarian rule. Only 100,000 of them were lucky enough to survive. To Auschwitz alone, 445,000 Hungarian Jews were sent.

On the eve of the Second World War, 3 million 350 thousand Jews lived in Poland. About 3 million of them were killed by the Nazis and their allies. Out of the 350,000 survivors, 200,000 escaped to the Soviet Union, and approximately 100,000 were saved by partisans, in camps, etc. The stages of this sorrowful journey are tragically known: Treblinka—870,000, Belzec camp—600,000, Sobibor—250,000, Majdanek—60,000, Auschwitz—1,275,000.

Before the war, 137,000 Jews lived in Slovakia. 40,000 of them went to Hungary when it annexed Transcarpathia. 90,000 Slovak Jews were deported to Auschwitz, Treblinka, and Sobibor. A total of 110,000 Jews in Slovakia died in concentration camps.

Out of 350,000 French Jews, 77,000 perished. Some people escaped by emigrating to Spain, Switzerland, and North Africa.

Before the occupation, 90,000 Jews lived in Belgium. About 40,000 of them were sent to death camps in Poland, and 25,000 emigrated to France to share the fate of French Jews.

Of the 140,000 members of the Dutch Jewish community, only 35,000 survived the war.

Before the war, 3,500 Jews lived in Luxembourg. Almost 2,000 of them were sent to death camps.

Of the 750,000 Jews in Romania, 350,000 were killed. Initially, the pogrom was organised by the Romanian authorities. Later, the actions of the Germans and Romanians were coordinated.

Before the war, 78 thousand Jews lived in Yugoslavia. 60,000 of them perished in Treblinka and Auschwitz or were killed by Croatian nationalists—*Ustaše*.

Of the 77,000 Jews in Greece, about 65,000 perished. Most of them died in Auschwitz.

In some European countries, society managed to save Jews from genocide.

7,200 Danish Jews were transported by boat to Sweden. Almost 500 Jews captured by the Nazis during a raid were thrown into Theresienstadt. In 1945 they returned to their homeland alive.

The Jews of Finland — 2,000 people — were saved because the government did not comply with Hitler's demand to deport Jews from the country.

Italy's 57,000-strong Jewish community largely survived thanks to Benito Mussolini's refusal to send Jews to their deaths. During the German occupation of northern and central Italy in 1943, about 8,000 Jews were killed.

The Jews of Bulgaria, 50,000 people, survived the terrible years almost without loss. This was facilitated by the parliament, church, and royal court of this country.

And the last thing. Before the war, 1 million 750 thousand to 1 million 800 thousand Jews lived on the territory annexed by the Soviet Union, including about 200 thousand refugees (in general, there were 2.75-2.9 million Jews in the USSR at that time). About 1 million 100 thousand Jews managed to evacuate to the east. The rest, almost all of them, perished. To these should be added 120,000 Jewish servicemen who died as soldiers in the Soviet army, and another 80,000 who were shot in prisoner-of-war camps.

This is a terrible martyrology. I took most of its data from Yitzhak Arad's book *The Holocaust* (Jerusalem, 1990).

Attempts to comprehend the tragedy in Jewish and world thought are almost unknown to our public. Realising that the topic is inexhaustible, I will focus on some of its issues.

The tragedy of European Jewry took place with the astonishing indifference of the peoples and governments of the civilised (?) world.

I will cite just a few facts:

- Two international conferences on refugee issues (in Switzerland and Bermuda) turned into a farce and clearly showed the Germans that the world was not ready to help the Jews.
- At the beginning of the war, the US State Department made great efforts to prevent information about Nazi atrocities from reaching the media — government officials feared that society would demand help for the victims.

- The ships *St Louis* and *Struma* with Jewish refugees on board were denied permission by England and then the United States to arrive in Palestine. The people from the *Struma* died, and those from the *St Louis* miraculously survived, but not thanks to the Americans or the British.
- During the entire period of the genocide of the Jewish people, the Allied powers did not adopt a single document condemning Nazi atrocities.
- The countries of the anti-Hitler coalition did virtually nothing to prevent the deportation of Europe's Jews to concentration camps in Poland. Even hundreds of paratroopers from Palestine who expressed a desire to save their brothers and sisters were not allowed to take part in the fighting. "The camps could not be bombed for strategic reasons, Jews could not be given weapons for political reasons," which would mean recognising Eretz Israel, writes E. Berkovich.
- The Jews who remained on Soviet territory knew virtually nothing about the anti-Semitic genocide committed by the Germans in Europe. Who was to blame? Of course, Stalin's totalitarianism, which destroyed civil society, including all forms of Jewish association, and kept its citizens in an information vacuum.
- Even to the offer to take in 20,000 Jewish children, America said "no." (But maybe this is a coincidence? Again, the facts clearly show that it was not! An opinion poll in April 1939 showed that only 8.7 per cent of citizens voted in favour of increasing the emigrant quota, while 83 per cent voted against it.)
- Both the church and the Pope in the Vatican were silent. Some of the priests repeated the anti-Semitic dogmas of the past: "This is a punishment for the Jews for the death of Jesus." (The activities of individual priests to save Jews were their personal position as citizens.)

I think that's enough information. In my opinion, it contributes to a clearer understanding of those times. (It is not superfluous also in today's thoughts and hopes of our peoples that the world will help us. I am sure that only we can help ourselves. And no one else).

How do we understand this indifference of some people to the deaths of others? How to explain it?

Perhaps the answer to this question will be the powerlessness of the European peoples in the face of Nazism, and the mechanism of solidarity of peoples in the name of preserving civilisation and life on earth, which was not powerful enough at that time (and even now), the immoral position of a number of states and peoples " it's no concern of mine " (the illusion that when others are killed, you still have a chance to survive), the historical confrontation between Jewish and Christian civilisations, and the tragic politicking of state leaders, which cost hundreds of thousands and millions of lives...

Perhaps this list can be continued. But the question: "Will humanity take this lesson into account?" is perhaps the most pressing question today. Unfortunately, we can't bring back the dead, so at least let the living survive....

Another aspect of the tragedy is worthy of attention: how did it happen that millions of people went meekly to their deaths? And did they go meekly? Or do we know almost nothing about this either?

One of the most conscientious researchers of this topic, the Israeli writer K. Shabtai (incidentally, he himself miraculously escaped the concentration camps), analyses this topic in detail. He writes that the Jews of Europe had virtually no opportunity to fight. He also talks about the behaviour of people of other nationalities in Nazi camps (there were about 5 million of them). And although they were in better conditions than the Jews, there were practically no uprisings among them: hunger, abuse, cold, and absolute disenfranchisement demoralised people. Almost without resistance, the Germans exterminated both the Polish intelligentsia and the Polish officer corps. And what about the millions of soldiers of the Soviet army who were taken prisoner in the first months of the war? Do we know anything about their uprisings? Almost nothing.

The possibility of self-defence depended on many circumstances. You had to have hope, some resources, and weapons. After all, the Warsaw Uprising took place only after five years of captivity. Jews lived in different countries, had no state of their own, and when the Germans came, they were deprived of their civil rights and handed over to the Germans and local "genlemen" for execution. At that time, Berkovich wrote in the aforementioned book, the whole of Europe went mad with hatred and bloodlust. And in the centre of this orgy was a nation that had no national leadership and no military traditions.

The diabolical, cynical Nazi programme of extermination of the Jews was designed so that the victims did not know that they were being transported to their deaths until almost the last days. And once in the camps or ghettos, they no longer appreciated life, which was terrible and humiliating, and many longed for death as liberation.

And yet there were acts of resistance, even in these terrible conditions. The world knows about the uprisings in the Warsaw ghetto and in Vilna, Lviv, Krakow, Będzin, Brody, Tarnów, Hrodna... There were also uprisings in Treblinka, Oświęcim, and Sobibor. And how many uprisings remained unknown because all the rebels were killed? Almost by accident, it became known that the last of the prisoners of the Szawne camp attacked their guards unarmed and almost all of them died.

Despite the danger, there were dozens of Jewish partisan units in Poland, Belarus, and Ukraine... As in many other cases, this is almost unknown to our citizens.

And how many acts of human dignity were there among the doomed — from Janusz Korczak's last march with his children to the same path of the Warsaw rabbis with their brothers to death (they were offered the possibility of salvation, but refused it).

This topic is infinitely broad, and I understand that any pen is powerless to comprehend a tragedy of such a magnitude as the Shoah. Perhaps only in a hundred or two hundred years will researchers be able to approach it objectively. For contemporaries, it still hurts, it still calls out to them. These are the fates of loved ones: parents, grandparents, blood relatives.

***

The Catastrophe of European Jewry has its own symbols. Babyn Yar is one of them. There is no serious scientific research on this topic. Even the number of those killed is estimated at 34 to 200 thousand. Europeans know the victims by name, while we still count the number of victims of the Second World War on the territory of the former Soviet Union from 20 to 40-50 million. Babyn Yar has become a symbol of tragedy for the world. For the Soviet authorities, it was one of the "objects" that they wanted to get rid of (like Bykivnia, like the Kyiv-Mohyla Academy, like Katyn...). And then there was the public struggle for a monument in Babyn Yar, the government's ignoring of a number of brilliant projects, and the installation of a symbol from the sculptural classics of Stalinism that has no sign of the Jewishness of this tragedy. And then there were attempts to build an amusement park on the bones of the victims. Miraculously, it was not built. And then there was the cynical crackdown of people who came to this place of God on the anniversary of the shootings... I am writing about the chronology of cynicism, the desecration of the memory of the people, the mockery of the most sacred thing — the ashes of the dead — and I understand that at that terrible time there was nothing special about it... Wasn't the memory of other peoples killed just as terribly, when there was no history of the UPA for Ukrainians, no books by Hrushevsky and Vynnychenko, when Ukrainians themselves were killed not figuratively but physically by the thousands just because they did not agree to be *mankurts*? And what a terrible story of the peoples deported by Stalin: Crimean Tatars, Germans from Ukraine and Russia, Kalmyks...

All of this is true. I don't stick out my pain and the pain of my people. But I want to, I need to know about it. And my children must know. And you, and your children, readers. So that this will never happen again. Never! To any nation in the world.

***

The illusions that people had in the early 20th century — that the harmony of nations, states, and economies was about to come —

dispelled very quickly. None of the stages of human life was as terrible and hateful as this one. The insanity of the First and Second World Wars, the Gulag and Kampuchea, the genocide of Armenians and Jews, the artificial famine in Ukraine and the terrors of Maoism continue today in Yugoslavia, Armenia, Azerbaijan and Transnistria.

Is this the inevitable path of human development? On the eve of the new millennium, are we unable to stop this chain reaction of destruction of each other?

I understand that there is no universal answer to this question. Each problem, each contradiction must be resolved in its own way. And it is no coincidence that in order to survive, to somehow coordinate the actions of different states and peoples, the United Nations was created, the Helsinki Process for Cooperation and Security in Europe was launched, and intensive searches for other ways of understanding on Earth are ongoing. And the search for new ways of humanity consists of the search of each nation, at each particular stage of its history.

At the stage when the people of Ukraine are creating their own state, when the tragic experience of the past must be comprehended as deeply as possible, when there is hope for the revival of the cultures of the peoples of Ukraine, including the Jewish one, I ask people about the Holocaust, about Babyn Yar, about the ability of humanity to take into account the tragic lessons of the past, about hopes, if not for happiness in the future, then for survival. People should have answers to these questions.

I am very grateful to everyone who answered my questionnaire. Some of those responses I present to the readers. But first, the questions.

I. What does Babyn Yar mean to you? How did it enter your life experience? Is the memory of Babyn Yar still alive for you?

II. Do you think that the people of Ukraine and the world remember the tragedy of Babyn Yar as a genocide of Jews, the murder of innocent children, women, and the elderly? Or is this sea of blood no longer visible among the many madnesses of the twentieth century?

III. Lessons from Auschwitz, Treblinka, Babyn Yar... Is this not a metaphor? After all, Kampuchea, Sumgait, Baku have just happened... Have we learnt the lessons of history? If not, do we still have hope for this?

V. In your opinion, is humanity able to protect itself from suicide on the threshold of the third millennium? Will people create barriers to the madness of murder? What do we hope for?

Gelii Aronov, writer (Kyiv)
I. When I was much younger, I could answer this question unequivocally: "Pain, wound, grief". All of this, of course, remains today, but over the years, the seemingly inappropriate feeling of shame has joined and even become equal to it. After all, "the dead have no shame", and the victims, participants and accomplices of the tragedy are mostly no longer among the living.

And yet — shame, shame for the people who ceased to be human because they realised their power and backed up this realisation with spilled blood. Shame for the people who so quickly (in a matter of days!) sided with the power and, if not with zeal, then willingly accepted the role of accomplices. Shame for the people who deceived the doomed by silence or outright lies, and the direct lies of the Nazis can be explained by their logic, but the lies of the "native authorities" who knew about the fate prepared for their citizens but did not consider it necessary to tell them the truth: "You are doomed! Save yourselves!", is even harder to explain. Were they afraid of panic? Did they not want to embarrass the abandoned city? What are these reasons worth compared to the opportunity to save thousands, or even hundreds, even dozens, even one? No, this cannot be called anything other than treachery, and I am ashamed of the people who have been silent about this for 50 years.

I am also ashamed of the people of Kyiv who were not affected by the action on 29 September 1941. I know that among them there were those who were horrified, those who sympathised, and those who saved. I am not talking about them, nor about those who gloated, betrayed, looted. I'm talking about the many, many people who perceived the tragedy without joy, but also without much sadness, almost indifferently, routinely. I understand that they had already been trained by their entire Soviet life to react only on command, I understand everything. But it's still a shame.

II. I once formulated the "geometric law of memory". It goes like this: "The strength of the memory of an event is inversely proportional to the distance from the point where it occurred to the point where the potential memory keeper is located." In accordance with this law, the memory of Babyn Yar is already limited to a very narrow circle of people who are somehow connected to Kyiv, or more precisely, to Kyivan Jewry. I have personal observations that show that people who lived near Kyiv (within a radius of 25-50 km) at the time of the tragedy took the news of it as just another reality of war, nothing more. To the descendants of these people, the term "Babyn Yar" means virtually nothing.

III. This question could be answered in two words: "Sumgait and Baku". This would also be the answer to question IV. Nevertheless, the lessons of history are a reality just as much as history itself is a reality. People who are able to think historically and who know history are able to draw conclusions from it. It is they who, by understanding the temptation to self- and mutual destruction inherent in human nature, are able to create barriers to genocide. There is nothing supernatural about them; unfortunately, these are the same democratic mechanisms designed to prevent the unleashing of baser instincts, to prevent the creation of social or national formations that are not based on universal values.

Alik Babionyshev, historian (USA)
I. Babyn Yar (like Auschwitz, Kolyma, Pol Pot's Cambodia) is one of the black holes of the universe that threatens to swallow human history, a trap on the path of civilisation, which calls into question the very fact of progress in human development. I found the story of the struggle for his memory in the Khrushchev-Brezhnev era to be important: people gathering on the anniversaries, resistance from the authorities, attempts to cover the ravine with sand, and finally the ugly monument. All of this is the fate of my generation, its awareness of its responsibility.

II. I think there should be no crime of this kind that has no monument (memory). If today it seems that we are facing a continuous sea of blood and violence, it is the duty of historians to recreate the true picture, to remember every victim, regardless of nationality.

III. Humanity as a whole learnt a serious lesson from the Second World War. But it was understood to a sufficient extent only in developed countries. Third world countries did not learn it, because nationalism seemed to them to be their own way of development. This applies to the peoples of the former USSR, and partly to the people of Israel.

IV. A real reassessment of values, which is inevitably happening in the world with the increase in the level of civilisation, is seen as a survival mechanism. The modern hierarchy of values can be defined as: man (personality), nation (culture, history), state (society). Recognition of the absolute infinite value of an individual serves as a moral barrier to the self-destruction of humanity in the near future. The mechanism will be the enormous scientific and economic potential of developed countries.

Mykhailo Biletskyi, researcher (Kyiv)
I. It so happened that Babyn Yar was one of my first childhood experiences. More precisely, not Babyn Yar itself, but the atmosphere of expectation. I remember how on one of the first nights after the Germans entered Kyiv, our neighbours in a communal apartment on Pushkinska Street for some reason — certainly out of inexplicable fear — burned their religious books in the oven; I still remember these thick, heavy-bound books with strange Jewish letters. A few days later, these people were killed in Babyn Yar.

I was six years old at the time. I don't remember any conversations about it in my childhood, but I think that on a subconscious level, mass murder of innocent people was included in the child's picture of the world as an integral part and norm of this world. Perhaps for this reason, as a schoolboy, I felt the spirit of the camps hovering over my country and believed in the Holodomor in Ukraine from the first words I heard about it.

I still believe that the main problem and the main curse of our century is the killing of innocent people, which continues to this day. And the main goal for the countries where they take place, and for all of humanity — even more important than making people well-fed and rich — is to stop these killings.

II. I think that in the European consciousness of the twentieth century, the genocide of the Jews plays a special role: not the first in time, it was the first to stir public consciousness and conscience; it was through it that the other genocides, such as Stalin's, Pol Pot's, and Lenin's, were perceived. I cannot say to what extent this genocide is associated with Babyn Yar.

III. The memory of mass genocides as a state of conscience is present in some people and absent in others. It is not the same for different peoples. I would like to think that at least among the peoples of Western Europe and North America, it is strong enough to exclude the possibility of Babyn Yar being repeated in their countries. (Although how can one not think of Lieutenant Kelly?)

I can't speak for the Asian and African worlds — sometimes it seems that they have not heard of these problems at all.

But it is especially painful to see how poorly the lessons of Babyn Yar have been learnt in the geographical and human space of which I used to consider myself a member, now called the former Soviet Union. Thousands killed, hundreds of thousands of refugees. And there are no forces in sight that could stop it.

It is necessary to realise that responsibility for mass murders committed in non-democratic and not sufficiently civilised countries also falls on democratic and civilised nations. Their indifference and inaction serve as a backdrop that allows these killings to take place. Europeans and North Americans often show a strange indifference to the blood shed outside their continents, as if this blood has a different price there. We don't remember John Donne's words well: "The bell is tolling for you". How many people remember the genocide, comparable to the Jewish genocide, that fell to the lot of another people, the Armenians? Or will humanity remain silent this time, accepting the imposed thesis that the fate and very right to life of a national minority is an internal matter for a sovereign state?

I believe that the only way to end the ongoing genocides is for all of humanity to recognise its responsibility for them. An effective mechanism of international control and intervention in the event of genocide and massive human rights violations must be developed. Humanity must wean totalitarian regimes from their traditional view of mass crimes as their internal affair, which does not allow for interference. The defence of the Kurds against Saddam Hussein is the first example of this kind, and it is encouraging.

Unfortunately, such a mechanism can only be effective if the criminal regime and criminal society are several orders of magnitude weaker than civilised nations, that have united.

IV. How can we ensure that a monster state that kills its citizens and threatens all of humanity does not arise again? Given the current level of armaments, it is a deadly threat. This is one of the main problems of humanity's survival. The likelihood of such a state emerging is not so small. In particular, somewhere in the vast expanse of our disintegrating empire. For me, the openly proclaimed plans of a former candidate for the Russian presidency and, in the future, for the Union presidency (who, by the way, received seven million votes) to genocide the Baltic peoples were a terrible symptom.

Of course, I do not know the answer to this question. I only wish that all of us—and especially politicians in unstable and potentially dangerous societies—would keep this threat in mind all the time. And cared about its elimination much more than about numerous other political goals. And we always want to hope. And even if there are no reasonable grounds for this, we can still hope in God.

Taras Vozniak, writer (Lviv)
I. Babyn Yar as a moral maxim appeared to me gradually, and not directly as Babyn Yar, because there were many others. First of all, I had to realise the existence of the Jewish people itself, which is not at all as clear as it seems to some. For a boy born in the Galician province, Jews and Jewishness were rather an Old Testament people and, perhaps, some echo of the Christmas holidays. That is, something more fairytale than real. Only later did they appear out

of biblical uncertainty: in the conversations of older people, whose memories, as well as their present, remained in the 20s and 30s of interwar Poland. And only then, through some kind of silence and the mention of someone in the middle gender, like a child or a wordless creature, did some vague outline emerge. It was difficult to put together the cheerful and funny image of the Vertep and that silence. It was only in a certain higher education course that I was surprised to discover that not everyone who spoke Russian was Russian. However, what is important in this provincial story? I think it is this stingy silence. Silence as an awareness of what happened, which does not allow for cheap street repentance and as a kind of taboo memory that gives us another chance to live on. And at the same time, still feel our common guilt and our universal fallenness.

II. Memory is different. There is grief, and there is memory as a statement. The mere statement of this fact in the minds of millions, if it is devoid of moral evaluation, is a kind of cynicism that many people, both in our country and abroad, are not without. Sometimes it is quite unpleasant to meet researchers of this kind. Just like with hypertrophied and often professional mourners. Their moral attitude to what happened is also often insincere and is a stereotype of the mass consciousness. It is important that memory becomes a personal act, moreover, an intimate one. There can be no group remorse or grief. Therefore, I would approach the question of the memory of Babyn Yar more qualitatively than quantitatively — have we let it pass through our hearts, or in the Christian paradigm — do we sympathize with the suffering of Christ? Has at least one of us come to that penitential compassion as a shared experience of his passions, when it burns with shame that you are here and he is there on the cross? How many of us bleed with the stigmata of faith? And thus love and repentance. So how much memory do we have as a compassionate stigma? I don't know.

III. The first word of the question contains the answer. What is a lesson? It is something that happened and was recorded as an answer to a question. The recurrence, after Oświęcim, Kampuchea, and Sumgait, should lead us to the conclusion that what history teaches us is that it teaches us nothing.. But who has learned this lesson? We are used to answering that *we* did. And what is this "we" — the people? Yes, there is a moral negation of genocides in the public consciousness. But it works only at the level of consciousness. As a people or as a public consciousness, we deny everything that happened. But does each of us, in the depths of his soul, have an experience of this denial? Has he learned this lesson as a person? Would this lesson become intimate? Many people simply did not think about it. They didn't care. Many people have not developed their intimate self and live in the social, and therefore superficial, world without knowing what is in their soul and what they are capable of. This underdevelopment of the soul is the reason why genocide is recurred so often. Do we have any hope of learning the lesson? But in order to learn it, we need not passive hope, but daily mental labor. Perhaps a kind of "education of feelings." Therefore, I would define hope as a labor of the soul and work on both one's own and another's soul.

IV. With the invention of the atomic bomb, humanity for the first time found itself in a situation where it could physically destroy itself. Technology, which man had dominated, dominated man. On the one hand, this made humanity mortal, but at the same time responsible for its life. That is, it became an adult. Mortality means responsibility for the life you have been given, even if you can neglect it. The same applies to all nations, which, from a purely technical point of view, are also not so difficult, or at least possible, to exterminate. So the question is: who was given a weapon of self-destruction — a child who was unconscious of his actions or a man who accepted the gift of life in order to preserve it? Sooner or later, an adult child with undeveloped gratitude as a response to the "gift of life" may find himself or herself at the button that launches the missiles. So our hope can only be to develop this gratitude, which is possible only if each of us has developed spirituality.

Semen Gluzman, human rights activist (Kyiv)
I. My first memory of Babyn Yar is my father's story. His father died there, not a commissar or a NKVD officer, but an old man who used to work in factories. So my first knowledge of Babyn Yar was more

"informational" (the specificity of my age at the time as a child, the "historicity" of the fact itself).

Babyn Yar entered my own life experience in a very specific way in my youth (in the sixties). Visiting Babyn Yar on 29 September was an almost heroic act at the time, coupled with career troubles for many (a close friend of mine, a member of the CPSU, was painfully worried that he could not go there with flowers for fear of ruining his career plans). It was there that I got my first first-hand impression of the place, role, and focus of the KGB, and my first first-hand observation of state anti-Semitism in action.

In the late 1960s, on a quiet winter evening, Viktor Platonovych Nekrasov told me in detail about the horrors of post-occupation Babyn Yar and showed me photographs he had taken at the time.

I get along with all this quite easily. Why? Because I realised a long time ago that the problem is not with the Germans or Ukrainians (Russians, Chuvash, New Zealanders...) who shot people at Babyn Yar (just as, in another sense, the problem is not with the Jews who served in the Cheka-NKVD-MGB). The problem is in the circumstances, in history, that is, in the system of totalitarianism. During the Brezhnev era, I shared camp routines with policemen, including those who shot from the walls of the Warsaw ghetto; it was difficult to get used to, but necessary. It helped to have a clear vision that these old men were now faithfully serving the new Moloch, the communist one. Pitiful cogs of history. Why should I hate them, those who paid for their own lives with the deaths of others (captivity, starvation, the choice of "either/or"), if I live absolutely calmly among the people who tortured me, who killed my friend Valery Marchenko? I understand that from the point of view of romantic literature, this can be condemned, but this is life. I sincerely believe that we need to live with all this calmly. Otherwise, there will be new blood, a new reason for revenge. Remembering does not mean hating.

II. I think that the memory of Babyn Yar in the former USSR is minimal. This was the aim of our former authorities, and they were quite effective in everything but the economy. Unfortunately, not only history has been distorted, but also the functional systems of the brain that *Homo totalitarius* uses to perceive the world around us and evaluate it. And here, of course, the problem is not only in the attitude towards Jews.

III. There is a chance to learn the lessons of history. But it is not in the courts or in the publication of archival documents. Not only in them. It is also in the way people will live today. And tomorrow. And whether an independent Ukraine will be a truly rule-of-law state. Fundamentalism (even if it is of the Eastern European type) as the basis of state independence cannot lead to anything other than new suffering and new years of bloodshed. It is madness not to understand this.

IV. Here, the answer has always depended on the personal views of the person answering, his or her life experience, and hopes. I am most likely a realist (synonymous with pessimist). I want to believe, I really want to believe.

What can I hope for? On myself. Only on myself. On my daily work. In my opinion, the worst sin of our society and our people is indifference. History is blind, the future depends on us. It depends on us in many ways — if we build a state that respects human rights to the maximum extent possible. There is no better recipe yet.

Marina Zavadska, writer (Slovakia)

When I was twelve years old, I asked my mother to give me a book from the Second World War that would not only tell about the advance of the armies, but would be factually accurate. I was already bored with Soviet books on this topic. Then she gave me a book by Anatolii Kuznetsov called "Death awaits in the ravine" (Babyn Yar, Prague, 1968). At the time, this work was published in the USSR only in the magazine *Yunost*. I already knew the documents from the labour camps, I knew about the mass graves in the Slovak village of Kremnička, about the concentration camps, so I was prepared for the fact that reading this book would not be easy. But in the opinion of one of my (at the time) peers, it was something new and scary.

Since then, I have read many books on this topic and am actively involved in their preparation. I cannot say that I became interested in modern history because of Babyn Yar. But it, along with

Anatolii Rybakov's *Heavy Sand* and many books by Czech and Slovak writers, made a great impression on me. And when I overcome the thick sets of laws of the fascist Slovak state, a lot of applications to the Hlinka Guard (the Nazi party's militia), and the documents of Aryanisation, I feel that I am working not only for myself.

Babyn Yar is one of the many places of human suffering during the Second World War. It is impossible to demand that the whole world remembers it, as it does not remember the dead four-year-old children from Kremnička, or even all the mass extermination camps. But we should strive to let the world know how all this could have happened. What should be avoided is the possibility of denying human rights to a group of people, including the basic right to life. Death is terrible, but much preceded the death of these people. By gradual restrictions and prohibitions (to earn money, to have a home, to buy food...), people were denied life. Death was just the logical consequence of this crazy ideology.

I'll go back to the book in question. It contains a wonderful picture of the relationship between three young friends: "And a little further on, I suddenly read something that I could not believe my eyes: Jews, Poles and Russians are the worst enemies of Ukraine. In front of this poster, for the first time in my life, I thought about who I was. My mother is Ukrainian, my father is a pure-blooded Russian. So I am half Ukrainian and half Russian. It turns out that I am my own enemy. My best friends were Shurka Matses, who was half Jewish, and Bolek Kaminski, who was half Polish. I could not understand this."

All of them were half "Aryan" Ukrainians, whom the world did not persecute at the time and who could be said to be favoured. They were their own enemies. Today, each of us is Slovak, Russian, Jewish, Ukrainian—and human at the same time. The enmity between us is no longer on the level of "Russian-Jew" or "Slovak-Russian", but "human to human". We all have this human dimension in common. And so for each of us, any conflict is self-destructive. We no longer have anything to stand out.

In the case of Auschwitz and Treblinka, the world had a lot to shut out, there was war, unreliable information, and no way to get into the centre of the violence. The victims did not have their own states behind them, maintaining diplomatic relations with their tormentors. A similar case today would be, and is, proof of the failure of civilisation and humanism around the world.

However, I think that the first lesson can be drawn from your challenge. If we put Babyn Yar and Auschwitz on the same platform, I think it is wrong to write about the "Jewish" genocide. The concentration camps were first filled by German democrats, and later by anti-fascists of other nations. Including Jews. To divide them at this point into Jews and non-Jews would be as insane and necrophiliac as shooting "in the name of the people and faith" in Karabakh. Conclusions can be drawn immediately.

The Czech psychologist Miroslav Plzak says that if the conspiracy of the worthy is not revived in the world, we will become defenceless. It depends on our attentiveness, activity or inactivity whether a teacher will give a student a bad grade because he or she does not agree with his or her view, whether our children will refuse to sit at the desk with a classmate because he or she is a Gypsy, or whether a drunken neighbour will beat his child to death tomorrow. We need to realise that a lot depends on the degree of our responsibility every day. Perhaps even everything. And if we manage to deal with these seemingly mundane situations, I think that in the event of a threat, all of humanity as a whole has a chance to survive.

Ritalii Zaslavskyi, writer (Kyiv)
I. First of all, it is neither a symbol nor an abstraction. At least for me. My grandparents, in whose house I spent my childhood, died in Babyn Yar. This is the first thing. Secondly, it was fate that my entire post-war life was spent next to this cursed ravine. I used to wander there every day, I knew every path, I saw a transparent ditch, the bottom of which was covered with bones, so the ground was not visible. At first, everything around was deserted, then, starting in 1966, people gathered, they were dispersed, and sometimes authorities tried to use them to hold cynical rallies, the essence of which was that anyone but Jews died in Babyn Yar, or at best, "including Jews". This is how all this entered my life experience. And how did I get along with this experience, you ask? I didn't get along with it, I live with it, I live every day and every hour!

II. The memory of the Babyn Yar tragedy as a genocide of Jews is acutely present primarily in the Jewish national consciousness. I mean the general, popular consciousness. For Jews, Babyn Yar is not only the past, but also a constant fear of the future. Of course, people belonging to other nations are not indifferent to this tragedy, but here we can only talk about a few, about conscientious intellectuals who are tortured by the imperfection of life in general. Everybody is feeling bad, everybody is living hard, and the mass consciousness of other nations is not very burdened by the memory of the Jewish tragedy of half a century ago. I am not saying this to reproach anyone; I am simply stating a fact. On the contrary, I can understand people who are absorbed in the impossible existence of the present, in the difficulties of the daily struggle for survival.

But at the same time, it is also incorrect to say that "this sea of blood is no longer distinguishable". These are the reasons for the concerns that have inspired the questions in this questionnaire. Otherwise, why would they be sent out?

III. What it means: "Have WE learnt the lessons of history?" Who is this "WE"? All *WE* are many *I*. Some have learnt, some have not, some consider Babyn Yar to be the past, horrible, but the past. Others consider it the future. But many people are just annoyed: isn't there too much talk about it? Maybe it's enough? There's no "we" in that!

IV. I don't know whether humanity will develop a survival mechanism on the threshold of the third millennium, no one knows. It is trying to. With the help of the UN; and also by indulging in reflection, debate, and self-reflection. Yet every time people came to the edge of the abyss, floundering in pools of blood, they suddenly stopped. Perhaps the instinct of self-preservation will save us now. Or perhaps it will not. The means of instantaneous destruction of all things are too terrible. Will they always be in safe hands? And even now, are they in safe hands? Unfortunately, state and national ambitions often outweigh reason and common sense.

Yuri Karabchievsky, writer (Russia)
I. There are phenomena on earth that make life unbearable. Not at the moment, not for anyone in particular, but life in general. Babyn

Yar is one of them. To live in the world while Babyn Yar exists is impossible, shameful, unworthy. But we live. I don't know why. We have a certain mechanism independent of us that establishes a shameful balance of bad and good, although in fact there can be no balance, this is obvious. Babyn Yar, even if it were the only case of mass murder of people, would outweigh all the good of all time. But this I say now, slowly thinking. And then, when I found out about him, and even more so, when I saw that terrible monument, with a muscular sailor and a courageous partisan, I thought, frankly, not so much about the torment of those who were killed there (not quite there, in another place, I know...), but about the abomination of our current relatively peaceful existence. It said, if I am not mistaken: "In this place, German fascists killed 100 thousand Soviet citizens." This "Soviet citizens" was the worst. It was the repeated extermination of those thousands of Jews already killed once, less, perhaps, cruel, but no less cynical. Jews came here — to remember Jews, anti-Semites came here — to curse Jews, but there seemed to be no Jews, they were not just shot once and thrown into a ditch on each other — they were permanently erased from memory, expelled not from life any more, but from death. That, in my opinion, is the worst thing in this story. I did not really like what Yevtushenko wrote then, thirty years ago, but now I feel differently about this poem. This is the case when poetic virtues become secondary, and conscience, decency, courage come out in advance. I generally treat him differently, but here is exactly the case when he really "said for everyone..." And it is still impossible to live...

II. I remember that when I told about Babi Yar to my, for example, fellow workers from the factory or other ordinary Soviet citizens, they could not understand my indignation in any way, they were surprised, and very sincerely, why it was necessary to distinguish Jewish victims individually: all peoples suffered, there were many Russians who died. And when I told them that no, these are different things, that, of course, is a pity for everyone, but the Germans killed the Russians as their enemies and only in those, mainly, cases when they were their enemies or seemed to be. But Jews were killed as Jews, for the fact of birth — and this is a completely different matter. They shied away from me, as if they were afraid of something, and tried to transfer the conversation to another topic. And they were not cold, indifferent people, they were mostly decent people, not evil, and not even stupid. I have very little optimism about the compassion of one people for another. Man to man—yes, he can sympathize sometimes, even with selflessness and sacrifice. But a people to another people—no, they are too heavy, too inert and too egocentric structures. A person can be selfless, a people cannot. It is always locked into its own needs and will never knowingly harm himself. And it cannot feel another's pain as its own.

III. I was in Armenia during the events in Sumgait, Khojaly, Baku, Kirovabad. I talked with a girl who was raped by eighteen people, and her sister was hiding under the bed. And with the brothers, in whose eyes their father's head was broken, and on a mattress they dragged him, covered with blood, from room to room, retreating in front of a crowd of pogromists, and when there was nowhere to retreat, they rushed at the attackers with knives, and these suddenly retreated. It was 1988, three years ago. And recently, in an Armenian village in Karabakh, a thirteen-year-old boy was killed, having previously cut off his ears. No, I don't believe in any lessons. Lessons are taken only by those who are already taught. And you can only teach someone who wants to learn. We want to see evil under a separate sign to know for sure—here it is. But it occurs in a completely unexpected place. For example, we say to ourselves: "Of course, Islam is a cruel religion, especially ethnopsychology." But Georgian Christian militants abuse Ossetian Muslims—and all our constructions break down. And then Muslim Uzbeks slaughter Turkish Muslims... And yet, apparently, in all these cases, we are dealing with a manifestation of what could be called Asianism, without offending either individuals or entire peoples. Perhaps in this unification is the key and some kind of hope? I mean, Europeanization.

IV. There is an undoubted evolution. Europe, after all, with all the deviations, is incomparably more protected now from bursts of popular idiocy. Needless to say, "Europe" is no longer so much a geographical concept as a legal and sociocultural one. England, France, Japan, Taiwan, Holland and so on. If there is a way, then it is in Europeanization, but this is a theoretical, contemplative way. Frankly, I do not think that in the near future all peoples and countries will follow it. Still, our—each of us—salvation in this life lies in the limitations of our imagination. if we didn't have this protective reflex, we should all have committed suicide, barely knowing about Auschwitz, Sumgait and Babyn Yar. "It's scary to live in this world—there is no comfort in it. The wind howls at dawn, the wolves gnaw at a hare." But instead of returning the ticket, like Ivan Karamazov, we put a plate with potatoes and chicken on the table in front of the TV, chew and watch the next mutilated corpse being dragged, not forgetting, however, to shake our heads with contrition. I do not know, perhaps, if we are already so tenacious, we must at least speak, not be silent, and not only on certain dates, and not only en masse, and not only after, but better at the same moment. Do you remember, when asked from the audience three or four years ago, what he hates above all, Yuri Vlasov answered briefly: "Collective insight!"

Grigory Kotsur, writer (Kyiv)
I. For me, the tragedy of Babyn Yar is one of the most terrible events in our history. That's how my life experience (and not only mine) perceived this event. Can it live in my memory? Of course. It is impossible not to remember this

II. Babyn Yar is certainly a genocide, the embodiment of the official policy of fascism towards the Jewish people. From this point of view, ideological tricks, another interpretation of this fact, attempts to take away from the Jews the sad privilege of being the main victim—all this is hard to understand.

Is this sea of blood invisible in the memory of the peoples of Ukraine and the world? Undoubtedly, no sea of blood can erode from human memory—even if there are crimes of this magnitude committed later.

III. Have we learned the lessons of history? Unfortunately, life shows us that humankind ignores those lessons, at best—learns them in part. So, for example, if the initiators of the October events of 1917 were to study the history of the French Revolution in the exposition of Thomas Carlyle and realize the inevitable consequences of the forcible imposition of recipes for universal happiness, their driving enthusiasm would be somewhat diminished. Unfortunately, this did not happen.

IV. On the threshold of the third millennium we have Karabakh, events in Yugoslavia, etc. The scale of the ecological danger to humanity is ahead of their awareness. In general, a person is arranged in such a way that he or she perceives adequately only an immediate, today's threat to his existence. Barriers? They are well known — spirituality, culture, science. But for them to be effective, we probably need some more stages of human evolution.

Myroslav Marynovych, writer (Lviv)
I. Babyn Yar entered my life as a young man as a tragedy "with a double bottom": officially — as a mass grave of SOVIET citizens, and unofficially (as mentioned almost in a whisper, with a taste of protest against the authorities) — as a bloody trace of the genocide of JEWS.

Babyn Yar, along with other symbols of satanic cruelty, became for me evidence that humanity is actually seriously ill with a special type of epilepsy. From time to time, with sad regularity, it must break down, fall (remember, epilepsy is popularly known as "falling sickness") in a convulsion of terror, sadism and horror, in order to wake up and, wiping the bloody foam, atone for grave sin. The word "must" here is a tribute to history, but not a fatal forecast for the future.

II. Yes, Babyn Yar is a symbol primarily of the genocide of the Jewish people. And any silence of this fact not only fills the soul of the Jew with pity and resentment, but also distorts world history. I suppose, however, that in the minds of many more citizens of the former Soviet Union, the word "Soviet" obscures the expressive national orientation of the massacre in Babyn Yar.

But the acuteness of awareness of national grief often causes another aberration of history — awareness of oneself as "the most offended people." Such a problem faces many nations, not just Jews. For example, no matter what torment my Ukrainian heart felt from the photographs of the half-decomposed corpses of the victims of the famine of the 1933 or from the awareness of the bloody mowing in my people during the Gulag harvest, I have no right to forget neither Babyn Yar nor the tragic Promethean attachment of Armenians to the Caucasus Mountains and the horror of their equally regular genocides. I dare not forget about the Kampuchean experiments and the torn body of the Kurdish people.

There is something contrary to God in trying to exalt one's suffering above the suffering of others. So it is possible not to notice half-decayed Ukrainian embroidered shirt in ditches of Babyn Yar or a small Star of David, for example, in Drohobych dungeon of NKVD.

IV. Answering the question of how to protect the humankind from suicide, I still cannot get around the religious perspective of the world, which I trust and without which I cannot think of a future. Humanity is not Baron Munchausen and will not pull itself out of the quagmire by the collar. The phenomenon of outside help, the parental hand must necessarily appear. But this requires one prerequisite: a person must be capable of a powerful volitional effort towards the Good, to which Heaven will respond.

If we pin our hopes on Evil, which in our time is manifested in ethnic or religious hatred, military aggression or violence, then Evil will respond to us. But it will be the last twilight of the world, after which night will come.

But if we want the triumph of Good, we must reveal it in ourselves, in people and in the wise formulas of cohabitation. Everyone must become a messiah to himself and trust in the laws of the Good, without looking at how many people around him went the same way. Unfortunately, this task cannot be divided into clear paragraphs of the political program. It is not the political party that will save us from disaster, but the human heart.

Mykhailo Moskalenko, writer (Kyiv)
I kept the memory of Babyn Yar — my personal memory — from my immediate childhood impressions and memories. I was born in 1948 in Kyiv, on Lukyanivka, near the *Ukrkabel* plant. My grandfather and grandmother are buried at the Lukyanivka cemetery — a few hundred meters from Babyn Yar. From the age of 5-6 years I

knew—because everyone knew—about the mass executions of Jews in the fall of 1941, and about the extermination of people of different nationalities in the same ravine and in the Syrets concentration camp of 1941-43, and about the execution of the *Dynamo Kyiv* football team, which defeated the German *Luftwaffe* team in occupied Kyiv. The famous Kurenivka disaster of March 13, 1961, that clay whirlwind, which I witnessed, was perceived by many people as "revenge of the earth" for two decades of official silencing of the Babyn Yar tragedy. When I remember this, the lines from Ivan Franko's masterpiece, the poem *Moses* (one of the highest achievements of Ukrainian literature of all time, based on Hebrew history) come to my mind: "You, generation of blind men, understand and remember: if you destroy the living soul, the stones will speak." And I am part of the "generation of blind men", too—after all, the whole truth about Babyn Yar comes into the light of day only now. In the 60s, Ilya Ehrenburg, Evgeny Yevtushenko, Anatoly Kuznetsov, Ivan Dziuba, Viktor Nekrasov laid the foundation for this. But much of what they said to the world in the 60s, especially about the tragedies on Lukyanivka, Kurenivka and Syrets, was well known "unofficially." Although, of course, not all. This is a component of my spiritual experience. Now I live on Demyan Korotchenko Street, and my windows face the Babyn Yar.

II. It is difficult to talk about the peoples of the world and of the former Soviet Union. It is easier to say about the peoples of Ukraine. The memory of the tragedy of Babyn Yar, of the genocide of the Jewish people, is undoubtedly alive. And, moreover, we understand that Babyn Yar is only the most noticeable peak of the terrible iceberg, whose full extent is gradually becoming clear. After all, not only Kyiv, but almost every other city in Ukraine, and far from only Ukraine, has its own Babyn Yar. And yet, even after the Armenian genocide of 1915, even after the Ukrainian genocide of 1933, the Jewish genocide of 1941 and the tragedy of Babi Yar, in the first place, cannot fade in people's memory. I am convinced that the blood shed here will not be forgotten.

III. The lessons of Auschwitz and Babyn Yar are not a metaphor. I am sure that the vast majority of people of Ukraine of all nationalities have learned these lessons. In the 20th century, several tens of millions of people were killed in Ukraine. Demographers, it seems, have not yet calculated a final figure for Ukraine — they have not summed up the military losses of all warring parties and the victims of the civilian population of the First World War and the Civil War, of famine 1921, repression of the 20s — early 30s, collectivization, the Holodomor of 1932-33, the Stalinist repressions of 1937-38, the NKVD terror against the Western Ukrainian population of 1939-41, military losses of the Second World War, Hitler's terror in the occupied territories of Ukraine, and in particular the genocide of Jews, the fratricidal war in Western Ukraine 1943-53 pp., the famine of 1946-67, the post-war Stalinist repressions, including the extermination of prisoners of war, the struggle against "cosmopolitanism" and — at the same time — against Ukrainian "bourgeois nationalism." I think that the democratic movement of Ukraine therefore opposes anti-Semitism in all its manifestations precisely because the bloody lessons of the history of the 20th century call for harmony and true friendship and mutual understanding of the peoples of Ukraine. Only this gives hope for the survival and future of the Jewish, Ukrainian, and other peoples of independent Ukraine. The fact that the Ukrainian state is built around a general democratic, not a particular national idea, makes it possible to hope for the best: the Jewish and Ukrainian peoples will cease to be a bargaining chip, a card in an imperial game.

IV. Humankind can avoid suicide if common sense prevails. Andrei Sakharov answered these questions best of all, it is difficult to add anything to what he said. Of great importance is the break in thinking, which made possible significant changes in the process of disarmament of nuclear superpowers.

Grigory Pomerantz, writer (Russia)
I. Babyn Yar is the place where my mother could lie. She left Kyiv timely, but she could be to late. This is the place where the Kyiv *nomenklatura* wanted to build a stadium.

II. There is no common memory of genocide. The Germans were horrified by what their fathers and grandfathers did. The Turks are not horrified, and still hate Armenians. I simplify a little, but this is the position of their government and leading newspapers.

In the 20th century, there were many massacres, murders of entire categories of people, harmful from the point of view of semi-science. Sometimes they were killed on ethnic grounds, sometimes on social grounds. The latter should not be called genocide, but stratocide (for example, the elimination of *kulaks* as a class). I'm not going to judge what's worse. In my opinion, Vasily Grossman wrote about this most correctly: both are equally terrible.

III. All mass murder is based on the idea that personality doesn't matter, that class or people or nation or race is more important. This is a very old hierarchy of values. A tribe that defeated another tribe could completely destroy it. Then it was not called genocide. Traces of tribal wars were preserved both in the Bible and in a Slavic chronicle: "They died like Avars, and there were no tribe or descendants left." From time to time, such an idea later mastered the masses (for example, the Haidamaks who captured the town of Uman).

Today, in connection with the collapse of the communist superpower and the growth of national consciousness, there is a return to tribalism. It seems to people that they were exiles in a non-national state, and in a new, ethnically pure one, they will find themselves. So the Communists dreamed — to find themselves in a just proletarian state, without superfluous, exploitative classes. The new world is no worse than the old. True liberation from Bolshevism is liberation from the spirit of hatred. This is not in one idea or another, but in hatred of someone else's, socially or nationally alien — anyway. The real liberation from totalitarianism is in the hierarchy of values, which was established two thousand years ago: "I brought not peace, but a sword. I will divorce a father and a son." Personality is existentially deeper than the people. The personality is directly rooted in God, and the deepest root of the personality is not in the national soil, but in the sky. This does not mean that a nation or family does not matter, but their importance is lower than the dignity of an individual. Until this is realized, the shooting in Karabakh, in Ossetia, in Transnistria will not stop. The conflict in

Crimea is revenge for the gross violation of the rights of Tatars, convicted not as individuals, not for individual crimes, but collectively, as a whole people. Now the two peoples who divided the Tatar houses among them were ruled by hatred. Without a way out of hatred there will be no peace.

IV. We are on the verge of the greatest crisis in human history. For the first time, humans have the means to destroy the entire biosphere. Our sense of responsibility is lower than our technical capabilities. Nations are like teenagers who have learned to shoot. What to hope for? Awareness of danger and growing sense of responsibility. The rise of global consciousness. If there is no global consciousness, if the values of man and mankind stand below national interests, national prestige and national pride, we will certainly perish. This is true for the planet as a whole, and for that part of it that was once the Russian Empire.

Marlena Rakhlina, writer (Kharkiv)
I. Babyn Yar is for me a symbol of the atrocities committed against the Jewish people. As a matter of fact, it had nothing to do with me personally, that is, none of my relatives or even acquaintances died either in Babyn Yar or in Drobytsky Yar (near Kharkov, where I live). But we live not only with what happened to us personally. In addition, I have enough reason and imagination to understand that all this is just a matter of chance, and therefore I feel it as if myself and my loved ones really died in Babyn Yar.

II. If the tragedy of Babyn Yar had not been hushed up, and for so long that only 50 years later we are talking about it frankly, I would have put it in the line of bloody events in the history of mankind. But the cynicism of that silence, the cynicism of the fact that we ourselves could remember everything that happened only 50 years later, makes it unheard even among the tragedies of the 20th century.

III. Of course, this became a metaphor. I would very much like to think otherwise, but I have to agree that the main lesson of history is that humanity does not learn from it. Otherwise, why did Kampuchea, Sumgait, and Baku become possible?

IV. I don't know! I have no reason to think that we are close to this now, just on the threshold of the third millennium, and when I read the prophecies of the geniuses of the 20th century about how happy people will be in the future (like prophecies of Chekhov whom I sincerely respect), my heart hurts so much, like cut with a blade.

That's all, but since I have been writing poems for many years, and even published three poetry collections, let me add a poem to my answers to your questionnaire.

I'm a Jewess
In my distant happy childhood
I didn't know I was Jewish:
Hitler explained all this to me,
and then Stalin joined him.
They were good people,
and diligent, believe me!
They taught me so good,
that I remembered for the rest of my life:
I'm not Russian, I'm Jewish!

I am a Jew and a daughter of Jews,
And my children are Jewish, too.
It means that our fate is prison
And persecution or exile,
And the contempt of the non-Jews;
Choose what you like best!

I'm used to this knowledge,
I realized my significance,
And I am proud of my people,
Of their wisdom and talent,
Of their universal destiny,
Of their great skill
To be at home among strangers
And be strangers among natural Jews.

But there's something more important:
We invented God, the God's Son was born among us;
The Spirit of God has filled my people,
And since then it blows where it wants.

Yevhen Sverstyuk, writer (Kyiv)

I. Babyn Yar is in my mind a place of a terrible crime, for which is difficult to find a name. War has taught people to devalue and neglect the sacred gift of life. But here we have something more than that: this is a challenge to God's creation.

II. I think that this tragedy is perceived by most people relatively, in quantitative terms, although the number here is less significant.

III. To some extent, historical memory awakens consciousness, especially if it is associated with the International Tribunal. But is that a lesson? Baku seems to me a "considered" lesson: there was already punitive indecision.

IV. Recent events lead to optimistic reflections on the human mind. But it is difficult to explain all this by the human mind. It seems that this mind is placed in front of a broken trough. I wonder if people will be able to stop silent suicide without war, if they will escape from the epidemic of consumerism and return to spiritual sources.

Yakiv Honigsman, historian (Lviv)

I. Babyn Yar is one of the stages, or rather one of the links in the general strategy of genocide (extermination) of Jews in Europe, planned by Nazi Germany even before the outbreak of World War II. This policy began to be implemented even before the war, gained more and more outspoken character on the eve of the war (Kristallnacht on November 9-10 1938, eviction of Jews from Germany, pogroms in cities bordering Poland, etc.), was cynically implemented in the first year of World War II on the Polish territory captured by German fascists. After the attack of Nazi Germany on the Soviet Union, in the summer of 1941, this policy began to be applied to the Jews of western Belarus, western Ukraine, and the Baltic states. (Mass executions of Jews in towns and cities of the occupied territory of the Baltic states, western regions of Belarus and Ukraine, the destruction of "small ghettos" in western Poland and later on the occupied territory of Ukraine and Belarus). The Kyiv tragedy, unlike the catastrophes that took place in the summer of 1941, is distinguished by the fact that it was carried out within a few days, without prior isolation of Jews in the ghetto. It was "well" planned and, in German, "well" organised, based on the extensive experience gained by the barbarians in previous "actions" against Jews. Babyn Yar once again confirmed the irrefutable truth that if Jews had had their own statehood, such a tragedy would not have come to pass. All hopes for the humanity of Western democracies and Soviet "internationalism" turned out to be empty illusions.

It is impossible to get along with the catastrophe of a people. We must remember this and draw appropriate conclusions. This means that we should not rely on "public disavowals of anti-Semitism" but on more realistic guarantees of the security of the Jewish people, as well as other ethnic groups. Stalin repeatedly publicly denied anti-Semitism, but in practice he carried out a real spiritual genocide of the Jews of the USSR, mass terror of all unwanted people, first Poles, Ukrainians, Germans, Jews, then other ethnic groups and their intellectuals, the spiritual aristocracy of these peoples — the brains of national minorities.

II. For the peoples of Ukraine and other peoples of our country, the memory of the Jewish catastrophe in Kyiv and other cities is very darkened and obscured. For Soviet people, the memory is tainted by the numerous "actions" of Stalin's terror against various groups of people of many nationalities. Too many crazy things happened in the 1930s and after the war in relation to the intelligentsia of the Ukrainian, Jewish, and other peoples. This policy is still being used to suppress people's memories. Therefore, we cannot talk about the memory of the murdered Jews at Babyn Yar. Many people have become indifferent to this tragedy. The reason for this is that for 50 years it was not only not talked about, but attempts were made to erase it from our memory, to distort the facts, and to obscure the events associated with the catastrophe of world and Ukrainian Jewry.

III. Auschwitz and other places of mass extermination of Jews have become symbolic sites of tragedy, of the historical catastrophe of Jewry. Other nations have experienced similar catastrophes, too. Unfortunately, there is no guarantee that they cannot happen again. If neo-Hitlerite organisations in Germany and fascist groups in the USSR could emerge after such a catastrophe, there is no guarantee that genocide against Jews or other peoples will not happen again. This suggests that many people have not taken into account the lessons of history. History and its tragic pages can repeat themselves.

IV. In order to prevent the catastrophes that occurred during and after the Second World War from happening again, and to prevent such tragedies in the future, it is necessary to create reliable barriers to such madness on the scale of the whole of humanity and the whole world. It is necessary to develop a criminal code against all carriers of anti-human concepts, to judge people who preach ideas of racism, anti-Semitism, hatred of other peoples and ethnic groups as harshly as possible. Moreover, these laws should be practised in all countries. So, these laws should be adopted internationally with the warning that ignoring them will result in sanctions against the country that refuses to enforce them against their violators. Only in this way can we hope that the past madness will not be repeated.

***

At the same time, I want to talk about a phenomenon that has not yet been studied, which I call the "PRICE OF LIFE". I am talking about cases of helping the doomed (Jews, Roma, mentally ill, and others), when both those whom one tried to help and those who tried to do so (sometimes together with their families) were killed.

In contrast to what happened in Central Europe, Nazi laws and regulations in the East declared that the only punishment for helping the enemies of Nazism was death.

Yad Vashem, the Israeli Institute for Holocaust Research and Remembrance, has collected thousands of testimonies of Jewish rescue during World War II. For the most part, these are materials about events about which there is sufficiently convincing evidence, so the algorithm proposed for the study and awarding of the Righteous Among the Nations excluded those cases in which potential witnesses were killed by the Nazis along with those they were trying to save.

According to the staff, there are thousands more cases in Yad Vashem's archives in which the title of Righteous Among the Nations was not awarded for various reasons: the witnesses did not live to see the decision, some circumstances were not convincing enough for the distinguished commission, etc.

In the archives of the Centre for Jewish Studies, we also have testimonies of more than 120 people who were killed by the Nazis for trying to help doomed Jews. Their names were found by our staff members Zhanna Kovba and Anna Prokhorova, who conducted a thorough research of archival documents, both Ukrainian and German, analysed research by local historians, and collected testimonies from neighbours or relatives (oral history).

As far as I know, similar research was conducted in Poland even earlier. After all, in the "Jolly Barrack," as this country was called in Soviet times, the conditions for researching history were much more liberal than in the Soviet Union, especially in Ukraine, where the topic of the Holocaust and the rescue of Jews, like many other historical topics, was taboo.

It is only in recent decades that the topic of Jewish rescue has been given its own meaning. It is clear that, after more than half a century, much evidence has been lost, and many potential witnesses have passed away and have not told what they knew. Here are just a few of the records of stories of failed attempts to save the doomed that Anna Prokhorova has made available to me:

1. The story of the Kulak family from the town of Huziiiv, Bolekhiv district, Ivano-Frankivsk region.
The Kulak family was wealthy and respected. The three of them ran the household: Anna, Mykola, and his younger brother, Stepan. The family had four young daughters (the eldest was 6, the youngest was only a year old), and Anna was expecting her fifth child. The Kulaks took in as many people as a specially built bunker could accommodate, hiding them and feeding them. However, in the spring of 1943, policemen appeared in the courtyard of the estate. During the raid, the Germans, without going down into the bunker, threw grenades and shot at the Jews, grabbed Mykola and Stepan, forced them to drag everyone out of the hiding place and bury them half alive in the yard, and then took the brothers to the Gestapo. They never

returned from there. Anna was lucky to escape that day. Some time later, she gave birth to a son, Mykola, who never knew his father.

2. The story of Kateryna Sikorska from Lviv.
Kateryna Sikorska hid the two sons of a doctor she knew, Anatolii and Leonid Kresel (14 and 15 years old). She also helped Mykhailo Kliar (50), a photographer who managed to escape from the ghetto. Kateryna and her daughters Iryna and Khrystyna hid and fed the men from July 1942 to March 1943, before the Gestapo came to their house one day. Kateryna was not at home at the time. Her younger daughter Khrystyna ran after her mother, and together they hid at the neighbour's house. At that time, the Germans interrogated and beat Khrystyna's older sister Iryna, but the girl did not confess to the location of the cache. However, the hiding place was discovered anyway, the Jews were taken to prison, and the owners managed to escape that day, but the Germans were waiting for them the next day when the Sikorski returned for their belongings. Kateryna was arrested and sentenced to death. The lawyer told Kateryna's daughters that if the family had money, something could have been done, but they did not, and Mrs Sikorska was shot.

There are dozens of similar tragic stories to tell. However, it is important to at least try to outline the motives of those who helped others at the risk of their own lives:

1. The desire to repay.
Ukrainians and Poles often helped their former teachers or managers of organisations that had treated their employees well in the past. For example, Theodoria Korzh from the town of Zboriv in the Ternopil region tried to save the family of Sarah Pulover, who had been her teacher at a tailoring school before the war. And Wasiuta Węgrzynowska from the village of Zahaypil helped the owners of the farm where she worked before the war.

2. Helping friends or their relatives.
Such help was often provided. For example, Anna Konska from Przemyśl knew the deceased parents of a fourteen-year-old girl, Donia Zwebern (Tweben), and so she hid her in her home.

3. Adherence to God's laws and human values.
One of the motivations for the behaviour of certain people and communities was the desire to follow God's laws and human values. Mefodii and Kseniia Bohatski from the village of Dovhovolia (in the present-day Rivne region) were believers—Baptists. As believers, they considered it their duty to save all the Jews they could and thanked God for the opportunity to do so.

4. "We couldn't leave them without help."
There were people who answered the question "Why did you risk everything to try to save them?"—"We couldn't leave them without help." I call this motive the "phenomenon of historically formed tolerance". It is most pronounced in cities and towns like Bolekhiv in Ivano-Frankivsk region, Minkivtsi in Khmelnytsky regiion, and Przemysl in Lviv region, with their diverse population and the combination of different cultural traditions. In such towns, there were usually a church and a synagogue next to each other, and various educational institutions and printing houses. During the Holocaust, people who grew up in an atmosphere of property and traditional tolerance and freedom saved their former Jewish neighbours and colleagues because they could not help but do so. Through all the trials—by the authorities, poverty, and tragedies—the elderly preserved the humanity, tolerance, and rejection of condemnation, betrayal, and denunciation that had been rooted in generations, and defended the belief that "we and the Jews share the same blood." Almost every family saved someone, helped someone. And what is very important, people knew that Jews were being hidden in this or that house, but they kept silent (at least we could not find a single case of betrayal or denunciation).

Among those about whom we have testimonies were those who collaborated with the Polish or Ukrainian underground. For example, Yonna Sepravsky from Lviv managed to obtain documents through the Polish underground for a Jewish girl, Miriam, whom she was hiding, and Antonina Kulakovska from Rivne, thanks to her connections with the Ukrainian underground, was able to warn and hide Ivraim Fishman on the day of the mass shooting of Jews; she was later executed by the Gestapo.

A special mention should be made of atypical rescue situations. The interpretation of human actions by Soviet historians, depicting a black-and-white picture of events, is the heroism of Soviet soldiers and the despotic Nazis and police. This format does not include the humanity of German soldiers and policemen, and all those who collaborated with the occupation authorities in one way or another.

People could cooperate or simply coexist with the Nazi authorities in order to be saved. For example, the head of an orphanage in Vinnytsia, Lydia Postolovska, whose pupils and staff included 19 Jews, had to cooperate with the occupation authorities in order to feed 70 children, not to mention save the Jews.

Many of the people I have mentioned were repressed by the Soviet authorities for collaborating with the Germans. Their names, as well as the names of all those courageous and desperate people who risked their own lives and the lives of their families to save others, urgently need to be immortalised in the memory of our society, because their actions are priceless from the point of view of humanity.

17. Russia's Use of Holocaust History to Discredit Ukrainians and Ukraine

In the first half of the 1930s, after Nazism came to power, German intellectuals sneered: "Who would believe the nonsense they are talking? Who would believe the propaganda dumb things from Goebbels?" However, over time, as the propaganda became more powerful and other sources of information were restricted, step by step what seemed unreal at first became a reality: German society professed the Nazi ideology.

Similar processes are taking place in Russia today. Access to the world's media is severely limited for Russians, and rashist propaganda is heard on TV, the Internet, newspapers, textbooks, literature, games for children and adults...

"History and political memory play a crucial role in contemporary Russian ideology, shaping collective identity and motivation for political decision-making," writes Ukrainian researcher Viacheslav Likhachev.

Russian ideologues have shaped the main narratives of their ideology, in which the Great Patriotic War (as they call the Second World War) occupies a central place in the official historical cult. One of the components of this ideology is the use of the Holocaust. For the outside world, this is an accusation addressed to all opponents of modern Russia of their participation in the Holocaust. Being fascists (rashists) in spirit, they accuse their opponents of fascism. Timothy Snyder has called this schizofascism.

The Ukrainian liberation movement is presented in this narrative as the main perpetrator of genocide. This is one of the justifications for denying Ukraine's right to exist. In Russian ideology, the Holocaust is interpreted differently than in civilised countries — as a Jewish tragedy. It is largely kept silent. Much more emphasis is placed on the heroism of resistance and the fact that the Red Army saved Jews from extermination (the role of other countries in the anti-Hitler coalition is silenced).

There is one more thing that happens that is virtually unknown in Western versions of the tragedy. The emphasis is placed on the fact that the main tragedy befell not the Jews, but the Soviet people. The stories of the Holocaust and the siege of Leningrad are presented as identical, although in fact they are fundamentally different. The former is based on racist ideology, while the latter is based on the inadequate actions of the Soviet government.

An integral part of these Russian theories is the interpretation of Ukrainian-Jewish relations, which continues the narratives of the Soviet era. The emphasis is on Jewish tragedies from different periods of history, blaming Ukrainians for them. The pogroms of the Civil War are necessarily called Petliura's. However, in those terrible years, pogroms were organised by virtually all the warring parties (Denikinites, individual gangs that had no national characteristics, the Bolsheviks, among others). Ukrainian nationalists are accused of killing Jews in the Second World War almost more often than the Nazis.

When analysing Soviet propaganda narratives about Jewish history, one of the leaders of the Ukrainian dissident movement, Yevhen Sverstiuk, said: "Few people today remember the Psalms of David, but everyone knows anti-Semitic jokes. This is evidence of the plebeianisation of the Soviet person."

The Soviet and Russian narratives also systematically falsified the history of Ukrainian tragedies by blaming Jews. Everything was done to avoid presenting the real picture of interethnic relations. The authorities pitted some against others. In the Soviet years, powerful ideological structures worked for this purpose, publishing hundreds of books, thousands of articles, dozens of documentaries, and so on. The archive of our Centre for Jewish Studies contains thousands of pieces of this literature. In today's Russia, all of these concepts are being spread vigorously.

For decades, Soviet and later Russian propaganda blamed the extermination of Jews not so much on the Nazis and Stalin and his supporters as on Ukrainian political leaders, descendants of Petliura or Bandera. The public was not supposed to know about the efforts of Petliura's government to counter the pogroms. A number of Porgomniks were shot on Petliura's orders. We at the

Center for Jewish Studies published archival documents that testify to this. Only when Petliura was no longer in command of the troops and his army was defeated by Bolshevik units did the pogroms begin to multiply. They were organised by numerous gangs, which were numerous in those years.

The Ukrainian national movement, of which Stepan Bandera was one of the leaders, also had anti-Semitic components at certain stages, as did virtually all right-wing parties in Europe at the time. Not to mention the fact that a number of countries were allies of the Nazis in this war: Austria, Hungary, Italy... Their involvement in the murder of Jews was much greater than that of the Banderites, whom Soviet and later Russian propaganda made symbols and the main perpetrators of the Holocaust.

Soviet and Russian narratives have always been and are false. There are many examples of this, both in history and today. Just one fact is that Stalin spoke of 7 million civilian casualties in the Soviet Union, while the world knew that 2.5 million Jews alone were killed in these lands. Everyone who understood at least something saw this lie. Even then, the theory of a heroic victory was born, replacing the truth about the tragedies of the war.

We, as the Centre for Jewish Studies at the Kyiv-Mohyla Academy, and the *Dukh i Litera* publishing house, have been countering these narratives to the best of our ability (we have published about 150 books). These books present modern theories of Jewish history and adequate versions of Ukrainian-Jewish relations to Ukrainian society. Our books are recommended for use in Ukrainian high schools. They are basic textbooks for bachelor's and master's degree programmes in Jewish studies at universities. The total print run of these books is over 120,000 copies.

The Soviet and Russian versions of the Babyn Yar tragedy are also part of the falsification of the memory of the Second World War. All of them silence the cooperation between Nazi Germany and the Soviet Union under the Molotov-Ribbentrop Pact. It was after this event that the Soviet population did not have information about Jewish tragedies in Germany or in the countries it occupied for several years. This contributed to the fact that many of those who died in the numerous "Babyn Yars" massacres waited for the "civilised" German military, not knowing that they would already never exist. Babyn Yar was not the first act of physical destruction of thousands of Jews during the Nazi invasion of Soviet territory. However, the Soviet authorities concealed these facts, and residents of Kyiv and Kharkiv were not informed about mass shootings in the territories captured by the Nazis earlier.

After the Second World War, the Soviet media accused Ukrainians of the shootings at Babyn Yar. But Jews, Roma, and the mentally ill were killed by special Nazi units. However, numerous Soviet and Russian publications refer to "Ukrainians, Ukrainians, Ukrainians...". The Nazis' accomplices were Soviet people, often prisoners of war, whose nationality (ethnicity) was never clarified.

After the end of the Second World War, the Soviet authorities concealed information about Nazi crimes against Jews for decades. The struggle for the memory of Babyn Yar lasted for decades and decades, just as the struggle for the memory of other tragedies of the Second World War. The authorities tried to replace the tragic truth of history with stories about the heroism of Soviet soldiers. In addition to the silencing of the Holocaust, there were manifestations of anti-Semitism in the postwar years: "doctors' cases", the fight against cosmopolitans, and the murder of members of the Jewish Anti-Fascist Committee.

Soviet and Russian propagandists largely shaped the concepts of the history of the Holocaust and Ukrainian participation in it that have been and continue to be spread throughout the world.

For various reasons, scholars in Europe and America had limited opportunities to study the actual course of events and the participation of various communities in the genocide of the Jewish people. At certain stages, foreign researchers did not have the opportunity to work with the archives of the Soviet Union at all. Much of the Russian archives are still closed today.

The Soviet and, today, Russian mass media had and still have a powerful network for disseminating their information. Much more than Ukrainian scholars and journalists have today. A few decades ago, the ratio between Russian and Ukrainian voices was even more disproportionate. Of course, in favour of Russia. There are many reasons for this. The first is the pseudo-statehood of

Ukraine for many years, when development of humanities, if they developed at all, was very slow, mostly in spite of, not because of, government policy. And while the situation has begun to change in recent decades, the balance of power is still far from being achieved, as fundamental narratives take decades, if not generations, to form. As a result, Soviet and later Russian narratives about the Holocaust and the guilt of Ukrainians in it are now being replicated around the world, far beyond Russia. The attention to these issues by Jewish communities, the world, and especially Israel, is understandable. But they, like other researchers of twentieth-century history in Eastern Europe, are largely dependent on established Soviet and Russian narratives.

Universities around the world have hundreds of departments of Slavic studies, de facto Russian studies, formed by scholars who profess Russian narratives. Many of these centres were created and operate with financial support and dependence on Russian money. Propaganda stereotypes are often replicated even by scholars who are enemies of communist ideology or Putin's Russia. It is also difficult for them to overcome their dependence on the powerful influences of concepts formed (falsified) over the years and decades in totalitarian (Stalinist), then authoritarian and now again totalitarian (Putinist) Russia.

Contemporary researchers emphasise that today's propaganda, amplified by the power of the latest mass media, is much stronger than the individual's ability to resist it. Scientists say that only about 20% of people are capable of resistance. The rest repeat the clichés of propaganda. Some Ukrainians took part in the crimes of Nazi Germany, but their role, both in Russian propaganda and in the replicated statements of Israeli leaders or politicians and scholars from other countries, is in most cases disproportionately exaggerated.

There were also numerous cases of Jewish rescue in Ukraine, about which the world knows very little. We have thousands of testimonies about this, and we try to tell about it as much as we can. The world does not know the facts of the rescue of hundreds of children in Basilian monasteries, which, unfortunately, we have not yet had time to tell convincingly, despite the fact that we have published a book about it, have similar translations of such books, documentaries and feature films, etc. I hope we will do this.

Every country has its own image of war. We know how the Poles interpret these events, how they are interpreted by the British, the French, the Russians. Even at a very general level, it is clear that these are completely different versions and it is almost impossible to build them integrally, looking for consensus. Each national community has its own myths that help the perception of history. For many years, stateless Ukraine had virtually no opportunity to form its image of war, this formation began only in the period of independence. This process is not fast and quite difficult, because our archives were opened only recently and the formation of domestic study of history, based on knowledge of the world literature, began not so long ago. It is very difficult for us to overcome Soviet stereotypes, because for a long time we were part of the Soviet world.

How can we resist anti-Ukrainian stereotypes? First of all, we must understand that the problem exists — a problem that cannot be solved quickly and requires the purposeful activity of scientists, politicians, citizens. Myroslav Marynovych once expressed the following opinion: "Only a strong democratic Ukraine can overcome the Soviet (Russian) myths of history, in particular in relations with national communities, including Jewish. We have been following this path for several decades together — Ukrainians and Jews, but there is no less long path ahead." We need scientific conferences aimed at finding the truth about the events of recent history. We need a comprehensive program that will cover the participation of liberal democratic scientists in the world to form adequate concepts of those events. There is a need for a targeted mass-media program in different languages to disseminate truthful information and refute Soviet and Russian falsifications. I hope that after the victory Ukrainian society will be able to pay more attention to this topic.

Today the world shudders from the atrocities of Russian barbarians in Ukraine, from the atrocities of Hamas militants in Israel. Could they have been foreseen to prevent them? I don't know. However, I place some of the blame for this on myself and other scientists and experts. Because we could not prove to the authorities of democratic countries the scale of threats and the inadequacy of world security systems. Unfortunately, it was not possible to protect numerous victims. Apparently, we are facing unprecedented challenges to world security. The previous mechanisms of peaceful coexistence of countries and peoples almost do not work. I hope that in the near future there will be new security mechanisms for humanity.

Leonid Finberg
30.10.2023

III
Memoirs

18. Ivan Dziuba

I don't remember how I met Ivan Dziuba. It happened around the second half of the 80s of the last century. But I remember very well how our relationship and cooperation began. Once, in the early 90s, we met by chance on Khreshchatyk. Ivan Mykhailovych told me that he was preparing a conference on Ukrainian-Jewish relations and invited me to join him in preparing the forum. To be honest, I was interested in this, because at that time I was trying to create and organise the activities of a number of Jewish centres and institutions. However, I had no public experience of organising conferences or speaking at them. Nevertheless, I responded because the offer was attractive to me. I wanted to get involved in this work. And we started working. Of course, the lion's share of that work was Ivan Mykhailovych's, because he knew almost all the researchers on the topic or public figures who had something to say. I also knew a number of people who were involved in Jewish history and culture, and step by step we began to put together a programme. At some stage of work we had dozens and dozens of names, and now, when more than thirty years have passed, I can say that they were stellar names. And so, we gradually worked our way up to holding a conference, which was held in 1991. The conference programme, in my opinion, was impressive. It brought together many people who were significant figures of that time. Historians such as Yaroslav Dashkevych and Martin Feller, former dissidents such as Yevhen Sverstiuk, Leonid Plyushch, Myroslav Marynovych... It is also worth mentioning Les Taniuk, a theatre director, writer, and political activist, as well as Leonid Plyushch, Mykola Riabchuk, Taras Vozniak, Myroslav Popovych, Oleksandr Burakovsky, Yakiv Suslensky, Oksana Zabuzhko, Semen Gluzman, Mykola Horbal, and Abram Katznelson.

Dziuba checked the names of the participants and edited the abstracts. I then took over the technical work and prepared the electronic version of the programme. I handed him two copies of the printed texts (computers and computer texts were not as widespread then as they would be in later years). Ivan Mykhailovych looked at these sheets and asked me, half-jokingly, but also half-seriously: "Leonid Kushelevych, are you sure that these copies are the same?" I said: "How could they not be?" "Okay, I'll check," he replied. A few days later, he brought me the same programme, but he had written it out by hand—he did not trust these technical means. However, later, in the following years, he learned how to work with computers and was already good at it.

***

I would like to tell you a little bit about the speeches at the conference. I understand that these are memories of Ivan Dziuba, but it is still largely his merit that such speeches and such people were there. I will quote what I believe to be the most interesting speeches. The keynote speech was by Yaroslav Dashkevych, who methodologically very clearly formulated the problems of researching Ukrainian-Jewish relations. He outlined what historians need to research in order to adequately present both the events of history and the problems of the present to free people and ideologically unbiased scholars. Dashkevich emphasised that Soviet pseudo-version and ideological concepts should be rejected forever: "We have convincing evidence that the nature of Ukrainian-Jewish relations was determined not by three or four years of bloody massacres, but by 356 years of more or less normal relations. Otherwise, it is quite certain that about a third of the world's Jews would not have gathered in Ukraine in the early twentieth century. It is difficult to imagine a situation in which almost 30% of the population would live in hell (as some foreign researchers sometimes try to portray Ukraine). The migration mobility of the Jewish population is well known: Jews have always had the opportunity in the seventeenth, eighteenth, and nineteenth centuries to emigrate from such hell under one condition: if it really was hell."

The speech of Yevhen Sverstiuk was also significant, as he outlined how Ukrainian-Jewish relations were interpreted in Soviet times.

"For the first time, perhaps, in history, the sons of Ukraine and the sons of Israel are meeting without intermediaries to begin cleaning the Augean stables. They have not been cleaned for centuries. There are stories of what happened and what did not happen, legends of enmity and unheard-of cruelty, of a Jew with the keys to the church and a Cossack with a rope in his hands. Instead of a horseshoe, the stereotypes of a Jewish extortionist and a Ukrainian butcher hang on the stable door.

The main thing is that there is not a single one of the thousands of thousands of facts of normal human cooperation between Ukrainians and Israelis in this stable—they were simply not recorded and remembered."

"Perhaps never before in history have the Ukrainian and Israeli peoples been so opposed as in the 'zone of internationalism'. The peoples have lost the true biblical basis that united them as a common sacred book of the Old Testament. After all, an illiterate Ukrainian peasant or Hebrew knew this book from childhood. In this century poisoned by hatred, who today knows the Book of Psalms of David, the Book of Proverbs of Solomon, the Book of Moses? But everyone knows the jokes about Abram and Moisha... And this is an image of the plebeianisation of our ethnic and spiritual culture—in a society with secondary and higher education."

Perhaps the most brilliant speech was that of Myroslav Marynovych.

"Both models of survival are incommensurable: Jews survive in dispersion among foreign peoples, Ukrainians survive on their land. The logic of one model does not follow from the logic of the other, and therefore the demon of misunderstanding dances at the junction of the models. Living among alien and often warring ethnic substrates posed a difficult imperative for Jews: to accurately identify the stronger. A mistake could have tragic consequences. Orientation towards the interests of the stronger party (ethnicity, political group, etc.) guaranteed Jews survival within the limits set for them by the stronger party. Since Ukrainians have often been the weaker party throughout their history, it is understandable that a persistent stereotype of Jewish hostility to Ukrainian national interests has developed in the popular mind. Those few exceptions, when Ukrainians briefly became stronger and received support from Jews, only confirm the general rule. The best way is not to be at odds with Jews who refuse to become strong themselves. Jews will fit into a strong Ukraine in a harmonious and non-destructive way."

These words were met with a standing ovation.

The conference was held at the Research Institute of Information Technologies. For several days, presentations were made, and discussions took place.

The day before, Ivan Mykhailovych and I discussed the programme in great detail, everything that needed to be done to make it happen. There was no doubt that Ivan Dziuba would moderate the conference. However, he fell ill, his asthma was exacerbated. And he told me: "Leonid Kushelevych, you will have to chair the meeting". To be honest, I was confused because I had no such experience. Nevertheless, the conference took place. For better or worse, I moderated a number of reports, and I was assisted by the more experienced Yuriy Shcherbak, Les Taniuk and other participants. As a result, an unprecedented forum for dialogue and understanding took place. It was extremely important and to some extent breakthrough.

I would particularly like to draw attention to Ivan Dziuba's text delivered at the conference. Conceptually, it was one of the most interesting. I was struck by the scope of the speaker's understanding of Jewish history and culture. We are talking about philosophical, cultural, and historical concepts, which were almost all innovative for Ukrainian humanitarian thought:

"The problem of Ukrainian-Jewish relations should be considered in several aspects. First of all, it is the relationship between our two peoples in Ukraine; secondly, the relationship between Ukraine and Israel as states; and finally, the relationship between representatives of the two peoples outside their national states. With regard to the first aspect, three main sets of questions can be identified. The first is the history of Ukrainian-Jewish relations in Ukraine, beginning with the days of Kievan Rus. The second aspect is cultural ties and mutual influences: the development of Jewish culture in Ukraine, religious and philosophical trends in Jewish thought, Jewish participation in the creation of Ukrainian culture, Ukrainian assistance to the development of Jewish culture, personal contacts between literary and artistic figures, etc. The third is contemporary political issues in Ukrainian-Jewish relations. And here is a natural transition to those other aspects—the prospects for establishing interstate contacts between the Ukrainian and Jewish diasporas in different countries of the world, etc."

"We need a dialogue between Ukrainian and Jewish intellectuals. We need a constant conversation at a high level of competence and morality."

"A Jew is an eternal dissident, an eternal dissenter. A Ukrainian is always complex, always the object of someone's claims. They are 'homeless'. They are 'strangers' (Marina Tsvetaeva: 'In this most Christian of worlds, poets are Jews'). Jews are strangers everywhere. Ukrainians are strangers in their native land. I'm not talking about individuals, of course, but about concepts."

"Some Ukrainians think that it is in the interests of Jews to discuss this problem, so let them complain about it. Some Jews think that it is in the interest of Ukrainians, so let them be concerned about it. In my opinion, both are wrong. Both Ukrainians and Jews need it equally. Even if all Jews move to Israel, this will be necessary not only for Ukraine and Israel, but for every Ukrainian and Jew everywhere: not only because we live on the same planet, but because each of us is a human being, and how can one be a human being without getting rid of mutual scores, wrongs, and sins?"

Later we managed to publish the reports of the conference participants. I was approached by the editor of the Rukh magazine *Svit* and offered to prepare and publish the reports in a thematic issue. Eventually, issue 3/4 of *Svit* was published. This issue is now a rarity. I had the opportunity to speak about this publication at a conference in the United States a few years ago on Ukrainian-Jewish relations. Mr Temerty, a Ukrainian philanthropist from Canada, offered to publish these materials in English. I do not know whether they were published or not, but that is another story.

***

The Ukrainian-Jewish conference was one of a series of conferences organised by Ivan Dziuba as chairman of the Ukrainian Studies Association. At the same time, similar forums were held on Ukrainian-Russian, Ukrainian-Polish, and Ukrainian-Chinese relations. I also remember the conference "Ukraine and the World". All of them were breakthroughs, innovations, completely unlike anything that had happened before in the academic humanities. I mean both the scale of the meetings and the speeches and dialogues of the most authoritative researchers. These were the first free, uncensored gatherings of scholars and public figures. The texts of the speeches published later became extremely important for the further development of Ukrainian humanities.

Ukrainian Studies Association, which was created by Ivan Dziuba, was one of the first structures of civil society in Ukraine. Today (30 years later) we can say that civil society is quite powerful and its influence on events is often no less than the activities of the authorities. But then it was the first, extremely important steps.

***

I would like to tell you a little bit about what I saw during Ivan Dziuba's tenure as head of the Ukrainian Studies Association. I remember this episode. We were sitting with him discussing some current problems, and his assistant came up to him and said: "Ivan, our accountant is cheating us. She is stealing money. I want to show you this on the documents. Do you see?" "I see." "Do you agree?" "I agree." "Let's fire her." "No," says Ivan, "what if we're wrong? "How?" she says, "let's look again". They look again—everything is correct. And again he disagrees. He had such respect for a person, such faith that a person cannot behave in a bad way, that he was looking for arguments in her defence again and again. It didn't matter that it was obvious to everyone else—he had to analyse everything himself. He was the last person to lose faith in a person.

The event I described happened just a few days before Ivan Dziuba was appointed Minister of Culture. And I thought: "My God, it's going to be so hard for you to run this ministry. If it's hard to make a decision to fire one person who is cheating you, how will you manage a ministry whose activities cover hundreds of thousands of people?"

I remember that Ivan really did not want to take this position. But he was persuaded, he was "forced" by Dmytro Pavlychko and Ivan Drach, who at that time were included in political activity much more than Dziuba. And he agreed. And later, in his memoirs, he wrote that these were the most difficult years of his life.

***

I would like to mention another important moment in Ivan Dziuba's life. I am talking about the period of formation and activity of the People's Movement of Ukraine (Rukh) in the late 80s and 90s. It was then that the foundations of a democratic Ukraine were being laid. The programmes of activities were prepared very carefully. The basic principles of the Rukh's national policy were formulated and written by Ivan Dziuba. The rights and obligations of the titular nation, the rights of national minorities were declared, and various aspects of national relations were carefully defined.

***

The Ukrainian-Jewish conference in Kyiv eventually continued in Jerusalem, where scientists from Israel invited us. The themes proclaimed in Kyiv were developed in new versions and with a new composition of participants. I remember one episode directly related to Ivan Dziuba — when one of the Israeli professors did not delicately react to a certain thesis of Myron Petrovsky. Several of our scientists tried to protect him from unreasonable criticism. Dziuba instantly turned to us and asked not to aggravate the situation and to seek understanding as delicately as possible.

With the same delicacy and reverence even to those with whom he disagreed, I encountered another time. Together with Geliy Aronov and Myron Petrovsky, we prepared the first number of *Yegupets* — an almanac of Jewish culture and Ukrainian-Jewish relations. The almanac opened with the text of Ivan Dziuba's speech in Babyn Yar in 1966. I dare to recall a few theses from this speech.

"Babyn Yar is a tragedy of all mankind, but it happened on Ukrainian soil. Therefore, an Ukrainian, as well as a Jew, has no right to forget it. Babyn Yar is our common tragedy, a tragedy primarily of the Jewish and Ukrainian peoples. Fascism brought this tragedy to our peoples. However, we must not forget that fascism does not begin with Babyn Yar and is not limited to it. Fascism begins with disrespect for man and ends with the destruction of man, the destruction of peoples — but not necessarily only with such destruction as in Babyn Yar."

"We recall the sacrifices and efforts of millions of Soviet people of all nationalities who selflessly worked to defeat fascism. We must think about being worthy of their memory, to be worthy of the duty that imposes on us the memory of many human sacrifices, hopes and aspirations. Are we worthy of this memory? Perhaps not, if there are still various forms of misanthropy among us, including the one that we call the worn-out, trivialised, but terrible word 'anti-Semitism'".

"We must eradicate all hatred of man, overcome all misunderstanding, and fight for true brotherhood all our lives. The way to true, not false brotherhood is not in self-forgetfulness, but in self-knowledge. Not to deny oneself and adapt to others, but to be oneself and respect others. Jews have the right to be Jews, and Ukrainians have the right to be Ukrainians in the full and deepest, not just the formal meaning of these words. Let Jews know Jewish history, Jewish culture, and language and be proud of them. Let Ukrainians know Ukrainian history, culture, language and be proud of them. May they know the history and culture of other nations, and may they be able to appreciate themselves and others as their brothers."

"This is our duty to the millions of victims of despotism, this is our duty to the best people of the Ukrainian and Jewish peoples who called for mutual understanding and friendship, this is our duty to the Ukrainian land on which we live together, this is our duty to humanity."

This material was provided to us by Roman Korogodsky. In addition to the text of the speech, he brought a review of this text, written by one of the respected Ukrainian humanitarians from the Institute of Philosophy. And I understand that the author wrote this review at the request of the competent authorities. He noted there that "anti-Soviet motives follow from the context of the speech." We asked Ivan Dziuba if we would indicate the name of the author of the review. He thought for a moment and said, "Maybe not." And then added: "But he could not write about context. He could only analyze the text. "

***

When Ivan Dziuba became Minister of Culture, we continued to communicate quite regularly, despite his busy schedule. And then one day he called us at home, I picked up the phone, and we got to talking. Ivan Mykhailovych said: "Leonid Kushelevych, it's hard to get through to you." I was surprised: "Ivan Mykhailovych, you have secretaries, don't you?" "No, Leonid Kushelevich, it would be inconvenient for me to call you through a secretary." I didn't know any other ministers like that. I didn't know them, and they probably don't exist. The same thing happened when Ivan Mykhailovych called us and my mother answered the phone. He always found time to talk to her, to ask her about her problems and life. "Lia Davydivna, how are you?" – he would say.

***

Ivan Dziuba for several years was a member of the Presidium of the Academy of Sciences of Ukraine, one of the academicians-secretaries of this institution. Once, at the end of the year, I came to visit him in his office – and he has a lot of annual reports of academicians and corresponding members on his desk. I asked if I could look, he replied: "Yes, look, please." There were huge volumes of texts by former communist ideologues. They continued to write their opuses, which by that time no one needed. I say: "Ivan Mykhailovych, it's fantastic – the country and we all live already a different life, but they continue to write these pro-communist and communist treatises!" He says: "You know, they write even more and with more intensity and energy than before. Although they practically get paid for it." I asked: "Can I take such materials for the archive?." He said: "Unfortunately, no, because these texts are in one or two copies and they should remain in the Academy's archive." I regret that I still did not rewrite at least the names of those texts for history. It was something... not that life after death, but a specific life that the country did not already know about. Thank God we were already living a different, new life.

At some point, I started meeting Ivan Mykhailovych more often. He and his wife Marta would invite us to their home, and this continued almost until the last months of his life. When I became a publisher, I started bringing Ivan Mykhailovych our books. At first, 1-2 books a month or two, and later — dozens of them (in recent years, we published 70-80 books a year). The gifts were received with great gratitude. And I decided for myself: just as we hand over the obligatory copies to the state libraries (Vernadsky, Parliamentary, Presidential, etc.), the Dziuba family will also receive their copies. Every time I brought a new batch of books, Ivan Mykhailovych would tell me about his impressions of the previous one. He often responded with reviews, either orally or in writing.

By the way, I have several such recipients who receive all our books. One of them is Bogumila Berdychowska in Warsaw. Her library is no less than that of any other Ukrainian intellectual. I hardly know any books that are not there.

***

Ivan Dziuba worked furiously. I don't know where he got so much time and energy. His legacy is a whole continuum of texts — innovative, accurate, of the highest quality. Maybe six months before his death, when he was almost 90 years old, he sent us a review of one of our books. It was brilliantly written, as were most of his texts. His work includes thousands of reviews, hundreds of articles, and many dozens of books. There are no signs of graphomania in them. As a rule, these are very important texts in each topic. If it is a monograph on Shevchenko, it is one of the most profound for understanding the work of the national genius. If it is a memoir, it is one of the best I have ever read, with good irony, a fantastic memory of the events that took place, and extremely accurate characterisations of the characters in the stories. I would also like to mention his portraits of politicians, artists and writers — they are on a par with the best texts for the most authoritative encyclopaedias.

Of course, every next generation reads mostly about the events of its time, but I am sure that those who are interested in the events of the twentieth century will definitely read the texts of Ivan Dziuba. I hope that some of them will be included in readers and anthologies for schools and higher education institutions.

***

At some point, I was lucky enough to become not only a good friend of Ivan and Marta Dziuba, but also the publisher of their texts. One of these books is Ivan Dziuba's *The Golden Thread* in our series "Cultural Figures" (which includes already almost 30 books). I approached Ivan Mykhailovych and asked him to compile a book of essays about his "heroes". Some of the articles are portraits of well-known writers and publicists in Ukraine, while others are about figures almost unknown in society. The book had a good response.

In 2020, I read Marta Dziuba's memoirs about Sergey Parajanov. I also knew that the Dziuba family archive contains correspondence with Parajanov and some of his manuscripts. I came up with the idea of publishing a book in the same series "Cultural Figures": *Ivan and Marta Dziuba about Parajanov*. This book contains Ivan Dziuba's conceptual articles about Parajanov's films, about poetic cinema, and Marta's articles are very accurate portraits of the people who were around Parajanov. And the figure of Parajanov himself — it seems to me that no one else has written about him with such an accurate memory as Marta's. The book was published fairly quickly, and Ivan Dziuba had time to enjoy it.

***

I think that Ivan Dziuba's main contribution to culture is what he himself defined as follows: "I am writing the history of Ukrainian culture on three continents". Gradually, year after year, he developed this project, but, unfortunately, this goal is so big that one person, even if it is Ivan Dziuba, cannot achieve it. A lot has been done, but the project is not complete. And this is a testamentary task for researchers of the next generations — to continue what Ivan Dziuba has done, to discover new names and new texts for Ukrainians.

I have my own sin in Ivan Dziuba's work on *Essays on Ukrainian Culture on Three Continents*. At one stage, I saw how hard he was working on these materials and offered to help him decipher the audio recordings. These were his dialogues with foreign research partners. And, unfortunately, it so happened that the person who undertook to do this turned out to be inadequate, mentally ill. Therefore, some texts were lost. I tried to find them, but unfortunately, nothing came of it. Ivan Mykhailovych was sad about the lost texts, but he understood that sometimes this happens and eventually forgave me.

Unfortunately, Dziuba did not have time to do much of what he had planned. He would show us boxes with hundreds and hundreds of letters from his correspondents and say: "I still want to prepare our correspondence with these authors for publication." I am sure that the researchers who will work with his vast archive will do so. This archive, which contains Ivan Dziuba's manuscripts and correspondence, must be preserved as a whole, as a national treasure.

***

Ivan Dziuba's libraries. I say "libraries" because thousands of books were in their suburban house (dacha), and other thousands were in their Kyiv apartment. Most of these books were carefully studied, and this is evidenced by numerous citations in almost all of his publications. Ivan Mykhailovych worked actively and fruitfully in the last years of his life. It seemed that old age was not about him. He wrote not only his academic and essayistic texts, but also did not leave unanswered the texts of the enemies of Ukrainian culture. He opposed Dmytro Tabachnyk and argued in detail against his anti-Ukrainian concepts.

***

I would like to speak separately about Ivan Dziuba's speech at Babyn Yar. Today, many people know about it, but in 1966, both Viktor Nekrasov and Amik Diamant gave speeches there, but only Ivan Dziuba's text has survived. Probably because it was the most conceptual and most accurate. As a sign of public opinion, Dziuba's speech at Babyn Yar was programmatic and alternative to Soviet schemes and dogmas.

***

Another episode from our relationship. On the eve of the eightieth anniversary of Ivan Dziuba, Olya Gnatiuk and I belatedly realized that a little more than three months were left before the anniversary. We wanted to prepare a celebration of the hero of the day, because even then we were well aware of his role and place in Ukrainian social and cultural life. We began to prepare the celebration at the Kyiv-Mohyla Academy. To do this, we agreed with Martha on cooperation, hoping from her to get the texts, photographs, etc. we need. We agreed that this would be our secret from Ivan Mykhailovych — we were afraid that he would do everything to prevent the celebration. He didn't like such honours, rituals, and high words. We knew this and planned a modest version of the greeting. At some point, Marta "ratted us out". I don't blame her: she was the closest person to Ivan Mykhailovych, his angel for many years of their married life, and she had the right to do so. A month before the anniversary, Ivan Mykhailovych said: "I know about your insidious plans." And he used his weapon: he wrote a text — instructions for the anniversary.

At that time, we had a book in honour of Ivan Dziuba almost ready. But his instruction turned out to be so brilliant that we decided to include it in the book as well:

"One of the biggest natural disasters of our society are the so-called jubilees — of individuals, institutions, parties, etc. Jubilees offend aesthetic tastes; harm health; include a powerful mechanism for wasting time — both for the celebrant and the reckless organisers of the jubilee; unacceptably reduce working capacity; demoralise society; split society on the basis of age, image and rating, ethical orientations, worldview, ideology, political beliefs, race and religious affiliation. And that's not all! So, in our opinion, the only real alternative to a jubilee can be an *anti-jubilee*.

The anti-jubilee procedure PROHIBITS: naming the anti-jubilarian; making toasts and congratulations; giving speeches, lectures, resolutions, astrological predictions, etc.; giving the anti-jubilarian anything except books.

IS ALLOWED TO: Drink non-alcoholic cocktails (except for the Molotov cocktail); play dominoes and cards; sing the anthem of democratic youth, the Soviet national song 'My address is not a house or a street, my address is the Soviet Union' and the Hutsul folk song 'We don't need sausage, we don't need butter—just so the star on the Kremlin doesn't go out'; play the balalaika and trembita; dance hopak and boogie-woogie".

We managed to print the first edition of the book one day before the birthday. Then there was a celebration. In my opinion, the event was a success. We satisfied all the requirements of the celebrant—we did not mention his name, tried to use all the literary terms, dozens of which he "approved" in his instructions for use on that day. These were academic, literary terms, and it was very difficult to link them to the event. In an attempt to bring down the pathos (which we had not intended), he suggested several children's riddles to determine the winner (by the way, it was Vyacheslav Bryukhovetsky who won fair and square). There is no way to list everything. I must conclude by saying that the event went well, cheerfully, to the delight of all participants. I think that Ivan Mykhailovych was also pleased, and the photos from that dinner, where he and Martha are fantastically beautiful, testify to this.

Unfortunately, my wife and I did not have time to attend Ivan Dziuba 90th birthday party, which took place in a very narrow circle, although we were invited. I had a meeting with a lawyer for my friend persecuted by the authorities, scheduled for that day. We could not postpone the meeting. And then—then we agreed on the next meeting, and, again, it did not take place. We were supposed to come to visit the Dziuba family on a certain day, but the day before, Ivan Mykhailovych was hospitalised. We dreamed of meeting after his recovery.

A few days later, Ivan Mikhailovich died. Unfortunately, I didn't get to say goodbye to him — I returned from a business trip at night and the same day began the Russian-Ukrainian war.

***

I am very glad that I had the good fortune to know Ivan Dziuba, and at some points to work with him. His memory will remain forever with me, with all our mutual friends and acquaintances, and with Ukrainian society in general. Ivan Dziuba marked the time in which he lived. The further we go, the clearer it becomes: if the previous era was the era of Vasyl Stus, the next one was the era of Ivan Dziuba.

Leonid Finberg
April 2022

19. Myron Petrovsky

My acquaintance with Myron and Svetlana Petrovsky happened about fifty years ago. Today I say »it happened in a past life«, calling so the period when I was engaged in engineering: I worked in factories, then built power plants. At one of the power plants I met a colleague—engineer Alik (Arthur) Kalmeier. We immediately recognized each other as like-minded people, especially with regard to the assessment of political processes in our country and world-view issues. One day Kalmeyer said that I absolutely need to meet his friend, Myron Petrovsky, literary scholar, expert in children's literature. I couldn't understand why would I want to meet him. I wasn't interested in children's literature.

Some time later, Kalmeyer and I went to the Petrovskys' new flat on Florence Street, where they had just moved. At the time, a four-room flat seemed a luxury. Later I learnt that the family got this apartment thanks to Svetlana's persistence in her battles with the city authorities. Those were the first days of setting up, making the flat habitable. I helped to unpack boxes of books, to adjust or craft something. The intellectuals' solidarity of those years is unforgettable: people who had previously held only a pen or a pencil in their hands acted without a shadow of a doubt as movers, repairmen and adjusters.

It was then that our first conversations with Myron and Svetlana began, which eventually grew into a long-lasting friendship. They asked me about my interests, my friends, my surroundings, my reading circle. Myron realised that my level of knowledge in the humanities was quite low and delicately offered me a few books from his library. These books became key for me in realising what was happening.

One of the first books was *Milestones* (Moscow, 1909), a book about the comprehension of the revolution by Russian intellectuals of the early twentieth century. In those years, such texts could be found only in special archives. I had never read anything similar in depth of analysis before. The polyphony of thinkers was also striking. I was most impressed by Bogdan Kistiakovsky's text, which was in harmony with my search and determined my interest in law and sociology of law.

The next discovery was Arkady Belinkov's book on Tynyanov (Moscow, 1965). Everything in it was surprising: the virtuosity of reading Tynyanov's texts, the author's brilliant stylistics, and the fact that the book managed to be published despite the censorship of the time. Belinkov's analytical method was very close to Myron. In many of his texts Belinkov broke through to the reader, masterfully circumventing the censorship barriers.

When I returned the books, we discussed them. I often asked questions, Myron commented. At that time Myron also told me about his friendship with Arkady Belinkov and showed me Belinkov's autobiography, which struck me. In time we published this autobiography and Myron's essay about Belinkov in *Yegupets* almanac. Year after year, Myron offered me new and new books: Mikhail Bakhtin, Aron Gurevich, Kornei Chukovsky, Samuel Marshak, Ilya Ehrenburg....

As time went on, I began to bring books to the Petrovskys' house, more often *samizdat*. For example, I shared books brought from Moscow, from Victoria Chalikova. She headed the Department of Scientific Communism at the Institute of Scientific Information of Social Sciences at the USSR Academy of Sciences (INION). There, books by Max Weber, George Orwell, Aldous Huxley, Mircea Eliade, sociologists and thinkers, authors of literary-philosophical dystopias and critics of Marxism—everything that was considered anti-Soviet literature—were published in tiny editions with the stamp "For official use". These books were intended for members of the Politburo of the CPSU Central Committee, humanities academics, journalists specialising in counter-propaganda, and figures on the Soviet ideological front. Victoria Chalikova's gifts were extremely important to all of us—and to Myron. Bringing books to Myron was as much a joy as giving him tobacco from my first trips abroad. For me, the smell of tobacco is forever linked to the image of Myron's pipe, Myron's books, Myron's study.

Much later, in 2019, I brought Myron my book *About everything and a little about myself*. It contained a little bit of autobiography, more stories about the formation of Judaic studies in

Ukraine, about the publishing house *Dukh i Litera*. This book contains my special gratitude to the Petrovsky family for many years of dialogue and study. Myron read the book carefully and thanked me for my kind words.

I often found myself witnessing dialogues between Myron and Vadym Skurativsky. I didn't understand everything in their conversations, and sometimes I didn't know the texts they were discussing at all. Frankly speaking, I was not always interested in the purely literary aspects of their conversations. But subconsciously I was learning the culture of dialogue, methods of analyzing texts, events, and biographies. I was amazed not only by Myron's dialogues with Vadym, but also by Vadym's numerous improvisations about world history, culture, and cinema.

I have witnessed the editions of Myron's books. All of them stand today on the shelves of our library with warm gift inscriptions of the author. Each inscription is as accurate as the texts of his books. Myron's attitude to words was absolute. His definitions of events, concepts, cultural phenomena — on the level of the most authoritative encyclopaedias. Myron was amazingly precise in his formulation of thought. This applied not only to written texts, but also to his spoken word.

I would like to talk about the atmosphere in the Petrovskys' house separately. Myron met his guests on the doorstep, helped them take off their outer clothes, and categorically did not allow the guest to do it himself. There was something very warm, touching and old-fashioned in this gesture, like a sign of a bygone time. Each of our visits began with the obligatory cheesecakes or a bun with jam, tea and breadcrumbs, which Myron dried himself. The guest was first fed and only then invited to talk. Almost always the conversations took place in the study, where the two of us and Myron — or the three of us, with Vadim Skuratovsky, — would gather. This was also part of the ritual. The subjects of the books Myron was working on were often the subject of conversation. His reading of "The Golden Key" or "The Cockroach", his cultural interpretations of circus and romance themes, famous literary works or cultural phenomena were genuine discoveries for me.

A gift for me and my wife were friends of the Petrovsky family, many of whom eventually became our friends. In this amazing apartment on Florence Street we met Yuri and Maria Shcherbak, Boris Lekar, Bogdan Zholdak, Geliy Aronov, David Miretsky, Mikhail Turovsky and Yuri Shanin...

In the late 1980s I left my engineering roles and engaged in the formation of civil society structures: *Rukh*, the Jewish community of Ukraine, the journal *Philosophical and sociological thought*. I organized expert surveys, and the intellectuals of Ukraine, Russia, Lithuania, Poland, who left the camps and prisons, answered our questionnaires.

In those years our friendly relations with Myron gradually turned into co-operation. In 1994, Geliy Aronov suggested publishing *Yegupets* — an almanac of Jewish history and culture. (Sholom Aleichem's Yegupets is Kiev, a small galut Egypt). Myron responded to the proposal to join the editorial board of the almanac, never ceasing to repeat: "What do I have to do with Jewish culture?" I remember how we all rejoiced together at the thin (about 200 pages) first issue of the journal, which opened with the text of Ivan Dziuba's speech at Babyn Yar in 1966. Ivan Dziuba's text was suggested for publication by Roman Korogodsky, along with a "closed review" by a prominent Ukrainian intellectual. The review, written at the request of the state security service, accused Dziuba of anti-Soviet subtext in his speech. We asked Ivan Mykhailovych whether to name the "reviewer" in the publication. He replied, "Probably not." Then he added bitterly: "He might not have written about a subtext."

For many years the almanac was edited by Myron and Geliy Aronov, and I brought new materials for publication. Myron contributed a lot to the formation of the almanac's publishing portfolio, finding new authors — Ritaly Zaslavsky, Inna Lisova, Yulia Veretennikova, Andrei Puchkov, Sergey Cherepanov, Yakov Lotovsky.... Myron became more and more involved in the preparation and editing of the almanac, which eventually published many of his landmark articles: reminiscences of Lila Brik and Arkady Belinkov, essays on the work of Boris Lekar and the last

Oberiuts, correspondence between Deitch and Rylsky, Chukovsky and Marshak....

As time went on, illness prevented Geliy Aronov from continuing the work he had started, and, starting with a certain issue of the almanac, it was only Myron who worked on the texts. I almost never interfered in his work with *Yegupets* materials — Myron was an experienced editor. He willingly worked with classical texts, but sometimes he did not accept innovative ones. Sometimes it became the subject of our arguments, but we always found compromise solutions. I am grateful to Myron Petrovsky for the years of our creative work together.

Myron Petrovsky's books *To the City and the World* (second, expanded edition) and *The Master and the City* (the cover for the book about Mikhail Bulgakov's Kyiv contexts was designed by Sergei Masloboyshchikov) were published in the *Dukh i Litera* publishing house, which is run by Kostyantyn Sigov and me. Myron's study of Janusz Korczak's life and work in Kyiv was published in a separate booklet.

In the last years of Myron's life, we often met, as before, and came with my wife Lena to the Petrovskys' house. Myron was acutely worried that he was no longer able to write down the texts he had previously thought out. He used to say: "When I sit down at the table, everything disappears". I offered him various forms of cooperation with colleagues to whom he could dictate texts. He rejected these proposals. His absolute demandingness for words became a barrier that could not be overcome.

We continued to meet even when Myron could hardly get out of bed and could barely walk. But he always met us at the doorstep. Lena and I came to see Myron on one of his last days. He could no longer get up, could hardly speak. But when he saw us, he tried to smile and barely audibly said: "Lenochka...", as if happy that he still could recognise the people around him.

20. Boris Lekar

A life-long story

(From the book "The World of Boris Lekar")
Boris and I were close friends. Some people are like a lens through which you view your own life. They magnify the main things, leaving everything else out. That's how you remember things best. Boris Lekar had this. A strange combination of dreaminess and rationality. And kindness at the heart of everything.

First, I tell you how I found a job for him in Jerusalem. Boris arrived there at the height of emigration, and it was very difficult to find a job; he did not know how to "settle down," as we say.

One day I got a call from Moscow. A group of Israeli culturologists had come to visit them to get to know the country. On the way, a suitcase with all the demonstration material went missing. You know how it goes. You have a lot to tell them, but nothing to show them. In Moscow, they somehow got out of the situation, and the next destination was Kyiv. We had to come up with something. So I collected everything I could around the city. I agreed with the Museum of Kyiv History, using it as a unifying idea: Kyiv-Jerusalem. I had a projector (we didn't have computers back then) and slides. The lectures were a great success. The head of the group was the director of the Centre for Jewish Art at the University of Jerusalem, named Narkis, and he was assisted by a lovely lady named Aliza Kogen. I showed them around Kyiv. They were very pleased. And then it occurred to me to say:

— My friend is an artist, an architect, and he's sitting in Jerusalem without a job.
— Oh, oh, that's for Aliza. She's an architect...

What a lucky thing! Boris was appointed to the university. It was a part-time job, but he didn't need any more than that, just what he needed to avoid reporting for duty every day. But what a business trips! Tunisia, India... dozens of other countries. Measuring and reconstructing plans of local synagogues. This helped him out a lot at the time. He worked at this centre for more than ten years. And, of course, he justified both my recommendations and their expectations.

But here, in Kyiv, Kharkiv, where Boris is from... If we compare, in a sense we all had the same childhood in a post-war country. We lived roughly the same way, the differences were insignificant. We studied at the same schools. One can imagine a certain biography of the generation to which Boris and I belong, its generic features.

***

I often recall images of my own growing up. My father was a skilled worker. He would leave while I was still sleeping, and when he returned, I was already in bed. All my time was spent in the yard, and I played football quite well, coaches would come up to me and invite me to the team. The game had two aims: to score a goal and not to hit a neighbour's window with the ball. It is clear what was more important. I think, more than one sports biography has been cut short by this misfortune. Maybe mine too... Or maybe because I got carried away with reading. My aunt from Moscow gave me *The Adventures of Baron Munchausen*. That's where I started, although the story I'm telling now is true. The baron would not have had enough imagination.

We lived poorly, and my Kyiv aunt was even poorer. She lived next door to us. Her husband returned from the war disabled, spent some time in hospitals and died. She raised her daughter, my cousin, alone. She was afraid of the financial inspector. The terrible word "financial inspector" stuck in my ears and stayed there. My aunt used to sew curtains at home. They were called "Richelieu", curly curtains for windows with all kinds of slits and festoons. It was a poor man's fashion at the time. We had an evil financial inspector. He was hunting for my aunt. I mean, not only for her, but I remember my aunt's horror. Someone like a fairy-tale monster. We used to open the door only after a conditional knock. Otherwise, everything would go quiet, and my sister and I would try to get under the bed.

This was about business. And now about justice.

We heated with firewood and stored it for the winter. It was stored in sheds. They were not stolen—there were locks, of course, but they were more for show. There was, so to speak, a social contract. You couldn't live without firewood in winter. Professionals would come to cut down the wood, work for half a day, and then sit down to dinner on the firewood. They would unwrap the food they had brought from home and open the common property—a quarter (*chekushka*, as it was called). Usually, the younger one poured it, and the older one held the glass. When he reached about halfway, the younger man would stop and ask with his eyes. The older man would try on the glass. "For you..." The younger one would add a little. "For you..." Finally, on the third or fourth attempt, the older said, "For me..."

This was about justice. Now about people.

We had a private household. Oddly enough, there were landlords. They kept house books. They collected money from the residents and paid the state. What was the benefit of this? I think it was very small. There were two landlords in our yard. Mexikantsev and Stepanov. Mexikantsev? I'm checking myself now. I think I'm not mistaken. I have no idea what his family did before the discovery of America. Probably, the former Aztec emperor was granted political asylum in our yard. The Mexicantsevs lived on the second floor. They kept canaries and didn't let us in. There was no one to let in, such was the poverty around. I remember also Stepanov well. I played football with his son. One of my first vivid life experiences was with Stepanov. They said he was a policeman during the war. In my time, he worked at a slaughterhouse. I can see him in the moonlight. I see him limping into the yard. He can barely walk. It's ten o'clock. It's the moon. They are already waiting for him here. His people. Customers. Stepanov begins to distribute the goods. He takes off his trousers and unloads the underpants. He takes out meat bones from everywhere, from the pockets, front and back. I look out the window: a frosty courtyard, dim light from the sky, black shadows. I don't know about Munchausen... But I'm conveying it accurately...

***

I started reading binge. I entered the Mechanical College and met a few other bookworms there. I had a friend, Misha Zaborovsky, whose father was the chief engineer of Kyivgaz. They had a library like this — no matter how many books you read, you can't read them all. But I tried...

Then we were sent to a plant. The team welcomed us with enthusiasm, as free helpers. But we've been warned: we had to be paid. The trade union was for us. But the plant didn't have money. We found a way out. We worked half of the shift for free, and the other half we made our own barbells. Where the metal came from is a naive question. The metal was there. That's not the trick. The trick is how to throw the iron over a two-metre fence. From the outside, there was a path along the fence. Our cordon was standing there, and people from the plant, with some effort, were throwing things over the fence... This was a sign of the times. One of my routes passed by the Karl Marx confectionery factory. At the end of the shift, sacks and bundles were falling over the fence. Involved persons shouted: "Dude, what are you stopping for? Come on, hurry up...." The guards were hurrying from a distance, and people were scattering. I wanted sweets. But my first acquisition was made of metal.

I came across the confectionery factory again in a hospital. I graduated from a technical school, then from a distance-learning institute (to be honest, it gave me little) and went to serve in the army. I had stomach problems, but I didn't shirk my duty. Before my service began, the military commissariat sent me to hospital. An elderly sad man, a Jew, was lying with us in the ward. He didn't talk much, he was preoccupied with his heart attack. He turned out to be a designer from a confectionery factory. He once invented a machine for making three-layer marmalade. I don't know if such marmalade had been made before him, on other machines, but his invention could have sweetened the life of the country. That was his dream. And he became an inventor for many years to come, until he had a heart attack. This marmalade is everywhere now, but

I'm afraid he didn't see it. Or the marmalade is not his. Or maybe the one from his machine was even better, I don't know.

***

Then I went to serve. There was a whole carload of people like me, one-year soldiers, ready-made specialists with higher education. Before we left, we were told that we would be divided into groups by speciality. Prepare yourself, take initiative, your desire will be taken into account to bring maximum benefit to the country's army and navy. We did not have time to prepare, although enthusiasts were already walking around with lists. The issue was resolved simply. As soon as the train started moving, the boss got drunk, and we were unloaded without any initiative from us, just alphabetically. With my letter F, I reached the very end of the route — to the north of the Kola Peninsula, to the point Afrikanda-1, as geologist Fersman humorously called it. But I had no regrets. I learnt Polish, spent a lot of time outdoors, in a sheepskin coat and with a carbine behind me. The service was not exactly in my speciality, our team guarded an airfield. Across the tundra from us was Afrikanda-2, a whole village, mostly military, where the main thing for me was the library. We went there from time to time, and I managed to organise a shelf for "intelligent" books in the library, so that I didn't have to look for them every time. It was then that the thematic plans of various publishing houses appeared, according to which books could be ordered for the next year. I asked the library to borrow these plans for just a week, so that I could fill out the postcards with my book orders, send them off, and receive the books already at the Kyiv address. A week has passed, and no one is going to Afrikanda. There is no occasion. I am tired. I went to our lieutenant. He said: "No, nothing is planned..." I must have looked miserable. "All right, keep your postcards with you. I'll think of something." And in the morning, they announced a combat alert. We grabbed our weapons, got in the car and rushed to Afrikanda-2. We drove around the town and stopped in front of the library. The lieutenant gets out of the car: "Let's go, but quickly". And I, just as I was, in a sheepskin goat and with a gun, ran into the library and handed in at last my orders.

***

After the army, I worked for many years in an organisation that was engaged in the construction of power plants, first thermal and then nuclear. We took part in the construction of Zaporizhzhya and Chernobyl NPPs. We were literally the first to arrive at the site and set up tents. We were called the Construction Management Organisation Department... We were engaged in calculations on how to optimally calculate the application of force. We lived on the road for years, watching the construction site grow from scratch. Thousands of people came from all over the country, set up tents, trailers, built dormitories and everything else they needed, including a cemetery. People were in a space where there was nothing yet, no infrastructure, nothing. The scale was grandiose, ancient Egyptian, something like an enormous anthill, with work on weekdays and weddings, births, funerals with an orchestra on Saturdays...

Rem Khenokh was the head of the construction of the Zaporizhzhya NPP, a great personality. I knew him because I worked with his son. In the same years, I met Boris Lekar, and once in a conversation I recommended him to Khenokh. Boris was the head of an architectural studio at the time. He came to our construction site, inspected everything, and offered something very different. I remember being surprised. Boris explained that he had no right to earn money for himself until he provided for his employees first. And for himself — in the very last turn. Among his employees were architects, a decorator, a sculptor. And he had to think about everyone, otherwise he would not have taken on the job. They did something together: a dining room, some murals, something else. And I was able to appreciate Boris's life principles. I think he never got anything for himself. I had a friend, Alik Kelmeyer. He introduced me to Myron Petrovsky. He brought me to his house, which eventually became my home. I met people there, such as Vadym Skurativsky, academician Platon Biletskyi and his wife, and the hosts — Svitlana and Myron Petrovsky. All of them were people of great humanitarian culture. At first, I was embarrassed. I remember campaigning for Biletsky to learn Polish. He just smiled. Apparently, he knew almost all European languages, Eastern European ones for sure.

One day, Boris Lekar came to visit. It was a children's birthday party. Boris was with a black poodle and entertained the audience. The poodle prepared a whole programme in honour of the holiday. He barked at all the numbers up to five and never went astray. Boris put a coloured cap on his head and acted as a clown. The children squeaked with happiness, and the adults laughed until they dropped. Boris was on a roll.

***

And more from those old memories. The poet Arsenii Tarkovsky came to Kyiv at the invitation of, as I remember, the Book Club, a group of enthusiasts, including myself. I had to show the guest around Kyiv, especially since he was interested in Ukraine, especially Kyiv. He had roots here. I had to find a good local historian. I didn't have to look far, my then new friend Vadym Skurativsky was a man of encyclopaedic knowledge. Those who know Vadym can confirm this. But he had his own peculiarities. He could talk for hours about every monument in Kyiv (and not only), literally cutting through one cultural layer after another. But to do this, he had to be taken to the right place and put there. He himself is an inattentive person, he could not find this place and get lost on the way. In the end, we asked Mykhailo Braichevsky, a venerable historian, author of the book *The Origins of Rus*. I was enchanted with his stories. He was on fire then. He told us the whole history of Podil: city fires, architecture, churches, who lived where... But Tarkovsky was really interested only in one topic: Hryhoriy Skovoroda. The traveller, philosopher and theologian of the eighteenth century. The face of Ukraine. I have extracts about him, and here I want to quote one of them: "His poverty cultivated in him a most useful heart and sowed in him the seeds of patience, which, when they bore fruit, made his life wise and happy." He was a follower of Marcus Aurelius. I got the impression that Tarkovsky came to Kyiv on purpose to, so to speak, get used to Skovoroda's teachings on the spot, to see the places where he lived (although Skovoroda travelled half of Europe and knew a lot of living and dead languages).

Then there was a literary evening, a meeting with Tarkovsky at the Institute of Civil Aircraft Engineers (as it was then called). The poet read poetry, answered questions, but selectively. He was reluctant to answer questions about his biography or his son, or even skipped questions altogether, but he spoke at length about the values that Skovoroda brought to the world. It was obvious that this topic lived in him.

We stopped at St Sophia Cathedral and went to the pottery workshops. There were some of them there. They had been warned in advance, so they were getting ready. A woman of fifty or so came out to meet us. At the time, this age seemed almost relic to me, and in general, there was something about this woman... It was easy to imagine her in the 1930s, wearing a red headscarf, in the fever of everyday life. Now all looked different, and the age itself testified to it. And she spoke, apparently experiencing it anew every time: "Initially, there was a project to organise a ceramic production here to bring potters from all over the world. But it didn't work out... Then we started dreaming about the Institute of Ceramics. But industrialisation began, and the energy went there. Then we got serious — the Museum of Ceramics... But there is a war here... And then..." The woman spread her arms to encompass her current modest estate. "That's how we live..." Tarkovsky listened attentively. And then he said: "The main thing is that the clay is not taken away..."

***

I was one of the first to come to Israel. There was no direct flight, so I flew via Cyprus. Boris rushed to meet me at the bus station in Jerusalem. He already had a car. We loaded up, he was sitting back, the car was standing. "Let's go." "I can't. I'm too excited." Some guy came up and pushed us out of the car park, and that's the only way we left...

Boris drove a car in a strange way. He explained to me that Jews didn't like green lights. That's why he tried to run red lights. He got away with it. His wife Nina also had a licence, and it was not easy to establish the identity of the driver behind the wheel of the only car in the family. Every two years Nina took penalty courses for driving offences. The last time she did it with the Minister of Transport of Israel. The law in Israel is the same for everyone.

Then Boris got an idea. "I don't have any new money coming in," he told me, "I've set up a travel fund. Every year, Nina and I go to a new country. I have laid out the money for ten years in advance. It turned out to be a little too little. I have to sell my car."

— Maybe don't sell it yet?
— No, right now...

It was obvious that Boris was afraid to change his mind. And so it was.

— I bought a new car, he said on the phone. "I've forgotten how to use public transport. Come and visit me. You'll see for yourself.

And I did. It was obviously a Volkswagen from the war years. It is not clear how it got to Palestine. The twin brother of our Zaporozhets—either a "beetle" or a "tin can"—I'm quoting the domestic names from memory, because there are no such vehicles in Kyiv for a long time. Plus the age—Boris's car was 40 or 50 years old. Not less than that.

It was impressive. Boris painted the beetle light green and painted white daisies on top. The beetle looked like a flower bed on wheels.

— The police know me,—Boris said nonchalantly.—There's no one else like my car in Jerusalem.
— In Israel, too.
— It's possible.—Boris wanted to remain objective.

The design did not save Boris from disappointment. The car turned out to have a character, that is, an appetite.

— It eats a lot of petrol. And there is no one to sell it to.
— Maybe you could repaint it," I suggested.
— There's another problem. — Boris complained. "The seats have no shock absorbers. I put cushions under it. It doesn't help. It's okay for me, but for Nina... Once she drives, she can't sit for two days.

Boris fought with insurance companies. They cheat people, just like everywhere else. Once, in my presence, he got into it with an another driver, and both of them got out. The driver was boiling.

— Listen, — Boris said to him, — what are you worried about? You'll get your insurance. I know how...
— How can you be so sure? — I ask.- Getting insurance is always a problem.

It turns out he had reasons. The insurers owed Borys money, but they were in no hurry to pay it back. He went there many times to no avail.

"Here's what I'm going to do," Boris told the insurers the next time he saw them and unfurled a large banner. "I'm going to stand in front of your office. And let everyone see that the crooks are here..."

And that's exactly what the banner said. Boris was immediately paid half of his money. He didn't expect any more. So he had good relations with the insurers...

***

Once he came to our house for a children's birthday party. The kids were acting up. My wife said: "How do we teach them to be together.?.." And Boris replied: "Together is good, but how do we teach them to endure loneliness..."

This was his painful problem...

He gave us Israel, even though he did not read newspapers or watch television. He had his own special connection with this world. You can see it quite clearly in his works. The desert, Jerusalem... the Dead Sea... What only an artist can do. Who needs it? He thought about this question more than once. Not rhetorically, the question had a literal meaning for him... Once he decided to create a community of artists and musicians. He was running around with this idea. And then he said (he was in Israel at the time): "What am I thinking? To unite the entire Israeli poor...

But this did not stop him. Hence his home exhibitions. Hence his work with hopelessly ill children... He was a consistent idealist, and, to be more precise, an idealist of goodness... As they say, feel the difference.

He missed Kyiv a lot. He had just arrived, stayed with us, we talked until three in the morning. When we woke up at eight, he was gone. He left unnoticed and came back a few hours later, completely happy. It was the beginning of winter in Kyiv, and the snow was not everywhere, so he would collect it in his palms and touch the walls to feel the cold... That's what he told us: "I went to see the snow...

Soon after leaving for Israel, Boris Lekar sent a strange letter to his friends. It was a large piece of paper cut into shapes, with a separate part for each person. The only way to read the letter was to get together and put the pieces together. This was exactly what Boris wanted – a friendly feast with his own, albeit invisible, participation. And so it happened...

But even before that... Kyiv Day, one of the new holidays at that time, was approaching. People were preparing to watch, and artists were preparing to show themselves...

— I think, — Boris said, — Arsen should exhibit...

Arsen is our son, he used to draw, but at six years old he was still far from having an exhibition.

— I'll take care of it, — Boris reassured. He was a respected figure in our son's life.

They both stood under St Andrew's Church. Boris with his watercolours, Arsen next to him. Our friends made Arsen popular. His works sold briskly at a ruble apiece, not like Boris's. However, Boris's prices were higher. We stopped Arsen when he was in a hurry to go home.

— Maybe I'll paint something else by the end of the day and have time to present it there...

At the time, I was engaged in the sociology of politics. The new country, Ukraine, aroused great interest. Once, an American professor, David Ross, a colleague of mine, visited Kyiv. We became friends. He organised a trip to America for a group of Ukrainian public figures and government officials. The professor was responsible for everyone and, naturally, paid for all. We stayed in New York for many days. We were about to leave, but David suddenly looked a little embarrassed.

— I don't know what to do. I paid for the hotel, and they gave me this... — David showed me some paper — A bill for using the TV. Some of you watched a porn channel, and you have to pay for it separately. And it's expensive. How much? Almost as much as the room. Here, look.
— It can't be. It turns out that the man was awake for six hours every night. And that was after being on his feet all day.
— Yes, — David agreed grimly. — They were surprised themselves. But they have counters.
— Let's see who it is.
— I've already found out, — David said. — It's one of your officials.
— God, how I hate them... — said our interpreter, who took part in the conversation. She was a person with a great education, a smart girl. David passed a thoughtful look over our faces. Something was going on in his head.
— I think it can't be right. A man has to sleep sometime.
— It can, — said the interpreter. — Now I understand why he was always sleeping on the bus. I thought he was hungover.
— You know your own people better than I do, — David said tactfully. — But how do we settle up?

This is a good question. After all, the delegation is here, the bus has arrived, and it's time to move. David sighed sadly and went to the receptionist. He came back happy.

— They think it must be a mistake. A person cannot stand it. They'll check the TV now.
— And what about us?
— They said you could go. I explained to them: a new country, friendly with America. They said let them go...

We grabbed our bags and hurried to the exit.

I remember this because Boris and I met in America—it was such a happy coincidence. We spent a wonderful evening together.

***

His last visit to Kyiv gathered a lot of people. Even surprisingly for our times. A whole club of friends. Boris brought his installations—toy mise-en-scènes that had an ideological and story-line basis. Let me just say that it was unusual. It started with customs. Boris presented a suitcase containing "cultural values" for inspection. He entered them in the declaration. The customs officer opened a box, rummaged through it and pulled out a plastic doll. He and Boris looked at each other.

— What is this?—the customs officer asked.
— It's a detail of the performance,—Boris said, keeping his face formal.

The customs officer put the doll back and opened the next box. It didn't matter what exhibit was inside—a rubber elephant, a celluloid palm tree, a skeleton of a roach, a candy... It could have been anything.

— And in the other boxes? Is it the same?
— No, everything is different. Toy furniture, toy dishes, toy cars...
— Close it and go through,—the customs officer said dryly.

The exhibition was held in the House of Architects, which was Boris' home. People had gathered. It was time to open. And at that moment the lights were turned off.

— What can I do? — The director, Boris's old friend, just threw up his hands. He was worried himself. — Our electrician quit, and even if he hadn't, he'd still be drunk... Where to look? It will take time.

And so it was. It was winter, six o'clock in the evening, thick twilight and a loud crowd. Not to mention the exhibits, you can't see each other. Boris came with his wife, he was busy celebrating, so we had to save the day somehow. But surprisingly, the people were not worried at all. Everyone thought it was meant to be that Boris had prepared some scenario and that the performance would start soon. So when the candles were lit (I tried to get them), they took it for granted. The first part of the evening was spent by candlelight (someone compared it to a church service), and when the lights finally came on, I think the audience was even disappointed.

Boris was a tireless inventor. It was a feature of his nature. This is how he fought his illness for many years — with laughter. There was no irony, no mockery in it, it was the laughter of general festive merriment. When everything was good and wonderful... Wonderful minutes and hours... On his tombstone (Boris encouraged artists to organise an all-Israeli competition on this theme), he depicted flowers and butterflies. And among the lions of Jerusalem (there was such an initiative), Boris was the most cheerful.

If Socrates...

Review of Leonid Finberg's book *On Different Things and a Little About Myself* (Dukh i Litera, 2018)
By Olena Stiazhkina

Meaning and goodness are born in practices, not in theoretical reflections on them, Tomas Venclova once said. This thought of the thinker did not leave me all the time I was reading Leonid Finberg's book *About Different Things and a Little About Myself*. And all the time after reading it—up to the moment of writing—as well. That's why I don't think I can write a review. Perhaps if you walk alongside a donkey carrying a cart of books uphill (where else?), you will get a journey. The donkey on the cover is a fragment of a painting from the Novoselytsia Synagogue, and the book cart is everywhere. Not just on the cover, but on almost every page—books, books, books. They built the past, present, and future, and they decorate paradise, if, of course, someone is waiting for it.

Next to the books are hugs for Ukraine as part of the world and the universe. Ukraine emerges through the humanity and pain of the post-war period, through the inability to breathe and be free in the late Soviet era, but also through opportunity. Through the opportunity to find books, to take them from other people's hands, to keep them, to share them, to grow, to overcome one's own cowardice, to escape despair by laughing at the system, to emerge through friendship with those who also read, who write, who draw, who study. In the twilight of Soviet madness, Leonid Finberg's books and people create networks of handshakes, networks of views and thoughts that allow Ukraine's future to be, and to be bright.

In the first part, which contains interviews with Finberg from different years, there is indeed "a little" about the author. However, the "different things" appear as a history of the unbroken tradition of Ukrainian intellectualism, and acquires lively voices, bright faces, and tangible intonations. In this part, Finberg's book is about immortality. Indeed. It's about the fact that there is no death, because all thoughts, smiles, small and big deeds remain alive. The characters speak, and you can communicate with them, argue with them, expect support, and even seem to be able to shake their hands and hug them. Finberg's people — in books and with books — are not marble monuments or granite tablets, they just are. And this is a miracle among the other miracles that appear on the pages of *About Different Things and a Little About Myself*. The denial of nothingness — the nothingness of Ukraine, the nothingness of Jews in Soviet times, the nothingness of truth, the nothingness of resistance — is an important component of the book. The denial of nothingness is not only and not just at the level of an idea, but through practice, through daily action, through the realisation of a dream — together with others, whose circle grows larger the larger the tasks that need to be accomplished. The garden of books, the dream space of childhood, is planted by the author and his friends, colleagues, and family.

Alongside the *Dukh i Litera* publishing house, whose editor-in-chief is Leonid Finberg, other publishing houses are also producing books. At the same time, the action aimed at filling the Ukrainian space with good and necessary publications, both modern and ancient, is not a story about business competition for the author. This is a story about solidarity, about a common cause, about sincere admiration for those who walk alongside and also publish books.

Finally, about business... I would include Finberg's book in the list of literature for business schools or schools in general. Because the author very convincingly (but without convincing anyone) says that life and dreams are not about martyrdom and constant overcoming of obstacles. And that business, like any other fact of life, can be for joy, for pleasure; it can be not about fatigue and escape, but about realised — happy — adventures, about a huge world in which to live comfortably, about a country for which nothing is spared, about people who do not chew each other for fame, money, orders, but always choose the path of cooperation, mutual assistance and become friends.

The practices that gave birth to the meaning and goodness of this book and its wonderful author have another important part, to which the pages of *About Different Things and a Little About Myself* are devoted. It is about saving an almost forgotten language and —

without exaggeration—resurrecting an almost dead language, a language spoken by the Jews of Ukraine, Poland, and other European countries. It is about Yiddish, about the Yiddish books that were rescued (both from their only readers, mice, and from translations from Yiddish into Soviet), read, translated without losses or censorship, and published. It is about how the Center for the Study of the History and Culture of East European Jewry at the National University of Kyiv-Mohyla Academy came to be, where this almost extinct language was taught, became alive and necessary, where Jewish studies took a prominent place among the educational programmes of Kyiv-Mohyla Academy, and where the return of the names of Jewish writers and thinkers became evidence of the formation of the Ukrainian political nation.

Travelling through Finberg's book is not about moving from point A to point B. Sunshine, wonder, irony, a gentle invitation to reflection, happy finds (real treasures), incredible acquaintances are on every page, and therefore the "assembly points"—places to join those who walk, read, work alongside—can be as convenient as the reader needs, as they suit their mood, needs, desires. You can start from the beginning. Point A—the beginning—will still invite you to a meeting. But you can also start from the end. Finberg is one of those truly kind people who have been professing the principle of "letting children" all his life. Or simply, "letting everyone." If you are in the mood to plunge into *samizdat*, into sociology, which was growing in the Soviet twilight, then the third part of the book, about how ordinary citizens discussed the 1977 draft Constitution in the press, is exactly what you need. A detached researcher's position, a sample of 1,500 letters, a fierce but subdued methodological framework, and a scholar's interest—and the chapter presents a colourful, expected and unexpected picture of late Soviet society, the process of constructing "public opinion" and the breakthrough of real human voices. And the "great celebration of the adoption of the constitution" turns into great sadness and regret. Fortunately, this text did not fall into the hands of the KGB and remained not only a reflection of the era, but also a powerful research study in a field that could be very fruitful for a new generation of sociologists and historians of the Soviet Union.

"It's about all of us," Taras Voznyak said at the book launch. And it is true. The name index contains more than six hundred names. And the book contains as many stories, almost every one of which is an ongoing dialogue. A dialogue with those who defended the Orange Revolution in 2004, who stood on the Maidan in 2013, with those who bury their/our dead in Babyn Yar and throughout Europe, talking about them, with those who write and translate books, with those who think of Ukraine as a society of free and dignified people.

This book is about those people who have the strength not only to live in an era of change, but to make these changes themselves, realising that someone has to plant, care for, and protect the garden they dreamed of in childhood, and that evil only looks unshakable, but in reality it does not exist. Where there is love, there is no evil.

And a little criticism. First, there is no "betrayal" in the book. There is no despair, no depression, no premonition of the Apocalypse. Only (sometimes) light sadness and transparent bitter pain. However, even alongside these are faith and hope, deeds and people, yesterday's results and plans for tomorrow.

Secondly, the genre. No one will ever be able to determine the genre of this book. Biography, memoirs, conversations, scientific research, success story, political satire, portraits of contemporaries, prefaces to other books — all of these and a little bit more. But what can we call it all? I get lost in search of the right word, and then I stop at the thought: "If Socrates had written a book, it would be impossible to define its genre, too."

UKRAINIAN VOICES

Collected by Andreas Umland

1. *Mychailo Wynnyckyj*
   Ukraine's Maidan, Russia's War
   A Chronicle and Analysis of the Revolution of Dignity
   With a foreword by Serhii Plokhy
   ISBN 978-3-8382-1327-9

2. *Olexander Hryb*
   Understanding Contemporary Ukrainian and Russian Nationalism
   The Post-Soviet Cossack Revival and Ukraine's National Security
   With a foreword by Vitali Vitaliev
   ISBN 978-3-8382-1377-4

3. *Marko Bojcun*
   Towards a Political Economy of Ukraine
   Selected Essays 1990–2015
   With a foreword by John-Paul Himka
   ISBN 978-3-8382-1368-2

4. *Volodymyr Yermolenko (ed.)*
   Ukraine in Histories and Stories
   Essays by Ukrainian Intellectuals
   With a preface by Peter Pomerantsev
   ISBN 978-3-8382-1456-6

5. *Mykola Riabchuk*
   At the Fence of Metternich's Garden
   Essays on Europe, Ukraine, and Europeanization
   ISBN 978-3-8382-1484-9

6. *Marta Dyczok*
   Ukraine Calling
   A Kaleidoscope from Hromadske Radio 2016–2019
   With a foreword by Andriy Kulykov
   ISBN 978-3-8382-1472-6

7. *Olexander Scherba*
   Ukraine vs. Darkness
   Undiplomatic Thoughts
   With a foreword by Adrian Karatnycky
   ISBN 978-3-8382-1501-3

8. *Olesya Yaremchuk*
   Our Others
   Stories of Ukrainian Diversity
   With a foreword by Ostap Slyvynsky
   Translated from the Ukrainian by Zenia Tompkins and Hanna Leliv
   ISBN 978-3-8382-1475-7

9. *Nataliya Gumenyuk*
   Die verlorene Insel
   Geschichten von der besetzten Krim
   Mit einem Vorwort von Alice Bota
   Aus dem Ukrainischen übersetzt von Johann Zajaczkowski
   ISBN 978-3-8382-1499-3

10. *Olena Stiazhkina*
    Zero Point Ukraine
    Four Essays on World War II
    Translated from the Ukrainian by Svitlana Kulinska
    ISBN 978-3-8382-1550-1

11 *Oleksii Sinchenko, Dmytro Stus, Leonid Finberg (compilers)*
    Ukrainian Dissidents
    An Anthology of Texts
    ISBN 978-3-8382-1551-8

12 *John-Paul Himka*
    Ukrainian Nationalists and the Holocaust
    OUN and UPA's Participation in the Destruction of Ukrainian Jewry, 1941–1944
    ISBN 978-3-8382-1548-8

13 *Andrey Demartino*
    False Mirrors
    The Weaponization of Social Media in Russia's Operation to Annex Crimea
    With a foreword by Oleksiy Danilov
    ISBN 978-3-8382-1533-4

14 *Svitlana Biedarieva (ed.)*
    Contemporary Ukrainian and Baltic Art
    Political and Social Perspectives, 1991–2021
    ISBN 978-3-8382-1526-6

15 *Olesya Khromeychuk*
    A Loss
    The Story of a Dead Soldier Told by His Sister
    With a foreword by Andrey Kurkov
    ISBN 978-3-8382-1570-9

16 *Marieluise Beck (Hg.)*
    Ukraine verstehen
    Auf den Spuren von Terror und Gewalt
    Mit einem Vorwort von Dmytro Kuleba
    ISBN 978-3-8382-1653-9

17 *Stanislav Aseyev*
    Heller Weg
    Geschichte eines Konzentrationslagers im Donbass 2017–2019
    Aus dem Russischen übersetzt von Martina Steis und Charis Haska
    ISBN 978-3-8382-1620-1

18 *Mykola Davydiuk*
    Wie funktioniert Putins Propaganda?
    Anmerkungen zum Informationskrieg des Kremls
    Aus dem Ukrainischen übersetzt von Christian Weise
    ISBN 978-3-8382-1628-7

19 *Olesya Yaremchuk*
    Unsere Anderen
    Geschichten ukrainischer Vielfalt
    Aus dem Ukrainischen übersetzt von Christian Weise
    ISBN 978-3-8382-1635-5

20 *Oleksandr Mykhed*
    „Dein Blut wird die Kohle tränken"
    Über die Ostukraine
    Aus dem Ukrainischen übersetzt von Simon Muschick und Dario Planert
    ISBN 978-3-8382-1648-5

21 *Vakhtang Kipiani (Hg.)*
    Der Zweite Weltkrieg in der Ukraine
    Geschichte und Lebensgeschichten
    Aus dem Ukrainischen übersetzt von Margarita Grinko
    ISBN 978-3-8382-1622-5

22 *Vakhtang Kipiani (ed.)*
    World War II, Uncontrived and Unredacted
    Testimonies from Ukraine
    Translated from the Ukrainian by Zenia Tompkins and Daisy Gibbons
    ISBN 978-3-8382-1621-8

23 Dmytro Stus
   Vasyl Stus
   Life in Creativity
   Translated from the Ukrainian by
   Ludmila Bachurina
   ISBN 978-3-8382-1631-7

24 Vitalii Ogiienko (ed.)
   The Holodomor and the
   Origins of the Soviet Man
   Reading the Testimony of
   Anastasia Lysyvets
   With forewords by Natalka
   Bilotserkivets and Serhy
   Yekelchyk
   Translated from the Ukrainian by
   Alla Parkhomenko and
   Alexander J. Motyl
   ISBN 978-3-8382-1616-4

25 Vladislav Davidzon
   Jewish-Ukrainian Relations
   and the Birth of a Political
   Nation
   Selected Writings 2013-2021
   With a foreword by Bernard-
   Henri Lévy
   ISBN 978-3-8382-1509-9

26 Serhy Yekelchyk
   Writing the Nation
   The Ukrainian Historical
   Profession in Independent
   Ukraine and the Diaspora
   ISBN 978-3-8382-1695-9

27 Ildi Eperjesi, Oleksandr
   Kachura
   Shreds of War
   Fates from the Donbas Frontline
   2014-2019
   With a foreword by Olexiy
   Haran
   ISBN 978-3-8382-1680-5

28 Oleksandr Melnyk
   World War II as an Identity
   Project
   Historicism, Legitimacy
   Contests, and the (Re-)Con-
   struction of Political Commu-
   nities in Ukraine, 1939–1946
   With a foreword by David R.
   Marples
   ISBN 978-3-8382-1704-8

29 Olesya Khromeychuk
   Ein Verlust
   Die Geschichte eines gefallenen
   ukrainischen Soldaten, erzählt
   von seiner Schwester
   Mit einem Vorwort von Andrej
   Kurkow
   Aus dem Englischen übersetzt
   von Lily Sophie
   ISBN 978-3-8382-1770-3

30 Tamara Martsenyuk,
   Tetiana Kostiuchenko (eds.)
   Russia's War in Ukraine
   During 2022
   Personal Experiences of
   Ukrainian Scholars
   ISBN 978-3-8382-1757-4

31 Ildikó Eperjesi, Oleksandr
   Kachura
   Shreds of War. Vol. 2
   Fates from Crimea 2015–2022
   With an interview of Oleh
   Sentsov
   ISBN 978-3-8382-1780-2

32 Yuriy Lukanov
   The Press
   How Russia Destroyed Media
   Freedom in Crimea
   With a foreword by Taras Kuzio
   ISBN 978-3-8382-1784-0

33 Megan Buskey
   Ukraine Is Not Dead Yet
   A Family Story of Exile and
   Return
   ISBN 978-3-8382-1691-1

34 *Vira Ageyeva*
Behind the Scenes of the Empire
Essays on Cultural Relationships between Ukraine and Russia
With a foreword by Oksana Zabuzhko
ISBN 978-3-8382-1748-2

35 *Marieluise Beck (ed.)*
Understanding Ukraine
Tracing the Roots of Terror and Violence
With a foreword by Dmytro Kuleba
ISBN 978-3-8382-1773-4

36 *Olesya Khromeychuk*
A Loss
The Story of a Dead Soldier Told by His Sister, 2nd edn.
With a foreword by Philippe Sands
With a preface by Andrii Kurkov
ISBN 978-3-8382-1870-0

37 *Taras Kuzio, Stefan Jajecznyk-Kelman*
Fascism and Genocide
Russia's War Against Ukrainians
ISBN 978-3-8382-1791-8

38 *Alina Nychyk*
Ukraine Vis-à-Vis Russia and the EU
Misperceptions of Foreign Challenges in Times of War, 2014–2015
With a foreword by Paul D'Anieri
ISBN 978-3-8382-1767-3

39 *Sasha Dovzhyk (ed.)*
Ukraine Lab
Global Security, Environment, and Disinformation Through the Prism of Ukraine
With a foreword by Rory Finnin
ISBN 978-3-8382-1805-2

40 *Serhiy Kvit*
Media, History, and Education
Three Ways to Ukrainian Independence
With a preface by Diane Francis
ISBN 978-3-8382-1807-6

41 *Anna Romandash*
Women of Ukraine
Reportages from the War and Beyond
ISBN 978-3-8382-1819-9

42 *Dominika Rank*
Matzewe in meinem Garten
Abenteuer eines jüdischen Heritage-Touristen in der Ukraine
ISBN 978-3-8382-1810-6

43 *Myroslaw Marynowytsch*
Das Universum hinter dem Stacheldraht
Memoiren eines sowjet-ukrainischen Dissidenten
Mit einem Vorwort von Timothy Snyder und einem Nachwort von Max Hartmann
ISBN 978-3-8382-1806-9

44 *Konstantin Sigow*
Für Deine und meine Freiheit
Europäische Revolutions- und Kriegserfahrungen im heutigen Kyjiw
Mit einem Vorwort von Karl Schlögel
Herausgegeben von Regula M. Zwahlen
ISBN 978-3-8382-1755-0

45 *Kateryna Pylypchuk*
The War that Changed Us
Ukrainian Novellas, Poems, and Essays from 2022
With a foreword by Victor Yushchenko
Paperback
ISBN 978-3-8382-1859-5
Hardcover
ISBN 978-3-8382-1860-1

46 *Kyrylo Tkachenko*
Rechte Tür Links
Radikale Linke in Deutschland,
die Revolution und der Krieg in
der Ukraine, 2013-2018
ISBN 978-3-8382-1711-6

47 *Alexander Strashny*
The Ukrainian Mentality
An Ethno-Psychological,
Historical and Comparative
Exploration
With a foreword by Antonina
Lovochkina
Translated from the Ukrainian
by Michael M. Naydan and
Olha Tytarenko
ISBN 978-3-8382-1886-1

48 *Alona Shestopalova*
From Screens to Battlefields
Tracing the Construction of
Enemies on Russian Television
With a foreword by Nina
Jankowicz
ISBN 978-3-8382-1884-7

49 *Iaroslav Petik*
Politics and Society in the
Ukrainian People's Republic
(1917–1921) and
Contemporary Ukraine
(2013–2022)
A Comparative Analysis
With a foreword by Mykola
Doroshko
ISBN 978-3-8382-1817-5

50 *Serhii Plokhy*
Der Mann mit der
Giftpistole
Eine Spionageschichte aus dem
Kalten Krieg
ISBN 978-3-8382-1789-5

51 *Vakhtang Kipiani*
Ukrainische Dissidenten
unter der Sowjetmacht
Im Kampf um Wahrheit und
Freiheit
Aus dem Ukrainischen übersetzt
von Christian Weise
ISBN 978-3-8382-1890-8

52 *Dmytro Shestakov*
When Businesses Test
Hypotheses
A Four-Step Approach to Risk
Management for Innovative
Startups
With a foreword by Anthony J.
Tether
ISBN 978-3-8382-1883-0

53 *Larissa Babij*
A Kind of Refugee
The Story of an American Who
Refused to Leave Ukraine
With a foreword by Vladislav
Davidzon
ISBN 978-3-8382-1898-4

54 *Julia Davis*
In Their Own Words
How Russian Propagandists
Reveal Putin's Intentions
With a foreword by Timothy
Snyder
ISBN 978-3-8382-1909-7

55 *Sonya Atlantova, Oleksandr
Klymenko*
Icons on Ammo Boxes
Painting Life on the Remnants of
Russia's War in Donbas, 2014-21
Translated from the Ukrainian by
Anastasya Knyazhytska
ISBN 978-3-8382-1892-2

56 *Leonid Ushkalov*
Catching an Elusive Bird
The Life of Hryhorii Skovoroda
Translated from the Ukrainian
by Natalia Komarova
ISBN 978-3-8382-1894-6

57 *Vakhtang Kipiani*
Ein Land weiblichen
Geschlechts
Ukrainische Frauenschicksale
im 20. und 21. Jahrhundert
Aus dem Ukrainischen übersetzt
von Christian Weise
ISBN 978-3-8382-1891-5

58 Petro Rychlo
„Zerrissne Saiten einer
überlauten Harfe ..."
Deutschjüdische Dichter der
Bukowina
ISBN 978-3-8382-1893-9

59 Volodymyr Paniotto
Sociology in Jokes
An Entertaining Introduction
ISBN 978-3-8382-1857-1

60 Josef Wallmannsberger (ed.)
Executing Renaissances
The Poetological Nation of Ukraine
ISBN 978-3-8382-1741-3

61 Pavlo Kazarin
The Wild West of Eastern Europe
A Ukrainian Guide on Breaking Free from Empire
Translated from the Ukrainian by Dominique Hoffman
ISBN 978-3-8382-1842-7

62 Ernest Gyidel
Ukrainian Public Nationalism in the General Government
The Case of Krakivski Visti, 1940–1944
With a foreword by David R. Marples
ISBN 978-3-8382-1865-6

63 Olexander Hryb
Understanding Contemporary Russian Militarism
From Revolutionary to New Generation Warfare
With a foreword by Mark Laity
ISBN 978-3-8382-1927-1

64 Orysia Hrudka, Bohdan Ben
Dark Days, Determined People
Stories from Ukraine under Siege
With a foreword by Myroslav Marynovych
ISBN 978-3-8382-1958-5

65 Oleksandr Pankieiev (ed.)
Narratives of the Russo-Ukrainian War
A Look Within and Without
With a foreword by Natalia Khanenko-Friesen
ISBN 978-3-8382-1964-6

66 Roman Sohn, Ariana Gic (eds.)
Unrecognized War
The Fight for Truth about Russia's War on Ukraine
With a foreword by Viktor Yushchenko
ISBN 978-3-8382-1947-9

67 Paul Robert Magocsi
Ukraina Redux
Schon wieder die Ukraine ...
ISBN 978-3-8382-1942-4

68 Paul Robert Magocsi
L'Ucraina Ritrovata
Sullo Stato e l'Identità Nazionale
ISBN 978-3-8382-1982-0

69 Max Hartmann
Ein Schrei der Verzweiflung
Aquarelle zum Krieg von Danylo Movchan
Paperback
ISBN 978-3-8382-2011-6
Hardcover
ISBN 978-3-8382-2012-3

70 Vakhtang Kebuladze (Hg.)
Die Zukunft, die wir uns wünschen
Essays aus der Ukraine
ISBN 978-3-8382-1531-0

71 *Marieluise Beck, Jan Claas Behrends, Gelinada Grinchenko und Oksana Mikheieva (Hg.)*
Deutsch-ukrainische Geschichten
Bruchstücke aus einer gemeinsamen Vergangenheit
ISBN 978-3-8382-2053-6

72 *Pavlo Kazarin*
Der Wilde Westen Ost-Europas
Der ukrainische Weg aus dem Imperium
Aus dem Ukrainischen übersetzt von Christian Weise
ISBN 978-3-8382-1843-4

73 *Radomyr Mokryk*
Die ukrainischen »Sechziger«
Chronologie einer Revolte
ISBN 978-3-8382-1873-1

74 *Leonid Finberg*
My Ukraine
Rethinking the Past, Building the Present
ISBN 978-3-8382-1974-5

75 *Joseph Zissels*
Consider My Inmost Thoughts
Essays, Lectures, and Interviews on Ukrainian Matters at the Turn of the Century
ISBN 978-3-8382-1975-2

76 *Margarita Yehorchenko, Iryna Berlyand, Ihor Vinokurov (eds.)*
Jewish Addresses in Ukraine
A Guide-Book
With a foreword by Leonid Finberg
ISB 978-3-8382-1976-9

77 *Viktoriia Grivina*
Kharkiv—A War City
A Collection of Essays from 2022–23
ISBN 978-3-8382-1988-2

78 *Hjørdis Clemmensen, Viktoriia Grivina, Vasylysa Shchogoleva*
Kharkiv Is a Dream
Public Art and Activism 2013–2023
With a foreword by Bohdan Volynskyi
ISBN 978-3-8382-2005-5

79 *Olga Khomenko*
The Faraway Sky of Kyiv
Ukrainians in the War
With a foreword by Hiroaki Kuromiya
ISBN 978-3-8382-2006-2

80 *Daria Mattingly, Jonathon Vsetecka (eds.)*
The Holodomor in Global Perspective
How the Famine in Ukraine Shaped the World
ISBN 978-3-8382-1953-0

81 *Olga Khomenko*
Ukrainians beyond Borders
Nine Life Journeys Through the History of Eastern Europe
With a foreword by Zbigniew Wojnowski
ISBN 978-3-8382-2007-9

82 *Mykhailo Minakov*
From Servant to Leader
Chronicles of Ukraine under the Zelensky presidency, 2019–2024
With a foreword by John Lloyd
ISBN 978-3-8382-2002-4

83 *Volodymyr Hromov (ed.)*
A Ruined Home
Sketches of War, 2022–2023
ISBN 978-3-8382-2008-6

84 *Olha Tatokhina (ed.)*
Why do they kill our people?
Russia's war against Ukraine as told by Ukrainians
With a foreword by Volodymyr Yermolenko
ISBN 978-3-8382-2056-7

Book series "Ukrainian Voices"

Coordinator

Andreas Umland, National University of Kyiv-Mohyla Academy

Editorial Board

Lesia Bidochko, National University of Kyiv-Mohyla Academy
Svitlana Biedarieva, George Washington University, DC, USA
Ivan Gomza, Kyiv School of Economics, Ukraine
Natalie Jaresko, Aspen Institute, Kyiv/Washington
Olena Lennon, University of New Haven, West Haven, USA
Kateryna Yushchenko, First Lady of Ukraine 2005-2010, Kyiv
Oleksandr Zabirko, University of Regensburg, Germany

Advisory Board

Iuliia Bentia, National Academy of Arts of Ukraine, Kyiv
Natalya Belitser, Pylyp Orlyk Institute for Democracy, Kyiv
Oleksandra Bienert, Humboldt University of Berlin, Germany
Sergiy Bilenky, Canadian Institute of Ukrainian Studies, Toronto
Tymofii Brik, Kyiv School of Economics, Ukraine
Olga Brusylovska, Mechnikov National University, Odesa
Mariana Budjeryn, Harvard University, Cambridge, USA
Volodymyr Bugrov, Shevchenko National University, Kyiv
Olga Burlyuk, University of Amsterdam, The Netherlands
Yevhen Bystrytsky, NAS Institute of Philosophy, Kyiv
Andrii Danylenko, Pace University, New York, USA
Vladislav Davidzon, Atlantic Council, Washington/Paris
Mykola Davydiuk, Think Tank "Polityka," Kyiv
Andrii Demartino, National Security and Defense Council, Kyiv
Vadym Denisenko, Ukrainian Institute for the Future, Kyiv
Oleksandr Donii, Center for Political Values Studies, Kyiv
Volodymyr Dubovyk, Mechnikov National University, Odesa
Volodymyr Dubrovskiy, CASE Ukraine, Kyiv
Diana Dutsyk, National University of Kyiv-Mohyla Academy
Marta Dyczok, Western University, Ontario, Canada
Yevhen Fedchenko, National University of Kyiv-Mohyla Academy
Sofiya Filonenko, State Pedagogical University of Berdyansk
Oleksandr Fisun, Karazin National University, Kharkiv
Oksana Forostyna, Webjournal "Ukraina Moderna," Kyiv
Roman Goncharenko, Broadcaster "Deutsche Welle," Bonn
George Grabowicz, Harvard University, Cambridge, USA
Gelinada Grinchenko, Karazin National University, Kharkiv
Kateryna Härtel, Federal Union of European Nationalities, Brussels
Nataliia Hendel, University of Geneva, Switzerland
Anton Herashchenko, Kyiv School of Public Administration
John-Paul Himka, University of Alberta, Edmonton
Ola Hnatiuk, National University of Kyiv-Mohyla Academy
Oleksandr Holubov, Broadcaster "Deutsche Welle," Bonn
Yaroslav Hrytsak, Ukrainian Catholic University, Lviv
Oleksandra Humenna, National University of Kyiv-Mohyla Academy
Tamara Hundorova, NAS Institute of Literature, Kyiv
Oksana Huss, University of Bologna, Italy
Oleksandra Iwaniuk, University of Warsaw, Poland
Mykola Kapitonenko, Shevchenko National University, Kyiv
Georgiy Kasianov, Marie Curie-Skłodowska University, Lublin
Vakhtang Kebuladze, Shevchenko National University, Kyiv
Natalia Khanenko-Friesen, University of Alberta, Edmonton
Victoria Khiterer, Millersville University of Pennsylvania, USA
Oksana Kis, NAS Institute of Ethnology, Lviv
Pavlo Klimkin, Center for National Resilience and Development, Kyiv
Oleksandra Kolomiiets, Center for Economic Strategy, Kyiv

Sergiy Korsunsky, Kobe Gakuin University, Japan
Nadiia Koval, Kyiv School of Economics, Ukraine
Volodymyr Kravchenko, University of Alberta, Edmonton
Oleksiy Kresin, NAS Koretskiy Institute of State and Law, Kyiv
Anatoliy Kruglashov, Fedkovych National University, Chernivtsi
Andrey Kurkov, PEN Ukraine, Kyiv
Ostap Kushnir, Lazarski University, Warsaw
Taras Kuzio, National University of Kyiv-Mohyla Academy
Serhii Kvit, National University of Kyiv-Mohyla Academy
Yuliya Ladygina, The Pennsylvania State University, USA
Yevhen Mahda, Institute of World Policy, Kyiv
Victoria Malko, California State University, Fresno, USA
Yulia Marushevska, Security and Defense Center (SAND), Kyiv
Myroslav Marynovych, Ukrainian Catholic University, Lviv
Oleksandra Matviichuk, Center for Civil Liberties, Kyiv
Mykhailo Minakov, Kennan Institute, Washington, USA
Anton Moiseienko, The Australian National University, Canberra
Alexander Motyl, Rutgers University-Newark, USA
Vlad Mykhnenko, University of Oxford, United Kingdom
Vitalii Ogiienko, Ukrainian Institute of National Remembrance, Kyiv
Olga Onuch, University of Manchester, United Kingdom
Olesya Ostrovska, Museum "Mystetskyi Arsenal," Kyiv
Anna Osypchuk, National University of Kyiv-Mohyla Academy
Oleksandr Pankieiev, University of Alberta, Edmonton
Oleksiy Panych, Publishing House "Dukh i Litera," Kyiv
Valerii Pekar, Kyiv-Mohyla Business School, Ukraine
Yohanan Petrovsky-Shtern, Northwestern University, Chicago
Serhii Plokhy, Harvard University, Cambridge, USA
Andrii Portnov, Viadrina University, Frankfurt-Oder, Germany
Maryna Rabinovych, Kyiv School of Economics, Ukraine
Valentyna Romanova, Institute of Developing Economies, Tokyo
Natalya Ryabinska, Collegium Civitas, Warsaw, Poland
Darya Tsymbalyk, University of Oxford, United Kingdom
Vsevolod Samokhvalov, University of Liege, Belgium
Orest Semotiuk, Franko National University, Lviv
Viktoriya Sereda, NAS Institute of Ethnology, Lviv
Anton Shekhovtsov, University of Vienna, Austria
Andriy Shevchenko, Media Center Ukraine, Kyiv
Oxana Shevel, Tufts University, Medford, USA
Pavlo Shopin, National Pedagogical Dragomanov University, Kyiv
Karina Shyrokykh, Stockholm University, Sweden
Nadja Simon, freelance interpreter, Cologne, Germany
Olena Snigova, NAS Institute for Economics and Forecasting, Kyiv
Ilona Solohub, Analytical Platform "VoxUkraine," Kyiv
Iryna Solonenko, LibMod - Center for Liberal Modernity, Berlin
Galyna Solovei, National University of Kyiv-Mohyla Academy
Sergiy Stelmakh, NAS Institute of World History, Kyiv
Olena Stiazhkina, NAS Institute of the History of Ukraine, Kyiv
Dmitri Stratievski, Osteuropa Zentrum (OEZB), Berlin
Dmytro Stus, National Taras Shevchenko Museum, Kyiv
Frank Sysyn, University of Toronto, Canada
Olha Tokariuk, Center for European Policy Analysis, Washington
Olena Tregub, Independent Anti-Corruption Commission, Kyiv
Hlib Vyshlinsky, Centre for Economic Strategy, Kyiv
Mychailo Wynnyckyj, National University of Kyiv-Mohyla Academy
Yelyzaveta Yasko, NGO "Yellow Blue Strategy," Kyiv
Serhy Yekelchyk, University of Victoria, Canada
Victor Yushchenko, President of Ukraine 2005-2010, Kyiv
Oleksandr Zaitsev, Ukrainian Catholic University, Lviv
Kateryna Zarembo, National University of Kyiv-Mohyla Academy
Yaroslav Zhalilo, National Institute for Strategic Studies, Kyiv
Sergei Zhuk, Ball State University at Muncie, USA
Alina Zubkovych, Nordic Ukraine Forum, Stockholm
Liudmyla Zubrytska, National University of Kyiv-Mohyla Academy

Friends of the Series

Ana Maria Abulescu, University of Bucharest, Romania
Łukasz Adamski, Centrum Mieroszewskiego, Warsaw
Marieluise Beck, LibMod—Center for Liberal Modernity, Berlin
Marc Berensen, King's College London, United Kingdom
Johannes Bohnen, BOHNEN Public Affairs, Berlin
Karsten Brüggemann, University of Tallinn, Estonia
Ulf Brunnbauer, Leibniz Institute (IOS), Regensburg
Martin Dietze, German-Ukrainian Culture Society, Hamburg
Gergana Dimova, Florida State University, Tallahassee/London
Caroline von Gall, Goethe University, Frankfurt-Main
Zaur Gasimov, Rhenish Friedrich Wilhelm University, Bonn
Armand Gosu, University of Bucharest, Romania
Thomas Grant, University of Cambridge, United Kingdom
Gustav Gressel, European Council on Foreign Relations, Berlin
Rebecca Harms, European Centre for Press & Media Freedom, Leipzig
André Härtel, Stiftung Wissenschaft und Politik, Berlin/Brussels
Marcel Van Herpen, The Cicero Foundation, Maastricht
Richard Herzinger, freelance analyst, Berlin
Mieste Hotopp-Riecke, ICATAT, Magdeburg
Nico Lange, Munich Security Conference, Berlin
Martin Malek, freelance analyst, Vienna
Ingo Mannteufel, Broadcaster "Deutsche Welle," Bonn
Carlo Masala, Bundeswehr University, Munich
Wolfgang Mueller, University of Vienna, Austria
Dietmar Neutatz, Albert Ludwigs University, Freiburg
Torsten Oppelland, Friedrich Schiller University, Jena
Niccolò Pianciola, University of Padua, Italy
Gerald Praschl, German-Ukrainian Forum (DUF), Berlin
Felix Riefer, Think Tank Ideenagentur-Ost, Düsseldorf
Stefan Rohdewald, University of Leipzig, Germany
Sebastian Schäffer, Institute for the Danube Region (IDM), Vienna
Felix Schimansky-Geier, Friedrich Schiller University, Jena
Ulrich Schneckener, University of Osnabrück, Germany
Winfried Schneider-Deters, freelance analyst, Heidelberg/Kyiv
Gerhard Simon, University of Cologne, Germany
Kai Struve, Martin Luther University, Halle/Wittenberg
David Stulik, European Values Center for Security Policy, Prague
Andrzej Szeptycki, University of Warsaw, Poland
Philipp Ther, University of Vienna, Austria
Stefan Troebst, University of Leipzig, Germany

[Please send requests for changes in, corrections of, and additions to, this list to andreas.umland@stanforalumni.org.]

ibidem.eu